CARY GRANT: The Lonely Heart

The stress of uncertainty over his parentage (Grant identified strongly with his father, whom he loved, and who died early in the actor's career), the plaguing agony of hiding his true nature from the world, created much of the tension from which Grant suffered. Conflict and stress provoked this charmer's manic and violent temper, his sudden moods of neurotic, deeply self-absorbed solitariness, his unreasoning hatreds and drastically consuming loves. Nothing for Grant was tepid or half-hearted; he flew to extremes; he was never really at ease.

A consistently devouring passion of his was for vaudeville. He learned at the feet of the masters: George Burns and Eddie Foy Snr among them. For all of his polished manners, Grant was British working-class to the end of his life: in his cockiness, obstreperousness, love of vulgar humour, fondness for fish and chips, sausages and mash and tripe and onions, and in his affection for old music-hall songs. His rare moments of happiness would find him banging away at a grand piano in his Beverly Hills living-room, shouting once popular refrains such as "Yes, We Have No Bananas", or "Up In A Balloon, Boys". It was this proletarian charm that endeared him to men and women alike; behind the perfectly tailored suits, the perfect tan and flashing teeth of the ultimate matinée idol, there was a tough, brash, sardonically humorous West Country lad screaming to be let out.

About the Authors

Charles Higham was born in London, the son of an MP. A former writer with the *New York Times*, his bestselling biographies include lives of Katharine Hepburn, Bette Davis, Errol Flynn and the Duchess of Windsor. The author of two acclaimed books on American-Nazi collaboration in World War II, *Trading with the Enemy* and *American Swastika*, he is also a recognised film and political historian and has received several awards including the Prix des Créateurs of the Académie Française.

Roy Moseley is one of the best-known show-business biographers on both sides of the Atlantic, dividing his time equally between London and Los Angeles. He is the author of the first biographies of Merle Oberon, Roger Moore and Rex Harrison, and of a personal account of his friendship with Bette Davis, *Bette: An Intimate Memoir*.

CARY GRANT
The Lonely Heart

Charles Higham and Roy Moseley

NEW ENGLISH LIBRARY
Hodder and Stoughton

Special acknowledgment to Victoria Shellin

Copyright © 1989 by Charles Higham and Roy Moseley

First published in Great Britain in 1989 by New English Library hardbacks

First New English Library paperback edition 1990

British Library C.I.P.
Higham, Charles *1931*–
    Cary Grant: the lonely heart.
    1. Cinema films.
    Acting.   Grant, Cary,
    1904–1986
    Biographies
I. Title   II. Moseley, Roy
791.43′028′0924

ISBN 0-450-51612-1

Printed and bound in Great Britain for Hodder and Stoughton Paperbacks, a division of Hodder and Stoughton Limited, Mill Road, Dunton Green, Sevenoaks, Kent TN13 2YA. (Editorial Office: 47 Bedford Square, London WC1B 3DP) by Cox and Wyman Limited, Reading, Berks. Photoset by Rowland Phototypesetting Limited, Bury St Edmunds, Suffolk.

Roy Moseley wishes to dedicate
this book to his mother and father,
with all his love and gratitude,
and to Jane, Glen, and Gavin Kern

Charles Higham wishes to dedicate
this book to Pamela, Madeleine,
and Philippe Mora

ILLUSTRATIONS

ACKNOWLEDGMENTS
1 Authors' Collection.
2 The Kobal Collection.
3 Martin Masheter Collection.
4 Philip Masheter Collection.

It has not always been possible to trace copyright. The publishers apologise for any inadvertent infringement and will be happy to include an acknowledgment in any future edition.

"What can one say about Cary Grant? – He went from rags to riches in one short jump – and filled us all with love and laughter."

— Katharine Hepburn

"As a child I wished I was a member of the Secret Service."

— Cary Grant

"He was the last of the great gentlemen."

— Timothy Hutton

"Anyone who is on Cary's side is, of course, on the side of the angels."

— Richard Brooks

PREFACE

In 1987, *People* magazine named Cary Grant, along with Greta Garbo, the greatest of the stars. Certainly, no actor, except possibly Clark Gable, has equalled Grant's romantic appeal; he had few peers in the art of romantic comedy. Despite the occasional news story suggesting some collision or other with a wife or girlfriend, his life appeared enviably bland, smooth, and marked by a virtually unbroken chain of success. Among the wealthiest of all performers, he owned houses in Beverly Hills, Malibu and Palm Springs; in London, he stayed at the Connaught; he was the owner of two Rolls-Royces and his clothes and shoes were hand-made for him.

For many of his contemporaries, and for subsequent generations, he was the nonpareil of elegançe and style. Men like Frank Sinatra and Ronald Reagan, George Burns, Bob Hope and Jack Benny were lost in envy of his sophistication, poise and air of breeding. Even the women, most notably his first wife, Virginia Cherrill, and his fourth wife, Dyan Cannon, who suffered from his marrying them, could find warm things to say about him when time had almost healed their wounds. The pain they feel in discussing him stems in part from the fact that they are still, after many years, hopelessly in love with him.

To many young men, Grant was a surrogate father, giving them tender and considerate advice. Among those who benefited from his guidance and consideration were Ted Donaldson, the gifted child star of Grant's admirable comedy *Once Upon A Time*, Barbara Hutton's son, Lance Reventlow, and Timothy Hutton, among the best young contemporary actors, brilliant in *Ordinary People*, whose father, Jim Hutton, Grant had befriended during the shooting of his last film, *Walk, Don't Run*. For Phyllis Brooks, the exquisite, half-forgotten blonde actress of the 1930s, most effective in *Rebecca of Sunnybrook Farm* and *The Shanghai Gesture*, he was the love of her life; even today, in her mid-seventies, widowed and with a happy family of grown children, she smiles, and the tears start in her eyes, as the memories re-emerge.

Yet Cary Grant cannot be said to have enjoyed the comfortable, glowing existence that his multitude of admirers imagined. Much of his life was painful, even tortured; his spirit was ambiguous, deeply compulsive, at times almost insane in its obsessiveness. Like so many actors, he was a mass of contradictions: he could be generous to a fault and unholy in his stinginess; passionately devoted and loving, yet unthinkably cruel, sadistic and destructive. He could be meticulous in his punctuality, letter-perfect on a film set, giving no trouble to producer, director or co-stars, or maddeningly emphatic over pointless details, holding up work for hours or even days on end over the position of a light or the cut of a coat or the material used in a doorknob. Casual and careless to the point that his own home would be the most dishevelled, poorly repaired and messy in the whole of Beverly Hills, he was so enraged by the presence of a trademark on the glass panel in a window that he had it removed at vast cost. He would fuss over the ironing of his shirts by a housekeeper, sending them back repeatedly for new pressing, yet his neighbours would notice him hanging out his washing with clothes pegs on a line.

In many ways, he took a pixieish pleasure in confusing everyone with his personal contradictions; in other respects, he was tormented by the conflicts in his nature. He was puzzled and disturbed all through his life by the mystery of his origins. He was circumcised in 1904 when circumcision was almost unknown in Britain, except for religious or extreme medical reasons. The operation had to be performed by a *mohel*, a special surgeon appointed by a rabbi through a local synagogue; and yet exhaustive research in Bristol, Grant's birthplace, shows no trace of anyone Jewish on either side of his family.

Documentary proof is lacking, but the authors believe strongly that Grant's true mother, whose name was almost certainly Lillian, was of Jewish birth. They believe that she was a seamstress, working in the same clothing factory as Grant's father. His closest friends, including Ray Austin and William Curry McIntosh, have confirmed that his visits to Elsie Leach, his supposed mother, were artificial and strained, that she never seemed to recognise him as her son, that she appeared to be completely indifferent to his career and to his life in California, and that she consistently refused to visit Los Angeles.

Certainly she was, in the early years, a cruel and despotic human being, whom the boy Archie resented as he grew up. One quasi-Freudian belief is that sons of mothers who have ill-treated them tend to wreak vengeance upon the women who love them for the rest of their lives. Whether or not this psychiatric explanation makes sense, the fact is that Grant tormented many of the women with whom he became involved or whom he married. His actions against them went beyond mere verbal punishment: he physically abused them, beating them and sometimes injuring them.

It has also been stated, with equal glibness, that bisexuality or homosexuality are the result of a dominating female presence in the life of a growing man. Again, the authors do not claim to be psychologists. We have made no attempt, in the text of this book, to explain why, throughout his life, Cary Grant became sexually involved with certain men, two of them of great prominence, others totally obscure. When he ceased to enjoy a sexual liaison with Howard Hughes (testified to by three of Hughes' lieutenants and his publicist, it can only have been brief and superficial) or, far more seriously, with Randolph Scott, he remained a good and true friend of these men throughout their subsequent relationships with women, and he owed much of his fortune to Hughes' skilled guidance.

Bisexuality is a subject that even today makes many people feel uncomfortable. A human being who moves, comfortably or not, between the poles of sexual experience is, to them, alien and unsettling: a creature beyond understanding. Hence the fact that, when books or articles imply or state that an idol of the world is sexually ambiguous, the resentment seems almost as fierce as if he were disclosed as being purely homosexual.

Yet the honest biographer cannot shirk the painful truth, even at the risk of being called deliberately sensationalist; in an area in which even compassion is suspect, the facts are unavoidable. And for a star of Cary Grant's magnitude, the pressure towards invention and deceit, cover-up and confusion, can be terrifying. An actor in private and public life as well as on the screen itself, a famous performer can suffer intolerably; he is forced to satisfy the fantasies of millions, live out a complex mythology and deny himself any utterance of the "love that dare not speak its name". Even today, in this supposedly liberal age, actors of note feel compelled to disguise their true natures, so that autobiographies have appeared, seemingly exhaustive, written with expert ghosts, in which not an inkling of a true sexual personality emerges.

The stress of uncertainty over his parentage (Grant identified strongly with his father, whom he loved, and who died early in the actor's career), the plaguing agony of hiding his true nature from the world, created much of the tension from which Grant suffered. Conflict and stress provoked this charmer's manic and violent temper, his sudden moods of neurotic, deeply self-absorbed solitariness, his unreasoning hatreds and drastically consuming loves. Nothing for Grant was tepid or half-hearted; he flew to extremes; he was never really at ease.

A consistently devouring passion of his was for vaudeville, for knock-about comedy, the excitement and glitter of the musical theatre. He learned at the feet of the masters: George Burns and Eddie Foy Snr. among them. For all of his polished manners, acquired as an actor acquires them, as it were phonetically, Grant remained at heart a working-class boy, with all of the moodiness and darkness of his West Country forebears. Family rumours hinted that he might have been of gypsy or Spanish blood, intermingled in the eras before genealogical records were taken. Be that as it may, he was British working-class to the end of his life: in his cockiness, obstreperousness, love of vulgar humour, fondness for fish and chips, sausages and mash and tripe and onions, and in his affection for old music-hall songs. His rare moments of happiness would find him banging away at a grand piano in his Beverly Hills living-room, shouting once popular refrains such as "Yes, We Have No Bananas", or "Up In A Balloon, Boys". It was this proletarian charm that endeared him to men and women alike; behind the perfectly tailored suits, the immaculately groomed hair, the perfect tan and flashing teeth of the ultimate matinée idol, there was a tough, brash, sardonically humorous West Country lad screaming to be let out.

In exploring the story of a remarkable life, which encompassed triumph after triumph, the authors have not attempted to smooth out the many bumps with slick explanations, or paper over the cracks with convenient invented detail. The acknowledgments and source notes pages will indicate the range of opinion, for, against, and in the middle, of over 150 people who loved, hated, slept or worked with this great star. The record is presented plainly, for the reader to interpret as he chooses. Our conclusion, for what it is worth, was that Cary Grant, despite his many very human failings, was a good and decent man. Let others argue if they will.

1

Archibald Alec Leach was born at one a.m. on Sunday, January 18, 1904, at 15 Hughenden Road, Horfield, Bristol. King Edward VII was on the throne and Theodore Roosevelt was in the White House; the Russo-Japanese War was about to erupt; cars and films were in the teething stage and the blazing red of the British Empire covered most of the world map. Night-workers were toiling in the factories and coal mines and cleaning the streets, but much of England was asleep; the pale flicker of gaslight gleamed in glass globes over Bristol's streets, and from the harbour, dominated still by the tall masts of sailing ships, there was the toot of a whistle, the sudden blare of a funnel signalling departure, and the powerful scent of the sea.

The house in which the child was born was on the northern edge of the city, where there were green hills and beekeepers' gardens and clumps of bare oak trees. Number 15 was one of a newly constructed row of narrow terrace houses fashioned of grey Gloucester stone. Proliferating in drab monotony, these cheerless semi-detached homes would soon swallow up the lush countryside like a dark pestilence. Renumbered from 8, Hughenden Road the week before the boy's birth, the house had a front parlour of twelve by sixteen feet, the back parlour was twelve by twelve, the kitchen seven by ten feet. A narrow staircase rose from the hall to a landing into which opened three small bedrooms. There was an outside toilet and a pump for bathing in the back garden which sloped up to a stone wall.

The weather was unseasonably mild in Bristol that

January. While London was swathed in yellow sulphur fog that choked the throat and burned the eyes, turning passers-by into barely glimpsed phantom figures shivering in the cold, Bristol air was clear, swept with a fine wind from the Channel, and the temperature was a tolerable forty-eight degrees.

Elias Leach, Archie's father, was thirty-two years old, delicately and weakly handsome, with light-brown curly hair, soft, dark, reflective eyes, chiselled cheek-bones, and a sensual mouth decorated with a neat moustache. He had a slight cleft in his chin and a wistful, captivating smile that few could resist.

He was the son, grandson and great-grandson of earthenware potters. He had followed his unlettered mother Emily's calling by working at Todd's Clothing Factory, where he was a suit-presser, receiving the garments off the assembly line, and steaming them in creases with hot irons for an average of ten hours a day. He found release from the pressure of the work by indulging in affairs with numerous young women and drinking himself into a pleasant stupor night after night in the local pubs.

Elias' wife Elsie Maria, whom he had married on May 30, 1898, was the daughter of a family of brewery labourers, laundresses and ships' carpenters. Her first child, John William Elias, had died on February 6, 1900, a few days short of his first birthday, in the violent convulsions of tubercular meningitis. It had been a terrible way to start the new century, and Elsie had become neurotic and tortured as a result of her bereavement.

The couple behaved strangely after Archibald Alec was born. He was baptised three weeks later, but his birth was not registered until three weeks after that. Still more oddly, they had him circumcised, a procedure which was almost completely unknown outside the Jewish community in Bristol in 1904. It is possible that the reason for the circumcision was medical: a closing of the foreskin which would have rendered urination impossible. Cary Grant believed later that the reason for the circumcision was that his father was partly Jewish, but, in fact, there is no record of anything in the family tree to suggest such a possibility. We believe that he was the illegitimate child of a Jewish woman, who either died in childbirth or disappeared. His own attitude to his possible Jewishness was extraordinarily complex throughout his life. He declined the leading role in the anti-racist film *Gentlemen's Agreement* because the hero was a Gentile posing as a Jewish person, and he felt that as a Jew he could not satisfactorily play the part. He gave substantial sums to Jewish causes on several occasions: in 1939, he presented $25,000 to the Jewish actor Sam Jaffe to give to the United Jewish appeal with the understanding that his Jewishness would not be disclosed. In 1947, he gave an identical sum to the new state of Israel, and announced that it was in the name of his dead Jewish mother. He told some friends and the actress Mary Brian, to whom he almost became engaged, that he was Jewish; he told many others, including Clifford Odets, that he was not. The mystery remains.

Perhaps because of trouble in paying the rent, perhaps because of Elias' bad local reputation, the Leaches moved twice before their son was five: to two subsequent addresses in the suburb of Bishopston, which was only a few streets away from Horfield. These drab semi-detached houses huddled together on narrow streets which ran directly into open country. Dominating the neighbourhood was the looming Bristol Prison, into which, day after day, night after night, the Black Marias trundled behind government horses, carrying convicts into a place where hope was rapidly abandoned. The only other building of consequence was the equally depressing Orphanage, which housed the innumerable illegitimate children whose unhappy existence was Dickensian and dark.

The familiar sounds of Bishopston were the clop of horses' hooves and the grinding of wheels as conveyances, ranging from enormous, top-heavy furniture vans to simple two-wheel flies, ground along the streets to the nearby Gloucester Road, the main artery in and out of the city.

Counterpointed with these constant reminders of a now deeply industrialised Bristol were the occasional sounds of nature emanating from the nearby rural districts: the hum of bees from hives in a neighbouring estate, the cawing of crows and the lowing of cattle.

The existence was cheerless and depressing. Elsie Maria Leach was a harsh woman, who rapped Archie's knuckles at the slightest opportunity and docked his sixpence-a-week pocket money if he should mark a table or upset a cushion. She cooked basic food: thick, lumpy porridge, kippers, bread and lard, sausages and mash, fish and chips, suet pudding of a gelatinous consistency, and made pots of too-strong tea which were covered by woollen cosies knitted in the shape of animals or birds. Elsie blamed Archie for taking the place of the child who had died.

Elias was feckless and irresponsible, disappearing for long periods of time to a mistress or mistresses in the port of Southampton, a few hours away by train. In later years, Cary Grant tried to belie the ugly truth of his upbringing by writing of his father carrying him into a chandeliered drawing-room to recite a poem. But there was no drawing-room, and there were no chandeliers, in the pinched houses he occupied for the first years of his life.

He wrote that he was kept in dresses until he was several years old.

It seemed to me that I was kept in baby clothes much longer than any other child, and perhaps, for a while, wasn't sure whether I was a boy or a girl. I wonder why little boys are ashamed to be mistaken for little girls. Why do they take such pride in being little boys? Do little girls take similar pride in their sex and not wish to be mistaken for little boys?

He made too much of this, disturbed as he was in later life by his ambiguous sexual nature. As it happened, it was characteristic of all Victorian and early Edwardian parents to dress their male children in girls' clothing during their infancy.

Another memory of those earliest days of life was the constant emphasis, in family conversations, on money. His mother nagged his father continuously over the insufficiency of funds for the housekeeping. The butt of clichés like so many children, he was told repeatedly that money "didn't grow on trees", and that one must "waste not, want not"; he would be almost painfully tight with money to the end of his life. He always kept in his pocket a length of twine of mysterious significance. Perhaps it was to remind him of the days when he and his family had nothing.

Even when, at night during a storm, he woke and saw his parents holding each other around the waist for once, resting from their many quarrels as they looked out into the rain, he didn't feel a sense of happiness or belonging. He wrote in his middle age, "And now, today, as I think of it, I recall the intense feeling of being shut off from [my parents'] unfamiliar unity."

He seems to have found consolation with his Uncle John (Jack) Leach, the fourth child of Elias' parents and the eldest son, who worked in a department store. He liked his elderly grandmother Elizabeth, who could neither read nor write. Her ugly house on Picton Street may, like his own, have had no bathroom and was cold and damp in winter, but he felt at home there, and objected only to being bathed naked in front of his grandmother in a copper placed in the kitchen, ashamed even at that four-year-old stage of exhibiting his genitals to a woman.

At four-and-a-half, Archibald Alec was sent to Bishop Road Infant School. A short walk from the Bishopston house in which the family was living, the grey stone establishment clung to the shadow of the prison on Victoria Road, and was scarcely more appealing in its featureless, almost windowless blankness. The child was frightened from his first day at school. Rendered nervous and introspective by Elsie's cruelty and neurotic instability, and by the fact that he had no father to depend on, he was a classic example of a misfit in the rough-and-tumble of young boys and girls.

As long as he lived, he never forgot the threat of the cane, the smell of the chalk dust, the aroma of varnish on yellow desks with their hinged tops, the squeak of an inscription on a blackboard, or the fearsome demeanour of the spinster teachers. But gradually he got used to the other children, and he grew stronger through constant exercise that ranged from compulsory physical training in the morning in a damp or freezing yard, to playing football with no more than the outline of a goal drawn in chalk on the brick wall behind him. His success as goalkeeper earned him the grudging admiration of his lustier fellow-pupils, and laid the groundwork for his lifelong hunger, the hunger that consumes all performers, to be loved by the crowd.

There were some moments of relief from the misery of his existence at home. He managed to slip away to meet his father at the Todd Clothing Factory on Saturdays and walk home with him and Elias' cribbage-playing friends. He would search in his father's pockets for sweets and joyfully fish one up, munching it hungrily. At Christmas, he had a consolation: the pantomimes. Elias, who liked to sing music-hall songs while Elsie pounded away at the piano, loved the theatre and took Archie to these annual Christmas presentations. *Babes in the Wood, Aladdin, Cinderella, Jack and the Beanstalk*, and *Puss in Boots* were notable among the entertainments seen in Bristol during Archie's first five years, at such gilt-and-gingerbread palaces as the Prince's and the Empire (and Hippodrome) theatres.

The boy loved pantomimes; they were his escape from a usually gloomy existence into the multicoloured dancing world of the theatre. Elias was a "Stage-Door Johnny", addicted to actresses. He was often backstage, flirting in dressing-rooms with the more attractive chorus-girls. He also formed a friendship with the well-known troupe of acrobatic dancers and stilt-walkers known as the Penders. Starting on the week of August 8, 1910, when Archie was six-and-a-half, the Penders were at the Empire (and

Hippodrome) theatre in a show entitled *The Long and the Short of It: A Screaming Absurdity*. The Penders' real names were Robert and Margaret Lomas. Working under the banner of Howard and Wyndham, Booking Agents, they appeared with Robert's brothers and ten-year-old daughter Doris, performing a harlequinade. Robert Lomas was to become the dominant influence, the shaping force of Archie Leach's life, and would be far more of a father to him, albeit a stern one, than his own parent.

Born of yeoman stock in Bury, Lancashire, in 1872, Lomas was the son and grandson of travelling players. The Lomas family had, for thirty years, criss-crossed the British Isles and continental Europe with a collapsible stage and props, and a canvas tent, alternating Shakespearean performances with a knock-about music-hall act. Until the turn of the century, the family had appeared in a popular act, "Fun and Antics in Monkeyland", in ape, gorilla and chimpanzee costumes, dancing and singing and pulling their heads off at the end of the act to disclose their grinning faces. Now they also provided an eccentric routine dressed as policemen, which was later echoed by the silent movie comedy ensemble the Keystone Cops.

In 1908, they had had a narrow escape when the Theatre Royal, Drury Lane, caught fire at the end of a performance and burned many of their props. Under the aegis of the genial Arthur Collins, a distant relation of the actress Joan Collins and general manager of Drury Lane, they had appeared year after year in Christmas pantomimes, scoring a triumphant success in *Aladdin* in the 1909 season.

Robert Lomas was five feet eight, muscular from years of acrobatic training, handsome and olive-skinned, with slicked-down black hair and strong, aquiline features. Archie Leach resembled him strongly, and imitated him in later years. Despite his broad Lancashire accent and somewhat coarse, pushy and aggressive character, Lomas was very much a dapper man-about-town. He chain-smoked expensive cigars, sported smart suits, and boasted

21

fancy hand-painted ties. He was flashy, a "toff"; he was "theatre", all the way down to his smart, fashionable spats. But he was also despotic, cruel, and a severe taskmaster.

Archie was enthralled by the Lomases in their *The Long and the Short of It*. He laughed and clapped and jumped up and down as Robert Lomas, in a grotesque mask of an old woman's face, wearing a Mother Hubbard dress, dropped his hat on the stage and the shortest of the nine dancers, ten-year-old Doris Pender, picked up the hat and passed it up the line. He was delighted by the harlequinade, with Robert Lomas as Harlequin and Margaret Lomas as Columbine, in scenes that included the explosion of a steam train and a commotion in which the half-nude towelled figures of the Turkish bath ran helter-skelter all over the stage. He loved the police act, in which the family, in their tall black helmets that kept falling off, ran across scenery rooftops, plunged down chimneys, shot up through trap doors, exploded through windows and hung perilously from fire escapes. At one stage a horse pulled a fire wagon across the proscenium as the entire family hung from its ladder. The Lomases tumbled and danced in the Russian manner, with their knees bent and their feet kicking high; they tangled themselves in human pretzels of limbs, and then disentangled and danced again. Miraculously fluid and limber, they instantly became the focus of the child's dreams.

At home, there were the pallid, grey light of days and the flickering gaslight at night; the smell of cooking, especially of cabbage; his father coming home drunk; his mother's hysteria and stinginess; her constant mourning for her lost elder son. The Empire (and Hippodrome) theatre was full of laughter and gilt and bronze, polish and red velvet and dazzling lights and sparkling, spinning acrobatic dancers. Seeing his son's happiness, Elias Leach saw a way out for both of them. He gave Archie to Robert Lomas as an extra member of his troupe; and, since his wife, according to the laws of the time, would have no say in the matter, he signed the necessary paper himself. He must have lied that the boy was ten: the authorities did not permit children of six to work.

For all his life, protecting both his father and Robert Lomas, Cary Grant decently lied that he joined the troupe at sixteen. Robert Lomas' decision to adopt the boy by including him at this tender age was both surprising and daring: if the true facts had emerged, he could have been fined or possibly even imprisoned for the offence, but he was a fellow Mason of Elias'. Lomas needed an extra player, because so great was the demand for his troupe that it frequently had to split up; the Christmas before, augmented by outsiders, a splinter group had appeared at the Prince's theatre, Edinburgh, in pantomime. Although he could barely dance or do more than perform amateurish somersaults learned in the school yard, the six-year-old boy, as far as can be determined, joined the Pender ensemble in the second week of performance at the Bristol Empire (and Hippodrome) in two shows a night at six thirty and at ten to nine, from August 15–20, in "Bob Pender's Little Dandies", described in the programme as "an expert dancing scena à la Russe". The Bristol *Times and Mirror* in its edition of August 16, 1910, reviewed the performance as follows:

Bob Pender's Little Dandies, half a dozen lads and one little lassie – Doris Pender – daintily attired, present a rather unique dancing scene, combined with acrobatic feats . . . They do their work briskly and skilfully, especially the damsel, whose terpsichorean feats are graceful and facile . . .

When the show closed, the troupe took off on an extraordinary journey. They were booked to appear at the Wintergarten Theatre of Varieties in Berlin. Since the Berlin show was to open on the 27th, they barely made it to the destination in time via train, ship and train again. It is easy to imagine the excitement of the six-year-old boy as he was propelled from dreary Bristol to a steamship, and thence to a new culture.

The Wintergarten was the largest and most extravagant music-hall in Germany. Cavernous, luxurious, a riot of red plush and gilt, with motifs of angels blowing trumpets and heroic male nude athletes carved into the walls and ceiling, dripping with six massive crystal chandeliers, the theatre was situated in the rambling old Central Hotel opposite the Friedrichstrasse Railroad Station. Run by the genial, mutton-chop-moustached impresario Franz Steiner, it could accommodate as many as 750 performers on the stage and over 1,800 in the audience.

Since there is no way that Archie Leach could have learned to stilt-walk in the time allowed, he had to sit upon the shoulders of either Robert or Margaret Lomas as they paraded up and down on stilts in their comedy routines. Among the enthusiastic first-night audience were the smart, sharp-witted thirty-year-old New York entrepreneur Jesse L. Lasky, and the jolly, twenty-two-year-old Leo Maase, chief European representative of the H. B. Marinelli Agency, which numbered Sarah Bernhardt, Réjane, and Anna Held among its galaxy of famous clients. The two young men from New York were hunting for talent for the Folies Bergère theatre, which was in construction on Forty-Sixth Street and Broadway and was scheduled to be opened the following April under the management of Lasky and his able partner, Henry B. Harris. Captivated by the Pender Troupe of Giants, they made their way backstage to append Robert Lomas' signature to a contract. He signed without hesitation, despite the fact that he was already under contract to the Moss-Stoll theatre circuit in England. Somehow, given the loose laws on contracts of the time, he got away with this. The troupe had a triumphant two weeks at the Wintergarten, and Leo Maase secured them an October engagement at the equally famous Olympia in Paris, France.

Meanwhile, they returned to England for a less inspiring tour of the music-halls. Though rocking with audience laughter night after night for twelve performances a week, the music-halls were ugly and depressing, seldom clean, and usually in need of a fresh coat of paint. There was a great deal of drunkenness backstage, and vigorous fornication in the seedy dressing-rooms. Stage-door-keepers allowed in a motley collection of friends and relatives, barmaids, soldiers and sailors. The air behind the scenes was thick with smoke, alive with bawdy conversation and the constant smacking of buttocks and frequent pinching of female flesh followed by loud, raucous giggles. The music-hall managers, who spent the day washing the windows and posting the bills, would turn up at night in tie and tails and make futile attempts to bring some measure of control to the bedlam backstage.

Travel was by train, and, as members of the Music-Hall Artists' Railway Benevolent Association, the Lomases travelled first-class for third-class fares. The windows were pulled up tight no matter whether it was hot or cold, and cigarette or cigar smoke rendered breathing almost impossible. The Lomas family, Archie and other outside members of the troupe were housed in "digs".

The music-halls had appreciative, noisy audiences, but people in the galleries would scream out ribald comments during the show or blow "raspberries", greatly upsetting untried performers. The tradition was to shout back at the gallery "birds" with equal vigour, and sometimes there would be confrontations in the alley outside the theatre, with a free-for-all and several men winding up in the gutter with teeth missing.

Learning to stilt-walk must have been an ordeal for the child. The stilts were one and three-eighths of an inch square, with "steps" inside, cut from a block of the same thickness as the ash or oak stilt. They were fastened by carriage bolts and washers. A two-inch wooden screw inserted near the bottom prevented the stilt from turning on the bolt. The stilts were tied around the waist with rope, and the feet, which were also tied, rested on the steps. Stages sloped from the back to the footlights and it was almost impossible to keep balance. Again and again the boy would tumble, only to be expertly caught by one or another of the Lomases. Occasionally, he would crash through their reaching hands and hurt himself on the hard wooden boards.

The Pender Troupe appeared successfully at the Paris Olympia in October; they were booked that Christmas for the Theatre Royal, Drury Lane, pantomime, *Jack and the Beanstalk*, starring the great vaudeville star George Graves. The Penders, of course, played the giants. Archie was among them, as the smallest performer, and he also appeared in a routine as a stork, wearing a bird-mask. He celebrated not only Christmas but his seventh birthday in the show, and the Penders were warmly reviewed, singled out from the cast for their marvellous antics.

2

On March 15, 1911, Archie sailed for New York with several of the Pender Troupe aboard the ill-fated *Lusitania*. Robert and Margaret Lomas, and some of the boys went on the SS *Oceanic*; Doris travelled with Archie. Both vessels suffered rough crossings through turbulent, windswept seas, and the *Lusitania* (destined to be sunk by a German torpedo) was top-heavy and rolled alarmingly in the swell. The seven-year-old boy's excitement must have been extreme as the troupe docked. When the Lomases checked into rooms on West Forty-Ninth Street, and began rehearsing at the Hudson theatre, while the finishing touches were being put to the Folies Bergère, the city was alive with over thirty major theatrical spectacles. Mrs. Fiske, the reigning star of Broadway, was a sensation in *Mrs. Bumpstead-Leigh* at the Lyceum. Hazel Dawn was the star of *The Pink Lady* at the New Amsterdam; Nora Bayes and Jack Norworth were the sweetly singing duo in *Little Miss Fix-It* at the Globe; and *Get-Rich-Quick Wallingford* was a comedy riot at the George M. Cohan theatre. Broadway in 1911 was still authentically the dazzling Great White Way, and everyone was saying that the Folies Bergère of New York would offer a spectacle which even the colossal show at the Wintergarten and the dramatic epic *Thaïs* at the Criterion could not hope to equal. At first rehearsal, the Lomases met the robust and dynamic Scot, R. H. Burnside, one of the great theatrical directors of his era, who put the company of several hundred players through their frenzied paces. The Pender Troupe of Giants would not perform their harlequinade, considered too slow and aesthetic for American audiences, but restrict themselves entirely to stilt-dancing. They would appear in two of the three "pieces", of which the expensive and opulent two nightly performances would be composed.

The pieces in which the Penders appeared were *Hell*, described as "a profane burlesque", and *Gaby*, a satire, starring the great Ethel Levey, that dealt with the notorious career of the French star Gaby Deslys, whose affair with the deposed King Manuel of Portugal was the talk of Europe. The Penders also paraded around in the midnight cabaret, which was performed in the theatre roof-garden, a specially enclosed area above the main auditorium, until two a.m. This was a gruelling schedule for the seven-year-old Archie and ten-year-old Doris, and the other children.

At the beginning of April, the Lomases and the rest of the huge and glittering company of 200 artistes and 100 chorus girls were allowed to rehearse in the still unfinished theatre in which they would be appearing on Forty-Sixth Street. Jesse L. Lasky wrote in his memoirs almost half a century later:

> Archie's (stilts) were so high he had to be put on them from a ladder and bend his head low down to show his head under the proscenium . . . Years later he reminded me that the ladder on which he started his rise to fame was the one he used on 46th Street to mount his stilts.

The Folies Bergère theatre was beautiful. It was furnished with pink, grey and turquoise seats, and had wall bas-reliefs of copper and gold. Two-thirds of the orchestra floor was cleared for terraces of tables for the diners who composed the audience; the balcony was similarly arranged, and only the back seats of the theatre or orchestra offered conventional seating. It was the first dinner-theatre in the United States.

Genial Jesse Lasky, red-faced Leo Maase and the elegant Henry B. Harris were present throughout many of the rehearsals; Maase had just arrived in New York to take up the position of head of the local Marinelli Agency. After just over twenty-three days of rehearsal, the opening night took place on April 27 at eight fifteen. For weeks before-hand, millionaires had been meeting the entrepreneurs and bidding large sums of money for the best tables in open office auctions. Some of the tables went for as much as $150 each, or at least $5,000 in present-day terms. The legendary Diamond Jim Brady arrived in his brand new Phaeton with his buxom mistress, Lillian Russell; there were representatives of the Mellon, Rockefeller and Vanderbilt families; the mayor was present; and so were leading figures of the Army and Navy.

The evening was a riot of colour and excitement. "Better or more lavishly costumed productions had never been seen", the soon-to-be-legendary Sime Silverman wrote in *Variety*. "The Folies Bergère sets one the agreeable task of searching about for new epithets, for none of the old stock [ones] seem applicable in this latest enterprise . . ."

The sensation of the evening was Ethel Levey's Spanish dance in *Gaby*, which parodied Deslys' more absurd "La-tin" impersonations, and there was a murmuring of puri-tanical critics, laced through the audience of the besotted and over-fed audience of four hundred, when girls be-sported themselves in flesh-coloured tights, and Jean Mar-cel's Gladiators, heroic physical specimens from Paris, appeared dressed only in fig leaves, indulging in a violent argument over their stage positioning in which one of the men fell onto the stage with a bleeding nose.

The combination of iridescent colour effects, deafening music, high-kicking chorines, broad comedy, can-cans, pro-digious acrobatics and animal acts was typical of the era. There was a disastrous event on that opening night. At the close of the '*Hell*' satire, the head of a standpipe exploded because of pressure, and 5,000 gallons of water burst out, rushed down a shaft and through the ceiling over the east exit-door, throwing the fashionable audience into a state of terror and drenching large numbers of diners. Theatre manager Harry D. Kline ran onto the stage mopping his sweating face and explained, to general laughter and applause, what had happened. The show went on, while the stage-hands and ushers did their best to towel down the soaking, but surprisingly cheerful, victims of the mishap.

As for the Pender Troupe, they were on stage for a total of nine minutes in three hours of continuous performance, followed by the midnight matinée. *Variety* called them "of the English style of grotesque comedy, with a sprinkling of acrobatics". *Variety* continued:

> The present little act might indicate that the Pender Troupe is capable of giving a pleasing and regular number. The ten people, one by one, appear on stilts . . . Each wears a large hooded mask with comedy face, while little hands are seen from the arms up in the air. The close is the grouping of the ten figures, in step one behind the other.

The Penders were especially popular in an antic encore to the "Down the Strand" number in *Gaby*, in which they wore London costermonger costumes, and they closed both the main performance and the midnight cabaret in costumes composed partly of Stars and Stripes and partly of Union Jacks.

Unfortunately, for all of its razzle-dazzle, cheerful vulgarity and richness of production values, the Folies Bergère flopped. The chief reason was that the ticket prices at the top level of $2.50 were too high for the masses of theatre-goers, who couldn't manage more than a dollar. The show was for the rich, and the rich who went to the theatre were limited in number and had many other entertainments to distract them. What was more, the show lacked the touch of genius which Florenz Ziegfeld was already bringing to his celebrated Follies. Whereas Ziegfeld integrated dance, comedy (the latter never to his complete satisfaction), ballet and light operatic effects into a stunningly complete whole, Lasky and Harris simply threw one act after another into the melting-pot, and failed to produce pure gold. Worse, they panicked, and the moment the show began to lose money they chopped some of their best French acts, made the entire company take salary cuts amounting to a total of just over $1,000, and put so much pressure on Ethel Levey to add elements to her performance that she found an excuse and left for London to appear with great success at the Alhambra. R. H. Burnside resigned in a fury because of too much interference. The quality of the food was reduced, and the courses brought down from eight to six. This annoyed the heavy-eating customers. Meals became enormously expensive and less good and the wine cellar was reduced. The introduction of the young Irving Berlin's Alexander's Rag-Time Band provided a temporary fillip, as did the voluptuous Mademoiselle Simone, who posed in what appeared to be nothing more substantial than a $20,000 necklace that reached to her knees.

The Penders left before the show completed its run, victims of another economy purge. Apparently the decision was made to return Archie to Bristol. He reappeared, no doubt in a state of disappointment and irritation, at the drab and humdrum Bishop Road Infant School that September while the luckier Lomases went on to do another pantomime, *Hop O' My Thumb* at the Theatre Royal, Drury Lane. It must have been painful for the boy to have to make up stories explaining his absence; more painful still to suppress the exciting truth and to show no hint of his newly acquired acrobatic skills in the school playground.

He found some consolation in attending Saturday matinées at the Metropole, Pringle's Picture Palace, and Claire Street Cinemas, where he could see the Keystone Cops imitating the Lomases, along with such comedians as John Bunny, who had a face like mouldy cheese, and the beautiful comedienne Mabel Normand. He loved knockabout comedy more than ever, and seeing these actors on the screen, racing in fire wagons or souped-up 1911 jalopies down the rambling, interminable suburban streets of Los Angeles past palm trees and scrub and telephone poles stirred longings in him for a distant world.

On September 30, 1912, now known as Bob Pender and his Dandies, the Lomases were back in Bristol, performing at the Empire Music Hall. In January 1914, Archie had another exciting evening when his father took him to see the great American star Fanny Brice in *Hello, Ragtime*, a revue at the Prince's theatre.

That same year, Archie joined the Boy Scouts, and obtained, when war broke out, a Junior Air Raid Warden badge. He won a scholarship to Fairfield Grade and Secondary School. His father could barely find enough money to pay for his cap, blazer and trousers; he had to buy them in second-hand stores. This was humiliating. And then he received a shock: he returned home one day to be told that his mother had died suddenly of a heart attack and had had to be buried immediately. He repeatedly asked where the grave was, but was never told. It was only years later that he learned she had been admitted to the Fishponds Lunatic Asylum. This was much the worse of the two existing institutions for the insane in Bristol. It cost only one pound a year to put someone into this bedlam. Conditions were filthy and disgusting, and the patients wandered about, dirtying themselves, screaming, and tearing at their hair. The apparent reason for Elias signing papers which committed his wife was that he now installed a mistress, Mabel Bass, sometimes known as Meg, in his house. Though still neurotic and disturbed, Elsie Leach was no more insane than he was. Perhaps less so, if one considers the appalling wickedness of his move in incarcerating her.

Archie began his career at Fairfield Grade and Secondary School. He was admitted on September 2, 1915. The school was a hideous Victorian pile surrounded by a large playground which has since largely disappeared. Poorly heated and almost airless in the summer, it was a bare, stark place, serving horrible food. However, the now cheerful, sportive Archie, who had learned much from his months in the music-hall world, mixed well, and with his good looks and sturdy physique that had been greatly improved by stilt-walking and acrobatic training, and sexy, long-lashed

eyes he vanquished many of the young girls and earned the
admiration of his fellow pupils. He was fortunate that
because of his family's penuriousness he was not subject
to the homoerotic pleasures of public school. And the
headmaster of Fairfield, the Mr. Chips-like Augustus Smith,
was a delight. Almost everyone loved the glorious "Gussie".
It is true that he would rap certain students over the
knuckles, among them Archie Leach, for such innocent
offences as eating an apple between classes; like most head
teachers of his time, he was a little too handy with a birch
rod. But few resented even his strictest punishments. He
was a benign despot, striding through the corridors of the
school with his mortar-board and floating black gown,
dressed in tweeds, his cheeks flushed with excitement. Archie was also very fond of George Stockell, the science
master, with whom he kept in touch for the rest of his life,
giving him a five-pound note on his retirement in the 1960s.
There was the moustachioed Henri Audcent, the French
teacher, the robust "Maps" Madkins, who taught geogra-
phy, the music teacher J. D. Arnold; the chemistry teacher
Henry H. Howett, known by the name of one of his famous
formulae as H3. And there was the vigorous Miss Truscott,
who taught brisk gymnastics, in which, of course, Archie
Leach was supreme.

Archie was a mischievous boy, whose chief offence, according to a schoolmate, the present Mrs. Lillian Pearce,
was that "he wouldn't do his homework. It was supposed
to take place for one and a half hours every evening.
Instead, he would go to the Prince's or the [Empire and]
Hippodrome". Mrs. Pearce adds, "He was a very popular
boy, he was clever at most subjects and expert at all sports."

Another schoolmate, who later became an assistant to
the art teacher Minnie F. Townsend, was Ellen Kathleen
Hallett. She remembers:

Archie was average in art, good-looking, but you can't
tell from the acorn what the oak will be. The room in
which I taught Archie was divided in half. The boys on

the left next to the corridor, and the girls on the right. I can still see Leach half-way down the classroom. He always said he wanted to join the circus. He wasn't troublesome. He was just a nice, ordinary boy. But I must admit I was annoyed in 1947 when I saw the film *Bachelor Girl* [called in America *The Bachelor and the Bobbysoxer*] and the famous Cary Grant was being interviewed by Shirley Temple and said he had been taught art at school by a Miss Hallett. I thought he should have asked me first!

Another pupil at Fairfield was a man who calls himself Ted Morley. He says:

Archie never had anything to do with any of the girls at the school. His best sport was "fives", a form of squash played with gloves. He played the school piano quite well, specialising in music-hall songs. He had very strong teeth and would perform a trick in which he would place a heavy object in his handkerchief and then pick it up by biting the two ends of the hanky in his molars. He was always scruffily dressed, but his hair was neat and plastered down with brilliantine. In those days, his nose was so upturned that when you looked straight at him you could see all the way up his nostrils.

In the evenings, Archie would work backstage in the various Bristol theatres, eager as always to meet the performers. He was a call-boy, yelling out when an actor or actress was due on stage, or would run errands, carrying cups of tea into dressing-rooms, or helping to fend off the "Stage-Door Johnnies". There was great excitement for him in the week of July 16–21, 1917, when Bob Pender's Nippy Nine Burlesque Rehearsal, as the act was now called, turned up for two performances a night at the recently built Bristol Hippodrome.* It takes no feat of the imagination

* replacing the Empire-and-Hippodrome, which was demolished.

34

to envisage the reunion. From November 19–24 of the
same year, the great magician David Devant returned to
Bristol where Archie had seen him perform at the theatre
in Bedminster, to do his famous tricks at the Hippodrome,
including the Feather Necklet, the Magic Mirror, the German Soldier, David Devant's Disembodied Spirit, and the
Artist's Dream. All of these acts were exquisitely done. The
Penders were on the same bill, and it is probable that Bob
Pender secured Archie the job of assisting Devant's lighting
experts to create the illusions.

Then almost fifty, Devant was at the height of his career.
His brooding, attractively ugly face was strong and forceful;
he exuded self-confidence and masculine good cheer. But
he suffered from recurrent nervous disturbances and
periods of actual madness.

Archie watched fascinated from the flies above the stage
as he trained the lights on the great magician. Devant tied
an assistant with a sixteen-foot ribbon, sealed the knots
with wax, and threw the ends to the audience. Then he
placed the assistant in a cabinet and drew the curtains. The
audience members never let go of the ribbon. Suddenly, he
told them to pull the ribbon, the curtains opened, and a
woman was standing there tied up identically. He showed
a beautiful girl, dressed as a moth, drawn to a candle flame
and appear to vanish into thin air. He produced two dozen
eggs from a seemingly empty bowler hat, reduced a six-foot
soldier with a flick of the wrist to a two-foot-sized wooden
doll, cracked a two-foot egg with a spoon, found another
egg inside it, and another and another, finally producing a
full-sized girl from the smallest egg of all. The highlight of
the evening was the Magic Mirror act in which Archie
assisted.

To a dramatic roll of drums, David Devant put on heavy
black robes. An audience member in identical robes stood
next to him. The two men gazed into an enormous mirror.
Archie was supposed to train a spotlight on the mirror,
creating an illusion of a flame like a red rose. The figure of
Satan would emerge from it, luring the two men in to meet

a beautiful, semi-nude girl who lurked in the depths of the coloured glass. But Archie trained the spotlight too low, exposing where the girl was hidden. The curtain was rung down, Devant was furious, and Archie was fired on the spot.

In March 1918, Archie was expelled suddenly from Fairfield. There are three versions of what happened. His own explanation, given in interviews over the years, was that he had been found improperly in the girls' lavatories. This version was clearly intended to build up his masculine image. According to Lillian Pearce, he was found in the girls' playground. She says that he was discovered there with two other boys, reason enough for immediate dismissal. She asked him years later why he wouldn't mention the name of the boys who were expelled with him, and he only said, "I don't give names away." Mrs. Pearce adds, "His expulsion was so unfair. Several of us girls were in tears over it, because we didn't like to lose him." Ted Morley gives a different reason. He says: "The reason for Archie Leach being sent away is clear. He was involved in an act of theft with two other boys in the same class in a town named Almondsbury, near Bristol."

Mr. Morley refuses to say what was stolen. But a clue may be found in the same film, *The Bachelor and the Bobbysoxer*, in which his art teacher was mentioned. Interviewed by Shirley Temple, his character says that he was thrown out of school for stealing "a valise containing paints". At the time it was generally known how anxious he was to become an artist. Since it is unlikely he and his friends would have risked breaking into a store, which even in those days would have been equipped with a burglar alarm, it is more probable that he stole the valise from a private home.

There are also different versions of the conditions of the expulsion. According to Ted Morley, Archie, as he was told the dreaded news by the head teacher, walked down the aisle through all the other students, who were assembled to hear the verdict. As he did so, he took a cigarette from

a case, put it in his mouth without lighting it, and left.
Lillian Pearce says:

> We all assembled in straight rows, girls on the left of the
> line, boys on the right. We were standing. Archie was
> called to the platform. He stood to take the quiet but
> firm punishment in words, but he was not upset in any
> way. He was told to go home. He walked down the hall
> halfway, then he suddenly turned to face headmaster
> Augustus Smith, and said, "Please, Sir, may I take my
> school books home with me?" He was told that of course
> he could keep his books, but not now. Mr. Smith said,
> "Go home and I will promise to send your books after
> you." And this was done.

This episode took place in March. Now that he was free,
and we do not know Elias Leach's response to this disgrace,
he instantly rejoined the Bob Pender Troupe. Although he
tried to colour the picture in later years by saying that he
ran away from home, there is no evidence of this. It was a
natural progression for him to go back to the world of the
stage.

His next appearance with the Lomases was at the Nor-
wich Hippodrome in Norfolk from May 13–18, 1918 in
twice-nightly performances at six thirty and eight thirty.
Among the attractions of the evening were Pathé's gazette,
the latest pictures, Marcel Caron, pleasing vocalist, and the
popular Alfred Wellesley, in comedy burlesque as "The
Mad Emperor". This company moved on to the Ipswich
Hippodrome two days later, performing until the 25th.

The tour continued, still with the same performers,
through the south and west of England; records of the
period are scattered, but the *Era*, the weekly magazine of
show business, recorded the troupe as being present at the
Hippodrome, Devonport, back in Bristol at the Empire, at
the Aldershot Hippodrome and the Aberdeen Palace in July
and August. The Christmas season of 1918 was spent at
the Prince's theatre, Edinburgh, where the Lomases, with

Archie, performed in *Cinderella*. The following year, they would be placed at Rotherham, Dewsbury, York, Doncaster, Liverpool, Dundee, Morecambe, Eccles, and back at Bristol again in September. They spent another Christmas at the Prince's in Edinburgh, this time starring in *Babes In the Wood*. In many performances, they featured a popular dancing cow, the rear-end of which was Archie Leach. On all fours, under a heavy canvas cow costume, he appeared to be having a marvellous time. He formed a close friendship with a midget member of the troupe, Sammy Curtis, who never forgot him, and who, over forty years later, was to meet him in memorable circumstances in London.

While on tour, the company was informed that they had been engaged for an appearance in New York. Archie was overjoyed to learn that he would be returning to Manhattan, scene of the wonderful experience in the Folies Bergère. The troupe was cast in the energetic review *Tip-Top*, starring the famous comedian Fred Stone, which would be presented at the Globe theatre in the late summer of 1920 by the impresario Charles Dillingham. By now, Archie Leach was as much a member of the family as Tom and Bill Lomas, Robert's brothers, Maggie, Bob's widowed sister-in-law, also called Maggie, and her son, also called Bob. Contemporaries recall that only Doris Pender, who was now nineteen, greatly resented Archie Leach – as a result of her father's favouritism – hating him till the end of her life.

That this favouritism was a reality can be proven by the fact that Robert Lomas chose Archie alone to sail with him on the first vessel carrying the troupe to Manhattan; the others followed separately, according to Lomas custom. Archie was by now the leader of the troupe, excelled only by Bob Lomas himself as an acrobat and stilt-walker. The harlequinade had ceased many years before, but he was still indispensable as a knockabout policeman, clown and general assistant behind the scenes. When on July 21, 1920 he set sail with Lomas on the SS *Olympic*, sister ship of the *Titanic*, from Southampton, scene of so many of his father's peccadillos, he was still, at sixteen, five foot nine, not grown to his full height, and his complexion was described as "sallow" in the passenger manifest. His black hair was parted in the middle, and his eyes were so nearly black that they were described as dark-brown in contrast to the eyes of the other passengers, which were merely described as brown. Oddly, he gave his next of kin as "C. Leach", a mystery since nobody with that initial can be found in his family. It is possible that the "C" was a mistake for an "E". Soon after he left, his father was to have another child, Eric Leslie, by his common-law wife, Mabel Bass.

The *Olympic* steamed into New York Harbour on July 28. Among the passengers were Douglas Fairbanks, Snr., and Mary Pickford, who had just returned from a six-week honeymoon in Europe, conducted in the glare of publicity. Accompanied by fireworks, streamers, and a brass band, an enormous crowd was gathered on the wharf to welcome the most famous couple in the world. Archie had formed a superficial acquaintance with Fairbanks, since they both had been working out with weights in the ship's gymnasium. They would keep in touch on and off through the years.

Archie Leach would recall many years later – as Cary Grant – his new sighting of New York:

The most prominent spire, in the year of 1920, was the Woolworth Building. If any happy medium, any fortune-telling gypsy, had prophesied I would marry the heiress grand-daughter of its founder, no palm would have been crossed with *my* silver.

But, for the moment, his marriage to Barbara Hutton was twenty-one years away.

The troupe obtained a long, narrow apartment on West Fiftieth Street, near the corner of Eighth Avenue. The weather was unseasonably mild for July, with temperatures amazingly in the lower sixties. The troupe reported for work at the Globe theatre, where rehearsals for *Tip-Top* had already begun. They were scheduled to act as crazy cops in an episode in a courtroom in which Fred Stone was involved in a farcical trial. But, apparently, the combination of constant rewrites and a low proscenium arch, which made stilt-walking difficult, resulted in Charles Dillingham informing Robert Lomas of a change of plan. The Pender Troupe of Giants would instead be cast in the colossal revue entitled *Good Times*, to open imminently at the Hippodrome, one of the largest theatres in the United States. Lomas and Archie Leach were not disappointed. Their only problem was the lack of time to rehearse an entirely different routine before the first night on August 9. The other members of the troupe had barely arrived in New York and *Good Times* called for a somewhat different approach than *Tip-Top*. Nevertheless, by frantically working day and night, the troupe managed to fit into the elaborate chiaroscuro of the larger musical event.

Charles Dillingham was a genial and charming producer, who instantly electrified Lomas, Archie Leach and the others. With his white hair, ruddy face, white moustache and handsome figure dressed in the height of fashion, he was a suave gentleman of the world, far removed from his chief rival, the shrill, vulgar, manic genius Florenz Ziegfeld. To the Lomases' great delight, R. H. Burnside, their talented director from 1911, was maestro of this new extravaganza.

The Hippodrome presented a remarkable spectacle to the energetic band of players. The theatre could accommodate several hundred people on the stage at once, and about a thousand in the audience. It had a huge revolving stage, and the most elaborate theatrical machinery available. There was a tank that contained almost a million gallons of water, a waterfall that could be produced in an instant, a complicated battery of multicoloured lights, vast prop-rooms and wardrobe departments, and cages for a variety of animals ranging from monkeys to leopards and elephants. The Ziegfeld Follies, for all its razzle-dazzle, was somewhat more intimate in mood: tasteful, with exquisitely choreographed dancers whom Ziegfeld always refused to place in straight lines, and magical illusions, and transformation effects. *Good Times* was closer to a circus than anything else.

The music was by Max Steiner, whom Archie met later, in the 1940s, when Steiner was one of the two reigning composers at Warner Bros. The show, written by a variety of hands, starred such popular figures as Poodles Hanna-ford, the most nimble of acrobatic performers, and Jack Johnstone, famous for his frantic bicycling routine. Like the Folies Bergère, *Good Times* was divided into three scenes, or pieces, which were entitled "The Valley of Dreams", "A Toy Store", and "The Magic Grotto". Among the fanciful and exotic effects the evening offered were chorus-girls blowing multicoloured bubbles through straws, followed by an enormous bubble bursting over their heads, Elizabeth Coyle as the Statue of Light posing before a sequined backdrop behind which the Shadows of Long Ago danced in silhouette, and Colourland, a marching procession which went up and down an illuminated stair-case. At the climax, set in the Land of Happiness, the stage was turned into a lake, and then, in turn, into a series of Venetian canals, into which, carrying the flags of all nations, scantily clad girls dived from thirty-foot-high boards or slid down chutes. It was a precursor of the spectacles which Busby Berkeley would introduce to motion pictures just over a decade later.

The Pender Troupe of Giants appeared only once, in the "Toy Store" sequence, which featured dolls from every part of the world coming to life and executing acrobatic routines. They were followed by Abdullah's Arabs, from whom Archie learned a special tumbling dance, similar to modern breakdancing, in which the fall was taken on the neck and shoulders and the dancers spun around on their upper backs, leaping with great agility to their feet, somersaulting and spinning around on their backs again. *Variety* said of the Lomases:

In marches and formations, starting with a midget and winding up with a stilted figure twelve feet tall, they . . .

lined up abreast in "pair of stairs" formation for comedy business . . . The troupe is distinctly European in comedy appeal, but got over as sight asset at the *Hip*.

Good Times was an instant hit and earned everyone rave reviews, even from the staid *New York Times*. But life in the apartment just off Eighth Avenue was not comfortable. Always there was the contrast between the thrill of performance and the drabness of temporary digs, with, for example, a long line for the one bathroom every morning. The Penders, for all Bob Pender's fondness for Archie, were severe taskmasters. Archie became house-mother, assisting Maggie Pender in washing dishes, making beds, cooking (mostly heavy stews), and sweeping the floors. The favourite of his foster father in the theatre, he was the maid off-stage. The one thing he was not responsible for was the laundry. At night, after the show, the whole family would line up at the kitchen sink to wash their socks and handkerchiefs, towels and shirts, and then they would proceed one by one to the ironing-board. The ritual continued until the small hours. The only member of the family other than Mrs. Lomas capable of sewing on buttons or knitting was Archie Leach.

Archie fell in love with Manhattan. He was dazzled by the great stars who were appearing on Broadway and occasionally managed to get a matinée off to see them. He formed friendships at the time. He very much liked Poodles Hannaford, who stood, with one foot on each of two horses, riding bareback around a sawdust circus ring at the Hippodrome, and he was horrified when, one afternoon, Hannaford slipped off and was badly injured. Archie never forgot the great equestrian. He formed a friendship with Francis Renault, one of the best female impersonators in the city. A rival of the great Julian Eltinge, Renault was very successful, wearing exquisite costumes, and a fantastic variety of wigs, specialising particularly in a sensational impersonation of Lillian Russell. Despite the fact that he was virile and muscular, billed as the "Last of the Red-Hot

Papas", he was unabashedly gay and enjoyed, because of his performance, the attentions of many stage-struck young men. Renault is believed to have become both lover and patron of Archie, helping him financially over the years.

More importantly, George Orry-Kelly became the young Leach's best friend, and, it was generally believed, his lover. Jack Kelly, as George Orry-Kelly was known, was Australian. He was born in the country town of Kiama, New South Wales, son of William Kelly, a tailor, who hailed from the Isle of Man, and Florence Purdue Kelly, on December 31, 1897. Of slightly below medium height, well-knit and stocky, he was a handsome, effeminate youth, with large, dreamy-blue eyes, brown hair, and a sparkling, energetic, if at times hot-tempered nature. Fiercely ambitious, he had been named Orry after an Isle of Man king as well as the Orry carnation that flourished in his mother's garden. He began his life as an actor, clothing designer and scenic artist, the protégé of the gifted Eleanor Weston, who ran the local theatre. He is still remembered by elderly people in Kiama, who own his oil landscapes of the bush, and the ties, silk shawls and cushions which he designed and painted for them long ago.

After a brief and unsatisfactory period in London, and a short-lived stint on the New York stage as a chorus boy, Jack Kelly was a struggling tailor's assistant in the garment district by the time he met Archie. The two men were strongly attracted. Orry-Kelly was barely twenty-four when they met, full of gossip and breezy repartee. His Australian accent had been sandpapered down to an acceptable mid-Atlantic sound. The young men (Archie was just seventeen in the early months of 1921) decided to live together. They settled on an apartment in a house in Greenwich Village, just behind the present site of the Cherry Lane theatre. They needed a third roommate in order to meet the rent, which was in the region of fifteen dollars a month. The person they selected as their companion was also gay: Charlie Phelps, known as Charlie Spangles. He was Australian too, and had known Jack Kelly in Sydney, when he had worked a concession on Bondi Beach. He had been a steward aboard the *Olympic* and had jumped ship to make up the household with his new friends. He recalled later, "The three of us lived in what was a kind of massive loft. I remember that Archie loved fish, particularly English fish, and used to go and buy Dover sole at the market, and plaice. He would cook it for us."

The three men began to entertain. While Archie continued in *Good Times*, Charlie Spangles appeared at the Metropole Club in Greenwich Village, in an act entitled *Josephine and Joseph*, in which half of his costume was male and the other half female. One side of his face offered a beard and moustache, and the other half had lipstick, rouge, and mascara on his eyelashes. Jack Kelly now earned a living painting murals, and drawing subtitles for silent films.

The run of *Good Times* ended on April 30, 1921. To his delight, Archie was told that the troupe would now appear with the Ringling Brothers Barnum and Bailey Circus, touring the eastern states for a period of three months, starting with a special gala opening at a fairground in Brooklyn. The sweet scent of sawdust remained a recurring memory for the rest of Archie's life. The Pender Troupe of Giants was ideally suited to Ringling Brothers, and the succession of clowns, tumblers, lion acts, bicyclists, girls climbing ladders of swords, trapeze artists, and brass bands leading processions of giants and midgets was a big experience for the seventeen-year-old, star-struck youth. Charlie Phelps kept house with Jack Kelly during Archie's absence on tour. He said later that he enjoyed his role as housekeeper, but there is no indication that he was having an affair with Kelly. According to John Marvin, who knew Phelps well, "It was only Orry-Kelly who was in love with Cary Grant."

At the end of the tour of the Ringling Brothers Circus that summer, Archie returned to New York for a few days before embarking on a series of appearances for Poli's vaudeville circuit, starting on September 5, travelling from

Worcester, Massachusetts, to Hartford and Bridgeport, Connecticut, with the Lomases. They closed the first half of the bill. A better opportunity came after the Bridgeport engagement when they were signed by the United Booking Office for the Keith Circuit, headed by B. F. Keith. This was a step up in the world. The troupe started a gruelling schedule of engagements. They began in Washington, DC, on a steamy September 26, proceeding to Brooklyn, at the Bushwick theatre, and then, glory of glories, to the Palace in New York, the most valued venue in the nation. They were well received there, and mentioned in several reviews, leaving the city on a tide of excitement, and proceeding to Baltimore, Philadelphia, where the Lomases had numerous relatives and where they stayed with Robert Lomas' second cousin Richard, on to Buffalo, and then across to Toronto and Montreal in Canada. The tour continued to Rochester, where they played at the Temple theatre in the dead of winter, January 1922.

It had been an exciting few months. They had worked with such adored entertainers as Trixie Friganza and Harry Langdon, who was also a screen success, Jean Adair, and Eddie Foy and the Seven Little Foys. All of these headliners warmly befriended the troupe. Archie was particularly fond of Jean Adair. He had first run into her in Detroit, and was taken with her comedic skill and lively Scottish charm. They met up again when they were billed together in Rochester, where, worn down by the constant shifts of locale, strenuous work and the second-rate food, Archie Leach's constitution finally gave out, and he was stricken with rheumatic fever. He lost weight, was unable to sleep, and tossed and turned with a high temperature. Miss Adair nursed him through his sickness, and he never forgot her kindness. But he did not recover sufficiently and the tour was interrupted for several weeks while he convalesced.

The Penders dropped out of the Keith Circuit. But they were rescued by an individual who would one day become one of Archie's closest friends and his business partner. Frank Vincent was the sleek, dapper, young and able joint manager of the booking department of the Orpheum Circuit under President Martin Beck. In his offices at the Palace theatre in New York City, he was a perpetually warm and charming presence, dressed in the height of fashion, sporting elegant spats, and radiating good cheer from his prematurely greying head to his well-shod feet. He took an intense liking to Archie; the troupe was accorded the great honour, through the Central Booking Office, of touring the Orpheum chain of theatres.

On March 27, 1922, the Pender Troupe of Giants was in St. Louis; later, Archie would make a splash in the Municipal Opera in that city. There were three further appearances, at the Majestic in Milwaukee, the State-Lake in Chicago, and the 105th Street theatre in Cleveland, Ohio, when, apparently, some crisis in the family sent Robert Lomas, his wife, and other family members, except one of his brothers, back to England. Archie elected to stay behind. He was probably mindful of the London strike of May 1921, which had thrown many performers out of work. But his decision to take his chances in New York was a dangerous one. He and Robert Lomas' brother Tom hoped to form an act, but, unfortunately, even the keen support of Frank Vincent didn't help, and it proved impossible to secure any bookings that summer. Archie returned to the apartment in Greenwich Village and resumed his relationship with Jack Kelly. According to George Burns, he would sell Kelly's painted neckties in the street to make a living. Somehow, he and Jack and Charlie Phelps managed to pay the rent.

A job became available. It was humiliating, but at least it was a way of earning a living. A figure of Times Square was the popular stilt-walker Fred Wilson. He was a cheerful Bostonian who liked to appear in a policeman's uniform, holding children high above the crowd as he comically misdirected the traffic. He advertised various theatrical attractions with a sandwich-board.

Frank Wilson fell ill, and Archie was approached by the Chamber of Commerce to take over. He was forced to accept. He would now be a taller figure than he had been on the stage. He would wear ten-foot supports, which meant that his head was sixteen feet in the air. The stilts, with size fourteen shoes at the end and flapping goliath trousers, made up a weight of fifty-six pounds and his elaborate costume added twelve pounds more. It was one thing to perform on stage with proper rehearsal and preparation, it was quite something else to force a passage through the dense crowds thronging the theatre district, without bumping into anyone, stepping on children, or being thrown off the stilts by the determined efforts of hoodlums.

The summer heat and the white New York sun beating through a haze of automobile fumes, were well-nigh insupportable under these conditions. Children mocked him, tugged at his trousers and tried to dislodge him. He would have lost his job if he had kicked them or hit them with his hat. He had to smile at all times, and announce, through a megaphone, what was going on at the various film or legitimate theatres.

The author, Samuel Marx, who became the head of the story department at MGM Studios, never forgot Archie. He says:

> I recall this handsome young man, whom I would recognize as soon as I saw him on the screen, walking on stilts outside the Capitol theatre, which was run by Major Bowes, later of radio fame, indicating to the crowds through announcements or sandwich boards (and the crowds were fascinated and curious), that there were all kinds of exciting stage activities to be found at the Capitol, including various live acts. My offices were at 1600 Broadway, and whenever I would come out of there, even on Sundays, I would see him and talk to him. I never forgot Archie Leach. He was always smiling.

Brooks Atkinson mentioned Archie, but not by name, in his classic history *Broadway* ("A man with advertising boards over his shoulders walked through the Times Square throngs on stilts"). Sometimes, Archie would have a starched shirt studded with bulbs which would flash electric-light signals on and off.

He worked at Coney Island when Fred Wilson returned to Times Square, hired by Thomas McGowan, general manager of Steeplechase Park. (He remembered that he was engaged by George Tilyou, the genius creator of the amusement park, or by his son, Edward, but Tilyou had been dead for some years, and Edward did not engage staff.)

He was supposed to parade up and down the Bowery, a boardwalk that ran from Feldman's Astroland all the way to Steeplechase Park, but, on Sundays, he would sometimes be allowed to sell hot dogs from a stall. He wore a sandwich-board (he denied it in later years) which announced on the front STEEPLECHASE THE FUNNY PLACE, and, on the back, 50 ATTRACTIONS FOR 50 CENTS. He remembered that he wore a doorman's uniform of green coat, red braid, and green jockey-cap with red peak and long, tube-like black trousers. But eye-witnesses confirm that Jack Kelly designed for him a fantastic suit of pink and white linen, cleverly prepared so that it would be of minimum weight in the heat. The stripes on the white background were three-quarters of an inch wide. There was a bright pink cutaway jacket, over the striped shirt, and the trousers billowed out in enormous bell-bottoms. Archie also wore a pink and white striped top hat.

Matthew Kennedy, today the Executive Secretary of the Coney Island Chamber of Commerce, has never forgotten Archie Leach as he strolled up and down the Bowery on his stilts. He says:

The kids liked to follow him like the Pied Piper. I was one of them. I was ten years old in 1922, and sold ice-creams. Archie felt his job was beneath him, and instead of laughing with us when we teased him, he would look snootily down his nose at us and try to ignore us. I used to shout up at him and he would barely respond. We used to rag him and pull at the stilts. And he certainly *had* his head in the air in every sense.

Coney Island was at the height of its excitement and success in 1922. The subway was bringing crowds by the thousands from the city on sweltering summer weekends, and the marvellous variety of rides, the garish pavilions, the whirling ferris wheels, the merry-go-rounds, the simulated mechanical horse-ride with the horses pulled on chains, and the razzle-dazzle of fireworks, freaks and dancing animals created a magic kingdom long before Disneyland was dreamed of.

3

For all its tinselly glamour, Archie Leach hated Coney Island. He made everyone feel his contempt for the job, and they, as well as he, were greatly relieved when he was made redundant on Labor Day. He was engaged for *Better Times*, the sequel to *Good Times*, and Bob Lomas returned from England to re-form the troupe, which was now to be headed by Doris, aged twenty-two, and her husband, the accomplished acrobatic dancer Jack Hartman. Once again, Charles Dillingham was the producer and R. H. Burnside the director of the show, which was, of course, at the Hippodrome. There were the usual number of animals, including elephants, horses, and the remarkable Jacko the Crow, who, according to one source, "batted barely a feather as he snatched balls and tiny Indian clubs out of the air".

There was the "Land of Mystery", featuring dancers dressed as skeletons performing against a pitch-black backdrop, "At the Grand Opera Ball", in which hundreds of performers danced through the horn of a giant phonograph dressed as the characters of world-famous operas, the "Story of a Fan", in which the dancers were costumed as multicoloured fans, turning into one single giant fan at the climax, and the "Fat Man's Fair", a re-creation of an old-fashioned summer carnival, set partly on a magically re-created river-bank complete with flowing water. Archie appeared with four other performers as one of the Meistersingers in "At the Grand Opera Ball", dressed appropriately as Wagner's characters. He also appeared in drag in another number, with Tom Lomas. Well received by critics and public alike, *Better Times* ran from its opening on August 31, 1922, to April 28, 1923. Immediately after the closing night, Bob Lomas returned to England for the last time; he was to retire eighteen months later and open a balloon, novelty and toy shop at Southend in Essex.

Jack Hartman, Doris Pender, Tom Lomas, Jim Lomas and Archie Leach formed, along with a few American recruits, what was now known as the Lomas Troupe. It played on the Pantages Circuit, starting in Spokane, Washington, on September 3, 1923. What happened to Archie during the six-month period in between the closing of the Hippodrome show and the beginning of the tour is unknown, except for two brief appearances he made, at the beginning of May, at Proctor's theatre in Elizabeth, New Jersey, and in a one-night special revival of *Better Times* for the US Chamber of Commerce Eleventh Annual Meeting at the Hippodrome. According to the theatre historian Herbert Goldman, it was widely rumoured that Archie was a gigolo in New York, servicing a rich woman. However, there is no evidence to support this.

The Pantages tour took the Lomas Troupe from Spokane and Seattle, Washington, to Vancouver, Tacoma, Portland, Oregon, and San Francisco, winding up in Los Angeles on the first leg of the tour on October 29, 1923. They were now top of the bill, along with the William Weston Company, Poppy Chadwick, and "The Musical Attorneys". It was Archie's first visit to Hollywood. He was fortunate in being able to contact Douglas Fairbanks, Snr., who invited him to visit the set of a new movie in production, *The Thief of Bagdad*, in which he saw the great star and athlete climbing up a trellis, a flying carpet on wires, a genie, a flying horse, and other marvels.

Archie fell in love with the strange and exotic settlement that lay between the desert and the ocean. The hard, white, glittering light, the unblemished blue sky, the low-lying, sand-coloured buildings and tall, nodding desert palms created an atmosphere not unlike that of Egypt as seen in the travelogues. Unfortunately, the troupe's appearances were brief, only four days in extent, and soon they were travelling on to at least a dozen other states before they wound up in Wilmington, Delaware in November 1924.

After a brief hiatus, the Lomas Troupe reunited early in the new year for yet another series of engagements that took them as far as Saskatchewan and Alberta. They were back in Los Angeles in May 1925, repeating the same circuit and again earning excellent reviews. The monotony of the tours was almost indescribable. For two years or more, in almost every part of America and Canada, Archie and his seven companions had to repeat, night after night, and twice on matinée days, an unchanging stilt-walking and dancing routine unrelieved by the harlequinade that had lent colour and character to the performance earlier on. At last, the tour came to an end and the troupe broke up. Exhausted, several members, including Jack and Doris Hartman, elected to return to England. Archie returned to Greenwich Village and Orry-Kelly. There, he formed a strong new friendship.

Don Barclay was an inspired clown and wit with an attractively ugly face and a tiny, well-knit and athletic physique. He began his career in San Francisco at the beginning of the century, where he sang and danced and sold newspapers to homeless survivors of the 1906 earthquake. He combined his talents as an entertainer with considerable skill as a cartoonist for the San Francisco *Examiner*. Working with medicine shows, carnivals, travelling Shakespeare presentations and burlesque shows, he scored a triumph in the Ziegfeld Follies of 1917 and 1918. Although it is claimed that he met Archie Leach in England in music-halls, there is no evidence of this. It seems to have been a publicist's idea, to help both their careers by linking them fictitiously together. By 1925, Barclay had achieved a considerable name in New York. His frantic and inspired playing was a much-admired feature of such shows as the *Greenwich Village Follies* and *Go-Go*. He encouraged Archie to break free of the drudgery of stilt performance and make his way into legitimate musical theatre. Meanwhile,

Archie found encouragement from Jack Kelly who was beginning to advance his career considerably. Kelly was starting to work in theatre design, and soon he would become the chief-costumier for Ethel Barrymore. Another friend, Phil Charig, was also making headway; he spent long periods of time in London, where he was beginning to establish a major name. One moment he was rehearsal pianist, the next he was composing songs for musicals. Archie Leach's first opportunity to cross the divide between vaudeville and "legit" came through the determined and very talented young Jean Dalrymple, who was then on the threshold of what would be one of the most illustrious careers in Broadway's history. Strong, good-natured, optimistic and forceful, this brilliant young woman had set up a partnership with Max Tishman and Dan Jarrott, her lover at the time, to put together comedy sketches which would be toured across the country in tandem. They did not involve singing and dancing, but only comedy situations.

Jean Dalrymple never forgot Archie Leach coming in to see her for a role in one of her playlets:

> The particular skit that I had put together with my partners was about the handsomest man in New York. The comedy developed from arguments over him by two women. Don't ask me to remember the rest of the plot!
>
> The agents kept sending us Rudolph Valentino types because Latin lovers were all the rage then. Archie walked in with his olive skin and slicked-down hair, and he obviously wasn't a Valentino type really. But he was adorable looking, and as soon as I saw him I said to my partners, "That's the one!"

Dan Jarrott, who was very handsome himself, was apparently irritated and jealous of Jean's interest in the young man and said he was quite impossible. He told her that since Archie had a Cockney accent (probably acquired from other music-hall colleagues) and walked oddly, with the bow-legged gait of someone who had spent years on stilts, there could be no question of casting him. But Jean Dalrymple was adamant. Max Tishman recalls:

> You should have seen the way Jean worked on him to get over that rubber-legged walk! You see, he would put one leg in front of the other as though he were balancing, and it looked peg-legged. His knees were so stiff he had completely forgotten how to cross a stage. If he ever knew!
>
> We put him together with a popular young actor, Jack Janis, who was blond to contrast with Archie's dark hair. He would show jealousy of the handsomest man in New York. Constance Robinson played one of the two girls. She was quite a name then.

Jean Dalrymple says:

> Archie was extremely nice and gentlemanly. Dan was always accusing me of falling in love with him. But he was living with another young man.* We used to have coffee together in tiny little coffee-houses, any place we could get a cup for ten cents. I didn't love Archie in the way a woman loves a man, but as a sister. He had terrific charisma. Constance Robinson and the other girl, whose name no one can remember, were crazy about him. But nothing happened between them.
>
> He wasn't dapper in those days. His suits were a little worn, a little shiny, but he did his best with what he had. His shoes were well-polished and his hair was always groomed with brilliantine.

Archie grew fond of Jean Dalrymple. The rehearsals were prolonged and difficult. It was hard for him to adapt to the techniques of comedy. But there were pleasant evenings when Dan Jarrott and Jean invited him to their rooms at the National Vaudeville Artists' Club on Forty-Sixth Street

---

* Orry-Kelly.

and later to Jean's apartment and Dan would sing in a lilting baritone voice and all the others would harmonise. Everyone was young, happy, and delighted to be alive in New York.

At last the act was ready, and Max Tishman remembers that they took off by train, $100 a week for each of the cast, out of which they paid for their digs. Tishman picked up the railway fares and made sure they had curtained sleepers which in those days were bunks placed along the corridors. "It was a joy to take train rides in those days," Tishman recalls. "The food in the dining-car was good, and the black help was outstanding." Both he and Jean Dalrymple remarked on Archie's pleasure in doing this tour, getting his feet wet for a future as a straight actor.

The Jack Janis Company, as it was known, began touring in May 1926, at the Strand, Atlanta, Georgia, then travelled through the southern states and then north to Wisconsin, Illinois, Ohio, Canada, and thence to appearances at the National, Orpheum, and Loew's houses in New York City and Brooklyn. The trio was well received, and Tishman remembers that they enjoyed full houses everywhere.

Back in Manhattan, two other members were introduced to the warm and cheerful circle of friends that centred on the Greenwich Village loft. These were George Burns and Gracie Allen. Burns' dead-pan, sombre calm in the face of Gracie's manic stupidity and dizzy, ceaseless line of chatter enchanted audiences and earned the pair enormous fame. At ninety-two, Burns still had vivid memories of Archie at the time. He first met him more casually in 1923, during the run of *Better Times*, when Archie's best friend was Fatty Arbuckle's wife Minta. Fatty, who had been ruined by a San Francisco scandal in which he had been charged with sexually attacking a young woman with a Coca-Cola bottle, was living in obscurity in Manhattan at the time. Minta loved to gossip, and so did Gracie, and Orry-Kelly was also a great source of news about public and private scandals of the time. Burns says:

I vividly recall Archie Leach and Jack Kelly. What are you going to do about Archie's . . . Cary's . . . homosexuality? I remember a party at Archie's in Greenwich Village, I was there with Gracie and Mary and Jack Benny. There were maybe about twenty people there, and a pianist, and I got up and sang. Minta Arbuckle hated my singing; I could see it in her face. That's all I needed, because then I wouldn't sing to anybody but her. I stood in front of her and kept singing and singing, and Jack Benny fell on the floor laughing. It was a funny thing, standing in front of this woman who despised me, singing love songs right at her. It didn't amuse Archie. He was fond of Minta.

Archie was fascinated by Burns. Always capable of learning from other entertainers, he observed his timing with the utmost care. Told of this, Burns said he was flattered, and then remarked:

What the hell is timing? Timing is Gracie finishes a joke and I don't laugh, and I just stare at the audience and smoke my cigar. And the audience laughs and laughs. And when the audience stops laughing at last, I stop smoking, and turn to Gracie and talk to her as though nothing has happened. That's timing. Can you imagine me talking while the audience is laughing? It would spoil everything. Maybe Cary liked the way my expression was flat while I was listening. The more disinterested I was, the more the people screamed. Maybe he took more from Gracie. He would have been better off. She was the talent. She never did anything twice. Nor did he.

Aware of the relationship between Archie and Orry-Kelly, George Burns mentions that they had a big quarrel one night after a party. He says, "Gracie loved scandal. I didn't. Those things didn't interest me. I'm not interested in anything that happened yesterday."

With Phil Charig composing for Jack Buchanan, the great

British star, in London, and Orry-Kelly beginning to work with Ethel Barrymore, Archie's circle was doing well. He began meeting the young and promising Moss Hart, who shared his sexual ambiguity. Tall, quietly genteel, well bred and discreet, with a quick, nimble wit, always dressed beyond his means, Hart was a delight, and would soon use elements of Archie in characters in his first stage success, *Once In a Lifetime*, co-authored by George S. Kaufman. Lester Sweyd, an odd, diminutive, high-powered character who was filled with a passionate and consuming interest in every aspect of theatrical history, was yet another in the rapidly expanding clique. He became a sort of chairman of the unofficial club, attacking anyone who dared question his judgments as he reigned supreme at the popular Rudley's Restaurant at Forty-First and Broadway, where four p.m. get-togethers over coffee for a gossip were common. Edward Chodorov, on his way to a career as a prominent playwright, Edward Eliscu, who would write the lyrics for such popular songs as "Orchids In the Moonlight", "Flying Down to Rio", and "Great Day", Preston Sturges, destined for a meteoric career in the movies, and the energetic would-be producer Oscar Serlin argued, laughed, flirted with ideas, attacked the reigning critics Alexander Woollcott and Percy Hammond, decided on the fate of the world and plotted tremendous dream careers. Soon their castles in the air would become real life palaces. Not one of them except, paradoxically, their leader Lester Sweyd, would fail to become famous.

Archie in many ways was a mascot of the group, seemingly the least gifted in terms of burning genius, but, in his alternate moods of great gloom and mischievous darting humour, vividly appealing to the others. He was the outsider, the underdog, the working-class Britisher among smart Manhattan sophisticates. They decided uniformly that he must be given a break. He was known familiarly to his friends as "Digger" or "Kangaroo", because, knowing the antipathy that existed between Englishmen of his class and raw, brash Australians, they liked to tease him by saying that they were sure he was posing as a Bristol man and actually hailed from the outback. When they heard that the weak, somewhat vacillating, but ambitious, young Reginald Hammerstein, nephew of the great Oscar and Arthur Hammerstein, was looking for an Australian type for the second male lead in the Otto Harbach-Oscar Hammerstein II musical, *Golden Dawn*, they and Orry-Kelly, who could of course lie that Archie was Australian, pushed him very hard for the part. Yet it involved at least a modicum of singing ability, and Archie could barely carry a tune. However, as soon as Reginald Hammerstein saw him walk into his office he knew that he was looking at a potential star in the making. By 1927, Archie had shed his callow, awkward manner and his strutting, bow-legged, cocky walk; he looked like a man-about-town and at the same time he had the roughness necessary in an Australian type. He had only to make a slight change in his vocal tones, abetted by Orry-Kelly, to be convincingly Aussie. And of course he had all of the superb physical characteristics that had become famous when journalists described Anzac soldiers of World War I.

Golden Dawn was an absurd contrivance about the white goddess of an African tribe, an excuse for a good deal of semi-nudity as the copper-skinned cast whirled about in ludicrously extravagant dance routines; there were sumptuous jungle sets and a variety of fake native masks and costumes to enliven this preposterous entertainment. The implied racism in portraying all the blacks on stage as mindless savages was, unhappily, typical of the era. The music by Emmerich Kalman and Herbert Stothart, who would later become the resident composer of MGM, was undistinguished, but the show featured the Metropolitan Opera Company star Louise Hunter, in a leading role, and, as a witch-dancer, Jacques Cartier created a sensation. He was described by the *New York Times*' Brooks Atkinson: "Flooded by an iridescent purple light, he leads a heathenish incantation before a pagan, African god, at the head of a chorus garbed in strange patterns and ceremonial masks."

Atkinson went on to describe *Golden Dawn* as "ponderous and mannered". It was an example of the showcase being more interesting than the show.

Hammerstein's theatre was opened for the occasion, a gothic cathedral with an organ console and an orchestra which rose and fell by means of a type of lift; stained-glass windows shone down on the audience with designs representing the figures of opera.

Golden Dawn cannot be described as a success, but it gave Archie the break he desperately needed, and Reginald Hammerstein announced that he would keep him under contract. Archie joined the prestigious William Morris Agency, and had as his particular agent Billy Grady, who also represented W. C. Fields, one of Archie's idols. Archie was pleased when he was cast in the show *Polly*, which was composed by Phil Charig. *Polly* opened in Wilmington, Delaware, in November 1928, partly backed by the duPonts; William duPont's daughter Marion would later figure in the life of Cary Grant. The reviews were devastating. June, the British star who had been imported for the occasion, was not equal to the demands of her role, and, although Archie received praise for his spectacular good looks, more than one reviewer pointed out the shortcomings in his musical and theatrical technique.

After an equally disastrous appearance in Philadelphia, Arthur Hammerstein closed the show following a November 17 performance, and brought it back to New York for rewrites and restaging. Much to his annoyance, Archie was dropped from the cast. Marilyn Miller, the blonde, pretty, self-indulgent Ziegfeld star, wanted him to appear in the hit musical *Rosalie*, but the Hammersteins refused to loan him out to Ziegfeld. Instead, they arranged, rather brutally, to sell his contract to the Shuberts.

J. J. Shubert, who had noticed Archie in performance, decided to put him into the cast of the Jeanette MacDonald vehicle, *Boom-Boom*, which was presented at the Casino theatre starting on January 28, 1929. Archie's was a small role in this French musical comedy farce with music, set on fashionable Park Avenue with a degree of risqué bedroom humour. Jeanette MacDonald, soon to become internationally famous as Nelson Eddy's co-star in a series of gloriously absurd movie operettas, turned out to be a good and decent friend. Although there was some artificially stimulated press gossip about rivalries between them, in fact there could be none, because Miss MacDonald was the buoyant star of the show, playing with great charm and expertise the various naughtinesses the playwright had created; Archie was no more than a supporting actor, whose singing was just barely adequate. However, his looks and figure earned him respectable reviews. On the first night, there was a tremendous stir as, halfway through her first song, Miss MacDonald was interrupted by the arrival of the Naval hero Captain Fried, who turned up with his crew in uniform and was shown into a box. The orchestra conductor abandoned the love duet and struck up "The Star-Spangled Banner".

Orry-Kelly designed Jeanette MacDonald's costumes for the show brilliantly. After a weakish two months in New York, *Boom-Boom* toured in Detroit, Chicago and points west. Archie broke off the tour to make a quick trip to England in the later part of the year, visiting his half-brother, Eric, in Bristol, who still kept Elsie's existence in the asylum a secret. He returned to New York late in the year and took up the role of Max in *A Wonderful Night*, which was again costumed by Orry-Kelly. It was based on Johann Strauss' operetta *Die Fledermaus*. On this occasion, the part called for the ability to sing. J. J. Shubert was so enamoured of Archie that he did the unthinkable: he placed him in front of a curtain and stood a practised singer behind it, who delivered the numbers with great expertise while Archie opened and shut his mouth. No critic suspected that this was taking place and he received some complimentary reviews on his improved vocal ability. He was on his way: he even started to get fan mail. Girls in the company made themselves available to him, but he seemed to be caught up in himself and in the specialised, predominantly homosexual group which surrounded him. There is no record of his having any love affairs with women at the time.

Orry-Kelly travelled to St. Louis to design for the St. Louis Municipal Opera Company. He had a violent quarrel about his salary with the Shuberts, especially Milton Shubert, who staged the shows, and returned to New York. Meanwhile, Archie toured in a show called *The Street Singer* in September 1930, humiliatingly demoted from the important role of George to the less important role of Jean Baptiste when John Price-Jones, who had been in the show on Broadway, rejoined the production on tour. *The Street Singer* was a musical comedy of Americans in Paris, which included, ironically in view of Archie's earlier career as a child performer, scenes set in the Folies Bergère. The tour ended in January of 1930. Soon afterwards, Archie signed for the summer season in St. Louis. Orry-Kelly had made his peace with the Shuberts and was returning there for a second season. They travelled together in Orry-Kelly's vivid yellow Packard.

Archie was pleased to find on arrival that his old friend and mentor Don Barclay had been hired to appear in several productions of the season. In many ways, the Municipal Opera Company was a misnomer: the twelfth season of the "Muni", as it was known, featured not operas but operettas and musicals. Like its predecessors, it was staged at the Forest Park theatre, an open-air amphitheatre set among flourishing trees, and flanked by verdant hills. The open auditorium seated as many as 8,000 people. Amplifiers were used to carry the performers' voices to the most distant reaches on the edge of the hills, and there was little or no protection, except for the players, in the event of rain. The St. Louis theatre-goers favoured extravagant, even absurd plots, lavish production values, and rich, many-coloured lighting effects. All of these were supplied in amplitude by the young and ambitious Milton Shubert, who, three seasons before, had introduced a revolving stage which provided a great spectacle. As Brooks Atkinson reported in the *New York Times* on May 30, 1930, there was no point in applying the normal conditions of criticism which would be appropriate to hermetically sealed theatres. It was simply a question of 8,000 people having a good time in a densely wooded park under the shimmering light of a brand new moon.

While in rehearsal, as Orry-Kelly fought in his customary manner with virtually everyone, particularly the embattled Milton Shubert, Archie proved to be a relaxed and easy-going member of the company. Photographs of him at the time show a softer, rounder, less ruggedly masculine face than millions of women would soon respond to in motion pictures. In some costumes, he even looked positively effeminate, as though he were aching to appear in drag. Yet already, at the age of twenty-six, he was at the height of his looks. No one could doubt that he would merely have to appear before an audience to captivate virtually every woman in it.

It is doubtful whether he did more than appear in this succession of shows, displaying his excellent face and figure in a variety of period and modern costumes, his barely adequate singing voice swallowed up in choruses or rendered tolerable because of the sheer size of the physical environment in which he worked, and the numbers of expert and graceful performers who surrounded him.

Archie was featured in *The Street Singer*, starring Queenie Smith, in which he repeated his performance as George, an American Pygmalion-figure in Paris, who plans to turn a flower-girl into a lady within three months. During the preparations for the show, Archie became a close friend of a small, plump Humpty-Dumpty of a performer, Frank Horn, who would one day be his secretary in Hollywood. Horn became part of his gay circle. He and Archie and Orry-Kelly would enjoy all the random gossip of the Rialto.

Archie also appeared in *Music In May, Countess Maritza, A Wonderful Night, Irene,* and *Rio Rita.* On June 5, the St. Louis *Post Dispatch* published a cast picture in its photogravure section, headed, "An afternoon on the stage of the Municipal Theater in Forest Park". Archie was fourth from the left, the next but tallest, and certainly the best-looking of the entire company. Crisply dressed in a tweed jacket, well-cut slacks and an open-neck shirt, he looked utterly relaxed and content. He was glowing from the good reviews and the loud, uncritical applause of 8,000 people a night. Milton Shubert and his wife Jean were encouraging, warming presences, despite the differences between them that would lead to a painful divorce. While in St. Louis, Archie published an article in the *Post-Dispatch*, his first essay into print. He provided a characteristic actor's fiction, describing his early career as a pugilist and falsifying virtually every fact to do with his upbringing. He also pretended that he had returned to England in the late 1920s to perform in repertory theatre, an error picked up by several of his biographers. The article's chirpy, buoyant tone was typical of the public Archie Leach, and the boldness of placing the piece in a local newspaper in defiance of all the facts was certainly typical of him. He must have rejoiced in the many favourable comments he received as the first performer in the twelve-year history of the Muni who had broken into the paper in this manner.

The season ended to general acclaim in August. Archie and Orry-Kelly returned to New York in the Packard. There, according to Orry-Kelly's friend Vincent Sherman (a young actor who would one day turn director and use Orry-Kelly's* skills in the film *Mr. Skeffington*, starring Bette Davis) Archie and Kelly together opened a speak-easy on the west side of Manhattan. In the still-continuing prohibition era, speak-easies were focuses of social life: a new arrival would have to give a sign or knock in a particular manner, a small peep-hole would open in the door, and they would be admitted. Police raids were frequent, and such bars operated under conditions of considerable danger, sometimes sustaining themselves through pay-offs to official men. Despite numerous obstacles, the two men

---

* The name Jack Kelly was no longer used.

managed to succeed in their underground activity for several months. At the same time, they began to cool towards each other. Archie began to have affairs with other men. According to Vincent Sherman:

> They had a code. If Orry-Kelly came home and could hear classical music issuing through the door, it was a signal that Archie was involved in an amorous occasion with a young man. If there was no classical music, it was all right to come in.

After some months of this, Orry-Kelly apparently had had enough and accepted an offer, conveyed to him by Jack Warner, head of Warner Brothers in Hollywood, via John and Ethel Barrymore, to go to the West Coast as a contractee, designing for the stars. His considerable reputation on Broadway and Ethel Barrymore's special fondness for him, plus the fact that many figures of the theatre who flocked to the California studios in the wake of the birth of talkies preferred to work with one of their own, influenced this major step forward in his career. He took the train west, and Archie promised to follow him soon. Their parting was without jealousy, bitterness or regret. They were part of the casual, free-wheeling life of the time, and didn't believe in heavy displays of emotion. They were young, attractive, healthy, and, despite the Depression, the world was at their feet.

Archie became deeply involved with Phil Charig, whom he continued to see even during the period with Orry-Kelly. Charig had written the music for *Nikki*, a show based upon *The Last Flight*, from the novel *Single Lady* by John Monk Saunders, a former World War I aviator of moody and unstable temperament who was married to the actress Fay Wray. William Dieterle had made an excellent movie from the material the year before. The touching story disclosed the tortured lives of former heroes, who were unable to adjust to the boredom and monotony of ordinary life after the war and had embarked upon a life of heavy drinking and suicidal, devil-may-care adventure. Their mascot was the pretty, sensitive and very feminine young Nikki, exquisitely played in the movie by Helen Chandler.

Unfortunately, the script did not lend itself to musical treatment, and Phil Charig's score was well below his best work. Nor was Miss Wray ideal in the title part; she had had no stage experience, and had only worked in films, and was nervous and uncomfortable before a live audience. *Nikki* proved to be an ill-fated attempt to reverse the trend of 1931 and bring a screen performer to Broadway. Archie, as Cary Lockwood, one of the three airmen, was as personable and charming as ever, but neither he nor the frailly handsome Douglas Montgomery could sustain this shaky vehicle satisfactorily, and the show failed, closing on October 17, 1931, after only eighteen days of performance. Moved briefly to the George M. Cohan theatre, it closed again at Halloween. Immediately after the run, Jesse L. Lasky, who had brought Archie to the United States as a child, decided to try him out in pictures. After the failure of the Folies Bergère in 1911, Lasky had turned his misfortune into an extraordinary advantage: he had headed west with Cecil B. deMille and Sam Goldfish (later Goldwyn) and with them had literally founded the movie industry. By 1930, he was a high-ranking figure of Paramount Studios, and he and his colleague B. P. Schulberg, both of whom had been following Archie Leach's career very closely, decided to give him the chance he had been waiting for.

They were presenting a series of short films at the time, many of which were designed to promote new screen performers. The demand for British personalities was strong, because the diction of so many American performers at the time was nasal and unappealing, and several silent-screen actors and actresses failed when they were heard as well as seen. Although Archie's diction remained an odd blend of Cockney and West Country, gratingly lower-class to English audiences that were accustomed to the dulcet tones of West End actors, to American ears it sounded educated and cultivated. A vehicle was found for him, a ten-minute, one-reel example of forgettable trivia entitled *Singapore Sue*.

Casey Robinson, later the doyen of Warner Brothers writers, scripted and directed the short. He told Charles Higham years later that he never forgot Archie walking in for the audition, handsome, cocky, confident, with shining eyes and perfect posture, a matinée idol to his fingertips. Robinson put him in a sailor's uniform and gave him a run-through on camera. Within minutes, Robinson knew that a new screen personality had been born. It wasn't merely a question of ideally photogenic features, the bone structure without which no leading man could possibly succeed on film, nor was it merely a question of a classically constructed physique, with the broad shoulders, sculptured chest muscles and narrow hips of the athlete. It was the extraordinary combination of aggressive charm and confidence, and underneath it a little boy's vulnerability, unease and even shyness that provided the sort of contradictoriness which Robinson knew few women could resist. Archie Leach wasn't overbearing or unduly forceful, he didn't seem to have the airs of someone who automatically expected people to be attracted to him. His aggressiveness was a mask; the camera saw through the mask to an insecurity within him. Women would not feel threatened or over-ridden by his personality, and yet at the same time they would warm to his apparently unequivocal masculinity. The result of the test was an immediate contract and an invitation to go to Hollywood.

With little to lose and much to gain, Archie, remembering his happy times in California in the mid-1920s, decided to go west. He had already sold the furnishings of the apartment he had shared with Orry-Kelly in the West Fifties behind the old Madison Square Garden; the lot had been bought by Vincent Sherman, who was getting married that year. He was living now at the Variety Artists Club, in rooms near Phil Charig's. They had formed a friendship with the conductor and arranger Lenny Hayton, who later married Lena Horne. Demetrios Bilan, then a young and talented actor, who later became Huntington Hartford's right-hand man on the West Coast, remembers the farewell party vividly. It was held at Hayton's apartment on West End Avenue; Archie and Phil Charig arrived together, quite obviously a pair, eager and excited over their new adventure. Next day, they left in Orry-Kelly's much-driven yellow Packard for the long journey through winter snows, deserts and mountains to the promised land of Southern California.

4

The two young men arrived in Los Angeles in the last week of January 1932. The city had been drenched by a severe storm that had caused at least one death; hailstones had fallen, and the streets were flooded. Los Angeles at the time was a city of just under 1.25 million population; its spider-web of streets spread far into the desert and along the coast, the badly paved thoroughfares lined by temporary-looking wooden or stucco-and-brick bungalows, the wide sidewalks punctuated by enormous black telephone poles.

Outside the city were the desolate Hoovervilles, camps of prefabricated shacks housing the army of the unemployed. By contrast, Hollywood and Beverly Hills sparkled with bright flowers, tropical palm trees, handsome Spanish-style villas and mansions in a riot of architectural modes, usually with swimming-pools. Houses in the most expensive parts of town could be bought for $25,000, including the use of live-in domestic servants, who were sold along with the property. A fine apartment with two bedrooms and a large sitting-room could be had for seventy-five dollars a month. The newspapers were filled with pictures and stories about the movie folk: in the week of Archie's and Phil's arrival, MGM and Paramount publicists had combined to whip up a mythical "Battle of the Exotics" in which Garbo, Bankhead and Dietrich, whose enormous, sultry faces glowered from the *New York Times* Sunday Supplement pages, were supposed to be vying for men, fame and public acclaim.

The dominant figure of Hollywood social life was W. R. Wilkerson, owner of the *Hollywood Reporter*, whose wife Edith ran a social column in the magazine that was filled with inside information. He then owned the Vendôme, a favourite restaurant of the stars, and would later buy nightclubs, and become a special investigative agent for the FBI, using his great fame and influence as a cover. The leaders of society were the Countess Dorothy di Frasso, sister of Bertram Taylor, head of the New York Stock Exchange, and the wealthy wife of Mussolini's friend Count Dentice di Frasso. Though still married to di Frasso, she was carrying on a widely discussed affair with Gary Cooper, who had only just emerged as a star. They were mentioned in every gossip column, seen in every nightspot: he rangy, equine, lean, with fierce blue eyes and a crinkly smile; she dumpy, unbeautiful, but possessed of an irresistible vitality, charisma and charm. Her jewels were legendary, her international circle of friends glittering. To know di Frasso and to be liked by her was a sure passport to social acceptance anywhere.

That week, the wedding in Phoenix, Arizona, of Paramount executive Benjamin (Barney) Glazer and the actress-singer Sharon Lynn was the buzz of Hollywood; among the guests were John Gilbert and Dolores del Rio. Tod Browning's lurid horror movie *Freaks*, with Prince Ranlof, the Living Torso, Pete Robinson, the Living Skeleton, and the Hilton Sisters, actual Siamese twins, was the most discussed picture in town. Howard Hughes' exciting *Sky Devils*, with Spencer Tracy and William Boyd, was the action picture of the hour. In a matter of days, Garbo's sensational *Mata Hari*, about the exotic spy of World War I, would open with a splashy première at Grauman's Chinese Theater, where stars would imprint their feet in cement.

Archie and Phil Charig found an apartment at 1129½ North Sweetzer Avenue, in West Hollywood; since the flat was not advertised that week, it seems that Paramount had reserved it in advance. The building still stands today. It was a brown stucco-and-brick structure laid back from the street in a series of courtyards flanked by tropical plants; the building front was relieved by imitation black Tudor beams that gave it a quasi-English look. The apartment itself was tucked into a corner, overlooking a flourish of trees. Sweetzer was just a short drive to Paramount Studios on Melrose Avenue.

During those first two or three days, after no doubt returning the car to Orry-Kelly, whose offices were at Warner Brothers Studio, north-east over the Cahuenga Pass and Barham Boulevard, in beautiful down-town Burbank, Archie checked into Paramount to see the production manager, Sam Jaffe, and the casting department. Once past the almost royal wrought-iron gate, he saw a surrealist spectacle. The enormous parking-lot was dominated by a replica of the forward half of a large ocean-going liner; the executive offices were built in the form of a Mexican palace that had a British oak-timbered façade and were flanked with a French garden of box hedges. In this parched, beige world there stood squat concrete buildings with no roofs, staircases that led up to the sky, half of a Renaissance dining-room, ladders leaning against a back-cloth of storm clouds, and the ground floor of an Austrian castle, next to a cell of a Moorish prison.

For years afterward, ignoring his previous engagement in New York, Archie would say that he had been hired after introductions and a screen test. Nevertheless, he would always give credit to the studio boss B. P. Schulberg for seeing his merits from the beginning.

Schulberg saw to it that he was cast immediately as the second romantic lead in *This is the Night*, an imitation of the current success, *One Hour With You*. He was to play Steven, a former javelin thrower and new actor at Paramount, whose wife is unfaithful to him during a complicated game of adultery and double-cross. Schulberg cast him simultaneously in the part of a man-about-town in *Sinners in the Sun*, directed by Cecil B. deMille's brother William; he could walk from one set to the other without changing his white tie and tails, talking his way through two entirely different scripts.

In the pressure-cooker atmosphere of Hollywood in 1932, there was no room for rehearsal. And there were only a few days before Archie would have to start work. Days to catch up with old friends: Douglas Fairbanks, Snr., who had returned from skiing with Charlie Chaplin at St. Moritz and was about to leave on an expedition to the South Seas with film star William F. Farnum to make a film about Robinson Crusoe; and Frank Horn, the amiable humpty-dumpty of New York City and St. Louis, who was finding it impossible to get work. The weather suddenly cleared as February began, and the sun shone like an enormous white bulb in the hard, cloudless blue sky, over the seemingly interminable avenues that led from downtown all the way to the beach, haunted by the clanging, swaying red car-tram, shadowed at evening by the frowning blue sierra foothills haunted by coyotes.

It was necessary for Archie to change his name. He was rechristened by Fay Wray, who put together "Cary", in part from the character he played in *Nikki*, and a Paramount publicist who found "Grant". Soon, Fay Wray would be internationally famous as the girl King Kong held in his paw on the top of the Empire State Building.

Cary began work. The schedule was relentless; he had to act two quite different roles with equal conviction, switching sets at all hours of the day and night, toiling well into the early morning hours every Sunday. He had to adjust himself to the contrasting temperaments of Frank Tuttle, a sophisticated Easterner, and William deMille, a distinguished gentleman in poor health who had once worked with David Belasco. To add to the pressure, Schulberg was not satisfied with deMille's rushes, and replaced him brutally with the smart young Alexander Hall.

In *This Is the Night*, Cary was co-starred with Lili Damita, a tempestuous French girl who at the time was emotionally involved with Prince Louis Ferdinand, son-in-law of the Kaiser, and was to marry Errol Flynn. One of the supporting cast was Thelma Todd, who became the victim of a much-discussed case of suspected murder. In *Sinners in the Sun*, Cary appeared with Carole Lombard, who swore like a marine in accents that belied her fragile and wistful appearance. Despite his generous salary, the equivalent of $7,000 a week in today's money, Cary, always obsessed with cash profits, began looking, during the early spring of 1932, into areas of possible investment. He met a young man named Wright Neale, who had dabbled in the men's clothing business, and together with him and the Glendale interior decorator, Bob Lampe, decided to cash in on the booming new Wilshire district, and open a clothes shop at 6161 Wilshire Boulevard, slightly to the east of Vermont Avenue. It was, on the face of it, a good time to start such a venture, since Bullock's and Magnin's department stores had recently been opened down the street, elevating a once-shabby neighbourhood into a fashionable shopping area much liked by the well-to-do citizens of the Hancock Park and Rossmore districts, and by lawyers, doctors and oil-men downtown.

The shop opened on May 20, and was named in a large, glittering electric sign outside, NEALE'S SMART MEN'S APPAREL. The capital was $5,268.72. The monthly rental was $100, paid to the lessor, Gertrude Seaver. The fixtures and fittings were expensive mahogany, even down to the panelling in the changing-rooms, and the frames of the three-sided mirrors. In an untypical act of extravagance, Cary ordered 25,000 green-and-gold matchbooks with NEALE'S printed on them, far more than he would need for the immediate future.

Arthur Lubin, later famous as the director of a talkie screen version of *Phantom of the Opera*, and newly arrived as a Paramount assistant producer, recalls an episode of the third week of May. It evidently took place on a Sunday. Mr. Lubin remembers that he had bought a new car and it suddenly broke down on the corner of Wilshire and Vermont. Looking around for a public telephone to call the Auto Club, he decided, in the absence of one, to go into

Neale's. As he strolled through the door, Cary Grant was standing there. Cary said to him, "While you're here you might as well buy a suit and be our first customer!" Lubin bought a zip-up informal jacket.

Wright Neale was known to Cary as "Sister". He signed all his notes to Cary at the studio with that name. Cary was never mentioned on Neale's stationery, or in the press, as co-owner. He remained strictly a silent partner, but he didn't hesitate to use his looks and charm to lure people off the street into the store on the rare days when he wasn't working.

At the same time Cary was making *This Is the Night* and *Sinners in the Sun*, he had to pose with pretty girls for photographs at the beach, or in various parks, or be seen lobbing a tennis-ball over a net (he didn't play tennis at the time) or tossing a beach-ball to a partner in Santa Monica. The studio was promoting him as an athlete, and, to improve his physique, he installed weights in his apartment and began working-out. He could still do handstands and tumbles with great expertise; his easy manner and flashing smile charmed everyone and he was meticulously punctual and never temperamental. Delighted with Hollywood and loving the sun, for a while he shook off the darker side of his nature.

In a lunch break, he met, for the first time, a man who was to play an important role in his life. Randolph Scott was appearing in *Sky Bride* on an adjoining sound stage; he had arrived two years earlier from his native Virginia, and had been given an introduction to Howard Hughes by his father. Hughes had taken the handsome footballer and university engineering student under his wing; it was common gossip in Hollywood that they had become lovers. Hughes, whose macho reputation was exaggerated, and whose countless affairs with women were largely the invention of his press-agents, secured work for Scott as an extra, then as a contract player at Paramount. *Sky Bride* was Scott's first important film for the studio.

Scott was well over six feet tall and weighed 195 pounds

of well-defined brawn. He had a long, humorous, horsey face, a lazy swinging walk, shrewd eyes and an air of calculating laziness. Self-assured and self-contained, he disliked emotional commitments, indulging the attentions of both men and women while possessing the soul of a cash-register. Since he could not act, film making was just an easy path to acquiring a personal fortune. The moment he had completed a sequence, and he was no longer required, he would stroll over to his canvas chair, sit down, stretch out his long legs and pick up the *Wall Street Journal*.

Scott and Cary were instantly drawn to each other, and decided on the spot to share an apartment. Phil Charig, who had no liking for Hollywood, moved back to New York without composing a single song for a film. Randy, as he was known by everyone, moved in with Cary in Phil's place. It was, for obvious reasons, not customary for handsome young film stars to share accommodation; in the local beehive of gossip, there would be loud buzzing about such a thing. The implications were all too clear; the studio publicists had to cover by issuing releases that their two new contract stars were cutting expenses by dividing the rent; the unsuspecting public didn't realise that, at $400 a week, each man could easily afford to pay what could not have been more than seventy-five dollars a month.

As if determined to create more untoward comment, the two men at first declined even to be seen dating women in public, and instead, with almost incredible audacity, turned up at film premières as a pair. It is possible that they were banking on the sheer overtness of this to allay suspicion on the theory that, if theirs were a real liaison, they would be guiltily hiding it. Whatever the motive, their behaviour did not go unnoticed, and there were frequent squibs in the columns that were surprisingly daring for the time.

Apparently, this situation prompted the studio to put pressure on the two men to find dates with whom they could be photographed in various exotic parts of Los Angeles. The ideal pair of women was quickly found. Cary and Randy had, as near neighbours, two gorgeous girls who had just arrived in Hollywood together, thus giving rise to a great deal of scandalous comment which amused them very much and was quite unfounded, but never actually discouraged. Sari Maritza and Vivian Gaye quickly became as much the talk of the town as their two escorts. Sari Maritza's real name was Patricia Detering Nathan. Born in Tientsin, China, she was the twenty-year-old daughter of the influential Major Walter Nathan, a prominent figure in the social whirl of Peking and Shanghai in the first three decades of the century. She met, in Berlin, another colourful young beauty, Sanya Bezencenet, who had Swiss and Russian antecedents and was an up-and-coming London literary agent. They formed a team.

Sari was named after two operettas by Emmerich Kalmann. She made a splash in a German film, *Monte Carlo Madness*, and she was hired by Paramount on the strength of this success. But, like Cary and Randolph Scott, she put out the story that she had arrived in Hollywood on a chance of getting work, and had been hired on the spot for her beauty.

The two girls were opposites. Sari was a bubbling extrovert, always talking, filled with delightful risqué gossip and alive with extraordinary energy; Vivian was reserved, cautious, moody, and somewhat introspective. Whereas Sari was not strongly attracted to Cary, Vivian fell in love with Scott. But, as Vivian makes clear today, the relationship among the four was innocent and sexless, consisting largely of spinning around in fast cars to the beach or mountains, dancing to the latest hits in modest nightspots, and playing tennis, swimming, or just running around in the sun.

Cary bloomed in this paradise of the common man. With the Depression going on all around, everyone he knew was bursting with health, suntanned, vigorous; the air in those blessed days was pure and free of smog; occasional bursts of rain only made the atmosphere more sparkling than ever. The accessibility of every kind of sport and the proximity of the mountains and the desert made Los Angeles possibly the most desirable place on earth, for all of the faceless, sprawling ugliness of the city itself.

The summer came, burningly dry and unvisited by wind. Cary continued working without a break. But instead of advancing his position as an up-and-coming actor, the studio capriciously rushed him into a dreary subsidiary role as an actor in a play within the film *Merrily We Go To Hell*. He wore an eighteenth-century costume and spoke rather foolish lines to Adrianne Allen while wearing a powdered wig, white silk coat, breeches and buckle shoes.

The stars in this story of a newspaper-man turned playwright having an affair with an heiress, were Fredric March and Sylvia Sidney. Cary watched March's impeccable technique, his polished movements and suave delivery: the result of years of honing and refining his art on the stage. March's co-star, Sylvia Sidney, was the talk of the studio. Born Sophie Kosow in the Bronx in 1910, the tough, ambitious daughter of Russian-Jewish immigrants, Sylvia was a hard hitter whose personality contrasted utterly with the fragile, dewy-eyed waifs she impersonated on screen. B. P. Schulberg had brought her to Hollywood after his wife, Ad, admired her in the Broadway hit *Bad Girl*. Much to the annoyance of Ad and her teenaged son Budd, who would one day write the classic *What Makes Sammy Run?*, Schulberg abandoned them for Miss Sidney, with whom he conducted a flagrant love affair, presenting her with one astonishing gift after another. He also paved the way for the lusciously sensual girl's vivid career at Paramount, casting her with great success in such classics as *City Streets*. Even to cast an eye on Miss Sidney in commissary or studio corridor could result in a male performer's or crew member's instant dismissal; Schulberg was even suspicious of the harmless director Marion Gering, who had directed *Bad Girl* and whom he had imported with Miss Sidney. At least his choice of director for *Merrily We Go To Hell* was safe: the lesbian Dorothy Arzner, who sported cropped hair, a monocle, a cigar and white tailored suits with sensible shoes.

That summer the studio was in the grip of bitter board-room fights, both in Los Angeles and New York City. The formidable executive Sam Katz was struggling against Schulberg, sometimes winning, sometimes losing. By February 1932, he had moved ahead in the race for power, appearing with a theatrical flourish before a meeting of executives and department heads in the Paramount Building in Manhattan to plead for loyalty in the company, in the judiciously silent presence of bosses Adolph Zukor and Jesse L. Lasky, who had nursed the company along from the beginning. Katz slashed production by twelve pictures and many millions of dollars, hoping to salvage the wreckage of bad administration. In another reshuffle, Katz was set up at the head of the theatre chain, while Zukor continued as president, and Jesse L. Lasky as head of production. Schulberg was put on his mettle by being made a member of the Paramount Board of Directors in March, urged by Lasky to improve the standards and constantly nagged by Katz. Whether in Fredric March's Laguna beach house or Sylvia Sidney's luxurious Beverly Hills ménage, or Cary Grant's and Randolph Scott's North Sweetzer flat, the discussions of what the future of the studio would be raged fiercely.

Sometime later that summer, with *Merrily We Go To Hell* completed, Cary and Scott decided to move to a more substantial residence. With a new friend, Mitchell Foster, a gifted interior decorator from New York who had formed a partnership with the movie star William Haines, they obtained a lease on a comfortable residence in the Los Feliz district, at 2177 West Live Oak Drive. It still stands there, beautiful and with a superb view, just north of Western, above the beginning of Los Feliz Boulevard before that street turns east towards Griffith Park. Griffith Park was, and would remain, the haunt of homosexuals, and was considered to be a major pick-up area.

The three men appeared to be comfortable; in July, Foster took off to Europe for a three-month buying spree for Haines after forming their partnership earlier in the month.

Cary began work on two more films at once; movies which, after the disappointment of *Merrily We Go To Hell*, were designed to greatly improve his career. He had by now earned the confidence of B. P. Schulberg, and had befriended Schulberg's son, now sixteen, to whom he gave small but welcome gifts. The problem was that Cary preferred the warm-hearted Ad Schulberg to Sylvia Sidney, but he skilfully played the game of alliances and did not offend his powerful boss.

The two movies he made now were *Blonde Venus* and *Devil and the Deep*. In *Blonde Venus* he acted the role of a superficial, wealthy playboy who supports as his mistress a married woman, an exotic nightclub singer played by Marlene Dietrich. He would walk from the set of *Blonde Venus* to his dressing-room while clad in white tie and tails, and change into a Naval uniform as a lieutenant aboard a submarine in an African Naval base in *Devil and the Deep*, the story of a tormented commander insanely jealous of his moody wife. These parts were played by Charles Laughton and Tallulah Bankhead; Gary Cooper played another lieutenant in love with Bankhead.

The director of *Blonde Venus* was the proud, haughty and stubborn Josef Von Sternberg. He had added the "Von" himself. Cary was fascinated by him. Pale-skinned, he had a shock of unruly dark-brown hair, poetic brooding eyes, and a carefully cultivated black moustache. His white, translucent hands were those of a poet. He affected an ivory-topped cane and poison-green coats. He stared at his actors from under theatrical black hats, his lids heavy and snake-like, his mouth a thin line of contempt, and his expression sour and jaundiced.

When he went to a restaurant, there had to be six large black grapes on the table or he would not sit down. He was frequently seen holding a volume of the poems of Hafez in the original Persian, a language with which he was not familiar, and he would stand in the Hollywood Hills, looking at the lights below and crying the words, "My Hollywood!"

Von Sternberg was deeply involved with Miss Dietrich, whom he had propelled into international fame as the vicious slut Lola-Lola in *The Blue Angel*. He was responsible for the Dietrich the world knows. She was a sensation in *Morocco*, in one scene defying the gossips by planting a kiss on the lips of another female character, an invention of her own. She became famous for her blank, mysterious stares into the camera, achieved by silently counting from 100 backwards. Her next success was *Shanghai Express*, as the fly-by-night Shanghai Lily. Obsessed with her daughter, Marlene decided she wanted to make a picture in which she would have a child, hence the creation of *Blonde Venus*.

Schulberg decided he would separate Marlene and Von Sternberg, and she was fired for refusing to work without him. While she was temporarily out of work, a kidnap attempt was made on her child. Schulberg relented, and *Blonde Venus* began, with Von Sternberg directing.

Cary was fascinated by Marlene. But when Charles Higham asked her in 1966 about her feelings for Grant during the making of the picture, she replied, "I had no feelings. He was a homosexual." Cary watched her in scenes in which he did not appear, particularly in a Penderish sequence in which she was dressed as a gorilla, pulling off her monkey arms to disclose braceleted wrists as she sang "Hot Voodoo". Von Sternberg had the scene done 125 times. Finally the "gorilla" slumped over. Marlene had fainted because of the heat. B. P. Schulberg walked onto the set and said, "Get the ape back in action. We're over budget!"

Von Sternberg put a huge sign up on the set reading ABSOLUTE SILENCE. When production manager Sam Jaffe walked on and said something, he was asked whether he had read the sign. Sputtering that he was the production manager, he was removed from the sound stage. Furious, he soon resigned.

Cary observed constant arguments between Marlene and Von Sternberg. They fought continuously, much of the time in German. In one scene, Marlene was supposed to walk in a room and throw her hat on the bed. She refused to do so, saying it was bad luck, like wearing green socks, whistling in a dressing-room, or quoting from *Macbeth*. Finally, she won. Someone wheeled in a couch, and she threw her hat on that instead.

Making *Devil and the Deep* was equally problematical. Tallulah Bankhead made token passes at Cary which he summarily rejected. This annoyed her very much, and like Dietrich, she began to set off a train of gossip about Cary's alleged lack of virility. The fact is, she wasn't his type and she was too old for him. She misbehaved constantly, deliberately fluffing lines, arguing with director Marion Gering, and laughing at the dialogue given her. In one scene in the submarine, she asked a radio operator, "Have you tried the radio?" When he replied, "The oscillator isn't working," she threw back her head and roared. The actor playing the operator was so upset he tripped against a water-cooler and shook the lights, and a camera fell on his head, knocking him out.

Cary hated Bankhead and her heavy drinking. The players had to struggle with tiny, carefully scaled-down sets of the submarine, which were flooded with water in several sequences, working through the night until as late as four in the morning. Laughton took a brotherly interest in Cary. When Cary was depressed by the somewhat meaningless parts he was playing in the exhausting summer heat, switching from part to part without sufficient preparation, Laughton made him look at everything in perspective, showing him by inference that his own suffering as a physically unattractive man made Cary's discomfort seem trivial by comparison.

On September 23, Cary and Randolph Scott attended the première of *Blonde Venus* at the Paramount theatre in Hollywood. Afterwards, they went to the Brown Derby restaurant on Wilshire Boulevard for supper. As they left, well after midnight, the stars clustered on the sidewalk waiting for the traffic light to change so they could cross the street to the parking-lot. Cary glanced over and noticed a pair of acquaintances, the lawyer, Milton Bren, and Bren's wife Marian. A couple was standing with the Brens. The actor was a well-known, handsome young homosexual actor; with him as a "beard" was the blonde and beautiful star Virginia Cherrill. Cary knew Virginia by name: she had appeared with great success in Charlie Chaplin's classic movie *City Lights*. Chaplin had discovered her at a boxing match and had cast her as the blind flowergirl in the picture. He became furious when she rejected his advances, and tried to scrap all the footage she was in after months of work, only to be told by his financiers that he must continue with her. The story was already the talk of Hollywood.

Milton Bren made the introductions. Cary was fascinated with Virginia. It is illustrative of the superficial nature of his relationship with Randolph Scott that he thought nothing of calling her three days later from Paramount at her home on Havenhurst Avenue in West Hollywood to ask her out to dinner. She was living there in an apartment with her mother, just a couple of blocks below Sunset Boulevard. Virginia had liked Cary's performance in *Blonde Venus*, and was attracted to his dark good looks. After some hesitation, she agreed to date him.

They were very much in contrast. Virginia was a carefully sheltered, well-brought-up young woman – she was twenty-four at the time – the daughter of a bank president in Carthage, a small town in Illinois. Very much the apple of her family's eye, she had never wanted for anything and she was widely adored at Northwestern University as a soft, sweet-natured, gentle, and ravishingly attractive girl. On an impulse, she had decided to come to Hollywood. She was joined, as a chaperone, by her mother, who was no show-biz parent; so far from pushing Virginia into a career, her mother had very mixed feelings about Hollywood. Virginia's suffering at the hands of Chaplin, whose contract with her virtually put her under lock and key, unable to see men or even appear in public for well over a year, annoyed Mrs. Cherrill greatly.

Cary, with over twenty years in show business, his easy-going, worldly sophistication and British background, fascinated the sheltered and sensitive young girl, but his moodiness also proved unsettling to Virginia. Before long, she found herself out of her depth, swimming in dark waters.

They had gone out together a few times, to parties in Beverly Hills and to more informal occasions hostessed by Vivian Gaye and Sari Maritza, when Virginia received an unpleasant shock. Orry-Kelly came to see her and issued her a serious warning. She knew him well enough to listen to him carefully. "He told me that I should be very cautious indeed before entering into a committed affair with Cary; he added that Cary was the lover of Randolph Scott, and that he was in a position to know it. I was so young and innocent I didn't give the matter a second's thought," Virginia says.*

Cary's evenings with Virginia were sweetly sexless and consisted largely of candle-lit dinners in medium-priced restaurants or weekend trips to the beach with Cary's gang. Even the fact that Cary now engaged a male secretary, a former actor named Larry Starbuck, and installed him in the house on West Live Oak Drive, didn't seem to ruffle Virginia's self-contained purity and unworldliness. She found herself spending a good deal of time in what was a fairly obviously homosexual household, blissfully unaware of everything that went on around her.

That autumn the studio boldly decided to cast Cary and Scott together in a picture entitled *Hot Saturday*; this was perhaps to help allay any possible rumours surrounding their cohabitation by explaining that they were working on a film together. *Hot Saturday* starred the fiery Nancy Carroll; Cary played a relaxed, cheerful libertine, and Randolph Scott a decent, upright boyhood sweetheart of the heroine. Both actors walked genially through their parts, giving little evidence of commitment or even interest. Dur-

---

* After she divorced Cary, Orry-Kelly came to her and said, "We both loved him and lost him, didn't we?"

ing the shooting, a journalist, Ben Maddox, dropped by their home. In fairly typical racist terms of the era, and hiding a good deal more than he undoubtedly knew, he wrote in *Modern Screen*:

> A late supper was served by an old-fashioned negro mammy cook who came with the house and referred to her new employers as "the young gentlemen". Cary and Randy are really opposite types, and that's why they get along so well. Cary is the gay, impetuous one. Randy is serious, cautious. Cary is temperamental in the sense of being very intense. Randy is calm and quiet . . . Cary tears around in a new Packard Roadster, and Randy flashes by in a new Cadillac. Oh-oh-oh how the girls want to take a ride!

There is no indication in the piece that the desire for a ride was being fulfilled; there was no mention of Virginia Cherrill in the article. Soon afterwards, observing a published photograph of Cary and Randy in aprons washing dishes, the venomous columnist Jimmie Fiddler announced that the two men were "carrying the buddy business a bit too far". Carole Lombard gave an interview to the *Los Angeles Times* in which she asked the question, "I wonder which one of those two guys pays the bills?"

Cary began shooting *Madame Butterfly*, a version of the opera done as a non-musical drama, with Sylvia Sidney in the title role. He hadn't finished the picture when he was suddenly cast in Mae West's movie *She Done Him Wrong*, in which he played Captain Cummings, a police-agent disguised as a missionary, investigating the activities of the voluptuous Lady Lou. Cary's casting in the picture was a major improvement in his career. Miss West always claimed that she saw him as an extra around the studio and cast him on the spot; the truth of the matter is that B. P. Schulberg had decided the combination of the new and impressive leading man and the aggressively sexual Miss West would excite audiences in those ribald days before the

Motion Picture Code effectively emasculated the industry. Miss West's songs were calculatedly daring in their overtness, including "My Easy Rider's Gone" and "I Like a Guy What Takes His Time". Asked many years later how she had enjoyed working with Cary, Miss West said, shrewdly, "That part kinda built him up with the ladies." She had always been fascinated by men of ambiguous sexuality; she had even had the nerve to present, in 1927, a play entitled *Drag*, about homosexuality, at a time when the subject was entirely taboo in the theatre. Cary was irritated by Miss West's childishly egocentric nature. Yet he acted as an admirable foil for her almost brutal approach to sex in the picture; looking him up and down in one sequence, she called him, "warm, dark and handsome", and in another scene she addressed him in a much-misquoted line, "Why don't you come up sometime . . . see me?" As soon as this racy dialogue became common coin, Cary was actually famous for the first time. There was no question of any attraction between the two performers. Miss West's personal life was somewhat austere and far removed from the sexual freedom she personified on screen. And Cary's life was already filled with the complexities of dealing with his household relationship with Randolph Scott and with his tender but quite uninvolving romantic friendship with Virginia.

On Christmas Day, 1932, Cary and Virginia attended a welcome-home party given by Gary Cooper and Countess Dorothy di Frasso for Douglas Fairbanks, Snr., following his return from the sojourn in the South Pacific during the shooting of *Mr. Robinson Crusoe*. In the handsome ballroom at Cooper's house in West Los Angeles, many of the great figures of the screen were present, among them Norma Shearer and her husband Irving Thalberg, head of MGM, Samuel and Frances Goldwyn, Fredric and Florence March, the Charles Farrells, the Clark Gables and the Lionel Barrymores, as well as Cary's old friends John Monk Saunders and Fay Wray. Cary arrived not only with Virginia but with Randy, Vivian Gaye and Sari Maritza, a bizarre grouping that caused much comment in the columns. Seemingly unexhausted by shooting the first part of *She Done Him Wrong* simultaneously with the last part of *Madame Butterfly*, Cary looked magnificent in white tie and tails, and Virginia spectacular in a backless black evening-gown with jewels flashing at her neck and wrists. The twenty-piece orchestra played tangos, two-steps and fox-trots. The party helped Virginia professionally: MGM had been doing nothing with her for almost a year, and she was acting at the time in *Fast Workers*, a second-rate vehicle of the failing former superstar John Gilbert. After the much-discussed evening, the studio put her into a better movie, *The Nuisance*, a fast-moving comedy-melodrama about a pushy shyster lawyer played by Lee Tracy.

The new year brought a crushing workload for Cary; even he began to weaken under the constant and relentless Paramount schedules. He was in *Woman Accused* with Nancy Carroll, based on a *Liberty* magazine serial written as a gimmick by ten well-known writers including a new acquaintance of Cary's, Howard Hughes' uncle Rupert Hughes. He went on to shoot *The Eagle and the Hawk*, with Fredric March; he was cast, in an inside studio joke, as Harry Crocker, name of a well-known local man-about-town and scion of a banking dynasty. He and Fredric March played airmen in constant conflict; the author of the story was his old friend, the air ace John Monk Saunders of *Nikki* days. In one sequence, during an explosion, Cary flung himself across Fredric March to protect him from the force of the blast – or so a high-powered studio publicity department claimed.

Perhaps because of the pressure of work, perhaps because of the strain of sustaining two relationships at once, Cary became exceptionally moody, testy and difficult in the first months of 1933. He was not appeased by the collapse of his men's clothing store; Wright Neale had done everything possible to save it, but it had gone bankrupt, beaten by the fierce competition from the big stores on Wilshire Boulevard. Most of Cary's and Neale's investment of over

$5,000 went down the drain, and there was a series of creditors' meetings at their lawyers' offices. The result was that Cary bought the firm outright, including good will and stock, from his distraught "sister" partner, for a little over $300. Soon, after he had paid off as many debts as he could, Cary closed up the doors and threw away the keys.

Virginia Cherrill remembers that he would often have outbursts of temper at the time; but, increasingly involved with him psychologically, and still blinded by her innocence, she ignored the warning signals and began to long for him to propose to her. His jealousy and possessiveness were disturbing, but again she failed to heed the dangerous indications of his temperament. He would appear on the set of *The Nuisance*, glaring at her in her love scenes; he was suspicious of the attentions of Lee Tracy, who, though he was a most gifted actor with an electric, driving personality, was by no means handsome or even attractive. These incursions into her daily work made Virginia increasingly nervous that spring. She asked Cary not to keep driving over from Paramount to MGM to spy on her. The result was a series of violent quarrels; Virginia might be unworldly, but she was certainly neither weak nor submissive. Painful though it was for her, she had to hold her own, and she struck back as strongly as she could.

Despite his unsatisfactory behaviour, Virginia was in love with Cary by the summer of that year. They continued to be seen everywhere at social events. During June, they were at a party at the Santa Monica Beach Club when they ran into the famous comedian, acrobat and wit Jack Durant. Durant told Virginia that when the occasion arose she should ask Cary to show her his extraordinary skill at tumbling. The opportunity came soon afterward at a ball at the Beverly Hills Hotel. Everyone was in white tie and tails. Suddenly Durant said to Cary in front of Virginia, "I bet you fifty dollars you can't do a *Temsuka*." It was an Arab word which Virginia didn't then understand. Cary said, "You're on." He got up and hitched his trousers and walked to the orchestra leader and asked for a drum roll.

The conductor signalled the drummer, and, as the roll began, Cary performed a double forward somersault involving a full roll of the body, the head seeming to hit the floor, the full impact of the fall actually taken on the neck. Everyone applauded loudly. Virginia recalls, "Cary got up and walked back to our table and said to Jack, 'Give me the fifty dollars!' and Jack peeled off the bills and gave them to him and everyone clapped again."

Not knowing Cary's supposed Jewish background, Virginia was convinced he was of Arabic origin. To this day, she insists he was an Arab. His deep tan never left him, and his facial features made her think of the Levantine immigrants to Bristol in the sixteenth century.

The work at Paramount was still not much better than road mending. In a desperate effort to save the studio from ruin, Adolph Zukor and his executives continued to overwork their stars, forcing Cary into *Gambling Ship* and *I'm No Angel* opposite Mae West.

In the summer of 1933, Virginia was on loan and proceeded to Hawaii to make a film entitled *White Heat*; she was reluctant to leave Cary, but the part was a good one, and for the first time since *City Lights* she would actually have a starring role. The veteran woman director Lois Webber, at one time among the highest-paid figures of the silent screen, was to make the picture for a small independent company named Seven Seas/Pinnacle. Virginia played a San Francisco socialite married to a sugar-planter in Kauai; frustrated and bored by the alternating rain and wind-driven dust of her environment, the restless Lucille Cheney almost succumbs to the charms of a good-looking Hawaiian boy. When her husband violently assaults the youth, the heroine's mind is disturbed and in a dramatic sequence she sets fire to the cane fields.

Cary's parting from Virginia was painful. He hated the fact that he couldn't keep an eye on her during the many weeks of location shooting which the film entailed. He telephoned her in Kauai, and tried to check up on her with the switchboard of the Japanese boarding house, a difficult task in those days of comparatively primitive telephone services. He was maddened by the unfounded conviction that she was having an affair with William Mead Lindsay Fiske, one of the producers, who would later be one of the first Americans killed in World War II.

Virginia remembers the unpleasantness of making the film and the unreasoning intensity of Cary's jealousy. She had to work day after day on a sugar plantation, covered in red dust blown by a savage wind. At night, she would return to the Japanese boarding-house to be scrubbed by the housemaid in an effort to remove the dust from her hair, skin pores and nails. Fiske would disappear, along with his co-producer, to a local brothel; the director went to her room, and Virginia was left completely alone.

In September 1933, Cary made an appearance as the Mock Turtle in a grotesque version of *Alice in Wonderland*. Encased in a suffocatingly hot costume with a papier-mâché shell, and a large head with false eyes through which his own could only dimly peer, he could not have been more uncomfortable, and the weird parody of an English classic he had liked as a child can scarcely have improved his spirits. He was testier than ever when Virginia returned from Hawaii; William Lindsay Fiske checked into the Beverly Hills Hotel, and Cary tipped the operators to listen in to his calls to Virginia. Despite the fact that the calls were strictly to do with the movie, Cary remained angrily suspicious.

5

Virginia went by train to San Francisco to shoot a couple of additional scenes of *White Heat*. Cary had her followed by detectives, and seemed to be more irritable than ever when he found that nothing she was doing in that city gave him the slightest grounds for suspicion. She discovered she was being followed, but was forgiving and understanding, perhaps even touched by the extent of Cary's possessiveness. When she returned to Los Angeles, Cary was at last resting between pictures and he decided that, once Randy Scott had finished shooting a film named *Broken Dreams* at Monogram, he would go to London with her and Scott, to introduce them to his old friends in show business. Newspapers reported an unseemly quarrel between Cary and Virginia on the set of Monogram where Randy was working; more than one columnist hinted that the argument was over Scott. But it was probably just a trivial difference of opinion.

They were to leave in late November. But, meanwhile, Cary and Virginia began an elopement that never resulted in a marriage. They took off to Arizona together, staying at the Biltmore Hotel in Phoenix; they had several arguments during the trip, which remained completely innocent of any sexual involvement. The truth was that they were simply tourists, travelling on to Juarez and Tucson to see the local sights.

They returned to Hollywood after ten days, on November 5, 1933. That same day, it was announced that Randolph Scott and Vivian Gaye would be married before Christmas. Simultaneously, Virginia had a furious argument with Cary, their worst to date; she took off to New York without warning, finding refuge in an apartment there with her friends Laurence Olivier and his wife, the actress Jill Esmond. Angry and frustrated, Cary flew to the city in a drunken and unshaven condition, bursting into the apartment and demanding Virginia return to Hollywood. He said the trip to England was off now and that she must forget all idea of it, but she said cheerfully she was going ahead anyway. Finally Cary explained that he had problems with his immigration documents and didn't dare accompany her in case he would be unable to re-enter the United States. Distraught and in tears, she sailed without him.

Impulsively, Cary flew back to Hollywood, picked up Scott and flew back again to join the French liner *Paris*, sailing for Southampton on November 23. The two men callously left Vivian Gaye behind. They also declined to bring Sari Maritza with them. On board the ship, they were housed in an elaborate first-class suite supplied by Paramount, risking untoward gossip by not occupying separate cabins. The British actor David Manners was on the same vessel. He recalls that the studio had installed a grand piano so that Cary could play and sing his music-hall songs during the crossing. The three men joined in lusty baritone choruses, remaining closeted in the suite for almost the entire crossing. The studio had also arranged a suite at the Savoy Hotel in London. Virginia stayed at another hotel. But apparently even the superficial Randolph Scott found the situation a little strained and returned to New York after only a week. Cary took Virginia to Bristol to show her Fairfield Grade and Secondary School and to the Picton Street house to meet his father. She also met his half-brother Eric. Genial and polite, Elias sat on a tailor's table in his work room to talk to the couple. Elias' mistress, Mabel, was present during the meetings; Virginia noted that Cary seemed to be respectful towards her. He still thought his mother was dead, and she was never mentioned during the brief but, for Virginia, touching visit. There were several family reunions that week. Everyone wanted to meet the local boy who had become a major Hollywood star. One of these parties was at the Grand Hotel, where Cary and Virginia were staying in separate suites. Another was at Picton Street, where, among many others, Elsie's brother David and nephew Ernest were present. During a walk with some of his cousins, Cary felt an impulse to go into a fish-and-chip shop; he probably enjoyed the newspaper-wrapped repast more than any elaborate meal in Beverly Hills. Still quarrelling and making up, Cary and Virginia went to Paris at the beginning of December. Edith Gwynn wrote in her *Hollywood Reporter* column, "Cary, poor fellow, has to (put up with) all those 'Come up and see me sometime' invitations. If only he were free to follow . . . But he isn't, poor lover." On their return to London, the couple were talking about getting married on Christmas Day.

They formed a close friendship with the tennis star Bunny Austin and his wife, attending several parties at their home. Cary was proving more difficult than ever: he refused to attend the London première of *I'm No Angel* because Paramount wouldn't pay him for his appearance at the cinema. And he was ailing at the time. His once perfect health had begun to decline: he began suffering from alarming symptoms of rectal bleeding. Simultaneously, he had a severe gum infection and an inflamed tooth that troubled him unbearably. It was a horrible Christmas week; after excruciating dental treatments, which at least solved his problem temporarily, Virginia persuaded him to see a Harley Street specialist who gave him a proctoscopic examination. He was horrified to learn that he had a pre-cancerous condition of the rectum. An immediate operation was called for which involved delicate surgery. He was admitted to a clinic in the Fulham Road. The surgery and its aftermath were very unpleasant. Virginia was constantly at the hospital, where Cary was tortured and restless, shocked to be stricken at such an early age, and nervous that there might be some leak of the information of his illness to the papers.

She herself was run down, exhausted by stress, suffering from severe laryngitis.

Perhaps because they felt that if they didn't they never would, the couple decided to marry as soon as possible. Doctors had told Cary he must stay in bed for at least four more weeks. The couple at last set the wedding-day for February 9. The nuptials took place at the Caxton Hall Registry Office. A large crowd gathered to see them; weak, exhausted, and still in pain, Cary arrived separately, only to find that Virginia was missing. She had been delayed by some last-minute problem with her clothing; he himself was unsuitably attired, hatless, tieless and wearing a dark-brown scarf tucked into his beige tweed overcoat. He appeared to have dressed in haste, and he needed a shave. Virginia looked pale and slightly dishevelled in a yellow-and-black checked suit and a sable coat. Asked by reporters how he felt to be married, Cary said: "We are both very happy. Now we are going straight to Hollywood. We have got to get back to work. We intended to get married quite a while ago, but my illness prevented that.* I am getting better now." A moment later, the crowd closed in, shoving so violently that Virginia's glasses were knocked off. The couple were separated, and for an unpleasant moment feared that they might miss the boat train to Southampton. But they managed to climb into a taxi and arrive at the station just as the train was about to draw out.

They returned to New York on the SS *Paris*. Just as they were on the point of sailing at midnight, Virginia received offers from two studios, Gaumont and BIP, for parts in new films, and hesitated, wanting to go back to London, but Cary insisted they proceed. They arrived in Manhattan on February 15, and spent the evening seeing the play *The Pursuit of Happiness*, which Paramount was considering as a possible vehicle for both of them. Cary was still somewhat weakened by his operation and suffering from the radium treatments when they took the train back to

---

* It was described as "influenza" in the press.

Hollywood. They stopped off briefly to visit Virginia's family in Dallas City, Illinois, a pleasant small town on the Mississippi River just sixteen miles from her birthplace of Carthage. They saw her aunt and grandmother and her brothers and sisters, most of whom lived and farmed around La Harpe. "Cary was fascinated by my folks and by that part of the country," Virginia says. "Of course, almost everyone was fascinated with him. But Mother was very jealous of Cary and there was much tension between them."

Surprisingly, Virginia moved into the house in Los Feliz, thus creating a bizarre ménage. After three weeks, they suddenly moved to the quasi-Spanish La Ronda apartments on Havenhurst, Randy taking Apartment Eleven, on the ground floor next to the Grants. "The Grants and Randolph Scott have moved, all three, but not apart," wrote the knowing Edith Gwynn.

From the moment they moved to the La Ronda, with its tropical flowers and ornamental fountain courtyards, Cary and Virginia were miserable. They argued day and night. Cary's jealousy reached manic proportions; he was jealous, even, of her charming and quite unpossessive mother. Virginia says she clung to a constant hope that a miracle would happen to save their marriage, but it didn't. "I knew if we went on together, we would both be destroyed," she says.

One afternoon, she and Cary drove to the beach. They were returning in the late afternoon along Sunset Boulevard with its winding curves. A man passed them in a car and waved in a friendly spirit. Without her glasses, Virginia couldn't see who the man was, but relaxed from the sand and the sun, always outgoing and free-spirited, she waved back. Cary flew into a violent temper and hit her with the back of his hand. She recalls that the blow was so severe it split open the inside of her mouth.

She was bleeding all over her dress. She insisted Cary drive her home and stop being so hysterical. He refused, and she knew her mother would only scold her, hating Cary as she did, so she ran off and went to stay with a girlfriend. The next day, Cary located her somehow and called her up as though nothing had happened, and asked her what she was doing there. Virginia said, "Don't you remember?" He replied, "I don't know what you're talking about." And Virginia says she honestly believes that he didn't.

In desperation, Virginia went to San Francisco to consult with a psychiatrist friend of hers, Dr. Margaret Chung. Dr. Chung explained without much profundity that Cary's violence was due to his deep emotional insecurity. Back in Hollywood, Virginia decided to give Cary another chance. Responding to his endless calls telling her she was just a silly, hysterical girl and that she should forget all about what she claimed had taken place, she moved back in with him at La Ronda.

Cary didn't improve. While shooting yet another insignificant movie, *Thirty Day Princess*, he was on the verge of a nervous breakdown, screaming hysterically night after night at his unhappy wife. One evening, they were to go to a party given by the distinguished Danish actor and former middle-weight boxing champion Carl Brisson, Brisson's wife and his twenty-two-year-old son Frederick, in whom Cary had a strong romantic interest. Virginia was putting on a pale-blue evening-gown and doing her hair in front of the mirror when Cary walked in and said, harshly, "You're always so goddamned late!" She replied calmly she was ready to leave. "He struck me to the floor so that my face fell on the iron fender in front of the fire," she says. "It was cut wide-open, and blood drenched my dress. I lay there in agony, as he walked out and drove to the party alone."

The Brissons and other friends kept calling Virginia all evening, wondering what was wrong with her and why she hadn't come to the party. All she could say feebly was, "Ask Cary." When he returned late that night, finding her bandaged and sobbing, he asked her what had happened to her. Had she had an accident? She realised now that he was suffering from dangerous symptoms of schizophrenia.

The tormenting relationship continued all that summer. Whenever Virginia would complain about Cary's behaviour the day before, he would say, "You imagined it. Nothing like that ever took place." Virginia walked out on Cary and returned to her mother on several occasions, most firmly of all on September 15, following an especially savage argument. Friends such as Vivian Gaye and Sari Maritza did their utmost to cement the rift, but it was useless. Cary became a very heavy drinker; on the set, he continued his habit of taking alcohol from coffee cups, but he fooled few at the studio. Virginia made plans to move to England, where she would make, the following year, an early vehicle for the very young James Mason, *Late Extra*, also known as *What Price Crime?* The script was worthless, but at least she would escape from Cary for a while.

On September 28, Virginia yielded to Cary's pleas to join her at a dinner party, but he got drunk during the meal, and, when they returned to their apartment at La Ronda, he charged her with paying him no attention all evening. He walked towards her, raising his hand as though to strike, and she ran out and returned home to her mother, calling the ever-vigilant columnist Louella Parsons to say that she was in consultation with lawyers. Virtually incomprehensible, stumbling over his words, Cary telephoned Virginia on October 4 and blurted out his longing for her to return. When she refused, he snapped out, "This will ruin me!" and hung up. Virginia was concerned. There was something about his voice she didn't like. She telephoned back and got the Filipino houseboy, Pedro; Pedro ran upstairs to the bedroom. Cary was stretched out on the bed, dressed only in undershorts, a large bottle of sleeping tablets almost empty beside him. Pedro called for the paramedics, and Cary was rushed by ambulance to hospital.

Because there was some question of foul play, police surgeon Dr. C. E. Cornell was summoned to the scene. A stomach pump was applied. Virginia is sure that, in his drunken stupor, Cary had faked a suicide attempt to frighten her into returning to him, but she was too strong to yield to this theatrical device. Cary was furious, screaming at anyone who would listen that she had betrayed him. He was barely able to finish his latest and perhaps dreariest film, *Ladies Should Listen*; he was beside himself with the thought that his wife should cling to her mother, and he was appalled when, in December, she sued for divorce and for maintenance on the grounds of cruelty, insisting that he give her a full share of their joint property (valued at $50,000), $167.50 a week, and that he not obstruct the course of their litigation. He refused to respond to her request, and even succeeded in withdrawing all the money from their joint bank account, forcing her to pawn her engagement ring and other jewellery and to borrow money, using her car as insurance.

Cary's divorce from Virginia became final on March 26. Pale, her red-rimmed eyes concealed behind dark glasses, she sat in Judge Charles Haas courtroom in down-town Los Angeles and, in response to a question by her lawyer, Milton Cohen, described the misery of her marriage. She said, so quietly that she was barely audible:

> He was very solemn and disagreeable. He refused to pay my bills. He told me to go out and work myself, and then discouraged me every time I had an opportunity. He was like this almost from the first . . . He told me he didn't care to live with me anymore, a number of times . . . He was sullen, morose, and quarrelsome in front of guests. He falsely accused me of not appreciating him or his efforts. He was inclined to drink quite a bit all during our marriage.

Her mother Blanche confirmed the many examples of Cary's insults to Virginia. Cary did not appear in court, and within fifty minutes Virginia was free.

Virginia decided to proceed to England to make her film on April 27, 1935. Cary had been walking through another role in *Enter Madame* with Elissa Landi, and was exasperated, not only by his private life, but by his career. Getting wind of Virginia's departure for New York by train, Cary flew there to forestall her. He was wrongly convinced she was having an affair with someone; any thought of a relationship was very far from her mind — she had had more than enough of personal stress. All she wanted to do was live in a different environment and work. Cary's excuse for being in Manhattan was appearing on the "Lux Radio Theater" in *Adam and Eve* opposite Constance Cummings. He received $1,750 for thirty minutes on the air. Unable to reach Virginia to dissuade her from departing, he lingered on in Manhattan, deciding to make the best of a bad situation. Then suddenly he gave up and entered into a new romance, with the international beauty Sandra Rambeau.

Shortly afterwards, Cary dropped Miss Rambeau for the equally attractive actress Betty Furness. The daughter of the radio pioneer George Furness, Miss Furness was raised in an expensive apartment on Park Avenue and had begun appearing in movies at the age of sixteen. Like Cary, she was between pictures, and when he returned at the end of May to make his next movie, *The Last Outpost*, she returned with him, to make *McFadden's Flats*. She was seen everywhere with him in Hollywood, although it is almost certain theirs was a platonic relationship; she says it was. They were seen dancing at the Trocadero on June 8, at a party that included Dorothy di Frasso and the newly arrived gangster Benjamin (Bugsy) Siegel and on June 18, Carole Lombard invited them to a gala event, held in the funhouse at the Venice Pier with a total of 300 guests riding the carousel, enjoying the peep shows, hurtling down slides, and plunging into a whirling bucket of steel thirty feet wide known as a social mixer, where Cary, Marlene Dietrich, Claudette Colbert, Caesar Romero, Frances Drake, Randolph Scott, and Vivian Gaye (who would soon break off her engagement to Randolph Scott and marry the director Ernst Lubitsch) tumbled into a heap as the rotary machinery stopped dead. George Cukor remarked at the end of the party that it was great to see so many "star fannies" close up; Dietrich wound up with her legs around Miss Colbert's neck; agent Phil Berg had a broken foot; and Richard Barthelmess was black and blue from head to foot.

Edith Gwynn commented in her column upon Cary's widely known and discussed bisexuality. Since she couldn't state it directly, she disguised the barb in an account of an imaginary party game in which the guests would come as famous film titles. Marlene Dietrich came as *Male and Female*, Garbo as *The Son-Daughter*, and Cary, audaciously, was represented as *One Way Passage*, a sly reference to his sexual inclinations.

Despite such barbs, Cary was at last beginning to relax. It was easier for him to enjoy a lighthearted, much-publicised "romance" with Miss Furness than to experience the tensions of a real marriage. To help promote *The Last Outpost* and their own careers, he and Betty Furness went to one tremendous social event after another, he in custom-made tuxedos from Bullock's Wilshire, she in enormous skyscraper-high hats. The ever-knowing Edith Gwynn told her industry readers, "Betty is still wearing a high hat . . . Be sure to ask Cary what is the height of indifference."

That summer, the gossips were concentrating upon another of Cary's friendships: one which, according to witnesses, was a more intensely personal one. He began an affair with Howard Hughes. Then twenty-nine years old, Howard Hughes had inherited the Hughes Tool Company at eighteen, and had used much of his oil-drill fortune to indulge passions for film making and flying. Tall, bony, with carved features and a thatch of dark, unruly hair, the taciturn Hughes had an odd, high-pitched voice. He wore baggy suits and poorly polished shoes, drove an assortment of shabby, second-rate cars, and lived not in Beverly Hills or the still fashionable Hollywood Hills, but in an unpretentious house among the old money in Hancock Park. According to his late aides, Noah Dietrich and Johnny Meyer, and to his ebullient publicist of the 1940s, Guido Orlando, who is still alive, Hughes was bisexual, but intensely guilty about his consuming sexual hunger and psychological divisions and always eager to blanket his more secret activities under a cover of being radically promiscuous. This determined attempt to build himself as a Don Juan in the public eye finally rendered his relationships with both sexes useless. A brief marriage ended in disaster; all attempts to maintain a household of any sort failed and his love affair with the beautiful screen actress Billie Dove collapsed. That tormented relationship ended because Miss Dove's former husband, the tough director Irving Willat, threatened Hughes' life if he continued to see her. Willat told Dietrich he knew that Hughes was "a faggot" and didn't want her life to be destroyed by marrying him.

Hughes' discovery of Randolph Scott had led to what appeared to be a brief relationship; now his sexual interest in Cary was intense. Hughes had returned to Hollywood that summer, in 1935, after working with American Airways (as it was then known) as a luggage-handler under an assumed name in order to learn the business from the ground up. He emerged rapidly as a brilliant aviator, achieving 225 miles an hour, an extraordinary speed for the period, in his 580-horsepower Wasp engine plane and he won his first major aviation prize at the All-American Air Meet in Miami on January 14, 1934.

He paid Cary the greatest compliment of taking him to his secret hangar at Grand Central Airport in Glendale. Closed to all but a handful of visitors, the hangar was the site of the building of its creator's beloved aeroplane, H-1. Though not large, just twenty-seven feet from nose to tail, the H-1 was beautifully streamlined, with specially shortened wings that would allow a great increase in flying speeds. Up to that time, almost all aeroplane landing gear was fixed in position during flight, but the H-1, under Hughes' loving guidance, had a pioneer form of retractable wheels. Again and again, during 1935, the plane was pulled apart down to the last nut and bolt and put together again to achieve maximum safety and velocity. All that Hughes could think about, other than Cary, was his desire to make the first flight in the H-1. Noah Dietrich was with him constantly, acting as his financial adviser, trying to restrict his expenditure on the plane, and trying to make him rest, as he would work all night, the following day and the following night without sleep, finally collapsing at his drawing-board.

It was in the midst of this most intense period of Hughes' life that he actually managed to break free from his obsession long enough to take Cary on a yachting voyage down the coast as far as Ensenada and back, and then up north to San Francisco; Paramount began to panic and the publicists called Edith Gwynn repeatedly to say that Cary's real interest was in a, probably fictitious, girl described as "Little Miss Moffett". Exactly what took place on the yacht will perhaps never be known, but the certainty is that Cary and Hughes formed, in those days at sea, a profound romantic friendship that would remain unbroken until the day of Hughes' death almost half a century later. Even during the notorious Clifford Irving affair, Hughes would be in constant touch with Cary, seeking his advice on how to deal with a painful situation.

At the same time, Cary remained very close to Randolph Scott; their relationship continued, and Randy continued to live at La Ronda. Soon, they would live together again. On July 30, Vivian Gaye married Lubitsch after many delays and the next day, Randy flew to his home in Orange, Virginia, after making no fewer than eighteen movies in the last twenty-four months. There, he ran into the richest local citizen, the forceful, tweedy Marion duPont, heiress to her late father William's vast fortune, which was almost certainly over $100 million. Marion benefited from the pioneer industrial genius of her forebears that included major developments in the field of chemicals and explosives, and the invention of nylon and rayon had made the duPonts wealthy beyond calculation.

Like her father, Marion was obsessed with horses, which were almost her entire life. In 1932, she had bought for an undisclosed sum the five-year-old Battleship, son of the internationally famous racehorse Man O' War. In 1934, Battleship had won the Grand National at Belmont Park, America's greatest jumping event, and again he triumphed at the National Hunt Club at Brookline. In 1935, when

Randolph Scott was in Virginia, Marion had temporarily retired Battleship to stud, placing him for one year on her breeding-farm before she would take the supreme gamble and enter him for the world's greatest steeplechase, the British Grand National at Aintree.

With her vigorous stride, square shoulders, tweed suits, close-cropped black hair and plain, mannish face, Marion duPont was scarcely a beauty. Yet her seeming lack of femininity, which led many to believe she was a lesbian, was quite deceptive. According to a close friend of hers, Seth Green, former publisher of the *Record*, the local newspaper in Orange, she had an insatiable desire for men, and in view of her lack of looks was prepared to pay any amount of money to acquire them. She had married a former jockey and trainer named Tom Summerville, and, after tiring of him, acquired other men, running her private life very much as she ran her stud farm. Randolph Scott, who looked rather like a horse, was the next on her list. It was, of course, out of the question that he would be attracted to her. But his relentless financial ambition was not satisfied by the succession of increasingly mediocre films to which he was assigned. Marion duPont offered to invest in him; there were rumours that she bought a substantial shareholding in Paramount to improve the level of his roles, but that is scarcely borne out by records, since, soon afterwards, he drifted away to Twentieth Century-Fox and RKO. Whatever the truth, he was suddenly a far richer man than he had been. Marion duPont never bothered with the niceties of the society of her time; she installed him in her legendary mansion, Montpelier, the former residence of President James Madison and his celebrated wife Dolly. There, she put in a sauna, a novelty in the United States at the time, and a private gymnasium with weights for her lover's use.

Cary met Marion during her brief visits to Hollywood that year; maybe because of her enthusiasm for racing, and her plans for the Grand National, he acquired a sudden interest in the sport, and was a frequent presence at the racetracks.

That August, perhaps in order to have access to Cary,

perhaps because of a genuine romantic interest in Katharine Hepburn, the ever-ambiguous and mysterious Hughes kept turning up on location at Malibu, California, where Cary was shooting the picture *Sylvia Scarlett*, with the actress. Cary was on loan to RKO and the film, a story of travelling players, was an example of self-indulgence by the homosexual director George Cukor. There were all manner of sly and outrageously risqué references in the writing to Cary's bisexuality, presumably included in the well-founded belief that the public would remain oblivious of his predilections. Miss Hepburn was disguised as a boy through much of the action, and Cary was shown fondling her while she was dressed in male clothing. Miss Hepburn regarded the matter of making movies as an extended vacation, and always insisted on bringing a cook on location to prepare lunch. George Cukor brought his own chef, and they vied with each other to prepare the best meal. Long breaks were taken for afternoon tea while the cast, including Cary, sat on long wooden benches at tables laid out with linen cloths on the cliffs above the sea. The actor Brian Aherne recalled:

> One day, we were sitting down to eat when a biplane roared up and settled on the landing strip. Out stepped Howard Hughes. He was supposed to be having an affair with Kate, but I think he was more interested in Cary. He came over and sat with us, using that odd, high-pitched voice of his. Kate and Cary would tease him by whispering such words as, "Pass the bread, please," right in front of him, and he'd wonder what was going on. He'd suspect them of romancing each other and would start to shout, and then they'd scream with laughter at his discomfiture.

Aherne said that Cary was relaxed and charming during the work, very much at ease with everyone. But there was one sequence at which he balked. The actress Natalie Paley had gone out swimming and had got out of her depth. She began waving and calling for help. Cukor said, "Go on in,

Cary, Natalie's drowning," and Cary replied, "I won't. It's too goddamned cold!" Everyone stared at him appalled. Hepburn laughed and dived into the sea. She pulled Natalie Paley out, and the first thing Natalie said was, "Why did *you* have to do this! I was hoping to be carried out in Cary Grant's arms!"

The picture was a freakish failure, notable more for its extravagant hints at the sexual peculiarities of some members of its cast than for its intrinsic merits. The producer, Pandro S. Berman, still groans and holds his head at the mention of the movie. He says he called Miss Hepburn and Cukor to his house and told them he never wanted to work with them again. How the movie got past the vigilant Motion Picture Code Board remains an unsolved mystery of Hollywood.

By now, Edith Gwynn was beginning to make more overt references to Cary's bisexuality in her column. She talked of "a long-haired town for males", mentioning on her short and deadly list Gary Cooper, James Cagney, Cary and Randolph Scott, singling out Scott's newly acquired curls for special mention. Cary responded by appearing at the Trocadero on the night of September 30, 1935, with Scott as his date for the evening. Apparently, RKO objected, because his next public appearance at the same nightspot was with Betty Furness, and, on October 20, Miss Furness accompanied him to the wrap-up of shooting party at Cukor's house on Cordell Drive.

On a Sunday in the final days of filming *Sylvia Scarlett*, Howard Hughes again paid Cary a supreme compliment: he took him (the only person so honoured) for a joy-ride in the H-1 over Los Angeles, achieving a speed of about 300 miles per hour. On September 12, 1935, Hughes decided to aim for the world speed record for a plane flying over land; the site chosen for the test was Martin Field, near Santa Ana, California. The judges were air-ace Amelia Earhart, Hollywood stunt pilot Paul Mantz, and National Aeronautic Association official Lawrence Therkelson. After an initial failure, Hughes, to Cary's excitement, posted world record speeds, reaching a maximum of 354 miles per hour. But in his passionate pursuit of victory, Hughes forgot that his fuel was low, and his engine failed before he could access the auxiliary tank. He made a forced landing but, to Cary's relief, was uninjured.

Immediately after *Sylvia Scarlett* was completed, Cary signed a contract to make a picture in England, *The Amazing Quest of Ernest Bliss*; it was an uninspiring script, but he very much wanted to return home. His father was suffering from a stomach disease which was sufficiently serious to cause alarm. Cary also wanted to see his half-brother Eric. Randy caused a new flurry of comment by seeing him off when he flew to New York on his way to London. He sailed on the *Aquitania* in November. While in London, before he started work on the picture, he saw a good deal of Virginia Cherrill, who had partially forgiven him. She was very sympathetic when he told her of his father's sickness, and this warmed him towards her, though with his amazing capacity to deny the inconvenient past, he showed no regret for what he had done to her. He travelled to Bristol where he found Elias in desperate health at his home, 13 Victoria Walk. Septicaemia of the bowel had set in along with gangrene, following a radical operation for cancer. Though not much over sixty, Elias was already shockingly aged.

Cary returned with a heavy heart to London to begin work on *Ernest Bliss* for Grand National Pictures under the direction of Alfred Zeisler. He was consoled partly by the presence, as leading lady, of the gentle, quiet and subdued actress Mary Brian. Born Louise Byrdie Dantzler, the twenty-six-year-old Texan had won a beauty contest, and at the age of sixteen had made a vivid debut as a winsome and touching Wendy in J. J. Barrie's *Peter Pan*. She had gone on to appear effectively in such celebrated movies as *Beau Geste, Forgotten Faces, The Virginian, The Royal Family of Broadway*, and *The Front Page*. But she lacked the weight and presence to survive at the top in the harshly competitive world of talkies. Nor did her gentle, recessive nature assist her in dealing with the cruelties and intrigues and back-stabbings of life in a major studio. By 1935, she was adrift, and the starring role in *Ernest Bliss* was her last chance for success and survival. By now, she was really past caring; the chief interest for her in making the film was Cary Grant.

On December 2, Cary received a phone call from Bristol to say that his father had passed away after a second operation. Cary, professional to the last, told Alfred Zeisler and Garrett Klement, the head of the production company, that he would not break the shooting schedule to take care of the funeral arrangements. But Klement insisted he leave for Bristol immediately after the morning shoot on the fourth. He played his scenes perfectly, giving no inkling of his severe stress and anguish; then he drove down to join the Leaches at the funeral. Some historians have stated that he learned of Elsie Leach's existence in the asylum at the time, but that is entirely contradicted by the available evidence. In fact, it was to be three more years before the truth was known.

Returning to his apartment in Park Lane, Cary found a beautiful note from Virginia Cherrill. He wrote to her thanking her for a gift and saying how fond his father had been of her and he wished he had invited her to the funeral. ("In fact, I seem to have some peculiar idea you were there this morning."). He added that he knew Elias would have liked Virginia to have attended, and had even expressed that wish previously saying he had wanted them to be there with him "in case anything should happen to him at the first operation". Cary added:

> But somehow I didn't quite know how to ask you . . . It was unfair to ask you to go through the ordeal too, dear. I was afraid the invitation might seem wrongly motivated. Everyone in Bristol thanks you for your kindness. They've been so sorry about us, and now are so kind and helpful in their little manner.

From what he wrote Cary obviously felt the loss of his father greatly. He had found the funeral exhausting.

* * *

He continued working on *The Amazing Quest of Ernest Bliss* with a heavy heart, still consoled by the thoughtfulness of Mary Brian. However, seen today, the movie only too clearly reveals the lack of even a hint of genuine romantic warmth between them. Their "romance" was nothing more than the invention of a skilful studio publicity department and the tender memories of Miss Brian herself. Soon, the situation would change.

She says, "When Cary came back to London after his father's funeral, it was as if he shut that period of his life away. I'm sure he was grieving, but he didn't talk about it." She remembers that they would spend Sundays together, walking out into the London streets, looking at the announcements of destinations on the front of the red double-decker buses, and flipping coins to see which one they would take. They would sit at the top of the bus at the front and travel as far as the bus went, to various suburbs of London that for Cary had always been mysterious, romantic and unknown. To help get rid of his grief, Cary would take Mary to his beloved pantomimes; she herself had almost been cast in a new production of *Jack and the Beanstalk,* in which Cary had appeared in London at the age of seven. When he told her of his exciting experiences in pantomime, she was very regretful she had not accepted the part of Jack. They also went out to music-halls together after a day's work; Cary would discuss with her the histories and personalities of all of the performers with whose talents and backgrounds he was so intimately familiar. He talked to her of his years of stilt-walking, and told her that music-hall was still the chief passion of his life.

The high spot of that London winter season of 1935 was Noël Coward's striking collection of playlets, *Tonight at 8.30.* Cary and Mary tried to get tickets, but even Cary's considerable name failed to prove influential; Noël Coward, who had visited Cary and Virginia in Hollywood the year before, answered Cary's pleas and arranged for him and Mary to see the show from the wings. Afterwards, Laurence Olivier and Jill Esmond joined Cary and Mary at a supper party. That same season, still fighting against his grief, Cary was seen with Mary at several other major social events. Ad Schulberg, who was in town, held a soirée for the couple; among the guests were Virginia Cherrill and her latest romantic interest, the enormously wealthy Maharaja of Jaipur, Fay Wray and John Monk Saunders, and so was Cary's great friend Douglas Fairbanks, Jnr. On December 13, the actress Kitty Kelly gave a party for Cary and Mary at which the Duke of Kent, Lord Milford Haven and actress Betty Balfour were among the guests. Cary again became close to Fay Wray and her husband, who was writing a script for Alexander Korda based on the life of Lawrence of Arabia. He wanted Cary to play the role; unfortunately, this idea never came to fruition, and the picture wasn't made until decades later by Sam Spielberg, with Peter O'Toole.

Making *The Amazing Quest* (as the picture was finally called in England) proved to be uninspiring for both Cary and Mary. At times, fond as he was of Mary, the tension and stress made him flare up. She says:

> I think he had a few emotional scars from his divorce from Virginia. He had a terrible temper, and then he'd come running back saying how sorry he was. He would be angry at someone, and take it out on someone else. He never hit me. His anger was short-lived.

According to Mary Brian, when Cary returned to New York on the *Bremen* on February 5, 1936, his feelings for her deepened, and they began what she now describes as a platonic romantic love affair. Mary was appearing in London in "The Charlot Revue"; Cary had returned to Hollywood to make *Big Brown Eyes*, a comedy co-starring Joan Bennett, to be followed by *Suzy*, with Jean Harlow. He found Randolph Scott depressed: in an odd parallel to his own life, Scott's father was also dying of cancer, and passed away on March 5 in Virginia. Only a few days later, Scott travelled on to Charlotte, North Carolina, to marry Marion duPont in a ceremony which neither Cary nor any other of their Hollywood friends attended. Simultaneously, in fact, Mary arrived in Los Angeles and was met off the train by Cary; the following night they were seen together dancing at the Trocadero. They became very friendly with Gene Markey and his wife Joan Bennett, whom Cary enjoyed working with on *Big Brown Eyes*. Mary Brian says of her relationship with Cary in the spring and summer of 1936:

> He had even called me on the ship as I came back from England to New York. Romance would be my word for our relationship. It was flowers and attention and two people completely enjoying each other and doing the same things. It was a very exciting, lovely part of my life. In a very innocent way I loved him and he loved me. And we would always be friends. It was a great capacity Cary had, keeping friends, and even girls that he had gone with, seeing them again with no embarrassment on either side. He met my mother and they got along well. Everything seemed fine.

This was probably one of the happiest times for Cary. He had no passionate entanglements, Mary was a sweet and undemanding friend, and Hollywood was at the height of its glamour and luxury. *Big Brown Eyes* and *Suzy* were conventional movies that made little or no demands on his resources of energy. The Trocadero was aglitter night after night with the stars, dancing fox-trots and quick-steps and waltzes to the orchestra led by the irresistible Spaniard, Xavier Cugat. Everyone table-hopped and gossiped and made sure they were mentioned in Louella Parsons' column in the morning. They were carefree days, far from the thunderclouds of the increasingly dangerous and threatening European scene. Cary began thinking seriously of proposing marriage to Mary.

It was in this period, the agony of his father's death gradually eased away in his memory, that Cary heard shocking news.

6

On the night of July 11, 1936, Howard Hughes was driving to his house in Hancock Park from downtown Los Angeles, passing a streetcar safety zone at Third Street and Lorraine Boulevard, when, impatient as always, he drew out behind a tram to proceed with his journey. He struck and killed a pedestrian, fifty-nine-year-old salesman Gabe S. Meylan. Hughes called Cary and other friends in desperation. He was charged with negligent homicide, but so great was his wealth and influence, that he got away with saying he had made a sharp turn to avoid an approaching car. He was acquitted at the preliminary hearing. Hughes was badly shaken by this episode and became more reclusive, depending more and more on Cary for his friendship and support, and in fact Cary was virtually his only intimate male friend during this time. Hughes' romance with Katharine Hepburn was not going well and Cary proved a consolation to him in his severe bouts of depression.

During that summer, Cary continually ran into a couple, the agent Walter Kane and the stunning blonde actress Phyllis Brooks. Born Phyllis Steiller in Boise, Idaho, the twenty-two-year-old Phyllis was not well known at the time. She had a radiant, free-wheeling, extroverted quality, a deep, throaty laugh, and a habit of tossing back her magnificent hair and pushing it down with her hand as she cracked risqué, charming jokes. She was the opposite of the reserved Mary Brian. At the time, she made no great impact on Cary, and in fact their meetings were so superficial that today she only recalls meeting him much later.* But she made an impression, no doubt of it. Everyone who met her automatically loved Brooksie, as she was known in Hollywood. Even in the company of so many dazzling young women, she stood out. She was the toast of the Vendôme and the Trocadero, and Edith Gwynn and Louella Parsons constantly mentioned her in their columns, pushing her career along. Hollywood was not a place in which people often gave a helping hand; but just about everyone wanted to assist Brooksie. They all felt she deserved to be a major star.

In August, Cary at last proposed marriage to Mary Brian, but she hesitated. Although she rejects decisively any suggestion that she knew about Cary's ambiguous personal life, she undoubtedly sensed that he was first and foremost consumed with himself and his career. And even after he proposed, Cary himself seemed shaky about his intentions. He had no sooner indicated his desire to marry Mary than he wondered if it was the right time for him to get married. Mary Brian says, "I wasn't pressing for it. I went to New York. I felt that if there was any indecision on Cary's part, it was certainly not the time for us to get together."

And she wasn't aware of another complication: even while dating Mary in England he had seen a good deal of young Frederick Brisson, who still fascinated him. Brisson was then twenty-four years old.

Phyllis Brooks went to New York to appear to great effect in the play *Stage Door*. She was launched as a name to watch; but the play closed quickly when its temperamental star Margaret Sullavan became pregnant with the child who is today the famous writer of the autobiography, *Haywire*. Phyllis returned to Los Angeles. Cary had just finished shooting *Wedding Present* with Joan Bennett, his friend and mentor B. P. Schulberg being the producer. He called Mary Brian only sporadically; the interest he had in her now faded. One night at the Trocadero, Phyllis was entertaining an old friend of hers from New York, Eleanor French, a society nightclub singer who was very popular at the Stork Club. Eleanor had always wanted to meet Cary Grant; when Cary stopped by the table to remind Phyllis of their previous meetings, Eleanor was enchanted. The Earl of Warwick, who was in Hollywood looking for an acting career, and was an old friend of Phyllis', called her and asked what he could do to entertain Eleanor French. Phyllis replied that he could help by giving a party and inviting Cary, in the hope that Cary would be attracted to Eleanor.

That same week, Randolph Scott, who had returned from Virginia to make *The Last of the Mohicans* after only a brief period with his wife, who had settled several million dollars on him, had taken a beach house at 1019 Ocean Front,* Santa Monica, and Cary moved in. It was an intriguing house, a typically odd California mixture of styles. The front patio and entrance corridor and walled garden suggested a Spanish hacienda. But, inside, there was an imitation Regency staircase that twisted up to the left in a semi-circle and a circular Regency hallway on the second floor, with bedrooms off to right and left. The rest of the lower part of the house was a cross between Cape Cod and English mock-Tudor in equal parts. The front of the house, leading on to a swimming-pool, tennis court and the beach, featured Cape Cod eaves and a heavy grey slate roof. Somehow the architectural jumble was appealing; it was at this house that the Earl of Warwick arranged the house-warming party to which Phyllis came with Eleanor French, deliberately unaccompanied by male dates.

It never struck Phyllis as incongruous that she should be received in what was quite visibly the home of two men of ambiguous sexuality. The only surprise she experienced was that Cary was attracted to her and not to Eleanor. Superficial and cheerful as ever, Randolph Scott seems to have cared no more about Cary's interest in Phyllis than he did for his own wife, who seldom visited him from Virginia. Scott went on to make *Go West, Young Man* with Mae West, acting out the heavily comic quasi-sexual scenes with his co-star with what seemed to be total conviction.

---

* Later renumbered 1039, it is standing today.

Not since the heyday of his marriage to Virginia Cherrill had Cary felt so warm an interest in any woman. All thoughts of Mary Brian were forgotten as he and Phyllis danced at nightclub after nightclub, rapidly becoming the most talked-about couple in Hollywood. Phyllis recalls: "We were in love. Cary said to me, 'If anything ever happens to us, I'm done. You are young enough to maybe find love again, but I will be lost.'" The obstacle to this burgeoning relationship was the dislike that Phyllis' mother had for Cary. Unlike Virginia Cherrill's mother, Phyllis' parent was a frustrated actress whose career had never taken off; Mrs. Steiller was a neo-Victorian, correct and moralistic, and she was not at all happy with the idea of Phyllis conducting an affair, no matter how innocent, with a divorced film star in whom countless women were interested. There is no indication that either Cary or Phyllis was concerned about Mrs. Steiller's attitude. With breezy charm, Phyllis simply waved away her mother's objections when she returned home late at night after exciting evenings with Cary at the Trocadero.

At this time, Cary renewed an old and close friendship from his vaudeville days. He had never forgotten the theatrical and movie manager Frank W. Vincent, who had booked him and the rest of the Pender Troupe into the Orpheum Circuit after Cary's illness in Rochester in 1922. A gentleman of the old school, Vincent had not ceased to keep a firm eye on Cary's career from the beginning. He had formed a partnership with the powerful agent Harry E. Edington, whose clientele included the mysterious Greta Garbo. Cary, always shrewd where money was concerned, secretly entered into a partnership with these two important agents, investing much of his savings in the business. The situation was unique and of questionable legality, since in effect Cary became his own agent, receiving a split of the ten per cent which went automatically to Vincent and Edington. Moreover, and still more surprisingly, he was now the agent for several major stars; the Edington-Vincent client list was spectacular and included such figures as

Marlene Dietrich, Douglas Fairbanks, Jnr., Leopold Sto-
kowski, the up-and-coming Rita Hayworth, and Joel
McCrea. The thought of secretly being the film agent of
Garbo and Dietrich was intoxicating. Cary would soon
make far more money from his under-the-table agenting
and managing than he would from his work as a screen
actor. And no one save his partners in all of Hollywood
knew the truth. Had they known, several of the stars would
undoubtedly have been furious, especially those under contract to his studio, Paramount.

In the early months of 1937, Cary continued to see
Howard Hughes whenever possible. On January 18,
Hughes flew the H-1, renamed the Winged Bullet, from
Burbank Airport to Newark, New Jersey in a coast-to-coast
record of seven hours, twenty-eight minutes, and twenty-
five seconds. Several years would go by before that trans-
continental record would be broken. President Franklin
D. Roosevelt received Hughes at the White House and
presented him with the Harmon International Trophy. The
elated Hughes returned joyfully to Hollywood to receive
Cary's congratulations at an elaborate party which Cary
gave at the Trocadero. Hughes immediately began plans
for an around-the-world flight; that summer, he applied
for permission for the journey from the Bureau of Air
Commerce, but to his intense fury and that of his friends,
including Cary, he was turned down. Such a venture was
considered too dangerous at the time, despite the fact that
Charles Lindbergh and others had successfully flown the
Atlantic, and that, by now, zeppelins were already making
regular crossings.

In the spring, Cary was working on *Topper*, adapted
from the popular novel by Thorne Smith about a couple
killed in a car crash who return in whimsical good spirits
to haunt their still-living friends. The film provided an
agreeable opportunity for Cary to renew his acquaintance
with the charmingly flustered Roland Young, who played
the title role with effortless artistry, and whom Cary remembered with pleasure from the filming of *This Is the Night*

five years earlier. Constance Bennett was his co-star. More flamboyant, reckless and extroverted than her staid sister Joan, she was engaged to be married to the Latin lover Gilbert Roland at the time. Troubled by the alcoholism, nervous breakdowns and hysterical crying fits of her sister Barbara, she was on edge and extremely temperamental during much of the shooting.

His co-star's behaviour proved unsettling to Cary, who liked above all a calm atmosphere on a set; her frequent lateness grated on him. Worse, he was politically at odds with the producer Hal Roach. He had admired Roach's work with the great slapstick comedians he had loved as a child, including the ragamuffin Our Gang, a group of kids (for whom, during *Topper*, he gave a party at the studio), Laurel and Hardy, and Harold Lloyd, whom he liked most of all. Cary was impressed by the stories Roach told of his early life as a mule-skinner, and as a gold prospector in Alaska. He liked Roach's inventiveness, aided as it was by the skill of the director Norman Z. McLeod, with whom Cary had worked on *Alice in Wonderland*. The many bits of business in the picture, carefully established in the screenplay, brought out the best in him; he laughed and clapped like a child at the day's rushes, which showed him seemingly transparent, involved in a series of witty gags.

Cary, who was of course opposed to Hitler and Mussolini, disapproved of Britain's appeasement policy, and was concerned about the advance of Fascism in Europe, began to take steps towards the commitment that would lead him to become a special British Intelligence Agent in World War II. Acutely aware politically, he was, interestingly a staunch Republican who, if he had been a citizen and allowed to vote, would undoubtedly have supported Alf Landon in the 1936 election. He knew, friends confirm, of the pro-Nazi stance of certain other prominent figures of Hollywood, including the producer Winfield Sheehan, who had recently left his post as head of Twentieth Century-Fox and would soon form a questionable association with the German Nazi Consul General in Los Angeles, George Gyssling.

Cary also knew of the dangerous activities of Victor McLaglen, who had won an Academy Award for his performance in *The Informer* and who was frequently seen riding through Hollywood on horseback or appearing at meetings in various parks as Commandant of the Hollywood Czars, a radically anti-Semitic, pro-Nazi group that was discovered more than once beating up Jews. And it was known to most people, including Cary, on the Hollywood grapevine led by W. R. Wilkerson and his wife, Edith Gwynn, that Walt Disney, whose upright defiance of the Hollywood unions was already earning him notoriety, had an admiration for Hitler that was reciprocated and would soon entertain Leni Riefenstahl, Hitler's favourite film maker, who had made the German propaganda films *Berlin Olympiad* and *Triumph of the Will.* Nor was Cary unaware of the political leanings of Gary Cooper, who in 1938 would go to Berlin and be entertained by Hitler. Yet, for some incomprehensible reason, Grant was blind to Dorothy di Frasso's role as Mussolini's agent and collaborator. He was taken in, apparently, by her repeated statements that she was really an enemy of the Italian dictator even though, at the same time, she was entertaining Mussolini and Field Marshal Goering at her Villa Madama near Rome.

As he appeared in scene after scene of light-hearted, empty-headed farce in *Topper,* Cary continued his careful surveillance of the Hollywood anti-Semitic scene. In yet another paradox of his life and nature, he was simultaneously behaving in a manner that shocked several of his friends. Even the columnist Hedda Hopper, a homophobe who hated Cary, could not bring herself to mention that he and Randolph Scott turned up at the Santa Monica costume-party given by Marion Davies in honour of her lover William Randolph Hearst on April 29, 1937. They were dressed as identical circus acrobats, neither Mrs. Scott nor Phyllis Brooks accompanying them.

Life continued at the beach house. Marion duPont was still uneasy during her visits there, feeling unhappy and out of place in Hollywood, probably only too keenly aware of what was going on between her husband and Grant, who, for appearance's sake, moved temporarily into the house next door. She spent most of her days at the racetrack, trying to suppress her feelings of disappointment in the world of the turf. But it didn't work: she returned to her home in Virginia that spring and did not come back. She didn't even mention Randolph Scott in her memoirs. Cary moved in again, and he and Scott seemed quite content to be photographed for fan magazines in and around the swimming-pool, playing beach-ball, cooking in matching aprons in the kitchen, washing the dishes together, and fooling around on the patio in a manner that left little to the imagination. They were still confident that the public would never suspect anything and that the more they flaunted their relationship the more everyone would think that if they had anything to hide they would not allow themselves to be pictured or written about in their habitat. During the prolonged absence of Scott on location that summer shooting the film *High, Wide and Handsome*, Cary continued to see Phyllis, who often motored down to the beach house, but there was probably still no physical affair. Cary did not always go out with her. It is probably indicative of the uncommitted nature of their relationship that, during the shooting of the film, *The Toast of New York*, Cary was seen from time to time with the voluptuous Jean Rogers, a minor actress whose chief claim to fame was playing opposite Buster Crabbe as the heroine of the serial *Flash Gordon*.

Cary was introduced to Jean Rogers during a brief trip to New York, where he was among the many British expatriates who welcomed the arrival of Alfred Hitchcock by ship. The great English director and his wife had never been to Manhattan before. Hitchcock was on his way to Hollywood for discussion with David. O. Selznick about possible future projects, following the great success of his British films, *The Lady Vanishes* and *The Thirty-Nine Steps*. Cary was fascinated with Hitch: the enormously rotund film maker was shrewd, hard-bitten, bright and sharp-witted, with a wicked, enjoyable sense of humour. Knowing that Cary was very tight with money, he delighted in deliberately passing him the bills at the end of meals in expensive restaurants. For once, Cary didn't mind: he was captivated by Hitchcock's talent and wanted one day to work with him.

That autumn of 1937, Phyllis Brooks was appearing, with Randolph Scott, as a radio band singer in a Shirley Temple vehicle, *Rebecca of Sunnybrook Farm*. Cary starred in *The Awful Truth* and *Bringing Up Baby*. *The Awful Truth* turned out to be his first major success, the picture that would launch him as a major international star. Yet the auspices for this antic comedy made by him at Columbia on special loan from Paramount could not have been less promising. The director, Leo McCarey, was an alcoholic of unstable temperament, whose Irish-American charm secured him one job after another, but whose wayward approach to film making exasperated even his warmest admirers among the studio executives. Ralph Bellamy, the accomplished, thirty-three-year-old former Broadway actor who had made his name in the *Ellery Queen* series of B-pictures, and in *Hands Across the Table* with Carole Lombard, appeared with Cary and Irene Dunne in the film. He recalls the chaos from which *The Awful Truth* was born. The script was rewritten three times at least, among its successive authors Dorothy Parker and her husband Alan Campbell. The final draft was cobbled together from the existing ones by a hack writer named Viña Delmar, who fortunately had retained sufficient of Dorothy Parker's witty lines to make the whole film work. But she still had no proper structure or proper progression of scenes, and McCarey, smiling incessantly in his crinkly Irish manner, seemed cavalier in his attitude and unconcerned whether the picture would work or not.

Cary, who liked thorough professionalism, pre-preparation and pin-point precision in every detail of film making, was exasperated from the beginning of the first day's work. When he walked onto the set for the first time, Irene Dunne was pounding away at the grand piano in a desperate attempt to play "Home on the Range", which Ralph Bellamy was bawling out in a bathroom baritone. McCarey was lying under the camera laughing at this grotesque display of amateurishness; the perfectionist Miss Dunne was on the verge of tears because she couldn't read sheet music and was appalled by her own clumsy vamping of the song. Delighted, McCarey yelled, "Cut! Print it!"

Irene Dunne began to cry. Ralph Bellamy, red in the face, walked over to shake hands with Cary for the first time. He recalls saying to Cary, "There's no script!" And Cary replied, "Then what are we doing here?" "I haven't any idea!" Bellamy exclaimed.

The random process of shooting continued well into the night. Cary was beyond fury, beyond embarrassment. He apparently didn't know that McCarey had method in his madness: he had spent much of his early career working for Hal Roach as a director of Charlie Chase farcical short films and, later, of Laurel and Hardy pictures in which much of the comic business was made up as he went along. Cary offered several thousand dollars and a free picture to studio boss Harry Cohn if he could be excused from the movie immediately. But Cohn held him to his contract. Day after day, McCarey would walk on the set with a few scraps of paper scrawled with notes, and would insist the actors memorise lines that he had cooked up on a drinking spree a few hours before. There would be a quick run-through, or sometimes not even that, and then the actors would plunge into their roles. It was nerve-racking for everyone, but, as the shooting continued, Cary began to realise that this free-wheeling approach, which would one day become standard in Hollywood, had its advantages. The fixed, claustrophobic, airless atmosphere of Hollywood film making was being broken apart; McCarey was bringing back the freshness, attractiveness and charm of his silent movies and of the glorious Marx Brothers picture *Duck Soup*, a classic of comedy. Harry Cohn was delighted with the rushes and, monster though he was, actually was heard to laugh at some of the gag lines.

But there were problems: Cary did not appreciate McCarey's anti-Semitism, crypto-Fascism and extreme anti-black racism; McCarey's attitudes grated on his nerves, yet he didn't fail to appreciate the man's extraordinary abilities.

Alexander D'Arcy, who played an exotic gigolo in the picture with whom Irene Dunne has a brief but provoking liaison, has vivid recollections of making the film. He recalls that Cary sometimes would step in and try to direct his performance, which he strongly resisted.

There was one particular time that I remember, when he took over. He tried to move me around and tell me where to stand. I had a very tough reaction: I didn't let anybody push me around, and to this day I don't. So I said, "Cary, you're not the director. If there's something to be changed, ask Leo McCarey and he will tell me, and then I will follow. I follow directors, I don't follow other actors." Cary didn't say anything. The matter never came between us again.

During the shooting, D'Arcy became aware of the wide-spread rumours about Cary's bisexuality. He was told by somebody on the picture that Cary was having an affair with a male pianist. D'Arcy says:

Everybody knew that Cary was homosexual. It was an established thing. I knew Cary and Randolph lived together as a gay couple. Cary was not obnoxious. His mannerisms were not feminine at all; he was a regular guy. I think Cary knew that people were saying things about him; I don't think he tried to hide it.

Making *The Awful Truth* turned out to be a joy. The story of a divorcing couple who really love each other and find excuse after excuse to get together again (in the last half of the picture) had a relaxed, carefree, open quality that makes it seem quite undated today. The dialogue that McCarey concocted had a marvellous naturalism, effortlessly delivered by the stars, and Irene Dunne, who seemed inhumanly noble in most movies, let her hair down charmingly under McCarey's careful coaxing. Only the ending, when the couple finally unite in a vacation lodge, seems strained; nobody could think of how to conclude the film, and a stage-hand was responsible for thinking of this somewhat protracted dénouement.

It was during 1937 that Cary began a major career in radio, then a superb dramatic medium whose standards were far higher than those to be found in television some thirteen years later. Apart from his appearance in CBS's *Adam and Eve* in 1935 with Constance Cummings, and occasional interviews with Louella Parsons on her gossipy "Hollywood Hotel" programme, Cary had done little in the medium in the preceding years. But now he began to enjoy the freedom of radio, the easy money it brought and the fact that he did not have to deal with tedious rehearsals, numerous takes, hot lights and quirky directors. In March, he starred with his former colleague Jeanette MacDonald in *Madame Butterfly*, on Cecil B. deMille's famous "Lux Radio Theater", happily renewing his acquaintance with the actress six years after the harrowing days of *Boom-Boom*. On October 15, he appeared in the audio version of *The Awful Truth*, and, on November 21, in *Medicine Girl*, adapted from a story by P. G. Wodehouse, with the troublesome Constance Bennett. It was the start of a forty-year, very happy association with CBS. The network's boss, William Paley, was among Cary's warmest admirers.

In the autumn of 1937 *The Awful Truth* was a success which netted half a million dollars, the equivalent of twenty times that sum today, in a matter of weeks. It proved to be one of the biggest box-office hits that Columbia had known. As his own agent, Cary kept the whole of his $150,000 fee, and he also retained ten per cent of the picture by special arrangement, an additional factor in making him very rich. At the same time, Randolph Scott had followed suit and was happily freelancing, leaving Paramount and going under contract to Twentieth Century-Fox, his career at that studio assisted by the substantial number of shares in it bought by Marion duPont before her disillusionment had set in. It became common currency in her home town of Orange, Virginia, that she had, in the words of her friend Seth Green, "bought the studio". This was, of course, an exaggeration.

The reviews for Cary in *The Awful Truth* were ecstatic; almost overnight, by the mere device of leaving Paramount, he had entered the big time. A former studio employee says:

> The biggest mistake Paramount ever made was not building Cary's career. Why did they throw him away? Why did they never let him be a star but only a minor leading man? Because certain of the executives were homophobes. They hated it when they found out he was bisexual. Even B. P. Schulberg, his mentor, gave up on him in disgust when it was found out. Cary was crying all the way to the bank.

At the end of 1937 and beginning of 1938, Randolph Scott was bothered greatly by a matter which was never made public. His sister, Catherine Strother Scott, was destitute while living in Ireland. She had been suffering from emotional disturbances not dissimilar to those exhibited by Cary's own mother or foster mother. She had been brought in by consular officials at Hamburg and Southampton, England, announcing herself as destitute. Every effort was made to persuade her to return to the United States, and Randolph Scott paid for her passage, but she still declined and the division of Foreign Service Administration authorised two FBI officers, one of whom was a woman, to escort her from the Parkside Hotel in Dublin to the ship *Antonia* at Cobh. At the last minute, Scott had informed Catherine by telegram that he would give her no money until she came back to the family in Virginia.

This agonising matter caused the normally unflurried Scott considerable concern. Catherine docked aboard the *Antonia* on January 10, 1938, and Randolph took care of her from then on. During the extreme stress of this, Cary had as usual to act as though nothing in his life was untoward. He was appearing in Howard Hawks' frenzied farce *Bringing Up Baby*, once again co-starring with the inexhaustible Katharine Hepburn.

Hawks proved to be fascinating. Tough, flinty, and lean with a face like a meat hatchet, he was a perfectionist who tolerated little interference from his actors. At first, Cary had not liked Hawks or his role of a paleontologist in glasses who gets into a series of uncomfortable scrapes. He had told the director that he didn't know how to tackle such a part; he certainly wasn't an intellectual. Hawks told him, "You've seen Harold Lloyd, haven't you?" Cary nodded enthusiastically. The question gave him a clue: he would be playing an innocent abroad, a brainy man in a world full of tragi-comic menace.

As work began on this story of a scientist, David Huxley (a deliberate reference to the famous family of that name), and his weird affair with Susan, an eccentric Connecticut heiress, Miss Hepburn made a serious mistake. Hawks said:

> She kept laughing. And she took the comic situations *too* comically. I tried to explain to her that the great clowns, Keaton, Chaplin, Lloyd, simply weren't out there making funny faces, they were serious, sad, solemn, and the humour sprang from what happened to them. They do funny things in a completely quiet, sombre, dead-pan way. Cary understood this at once. Katie didn't.

Miss Hepburn says: "It's true. I did keep laughing at my own lines. Cary Grant taught me that the more depressed I looked when I went into a pratfall, the more the audience would laugh."

Cary and Hawks conspired to teach Katharine Hepburn the delicate art of farce. There was a scene in a museum involving the skeleton of a prehistoric animal. The veteran comedian Walter Catlett, a big, overweight, moon-faced man in thick horn-rimmed glasses, suddenly began to tease

Cary, even at one stage kissing him off camera to the enormous amusement of Miss Hepburn. Hawks remembered: "Walter used every mannerism of Kate's, but with a deadly seriousness, and she was entranced. After that, she played perfectly, being herself."

Fritz Feld, who played a comic psychiatrist in the movie, remembers the pleasure of working with Cary, observing his effortless timing. He says:

Life in Hollywood in those days was easy. Howard Hawks would come in in the morning and say, "It's a nice day today. Let's go to the races." And Cary, who loved the horses, was especially delighted when we would pack up and *go* to the races. Kate Hepburn also amused Cary by serving tea, as was her custom, every afternoon on the set at four o'clock. After one scene Hawks had especially liked, he delivered the cast two cases of the best champagne. Those were the days!

Cary and Hepburn had as their co-star in the picture a leopard which constantly threatened to scratch them to pieces. Cary hated it. Katharine Hepburn had a tendency to spin around while talking, flaring out her skirts; the leopard would paw at her, frightened by the movement. At one moment it lunged so violently that Hepburn broke the heel off her shoe. She looked around wondering what to say next to cover this unscripted mishap. Cary whispered in her ear. Suddenly she said, referring to her heelless shoe and her hastily improvised heavy limp, "I was born on the side of a hill!" The leopard's trainer, Madame Olga Celeste of the Ringling Brothers Circus, said:

Neither Cary Grant nor Miss Hepburn were the slightest bit afraid of Nissa, my wonderful leopard. They both put resin on their shoe soles so they wouldn't skid at all and startle Nissa. By moving normally around her, they didn't disturb her. All three became friends by the end of the picture.

Cary, perfectly Harold Lloydish in his round, scholarly black horn-rims, played the part of an overgrown schoolboy to perfection; the result was a masterpiece of screen comedy, in which Miss Hepburn also provided a performance of pure gold. The reviews were extraordinary, headed by *Time* magazine's unrivalled rave ("*Bringing Up Baby* comes in second only to last year's whimsical high spot, *The Awful Truth*").

Phyllis Brooks often dropped by during the shooting to watch the antics of the stars; she will never forget the experience, and by now, seeing Cary work, her love for him was enhanced by an intense professional admiration. She longed to marry Cary, yet he was still skittish and uncommitted; she still had not the slightest suspicion of his relationship with Scott and ignored the rumours. However, she did experience a jolt when Marion Davies, apparently on instructions from William Randolph Hearst, who must have had considerable detective work done on Cary in England, told her that Cary was Jewish on his mother's side and that she should think seriously before marrying a Jew. Completely devoid of racism, she swept aside this warning, not blaming Marion for it but rather the notoriously pro-Fascist Hearst.

Their platonic romance continued, conducted largely in public, unruffled by the quarrels that had marred Cary's earlier relationships. On January 11, 1938, while *Bringing Up Baby* was shooting, Phyllis appeared with Cary at a tennis-match party attended by Mr. and Mrs. Douglas Fairbanks, Jnr., the Fred Astaires, and others. Immediately afterwards, most of these guests and dozens more turned up on January 14 for the biggest première in years, the opening of *In Old Chicago* followed by a double celebration (it was the night of studio boss Joe Schenck's wedding anniversary) at the Schenck house converted for the occasion by the decorator Jack Harkrider.

Three nights after that, the eve of Cary's thirty-fourth birthday, there was the almost equally spectacular Hollywood Hotel party, at which the guests arrived with blacked-up faces and danced to Louis Armstrong and his band. The Rumba, the Conga and the Big Apple were the dances of the hour. Phyllis began work on *Little Miss Broadway* with Shirley Temple, enjoying the work and disappointed only that Cary was forbidden by studio chief Darryl F. Zanuck to watch her; Zanuck was afraid Cary's presence might distract her and the ten-year-old Miss Temple, who had a hopeless crush on him. Yet another party launched the dazzling new La Conga nightclub, at which Cary and Randolph Scott yet again appeared boldly as a pair, and Phyllis trailed along behind in a mixed group that included Bing Crosby, Liz Whitney, and Dietrich. Still more parties were held by the Chinese Princess Tai Lachman. The partying went on and on that year before the curtain rang down on a gilded era. As Cary started shooting Philip Barry's *Holiday* under the direction of George Cukor on February 28, he and Phyllis still managed to find time and energy at the end of the day's work to go dancing two or three nights a week at the Trocadero.

Holiday had been made before and it lacked much of the sparkle of *The Awful Truth* and *Bringing Up Baby*. The complications of interlocking relationships in high society seem tedious now, despite the expert playing of Grant and (again) Katharine Hepburn. What had seemed spontaneous and relaxed in the earlier films now was strident and shrill. Cukor, always uneven in temperament and prone to sudden tantrums, was not at his most inspired, and Columbia's tyrannical Harry Cohn, who said that he judged films by the movements of his backside, squirmed continuously through the day's rushes, and complained in words of one syllable to anyone paid to listen to him. Cary's only relief from this tedious experience came on March 26, when he heard the pleasing news that Marion duPont's stallion Battleship, watched by its owner who had made a last-minute dash by zeppelin across the Atlantic, triumphantly galloped in by half a head to win the Grand National at Aintree, the first horse from an American stable to triumph in that event. Randolph Scott failed to share Cary's enthusiasm; that cold-hearted man didn't even bother to send his wife, Marion, a telegram of congratulation.

The reviews for *Holiday* were surprisingly good, the *New York Times* remarking that "Mr. Grant's Mr. Case is really the best role, although it is quite possible that neither Mr. Barry nor Columbia saw it that way." Unfortunately, neither *Bringing Up Baby* nor *Holiday* succeeded at the box-office. Yet Cary's reputation was enhanced by each. By mid-1938, he was being deluged with fan mail, Cary Grant fan clubs were being formed all over the country, and efforts, unsuccessful as it turned out, were being made to have him address women's clubs, present prizes at high school athletic meets, and attend the Academy Awards.

Mrs. Reginald Gardiner describes an episode of the time. Reginald was dating the actress Margot Grahame at the time: "One night, Margot was leaving the Mocambo night-club very late. She saw two figures pressed close in the parking lot. With a shock, she suddenly realised that two men were kissing. The two men were Cary Grant and Randolph Scott."

In May, Phyllis was shooting the comedy *Straight Place and Show* with the manic Ritz Brothers, while Cary mysteriously turned up at certain social events with Dorothy Lamour. But this was only because Phyllis was working at night and he could never resist going out; in her memoirs, Miss Lamour took great pains to make it clear that Cary never made the slightest attempt to seduce her. As it happened, Cary was already thinking seriously of marrying Phyllis. He told his friends the Hoagy Carmichaels, "I'm going to marry Brooksie and have all the children we can. That's what life's all about."

Murmurs of Fascism continued in Hollywood. On June 13, 1938, Edith Gwynn asked her readers, "Will that big MGM star explain why he posed with a swastika armband around his coat sleeve in Germany? The local [German—American] bund boasts of it!" She was probably referring to Wallace Beery, who had long been suspected of being a Nazi sympathiser. If, as seems probable, Cary was already doing some investigative work for British Intelligence, he cannot have failed to note this item and follow it up.

At the same time, Cary was preparing to shoot an adventure film, the classic *Gunga Din* under the direction of the subdued, slow-speaking, part American–Indian director George Stevens, one of the great loves of Katharine Hepburn's life. *Gunga Din* was, according to Cary's co-star Douglas Fairbanks, Jnr., a thinly disguised attack on the Hitler régime, represented in the screenplay by the evil Indian guru played by Eduardo Cianelli and by his cohorts. The plot, a mixture of *The Three Musketeers*, *The Front Page*, and Rudyard Kipling's *Soldiers Three*, was the story of three tough sergeants of the Royal Engineers getting involved in *Boy's Own* heroics and adventurous antics on the North West Frontier.

The film started shooting on June 27 and finished on October 19. The final scenes were done in a desolate, wind-swept landscape at Lone Pine, where a fort had been laboriously constructed. The dusty conditions were unpleasant, getting on everybody's nerves. Phyllis Brooks drove out to the location, pleasing Cary by her presence but greatly irritating Joan Fontaine, who was in turn frustrated by Cary's lack of romantic interest in her. Deliberate, precise and a perfectionist, Stevens began to go seriously over budget and schedule, and the studio bosses were panic-stricken. Pandro S. Berman, who produced the film, recalls that he was especially irritated with Stevens because he had replaced Howard Hawks with him on the ground that Hawks had been very much behind on *Bringing Up Baby*. Now, Stevens was proving just as bad. Yet Berman, suppressing his extreme nervousness and hypertension, allowed Stevens to have his head. The result was a film that was destined to be a colossal box-office success.

While *Gunga Din* was in progress, Cary, like the rest of the world, hung upon radio announcements of Howard Hughes' spectacular around-the-world flight which he began on July 10, 1938, in suffocating heat at Floyd Bennett Field in Brooklyn. Hughes stopped in Paris and then flew on to Moscow, his progress delayed by a damaged rear landing-strut. After flying over Siberia, skimming across terrifying mountain ranges, he at last reached Fairbanks, Alaska, returning over Pennsylvania to his final touchdown on July 14. He had achieved a world record in less than four days. He was welcomed in a ticker-tape parade through Manhattan with more than a million people yelling their greetings as he drove by with Mayor LaGuardia. Cary was among the first to call him with urgent congratulations, breaking off a sequence to do so. Everyone on the set celebrated with champagne.

During the shooting, Phyllis Brooks remembers: "Cary received an astonishing telegram. It told him his mother was alive and had been let out of the asylum. He was stunned, but he couldn't break shooting to go." Is it possible that he was now informed of the existence of his real mother: the Jewish woman who had given birth to him?* Circumstantial evidence to this effect may be determined by the fact that almost at that exact time Cary called Sam Jaffe aside and handed him a cheque for $10,000 for the Jewish Refugee Fund, to assist Jews in escaping Hitler. He specifically told Jaffe that he did not want any mention made of his Jewish origins, but that the gift was made in honour of his family. Jaffe was astonished but happily accepted the gift. There is a certain irony in the fact that when this money was handed over, Cary was acting in a scene with the anti-Semitic, crypto-Fascist Victor McLaglen, whose relish in scenes in which Indians are being massacred still makes the movie something of an ordeal to watch.

Gunga Din at last finished shooting on October 19 after 115 gruelling days. Cary, who had been very fretful, longing to leave on his dramatic journey to Britain, at last shook clear of the work and took off by plane to join the *Queen Mary* for Southampton.

---

* In *Who's Who in America*, until 1962, he listed his mother's name not as Elsie, but as Lillian Leach.

What exactly took place during Cary's visit to England in November of 1938 remains a mystery. In view of subsequent events, it is most likely that after meeting Elsie Leach, he located his real mother, Lillian (?), and she died. (In 1948, he would give money to the new state of Israel in the name of "My Dead Jewish Mother".) After a visit to Paris, he returned from Le Havre to New York on the *Normandie* on November 24, 1938, to Phyllis Brooks, who had just finished making *Charlie Chan in Honolulu*. He was in an oddly detached, calm, and almost resigned mood. Phyllis was in New York, staying with Dorothy di Frasso's brother Bertram Taylor and his wife, Olive. All three went to meet Cary off the ship. It was a joyful reunion, but Phyllis suddenly began to exhibit symptoms of severe influenza. She was bedridden with a high temperature and a severe headache; soon her condition worsened and she was diagnosed as having double pneumonia. She had struggled out of bed to accompany Cary and the Taylors to the hilarious knockabout surrealist farce *Hellzapoppin*. When she returned, her temperature was 105. She was given an injection of sulphanilamide and says she was only the second person to have taken the drug (the first was Franklin D. Roosevelt, Jnr.). It was fortunate that, unlike Merle Oberon, who took the same drug shortly afterwards and broke out into a devastating rash which threatened to destroy her beauty, Phyllis had no allergy. But her condition was still serious, and the drug did not work on her as well as she would have wished.

Cary was required to return to Hollywood immediately

for work on Howard Hawks' new picture, *Pilot Number 4*, later retitled *Only Angels Have Wings*, in which he would play an intrepid Howard Hughes-like flier not dissimilar to the character he had portrayed in *The Eagle and the Hawk*. With an extraordinary lack of consideration that was reminiscent of his behaviour towards Virginia Cherrill, he insisted that Phyllis accompany him. She was certainly in no condition to do so, and in fact her doctors forbade the journey. But Cary wouldn't take no for an answer.

Extremely weak, and barely off the danger list, Phyllis was taken to the train in an ambulance, lying on a stretcher and accompanied by a nurse. Aboard the train, her condition did not improve since the constantly jolting carriage on the uneven tracks made sleep virtually impossible. In those days, telegrams could be sent off a train. When she reached Green River, Wyoming, Phyllis cabled her mother, telling her to be sure to arrange for a wheelchair to be in readiness when the express arrived at eight a.m. on the fourteenth at the Los Angeles down-town depot. Mrs. Steiller was furious with Cary for forcing her daughter to undertake this dangerous journey. Matters were not helped when a rainstorm burst upon the train as Cary lifted Phyllis in his arms to make his way down the steps under the insecure protection of an umbrella carried by the nurse. Still very feverish, and back on the danger list, Phyllis was taken her mother's home in West Los Angeles. It says much for her devotion to Cary that she didn't hold this experience against him. Her sturdy constitution pulled her through the ordeal, and by early January she was back on her feet again.

Work on *Pilot Number 4* began. Hawks was on top of his form as he directed the powerful action picture. He and the art director Lionel Banks effortlessly recreated a South American jungle town, Barranca, set at the foot of the Andes, in the confinement of the Columbia Studios. Rita Hayworth and Jean Arthur were in the film. Both were far removed from their screen images: Miss Hayworth was subdued, shy, gentle; she had a fine intelligence. Jean Arthur was so highly strung and nervous that she would sometimes vomit with fear before coming onto the set. Hawks' impatience with any form of hypersensitive behaviour didn't help, but day by day she gave one of her best performances. Cary liked her immensely, and she continued throughout her life to regard working with him as a pleasure.

At the same time as he was making *Pilot Number 4,* Cary was seeing a good deal of Dorothy di Frasso again. She gave him details of an astonishing voyage he had co-financed, with Bugsy Siegel, Marino Bello, stepfather of Jean Harlow, who had died as a result of a clumsy abortion done by her mother with knitting needles, the British man-about-town Richard Gully, Harry "Champ" Segal, former ring manager and Bugsy's personal trainer, and several others. They had sailed south aboard the yacht *Metha Nelson* along the California coast to Costa Rica, where they searched the legendary Cocos Island looking for buried treasure. They found nothing except some rusty nails, mouldy boots and evidence of former treasure hunts. Annoyed that he had been shanghaied into this absurd expedition, Bugsy flew home from Guatemala. Just as the situation seemed to be deteriorating beyond recall, the *Metha Nelson* was struck by a typhoon in the Gulf of Tehuantepec. Cary listened enthralled to this bizarre narrative.

It didn't seem to concern him that Bugsy Siegel was understood to be a dangerous and murderous gangster. However, he was worried when reports leaked out of the Fascistic activities not only of Victor McLaglen but of a Nazi cadre associated with the actor. It was only at this late stage that tiny, obscure references in the press hinted at the truth of an extraordinary episode, an episode which illustrated still further the dangerous presence of Fascism in Hollywood. The Nazi underground group worked with the Los Angeles German Consul, George Gyssling, and the San Francisco German Consul, Manfred von Killinger. It had planned, along with members of the Silver Shirt Nazi group, a bomb plot against a number of prominent figures of the film industry including B. P. Schulberg, Sylvia Sidney, Fredric March, James Cagney, Charlie Chaplin, Jack Benny, Louis B. Mayer and Sam Goldwyn, many of whom were members of the Anti-Nazi League. Members would secure the dynamite from the police, among whom they claimed to have major contacts, and an associate would obtain shrapnel, iron filings and soap to make up the bombs. A relation of Victor McLaglen was tried in the Superior Court when his plot was discovered by a Jewish investigative group. He was found guilty on several counts, including soliciting the commission of a crime, and was deported. Not a word of his punishment appeared in the newspapers. So great was the studio influence that there was scarcely a whisper (except, of course, in Edith Gwynn's column, which went largely unread by the general public) of Fascism in the supposedly pure paradise of Hollywood.

The Martin Dies House Committee on Un-American Activities was already in town. It was held in disgrace in later years for the excessive zeal against Communism which resulted in the infamous Black List era, but never given credit for its pursuit of Nazi sympathisers. Although many of the records are still classified, it is believed that Cary Grant testified before the committee, indicating where certain Fascist cells had begun to flourish. Simultaneously, he was appearing in a short-lived radio programme for NBC entitled *The Circle*. It was a light-hearted discussion programme in which Cary played a figure called the Beadle, a jocular master of ceremonies, Ronald Colman often appearing with Carole Lombard on the panel. A more questionable panel member was Lawrence Tibbett, the famous opera star, whose politics leaned in the direction of Mussolini and Hitler. Noël Coward was also on the programme; he was in Hollywood, in January 1939, staying with Cary at the same time as he was working with the Deuxième Bureau of the French Secret Intelligence, as a special agent, his activities disguised by the apparent frivolity of his character. From statements made in a telegram to Roy Moseley by Sir William Stephenson, head of British Security Coordination (the equivalent of MI6), Cary was already working with Coward for the Intelligence Services. Cary presided over two broadcasts as chairman, the first on February 12 with Marian Anderson and Basil Rathbone, and the second with the distinguished John Gunther (author of *Inside Europe*), Tibbett, and Rathbone again. Groucho and Chico Marx were on several of the programmes, providing comments from the Jewish point of view. *The Circle* was unpopular, and it folded on July 9, 1939, a mere six months after Cary was forced to leave it because of the pressure of work on *Pilot Number 4*.

That summer, with war rapidly approaching in Europe, Cary and Phyllis Brooks were in New York where they received word of the excellent Hollywood previews and the advance reviews of *Only Angels Have Wings*. Phyllis sailed to England to make *Flying Squad*, co-starring Jack Hawkins; there was no trace of her illness by now.

Cary stayed in America for a series of still classified meetings in Washington, where he was issued a special Diplomatic Visa on June 12. He followed Phyllis to London on June 16, aboard the *Normandie*. At a captain's party he met, and was intrigued by, the Woolworth heiress Barbara Hutton, a hypersensitive, retiring, neurotic girl with a disastrous capacity to choose the wrong men. In London, Cary made no reference to Elsie Leach or Lillian in interviews, but he did slip away to Bristol to try to persuade Elsie to come to America for safety. She declined, saying that she would stand by England whether or not war broke out.

Phyllis' favourite cousin was married to the well-known Paris art dealer, Charles Carstairs. She and Cary paid several pleasant visits to Mr. and Mrs. Carstairs in the French capital. In July, they unofficially became engaged; Cary gave Phyllis a handsome diamond ring. She didn't dare inform her mother. They took off to the South of France, through Northern Italy and down to Rome by car to stay with Dorothy di Frasso at the Villa Madama. They were overwhelmed by the giant wedding-cake of a house, with its vast entrance hall, its display of Raphael paintings and its enormous swimming-pool flanked by cypresses. It was supposed to have been built originally during the time of the Borgias. Dorothy delighted in terrifying Phyllis with stories of hauntings by previous generations of owners, and one night Phyllis was startled when large double-doors blew open, seemingly of their own accord. The countess told hilarious stories about Goering wallowing in her famous gold bath, and Mussolini gobbling all the food at her table. Cary continued to believe that Dorothy was anti-Fascist; he was convinced by her loud diatribes against the Italian dictator. Her husband Carlo Dentice di Frasso was around at the time, handsome and bland, seemingly unflustered by her seditious remarks. He probably knew all too well what her real politics were.

Cary and Phyllis returned to New York from Le Havre on board the *Ile de France* on August 7, only twenty-seven days before war broke out. They announced their engagement publicly for the first time in Manhattan. They took a train to Hollywood, a much happier journey than their previous one.

Cary began making *In Name Only*, with Carole Lombard. It was a heavyweight soap opera about a wealthy socialite who falls in love with an attractive woman when his wife who married him for money proves increasingly cold. The story, which could have been the basis for an entertaining screwball farce, was turned into a sentimental melodrama in which only Kay Francis as the unscrupulous wife seemed to be at home. Her sombre, tearful presence lent a touch of distinction to an otherwise meaningless movie. Cary was much more at home in a radio version of *The Awful Truth*, in which Phyllis Brooks excellently played along with him, and in which Claudette Colbert also appeared in a special cameo.

That July, a significant partnership was formed in Hollywood. Alexander Korda, the gifted, but erratic, Hungarian producer, Douglas Fairbanks, Snr., Samuel Goldwyn and Walter Wanger set up an organisation in association with Korda's London Films that would, for the next seven years, be a front for MI6. Sir William Stephenson confirms that Cary Grant worked with this partnership to flush out Nazi sympathisers in California, nor can it be doubted that he found another major contact in Cecil B. deMille, who used his production unit at Paramount and his "Lux Radio Theater" as similar fronts. One of deMille's agents, Charles Bennett, prominent as a writer for Alfred Hitchcock and others, has attested to this.

In August, Cary was in New York, on a trip of mysterious import. Noël Coward, his chief intelligence contact in the organisation, had gone to London in July to confer with Sir Robert Vansittart, former under-secretary for foreign affairs, and special adviser to the government on Intelligence matters. Vansittart, who also used London Films as a cover, by writing screenplays, was Korda's control in London.

War broke out on September 3, 1939. Deeply distressed but not surprised by the news, Cary was back in Hollywood with Phyllis. Twelve days later, he started work on *His Girl Friday*, an adaptation of *The Front Page*, directed by Howard Hawks and co-starring Rosalind Russell. In early October, the local FBI agents Richard Hood and Frank Angell were busy investigating, as Edith Gwynn knowingly wrote, "a major studio in regard to the Nazi spy situation which [they] believe has a stronghold in that neck of town". The reference can only have been to Warner Brothers, which, paradoxically, had just embarked upon a major anti-Nazi propaganda film, *Confessions of a Nazi Spy*.

Errol Flynn was already embroiled in Nazi activities, protecting from federal agents' intensive investigations his German friend Hermann F. Erben.

Erben had first interested Flynn in the Nazi cause in 1933, when, as a German Naval Intelligence agent in the South Pacific, he had indoctrinated the Australian actor aboard the North German Lloyd Steamer SS *Friderun*. In England, Flynn had written passionate pro-Hitler letters, including one in which he stated that he would like to see the Führer in Britain to take care of the Jews; and in 1937, Flynn had accompanied Erben to Spain during the Civil

War, pretending to be bringing a large sum of money to the Loyalists in Barcelona. But in fact he was seeking to undermine the Loyalist cause, and he and Erben obtained hundreds of photographs of Loyalist installations, trucks and troop movements, delivering them to the German agent Bradish Johnson at the Hôtel Plaza Athénée in Paris. One of the eye-witnesses of Dr. Erben's, taking the pictures, which showed Flynn next to Loyalist gun emplacements, to the headquarters of German Military Intelligence in Berlin, was Count Vejarano y Cassina, who would be arrested as a Nazi spy and would successfully dupe Cary Grant.

On November 12, 1939, Alexander Korda arrived in Hollywood to continue work on his film, *The Thief of Baghdad*, while he proceeded to co-ordinate MI6 arrangements in Los Angeles. Not only was the situation potentially dangerous because of Nazi infiltration into the industry, which could be most effective in the event that England were to lose the war, but also Los Angeles was a highly strategic region. At Santa Monica, the Douglas Aircraft Factory was turning out war planes under the instructions of the Department of Air in Washington and was arming against possible attack from Japan, which at the time had entered into a tripartite agreement with Germany and Italy. San Diego was an important Naval base, where many of the most valuable American warships were docked, and San Pedro and Wilmington were equally strategic ports of call. There was a widespread and not unfounded belief that Mexico presented a potential danger to American security. Nazism was rife in that country, and General Maximino Camacho, brother of the President, was known to have Fascist leanings. Correspondents of the *New York Times* and the *Washington Post* sent back urgent warnings to their readers from Mexico City advising of the existence of a powerful Nazi cell operating inside a converted convent and running a propaganda radio station which beamed Hitlerian messages from coast to coast. Those who, even to this day, continue to ridicule the necessity for any counter-intelligence activities in Southern California do not know what they are talking about.

Not only Cary Grant was enlisted in the British cause on a Special Orders travel document RR. David Niven was sent to New York to investigate a German agent and the actress Carmel Myers joined Korda's and the FBI's investigative group, along with her husband, the agent Ralph Blum. Samuel Goldwyn's studios were an effective front, covering for such figures as Merle Oberon (Lady Korda), who would soon risk her life carrying messages to Europe in bombers and June Duprez, star of *The Thief of Baghdad*, who was used as an informer.

On September 15, 1939, Cary was working on *His Girl Friday*, with Rosalind Russell, who proved to be one of the most adroit comediennes that Cary had ever appeared with. It was typical of Cary that he should introduce gag lines into the script, lines in which Archie Leach and Ralph Bellamy, who was also in the film, were mentioned by name. Howard Hawks was so enamoured of his stars that he allowed them to ad-lib constantly. Towards the end of shooting, Cary introduced Frederick Brisson, who was now working with Frank Vincent and thus a junior partner of Cary's, to Miss Russell. She fell in love with Brisson and would marry him in 1941.

In the autumn of 1939, Cary's relationship with Phyllis Brooks began to cool. He made the mistake of having a lawyer draw up a pre-marital contract which stated that in the event of a divorce he and Phyllis would make no demands on each other. He made the condition in the agreement that Phyllis' mother must never enter the marital home, specifying that Mrs. Steiller was "very disruptive". He indicated, although it wasn't actually stated in the agreement, that it was time Phyllis gave up her career. Mrs. Steiller was furious. "She screamed for four days," Miss Brooks says. "It was a sad and dreadful time." Miss Brooks doesn't blame Cary for this disastrous decision to make her sign the contract. There was no way that she could forbid her own mother to enter her house. She was upset, and disappointed, but he wouldn't withdraw the agreement or relent in his attitude to Mrs. Steiller. Cary was depressed; both he and Phyllis seemed to realise that they were making a dreadful mistake. But there was no going back, no chance of a solution. Miss Brooks says:

I have sympathy for Cary in this matter, and I have sympathy for me as well. The prenuptial agreement undoubtedly did us in. Cary said to me, "I had one great love in my life, Virginia, then I found you. I knew that if anything ever happened to us I would be done. Most people never find one great love. I've had two. You are young enough to find another. I never will. See how all these threads knit together? I do."

Miss Brooks has some further comments on the affair:

He was imperfect as are all we mortals, but he was my love. He was careful, gentle, kind, tender and fatherly to me. So far as I knew, he was a loving and passionate heterosexual. He had a very strict moral code as to loyalty, fidelity and like virtues, and lived by them when I knew him.

The long and loving relationship ended. The pain was intense for both. Ironically, Cary's next picture, starting on December 3, was *My Favourite Wife*. It was begun by Leo McCarey, but after a few days he drove off in a drunken stupor from his house in Santa Monica, collided with another vehicle, and was badly injured, almost severing his right arm. He was replaced by Garson Kanin.

The sharp, energetic, twenty-seven-year-old Kanin instantly appealed to Cary. He was cynical and loquacious, far removed from the amiable, ambling McCarey. Kanin had been a vaudevillian, a fact which Cary liked, and he played the clarinet and the saxophone skilfully, two further attractions. This prodigious young man expertly took the reins. The movie was a reworking of the old chestnut *Enoch*

Arden, the story of a woman who, thought to be drowned in a shipping mishap, returns to find her husband and presumed widower about to remarry. She sets out on an ambitious campaign to destroy the relationship. Leo McCarey, who had written the screenplay with the husband-and-wife team Samuel and Bella Spewack, daringly included more than one sly reference to the Grant–Scott relationship. In a revealing sequence, Nick Arden, played by Cary Grant, goes to a swimming-pool to cast eyes on the chief rival for his returned wife's affections, Burkett, played by Randolph Scott. Seeing Scott on a diving-board, looking rather like Johnny Weissmuller's Tarzan, the character's reaction would normally have been one of dismay at seeing what he was up against. But Cary's eyes lit up at the spectacle and later, in his office, Nick Arden is shown unable to work, haunted by the vision of Burkett in swimming-trunks on what appears to be a kind of trapeze metamorphosis of the diving-board. Bert Granet, who was the script supervisor on the picture, recalls:

> We shot the pool sequence at the Huntington Hotel at Pasadena. Cary and Randy Scott arrived as a pair and, to the total astonishment of myself, the director, and the ultra-macho film crew, instead of taking separate suites moved into the same room together. Everyone looked at everyone else. It seemed hardly believable.

The staid Irene Dunne seemed oblivious to what was going on around her. She gave one of her best performances in the picture, especially appealing in the scene in which the wife returns from south-east Asia to observe her children splashing in the pool. She had left them as babies, and, some seven years later, they no longer recognised her.

Cary took a break from shooting to appear as Romeo opposite Irene Dunne's Juliet in the radio series, "Silver Theater". He also broke off work to attend the funeral service following the death of Douglas Fairbanks, Snr., on December 10, 1939. The loss was a great sadness to him.

He had never forgotten his first encounter with Fairbanks and Mary Pickford (whom Fairbanks had divorced four years earlier) aboard the *Olympic* in 1920, nor their countless meetings since. He gave his condolences to Doug, Jnr. and his wife Mary, and to Sylvia Fairbanks, the widow, and with typical professionalism, returned to work the following day to play an antic sequence in a honeymoon hotel in which he assumed female guise.

During the shooting, Cecil B. deMille offered Cary one of the principal roles in a patriotic epic of Canada, *North West Mounted Police*. DeMille's motive was two-fold, since not only would Cary be excellent in the picture, he would be available to work with deMille in intelligence activities north of the border. But Cary disliked the part as it was written, and gently declined it.

There was no woman in his life at the time; Scott was still dominant, and to cover for the gossip he dated Louise Stanley and Rosalind Russell and, after an interval of some years, Fay Wray, whose divorced husband, John Monk Saunders, was to commit suicide by hanging himself with a necktie. Miss Wray co-hosted Cary's elaborate Christmas party. Both then and at a subsequent New Year's Eve event, he tried vainly to contact Elsie Leach in Bristol, frustrated by the appalling quality of the wartime telephone connections. On New Year's Eve, Phyllis Brooks turned up unexpectedly and in a restless mood; close to five a.m., she was seen to have a stand-up fight with the feisty Australian actress Constance Worth, former wife of George Brent.

In February, Cary was at the housewarming of Douglas Jnr. and Mary Fairbanks; they had just bought the handsome Pacific Palisades home of Elissa Landi, the Italian-born actress who had ruined herself financially by excessive party-giving. On January 18, Cary and Constance Moore, a new friend whose talents as a band vocalist and radio singer matched her gifts as an actress, and who was married to the popular agent Johnny Maschio, celebrated their joint birthday at a big shindig at Cary's house. Phyllis Brooks again turned up uninvited. Edith Gwynn wrote, "Cary would not allow his former girlfriend . . . to touch as much as an eye-dropperful." That same week, Phyllis was seen in several nightspots dancing with Frederick Brisson.

My Favourite Wife ended shooting on February 11. The same night, Cary substituted for William Powell at short notice, giving a much-admired performance on the Radio Guild Air Show.

That month, a new visitor in town was causing a sensation which never leaked into the press. Hilda Krüger, former girlfriend of Dr. Joseph Goebbels and J. Paul Getty, among other oddly assorted figures of society, was presently enjoying a relationship with Errol Flynn. The FBI had her under surveillance as a suspected Nazi agent or sympathiser, tapping her telephone calls, searching her luggage and tracking her on her visits to the German Nazi Consuls General in San Francisco and Los Angeles. Whether Cary was among the several Hollywood personalities keeping an eye on Hilda Krüger's behaviour is uncertain. But in view of his position with MI6, he probably was. Among those specifically delegated to watch her was Cary's close friend, the accomplished English comedian Reginald Gardiner. Because of his polished, sophisticated and not particularly intellectual personality, Gardiner would never be suspected of being a secret agent. But he investigated Krüger by means of becoming her lover; examining her papers, he at one time accused her point-blank of Nazi connections. In his reports to the FBI, he stated that she was the most dangerous German agent in the United States. June Duprez, Marlene Dietrich and Carmel Myers also gave reports on Krüger to the authorities.

Cary left for New York by the freighter, *Tampa*, on March 16, 1940, via the Panama Canal, arriving in New York on April 2, after changing to the *Santa Elena* in Cristobal, Canal Zone. The passenger manifest shows he was on Special Orders, i.e., British Government service, on Travel Document RR 98872/178/99. Alexander Korda was in Manhattan and they were soon in conference on British matters, flying to London and back by bomber. On April

22, Cary began work on his next picture, *The Howards of Virginia*, shooting in Randolph Scott's home territory and later in Northern California and at Columbia Studios in Hollywood. He played a real-life character, Matt Howard, a friend of President Thomas Jefferson who was involved in hostilities between the colonies and Great Britain. The inconsequential script by Sidney Buchman and the unenterprising direction of Frank Lloyd were notably uninspiring to Cary, who gave one of his worst performances in the picture.

In May, Cary was back in Hollywood, again conferring with Alexander Korda on what must have been Secret Intelligence matters. He also renewed his earlier acquaintance with Barbara Hutton. She was born in New York on November 14, 1912, the daughter of Franklyn Laws Hutton and the former Edna Woolworth. Her mother died, leaving her about $60 million, when she was five years old. As a child she was surrounded by bodyguards, sheltered, fat and miserable. Her New York début in 1930 was the social event of the season and cost her father $50,000.

The constant pampering, an ability to indulge any whim, and the poor health that marked her life, had taken their toll even by the time she was twenty. She was neurotic, paranoid, cut apart by operations, fearful of everything. Yet at the same time she was also gentle, sweet-natured, and poetic: she even published a volume of verse, at her own expense. She married, at twenty, the so-called Prince Alexis Mdivani, one of the famous "marrying" Mdivani brothers, whose "princedom" consisted of a pig farm in Georgia, Russia. He received $1 million as a stud fee at the time of the wedding. Franklyn Hutton commented on him, "You know the old saying. One can't choose one's relations."

In 1935, announcing that her husband "threw money around like confetti . . . you know these titled foreigners", she divorced Mdivani announcing, fatally, that she would never marry again. Next day she married the Danish Count Kurt Haugwitz Hardenberg Reventlow and a year later,

Alexis Mdivani was killed in a car crash. On February 24, 1936, her son Lance was born and the following year, Miss Hutton renounced her citizenship, and became a Dane. The marriage to Reventlow was no better than that to Mdivani. There were constant quarrels over Lance and the couple were separated. When she again met Cary, Miss Hutton had just returned with Dorothy di Frasso from a vacation on Windward Island, the millionaire Chris R. Holmes' private atoll near Waikiki, Hawaii. Barbara was unhappy with her private life; she had recently finished an unsatisfactory relationship with the British golfer Robert Sweeny and had begun drifting meaninglessly from one social event to another. Deeply insecure, her wealth gave her no happiness. City after city, resort after resort failed to satisfy her. Miserable, she was looking for a new romantic relationship, and Dorothy di Frasso, who delighted in matchmaking, reintroduced her to Cary at a party at her house. Cary and Barbara had seen each other during his long relationship with Phyllis Brooks, but up to now there was no evidence of any attraction between them.

As it happened, there was no attraction now. Nevertheless, they liked each other, and began going out to nightclubs and restaurants, including the Trocadero, the Mocambo, and William R. Wilkerson's newly popular Victor Hugo. Cary was still living at the beach house with Randolph Scott, but this fact did not seem to bother Miss Hutton, who decided to stay in Hollywood for a time and subrent Buster Keaton's mansion at 1004 Hartford Way, in Beverly Hills. It was an imitation Italian villa with thirty rooms, terraces that were landscaped by a gardener who had worked for Pope Pius XII, a thirty-foot Romanesque swimming-pool flanked by classical nude statues, and a brook stocked with trout which the servants would catch and serve at the dinner table. There were three tennis courts and fifteen acres of lawns and flower bushes.

When the columnists began buzzing over this new romantic liaison, Cary and Barbara started to restrict themselves to friends' or their own houses. Barbara rejected the advances of the young Frank Sinatra in order to spend most of her time with Cary who began giving parties at her villa, at which she appeared as a somewhat reluctant hostess. The Kordas, Dietrich, Rosalind Russell and Frederick Brisson, Constance Moore, Johnny Maschio and Jimmy Stewart were among the frequent guests. These expensive soirées failed to appease Barbara's restless, dark spirit. She brooded constantly, and her temper was not improved when Cary proved notably reluctant to appear at parties which she gave for her own circle of friends. Again, there is no indication that theirs was a sexual relationship. Indeed, Miss Hutton, who was covered with internal and external scars from her serious operations, and who suffered from very delicate health, appears to have had little interest in any form of physical liaison. She was, at the time, concerned about the fate of her close friend, the handsome tennis champion Baron Gottfried von Cramm, who had recently been imprisoned by the German Government for homosexuality, and she was also struggling with her former husband, Count Reventlow, for custody of their son, Lance. Cary became a surrogate father for Lance, working out his frustrated paternal instinct in a deeply felt relationship with the four-year-old boy. He gave him gifts, played ball and went cycling with him, and joined Barbara in assailing Reventlow, who, FBI documents allege, was a serious Nazi sympathiser.

On May 25, Douglas and Mary Fairbanks entertained Cary and Barbara at another big party at their recently acquired Westridge House. Phyllis Brooks arrived as Randolph Scott's date for the evening, which caused much amused comment in the columns. The group which included Alexander and Vincent Korda, Walter Wanger, Samuel Goldwyn and Cary Grant was continuing to conduct its investigations into untoward political activities in Hollywood at the time. Since William R. Wilkerson was a chief contact for the group and for the FBI, his wife would provide little glimpses of her husband's activities in her column. In view of the secrecy of the operation, this was exceedingly ill-advised, and she seemed to have no scruple in pursuing her journalistic activities. On May 25, she reported: "Fifth column investigations going on in the studios will be a secret, with only the producer group behind them, and the FBI getting the responses as they come in." Four days later, Mrs. Wilkerson reported that the group had determined that eighty-five per cent of German servants working in the movie colony accepted the direct orders of the local German–American bund.

On June 9, Noël Coward, who was still involved in activities for Free French Secret Intelligence, significantly moved in as Cary's house guest for a lengthy stay. Apparently, Edith Gwynn's disclosure of this fact blew the cover of both of them because a few days later they staged a quarrel which they made sure she included in the *Hollywood Reporter* and Noël moved out. Principal photography on *The Howards of Virginia* was completed on June 24. The filming had dragged on for an unconscionably long time, and turned out to be a disaster for all concerned.

A significant event took place on June 20. W. S. (later Sir William) Stephenson, who worked directly with Sir Stuart Menzies and Sir Robert Vansittart for British Intelligence in Whitehall, arrived in New York aboard the SS *Britannic* through U-boat-haunted seas. He set up under the cover of British passport control officer, with offices at Rockefeller Plaza. During the next few weeks, he started to establish a complex system of spies, calling his organisation, for want of a better term, British Security Co-ordination. BSC was from then on the MI6 centre of operations in the North and South American continents. Cary Grant was enlisted as a key figure of BSC. Stephenson has confirmed Grant's precise role, which was to act, along with Alexander Korda and others as a special link with Noël Coward, who would be travelling through Latin America and the South Pacific on BSC business. Like Cary, Coward would be the last person anyone would suspect of espionage. Among those whom Cary specifically investigated was Barbara Hutton herself. She was in contact with Nazi Germany in the interests of Baron von Cramm, and her mail was intercepted and sent to FBI headquarters for inspection and filing. It is doubtful whether the FBI could successfully have organised a plant in her own household; therefore, the most likely person to have removed her mail and forwarded it on to the authorities was Cary himself.

At the same time, Alexander Korda was in Lisbon, setting up his own MI6 organisation there. Among others, Vivien Leigh, Beatrice Lillie and Leslie Howard would assist him in that region during the war years.

Cary flew to New York at the time to confer with Stephenson; he continued through a severe thunderstorm to Washington, DC, by air, where he met with the British Ambassador, Lord Lothian, along with the director and writer Herbert Wilcox, Brian Aherne, Sir Cedric Hardwicke and other British exiles. He was told that his best work would be in intelligence as he was considered unsuitable at present for war service in England. He returned to Hollywood.

There was a reason for investigation of Nazis in Hollywood that July. Werner Plack, an alleged Nazi agent and member of Dr. Goebbels' staff in Berlin, was in town under the guise of being a champagne salesman, a job originally occupied by German Foreign Minister Joachim von Ribbentrop. Sy Bartlett, a White Russian Hollywood producer, had a fist-fight with Plack at the Café la Maze, accusing him point-blank of being a German spy and forcing Plack to flee the country. At the same time, Errol Flynn was still going around town with his Nazi friend Hermann Erben, who even had the nerve to appear in German uniform and wearing a Hitler moustache, and this at a time when for any British citizen or subject to associate with an enemy of Great Britain amounted to treason. So complete was Flynn's power as a great film star that nothing seemed to affect his popularity even in an area dominated by Jews. When Flynn travelled to South America that summer, he was asked by various American ambassadors or consuls to comment on Erben's activities. In every case, he protected him, pretending that he was a Jewish refugee and a harmless eccentric screwball. He was supposed to be reporting on Fascism in South America for *Collier's* magazine, a device which enabled him to be in touch with Nazis in Mexico City without exciting suspicion.

At this time, Cary was shooting *The Philadelphia Story* with Katharine Hepburn and James Stewart, under the accomplished direction of George Cukor. Howard Hughes had secretly obtained the rights to Philip Barry's play for Miss Hepburn, and she in turn, after appearing triumphantly on the stage in the central role of Tracy Lord, had sold the property to Louis B. Mayer at Metro-Goldwyn-Mayer. Cary was cast in the important role of C. K. Dexter Haven, a wealthy socialite who sponsors reporter Macaulay Connor and camera assistant Liz Imbrie as they invade Tracy Lord's Philadelphia estate. The complicated story of intrigue, double-cross and romantic misadventure provided Cary with the part of a lifetime. He proved an admirable match for Miss Hepburn's elongated, highly theatrical heiress.

The cameraman on the picture, Joseph Ruttenberg, recalled:

> Everyone had enormous fun on the movie. The days . . . were sweltering that summer of 1940, but nobody cared. Cary got along very well with Kate Hepburn. She enjoyed him pushing her through a doorway in one scene [so she fell over backwards], so much that she had him do it to her over and over again. There was a scene in which she had to throw Cary out the door of a house, bag and baggage, and she did it so vigorously he fell over and was bruised. As he stood up, looking rueful, Kate said, "That'll serve you right, Cary, for trying to be your own stuntman!"

Miss Hepburn, Grant, and James Stewart were determined to play a practical joke on Cukor. The fussy director always preferred a very quiet set. One morning, Cary arranged for every crew member to make as much noise as possible, shouting, hammering and sawing planks of wood. Cukor was furious; he walked off to collect his temper. By pre-arrangement with Cary, Miss Hepburn put up her hand and the noise stopped. Then she signalled her fellow players, and the entire crew, to follow her up to the flies above the sound stage. When Cukor returned, the stage was deserted. He thought he must have gone mad, or wandered onto the wrong stage. As he turned to leave, Miss Hepburn and Cary gave a signal, and all seventy people in the flies shouted, very loudly, "Quiet!!!"

During the shooting, Cary was preoccupied by work at the Frank Vincent Agency: he helped to renegotiate a deal for Garbo at MGM and a new contract for Rita Hayworth at Twentieth Century-Fox, beginning with the film *Blood and Sand*, which Cary had been scheduled to make for Paramount in 1933. He advanced the career of Brian Don-levy, greatly improving his Paramount contract, and Mar-lene Dietrich's Warner Brothers contract the following year owed much to his influence. He helped organise her special loan from Universal to Warner for *Manpower*. The stars concerned still did not know that he was meeting with Vincent to assist them professionally. He refurbished the agency's offices on Sunset Boulevard, which became, under his guidance, the most luxurious in Hollywood. The furniture was antique; the carpets were deep and the panelling was of the finest oak. There was even a butler to greet important clients or guests, and a waiter in uniform to serve them in the handsome penthouse office suite.

Cary gave his salary for *The Philadelphia Story*, some $175,000, to British War Relief and the Red Cross. He was concerned and distracted during the film by word of the bombing of Britain by the German Air Force. He was concerned about Elsie, and he also must have been dis-tressed by the dangerous conditions in which his friends and associates in MI6, Alexander Korda and Merle Oberon, were flying across the North Atlantic to bring information about American appeasement to the headquarters of the organisation and Sir Robert Vansittart in London. Virginia Cherrill, now the Countess of Jersey, was in town following a rough U-boat-plagued voyage across the Atlantic. She was expecting a baby and had been evacuated to the United States by ship with Somerset Maugham's daughter, Liza. Landing in Montreal on July 4, she travelled to New York, where she had a miscarriage brought on by the ordeal of her journey. She saw a good deal of Cary in Hollywood and told him of her experiences. They were friendly now; Virginia had set aside much of her bitterness. She was at social event after social event, escorted innocently by a number of eligible bachelors, but she was devoted and faithful to her husband. Her chief concern was to get back to Europe and help with the war effort in London. It took her some months to obtain permission from the authorities to take the Pan-American clipper to Lisbon.

Phyllis Brooks was in Hollywood at the time; she says today that she continued to be in love with Cary and deeply regretted the termination of their relationship. The pain of seeing him so often at different nightclubs, frequently with Barbara Hutton, was too intense for her to bear. By September, she had left Los Angeles for New York, happy to accept a part in Cole Porter's musical *Panama Hattie* in order to free herself of an impossible situation.

It was a busy summer. Noël Coward returned to Hollywood and again stayed with Cary, planning trips to South America and to Australia on behalf of MI6. Cary covered for him, giving people the impression that Coward was simply a house-guest who was going to do concert tours. The truth was that Coward would use his nightclub and restaurant act, singing his matchless songs, telling his witty stories, as a front for his activities as a secret agent, reporting on pro-Nazi activities in Southern Hemisphere regions. Coward told the author William Stevenson:

I was fluent in Spanish and could "do" the whole of Latin America, where the Germans were very active preparing their campaigns in the United States. And so that's where

I started . . . reported directly to Bill Stephenson while I sang my songs and spoke nicely to my hosts. A whole lot of tiny things are the stuff of Intelligence. Smallest details fit into a big picture, and sometimes you repeat things and wonder if it's worth it. I travelled wherever I could go – Asia and what was left of Europe. And I ridiculed the whole business of Intelligence, but that's the best way to get on with it – ridicule and belittle ourselves, and say what an awful lot of duffers we are, can't get the facts straight, all that sort of thing.

Thus, Coward was in fact spying not only on South Americans but North Americans as well. Cary confirmed that that was his own role in a statement made to his closest friend, assistant and chauffeur Ray Austin some twenty years later. Grant and Coward would mix as much as possible in the Hollywood community, determining who was dangerous and who was not.

Winston Churchill had provided Coward with an excellent cover in case any German agent should penetrate his activities. Churchill let it be known on the grapevine that Coward had been dismissed from MI6 because he had sought to publicise his activities as an agent. This absurdity was swallowed not only by the Germans but by British journalists, who were encouraged to print it in their columns.

While Noël Coward was in Los Angeles, his collection of playlets, *Tonight at 8.30*, which Cary had enjoyed so much in London six years earlier, opened with an all-star cast that included Joan Fontaine in *Family Album*, Judith Anderson and Isabel Jeans in *Hands Across the Table*, and Roland Young, so excellent in *The Philadelphia Story* and *Fumed Oak*. William R. Wilkerson and Edith Gwynn hosted an elaborate party at Ciro's, which they owned, following the première. Even Garbo turned up. Frederick Brisson and his fiancée, Rosalind Russell, were there, and so were Alexander and Merle Korda, back from one of their perilous missions, and Johnny Maschio and Constance

Moore, but there were notable absentees on this supremely patriotic occasion. Errol Flynn did not attend, and neither, oddly enough, did Cary and Barbara Hutton. Cary's motive in not appearing might be interpreted as an ingenious method of supporting the widespread belief that he was opposed to the war effort and was failing to help it in any way. It is also possible that Barbara Hutton was having one of her nervous attacks and that he stayed home to keep her company.

During August and September, Cary renewed his earlier warm acquaintance with the mischievous Alfred Hitchcock, who was staying with his diminutive wife Alma at the Korda house while they began looking for a suitable residence. Korda had been dissatisfied with the house and had been in New York, London and elsewhere. Hitchcock was starting work on September 5 on an uncharacteristic comedy, *Mr. and Mrs. Smith*. Meanwhile, Korda was very busy building sets for *Lady Hamilton*, called in the United States *That Hamilton Woman*, the story of the ill-fated mistress of Lord Nelson, in which the legendary tale would be used as a thin disguise for a propaganda attack on Hitler, represented in the story by Napoleon poised to strike against the British on the other side of the English Channel. Cary was delighted to renew his happy acquaintance with Vivien Leigh and Laurence Olivier, co-stars of the Korda production. He visited the set, captivated by the fine craftsmanship of the art director Vincent Korda, Alexander's brother, who had designed the elegant settings of eighteenth-century London and Naples.

A new and deep friendship was formed in that season. Clifford Odets, the reigning playwright of the American stage, was in town, following a stormy, protracted divorce from Luise Rainer and a disastrous relationship with Frances Farmer. Author of a string of highly praised plays written under the aegis of the Group theatre, he had recently scored a great success with *Golden Boy*, which was filmed in 1940 with the twenty-two-year-old William Holden. Tall, dark, brooding, capable of flashes of wit and charm, but more often morose, difficult and profoundly introverted, Odets fascinated Cary as few men had ever done. He was the first serious intellectual with whom Cary had come into contact. Odets was deeply read in a number of different cultures; he had a commanding knowledge of music and painting; and a fluent, sometimes pretentious, but always stimulating, line of speech. Peering through scholarly spectacles, he would rivet people but then tend to exhaust them with his excessive knowledge which made them feel uncomfortable. In every possible way he was out of place in the film community. Yet his hunger for the bodies of beautiful young girls was insatiable, as burning and fierce as his talent in its demands upon him; at the age of thirty-four, he was at the height of his physical strength, and of his power as a dramatist, and few women could resist his fame, his looks and his lean, athletic physique.

Odets would remain the one human being who reached into Cary's soul and understood it. Although it would be several years before they would work together, they remained in touch even when Odets was in New York and even though their politics were in opposition. Odets was a creature of the traditional Left, Cary still a dyed-in-the-wool Republican.

Clifford Odets' son Walt comments upon his father's relationship with Cary. In conversation, he told Charles Higham:

Although I do not believe they had a physical relationship, I think I am right in saying that they had an intense love for each other. My father was also bisexual, and I know he and Cary discussed this. It tortured both of them and bound them together. Yet at the same time, whereas my father was extremely repressed in private, never revealing anything of the other side of his nature, Cary often acted quite overtly effeminate in our home, startling me and my sister. Of course, I'm talking about years later; I wasn't born until the late 1940s.

Some part of my father – that part of himself which

came from his very ambitious, immigrant father – clearly aspired to be Cary Grant, so to speak. This is partly what kept him in Los Angeles, hanging out with movie people. Cary, on the other hand, must have aspired in some serious way to be like my father . . . Both men seem to have been quite conflicted and pained about . . . private sides of themselves. This was one of the reasons that their friendship was often difficult – each was especially sensitive to the other's expectations, because those expectations also came from within.

Cary continued to associate with Dorothy di Frasso that year. He seemed unwilling to admit to anyone what her purpose in Hollywood was: to use it as a point of departure for Mexico, where she was already engaged upon a highly questionable enterprise – financing an explosive device which she and Bugsy Siegel hoped to sell to the Italian Government. And this at a time when Italy was at war with Great Britain and President Roosevelt's policy was to give all possible assistance to the British. Or was Cary only pretending to support the Countess, while in fact really investigating her and her activities?

On October 10, 1940, Cary began work on a new film, *Penny Serenade*, with Irene Dunne. The director once again was George Stevens. *Penny Serenade* was the story of a young couple, a journalist and his sensitive, good-natured wife, who struggle against poverty in the United States and Japan. Following an earthquake in Tokyo, the wife loses her first baby in a miscarriage and the couple return to New York. They adopt a child only to lose it in tragic circumstances. The parallels with Cary Grant's life are startling: Elsie's loss of her first baby, Barbara Hutton's long-unsatisfied hunger for a child following the post-natal problems after the birth of Lance Reventlow, and Cary's own penurious origins all provided potent echoes of present and past. Stevens' delicate craftsmanship animated what could have been an intolerable soap opera; the story, told in flashback as the unhappy wife plays a series of phonograph records that evoke the past, the circular trademark labels irising out into remembered heartbreaking images, ensured a magical surface of effects. Cary's feckless, unreliable charmer provided an ideal foil for Irene Dunne's correct, pure-hearted wife. His playing was so expert that a few months later he was nominated for his first Academy Award.

On November 18, the Countess di Frasso threw a magnificent birthday party for Barbara Hutton, co-hosted by Cary and attended by Douglas and Mary Lee Fairbanks, the Ronald Colmans, Jack and Ann Warner and Darryl and Virginia Zanuck. The party was a farewell bash for Virginia Cherrill, who left for New York and Lisbon on November 24. Three days later, it was reported by Associated Press that Mussolini had paid the Countess di Frasso $2 million for the Villa Madama at the same time she was complaining loudly that the Italian Government had expropriated the residence.

On November 27, Barbara Hutton flew to Charleston, South Carolina, to see her ailing father, Franklyn Hutton. Cary was unable to travel with her because of additional scenes for *Penny Serenade*, but he sent sympathetic get-well messages with her. For years an alcoholic, Franklyn Laws Hutton was stricken at sixty-three with cirrhosis of the liver. He died on December 2, and, despite Barbara's last-minute flight to his bedside, he expressed his disapproval of what he thought to be a physical affair with Cary Grant by cutting her out of his will, leaving her nothing. She, of course, had inherited a considerable fortune, over $200 million, under the terms of her late mother's estate, but the decision was still a bitter blow and she sued trustees for $530,000 plus five per cent accrued interest, indicating that she had lent substantial sums to her father over the years. Irene Hutton, her stepmother, repaid the debt in full.

Barbara was involved in complicated arrangements with Nazi-occupied Denmark in order to secure her divorce from Count Reventlow. As a Danish citizen, she was not entitled to make deals with the German occupying Government, without committing treason. The Copenhagen Courts were of course under German jurisdiction. A spokesman for Miss Hutton in New York made the unfortunate and much-quoted remark, "Hitler Blitzkrieg or no Hitler Blitzkrieg, Barbara's divorce will come through according to Hoyle."

What Cary thought of this is unknown. Neither the State Department nor the Federal Bureau of Investigation was at all happy about this dealing with America's potential enemy, and a substantial documentary file was opened on Miss Hutton. There was still no serious indication that she and Cary would be married when the decree became final.

Barbara was depressed that Christmas of 1940, not only by her father's death but by a close friend's fatal injuries in a car accident. She was under a cloud, and Cary went alone to a party at Dorothy di Frasso's where a boxing-ring, erected on the lawn, featured a series of brutal fights in which ancient retired boxers beat each other to pulp while everybody screamed with delight. Occasionally, Barbara would surface from her mood of depression to give a party of her own. She retreated into her shell again when guests stupidly asked her how she felt to be the heiress to her deceased father's fortune. Although she never snapped back with the statement that he had left her nothing, she was seriously embarrassed by discussions of money and hated it when people would say, "You're quite a nice gal, even with all that cash," or "For all that money, you're quite normal." Occasionally, she would display some wit. One night, at a dinner party, with Cary at her side, she was shocked to hear someone ask her, "How does it feel to have so much money?" She replied, with deadly swiftness, "It's terrific." The smile froze on the inquirer's face.

As a result, Barbara only had very intimate small groups to her house from then on. She had to be sure she knew every guest, and no one was allowed to bring a stranger. She refused to talk to the press because she was irritated by the constant mentions of her forthcoming nuptials. And of course, since Cary was involved in secret war work, it was essential that she keep the lowest possible profile and make sure that no strangers entered the house.

Contradictory as always, after several weeks of reclusiveness and giving no major parties, Barbara spent a fortune on Cary's birthday event on January 18, 1941. Constance Moore was equally honoured. She also was born on January 18. The walls and ceiling of the house were draped with hundreds of yards of white satin, while the pool was surrounded with beautifully set tables displaying flourishes of dark red roses. The waiters were in red and white; the champagne flowed freely; and two bands played the current dance music until the sun began to gleam on the palm trees and tropical shrubs. Barbara was dazzling in a gold Chinese formal dress and a blaze of emeralds. Cary was resplendent in white tie and tails. It was an evening to remember, but soon after it Barbara slipped back into seclusion again.

Cary's winter was brightened by the extraordinary reviews for *The Philadelphia Story*, which had opened just after Christmas at Radio City Music Hall. Bosley Crowther in the *New York Times* had written:

> All those folks who wrote Santa Claus asking him to send them a sleek new custom-built comedy with fast lines and the very finest in Hollywood fittings got their wish just one day late with the opening of *The Philadelphia Story* yesterday ... This [film] has just about everything that a Blue Chip comedy should have ... and a splendid cast of performers headed by Katharine Hepburn, James Stewart and Cary Grant [who] is warmly congenial as the cast-off but undefeated mate.

Glowing from the public's response to the film, ideal escapist fare when war threatened, Cary cheerfully said farewell to Noël Coward on January 19, 1941, as Coward set off for Australia, fully briefed by William Stephenson for his dangerous mission under the guise of a concert tour. His messages from the Antipodes were relayed to Stephenson's British Security Co-ordination operation at the Rockefeller Center in New York.

A memorandum from R. L. Bannerman, Special Agent in Charge, New York Division of the Foreign Activities Correlation (Secret Intelligence) Division of the Department of State reported that Stephenson was working through both the British Purchasing Commission and the British Consulate, supervising the anti-sabotage protection of

British war orders from factories to the ports. At the same time, Stephenson gathered a staff of liaison officers who would cooperate with the various federal agencies. He would not only assure the security of British materials purchased on Government orders, but would establish general anti-sabotage security with the local police and the FBI.

Bannerman's memorandum concluded with the words: "Mr. Stephenson has so far refused to reveal the exact whereabouts of his office and the entire matter has been handled with the utmost secrecy. However, his private phone number is Circle 6-8580. This covers all information available without making a direct inquiry." It is easy to see from this document that not only was Stephenson with his operation including Cary Grant spying on the Americans, but the Americans were spying on him.

In the course of his paradoxical career, Cary was not only working in consultation with Stephenson, but at the same time he was in closer touch than ever with Bugsy Siegel. In the summer of 1940, Siegel, much to the distress of Dorothy di Frasso, had been indicted for the murder of the gangster "Big Greenie" Greenberg. On August 16, police had turned up at Siegel's Bel Air estate and found him hiding in the attic. He was interned in the county jail in down-town Los Angeles. Police found a Smith and Wesson .38 revolver and a .38 Colt automatic in Bugsy's strongbox, but on December 11, Assistant District Attorney Vernon Ferguson moved for the dismissal of the indictment, and John Dockweiler, the newly elected DA, also brought influence to bear. The journalist Florabel Muir alleged in her syndicated column that Siegel had contributed $30,000 to the Dockweiler campaign. Bugsy was released and within minutes was on his way to George Raft's house in Coldwater Canyon, threatening his life with a gun and charging Raft with having informed on him. He claimed that Raft was interested in Bugsy's girlfriend Wendy Barrie.

Almost as though he wanted to give Siegel some respectability, Cary invited him to various parties, and encouraged him to strike a new figure in society as a dandy, wearing handsome shirts, suits and silk pocket handkerchiefs. Siegel and di Frasso were seen as often at Barbara Hutton's mansion or Cary's beach house as they were at George Raft's home.

At the same time, Cary began work on *Suspicion* for Alfred Hitchcock. Based upon Francis Iles' novel *Before the Fact*, the film had been planned for years, first with Louis Hayward as its star, and then with Robert Montgomery and Laurence Olivier. It was the story of a disreputable, lying and treacherous husband whose charming self-indulgences at the racetrack succeed in squandering his new wife's insubstantial savings. Johnny Aysgarth was the sort of superficial, winning scoundrel Cary Grant could play in his sleep. The more difficult role was that of the wife, whose original naïveté has to be seen to be eroded inch by inch until at last she becomes convinced that her husband has killed his best friend. The ending was never correctly re-solved. In fact, the one imposed by RKO, the producing studio, was absurd: Aysgarth turns out to be innocent of any crime, his wife's terror totally unfounded.

The shooting began on February 10, 1941. Cary was again not impressed with his co-star, Joan Fontaine, of *Gunga Din* days. She herself was suffering from an unsatis-factory marriage to Brian Aherne, whose coolness towards her was a constant irritation. Hitchcock knew exactly how to use her nervousness and anxiety.

But he could not foresee her difficult temperament or her repeated absences from the set on the grounds of illness. Cary was exasperated by what he wrongly felt to be her fancied sickness. Professional to the core, and impatient of star tantrums and real or imagined ailments, he wanted to get on with the job and finish it with the least number of delays or aggravations. Cary was in a foul temper by the time the picture was finished. He tried to appease himself by going to the boxing matches with Barbara, attending a party given by Dietrich for the newly arrived German author Erich Maria Remarque at her Beverly Hills Hotel bungalow, and going to a farewell shindig for Dorothy di

Frasso, who left for Mexico with Ann Warner and Mrs. Charles Feldman on board the SS *America* on March 26.

It was in Mexico City that the most intense FBI surveillance continued against the Countess. Among her house guests at her apartment was Richard Gully, cousin of Antony Eden, social secretary to Jack Warner and well-known Hollywood man-about-town. Gully recalls that he and the Countess were being watched day and night. One of the Intelligence agents in Mexico was the actor Eddie Albert, while the actress Rochelle Hudson acted as liaison for US Naval Intelligence. When Hilda Krüger moved to Mexico, and when the allegedly dangerous Maximino Camacho, brother of the President, came to stay with Tyrone Power in Hollywood, the observation increased.

Following the exhausting and rather tiresome experience of making *Suspicion*, Cary took a well-needed rest, but then he was called to London, flying with Alexander Korda there by bomber. He referred to more than one trip with Korda at the outset of the 1940s in his memoirs serialised in the *Ladies' Home Journal* in the 1960s. He was back in May, when he turned down a role in the film *Bedtime Story* opposite Loretta Young, and also a part in *Joan of Paris* with Michelle Morgan. He very much wanted to star in *The Man Who Came To Dinner* as the irascible Alexander Woollcott-like columnist and radio personality, Sheridan Whiteside, but the part went to Monty Woolley instead.

On May 20, several admirals representing the Navies of the Latin American countries were in Hollywood, entertained by various leading figures of the film industry. There was a big party at MGM, an evening event at Ciro's, and another at the home of Constance Bennett and her husband Gilbert Roland. It was at the latter party that Joseph Longstreth, a young literary agent out of New York, met Cary Grant, who, for some unknown reason confided in him:

Mr. Grant told me in great secrecy that he had discovered that Errol Flynn was a Nazi agent and collaborator. He said to me that he had exposed Flynn to the authorities but the decision was made to do nothing about it. I was amazed and riveted, and promised to say nothing. I have not until now. But he is gone . . .

How had Cary determined this? Possibly through Korda and Noël Coward, or perhaps through William R. Wilkerson. The previous November, Flynn, in an act of treason since his country was at war with Germany, had arranged a rental car for Dr. Hermann Erben (on November 15, 1940) to escape across the border into Mexico, where Erben joined the Abwehr, the German Military Intelligence organisation. Flynn already had considerable knowledge of this organisation and who to contact there. Flynn's former business manager C. J. Wood remembers Flynn's desperate efforts to get Erben papers to go to Mexico. By May of 1941, when Cary's conversation with Longstreth took place, Erben was already in China, as an important member of the Bureau Ehrhardt, the Nazi spy-ring in the Orient.

Flynn, in breach of the British Trading With the Enemy Act, corresponded with Erben through a mail drop in Istanbul, conveying his desire to join him in Japanese-occupied territory. It is known that Korda's staff specialised in intercepting messages from Japan and China, using experts fluent in both Japanese and Chinese. A former member of Flynn's crew has testified, under promise of confidentiality, that after his return from Pearl Harbor as a guest of Captain James Robb that spring, Flynn conferred with the German Hans Wilhelm Rohl on the matter of the military and Naval constructions at Honolulu aboard his yacht, *Sirocco*. The result was that crucial information on the whereabouts of the camouflaged buildings was given to the German agent Ulrich von der Osten, who in turn passed the information on to the Japanese.

Why was nothing done about Flynn despite Grant's reports? Possibly because it was felt he would be of more use as a representative of anti-Nazism on the screen than as the defendant in a lengthy and protracted espionage trial which could only affect public morale adversely and, given his immense popularity, might even make a martyr of him. There is also the possibility that he could unwittingly lead the authorities to other suspects who could be rounded up; and it must not be forgotten that Flynn had the powerful protections of the Nazi agent, Charles Howard Ellis, as Chief Passport Officer in New York and of Nazi collaborators in both Major Lemuel Schofield, head of the Immigration and Naturalization Service, and Breckinridge Long, Chief of the Visa Division of the State Department.

A new and pernicious influence entered the lives of Cary Grant and Barbara Hutton. Count Carlos Vejarano y Cassina, the darkly handsome twenty-six-year-old son of the Spanish Vice Consul in Hendaye, France, had been recruited by the intelligence branch of the Gestapo in Biarritz in the summer of 1940 to go to the United States and contact potential or actual Nazi sympathisers. He was also to seek to influence prominent socialites through his title and good looks and urge them to call upon their congressmen for a negotiated peace in Europe. Arriving in New York City on November 22, 1940, he had met Sir Charles Mendl, the British diplomat and friend of Barbara Hutton, who had given him an introduction to Cary and Barbara. He and his wife, the former Wilma Baard, daughter of a Hudson River barge captain, arrived in Beverly Hills in April, and instantly attached themselves to Cary, who with Barbara sponsored them in obtaining a handsome apartment in West Hollywood. J. Edgar Hoover, always determined to keep his own suspects under cover where possible, failed to report Cassina's whereabouts and intentions to the British authorities, with the unfortunate result that Cary and Barbara became the unwitting host and hostess of a Nazi spy.

It was a crowded spring. Howard Hughes was in constant touch with Cary, keeping him informed about the colossal growth of Hughes Aircraft, which, by May 1941, had a little over 500 employees. Hughes was obsessed with the D-2, originally a bomber but converted because of technical problems to a twin-engine fighter plane.

On May 26, Hughes got a hefty contract from TWA to

develop the Constellation, a new flying ship that would average 250 miles per hour. Hughes turned up – one of his rare public appearances – at Ciro's, where Cary and Barbara Hutton threw a celebration party for him, in which they were joined by Frederick Brisson and Rosalind Russell, who were saying goodbye to a close friend of Barbara's, Jean Kennerley, as she returned to England by clipper.

June 1941 brought a troublesome event: it turned out that much of the money Cary had raised along with Ronald Colman, who was head of the committee for British War Relief, had been stolen by a publicist trusted with its transmission to England. There is no record of any subsequent trial, so presumably the matter was swept under the carpet. Also that month, the British Secret Intelligence Service, working with the FBI and Carmel Myers, who had checked into the Beverly Hills Hotel on the ground that her house was undergoing repairs, determined that the hotel was largely staffed with German maids who, unknown to the owners, were in fact Nazi agents. All were secretly rounded up and deported; no word of this appeared in the papers.

That same month, Cary appeared in a "Lux Radio Theater" show *I Love You Again* for Cecil B. deMille, giving his salary to the Chinese War Relief Fund. For several weeks, Cary disappeared from the columns, and it seems he made another bomber trip to England, again with Korda. He was back on July 26, when he and Barbara Hutton threw a party for their favourite, Wendell Willkie. As Grant, Hutton, and their close friend, the film publicist Robert Taplinger, drove at a snail's pace in the long queue of cars to the Hollywood Bowl for the Willkie rally the next night, a man screamed at them through the half-opened window, "I wish Hitler would come and mop you guys up!" Taplinger jumped out and struck the man to the ground.

Grant was vocal to friends against the current investigations into the film industry by Senator Burton K. Wheeler of Montana and Wheeler's associate, Senator Gerald P. Nye. Wheeler, documents show, was in the direct pay of the German Government, and was involved in intensive efforts to achieve a negotiated peace in Europe. With support from the German Embassy in Washington, he was already bent upon the Presidency. Spearheaded by William R. Wilkerson, the industry almost uniformly fought against the Wheeler-Nye committee, which objected to anti-German content in American films. But ironically, at the same time, Louis B. Mayer's MGM continued to do business with Hitler in Europe and Winfield Sheehan, former head of Twentieth Century-Fox, was discussing the possibility of his taking over the film industry when Hitler was victorious.

On August 18, 1941, Cary left for Mexico by car. He travelled rather mysteriously, alone, Barbara Hutton following two days later. They checked into the Hotel Reforma in Mexico City. Perhaps by coincidence, perhaps not, Errol Flynn was also at the Reforma, at a most sensitive time in Mexican history. In her book *Covering the Mexican Front,* *Washington Post* correspondent Betty Kirk wrote:

> Seven hundred Nazi agents poured into Mexico from the United States, Japan, Central America and Spain. These agents were preparing for the Axis conquest of Mexico. German was heard on the streets, in cafés, bars, and nightclubs. German drinking songs rang out at the cocktail bars, followed by blustering shouts of "Death to the Jew Roosevelt!" Germany's coming victory was shouted to the sky.

From Mexico, Barbara Hutton made a serious attempt to contact Baron Gottfried von Cramm. Richard Gully recalls that she actually succeeded in reaching Mussolini on the telephone. Mussolini promised to help. He phoned Hitler, and Barbara delightedly informed her guests that she was confident von Cramm would be prevented from being killed in a concentration camp.

Thanks to her extraordinary influence at the highest levels in Germany, Barbara was permitted to talk directly to Dr. Heinrich Kleinschroth, von Cramm's personal trainer, from her house in Beverly Hills on her return with Cary in late September. Cary was present during all of these conversations. On September 30, J. Edgar Hoover wrote to the Assistant Secretary of State, Adolf A. Berle, the following memorandum:

> As of possible interest to you, there is set out hereinafter a copy of a letter from Countess Haugwitz-Reventlow, formerly Barbara Hutton, to Dr. Heinrich Kleinschroth which was received from a strictly confidential source.
>
> "How happy I was to hear your dear voice over the telephone the other day . . . I did not call you up again as frankly I was frightened to, as nowadays they have a record of all foreign calls, and as I am not a citizen* I dare not do anything that the powers might disapprove of. So please don't ask me to phone you again as I honestly do not dare to, and if ever the newspapers got wind that I have friends in your country, that I not only write to and wire all the time, but speak to as well on the telephone, I would hate to think what would happen to me . . . [The United States] is anything but neutral.
>
> "The night of our phone call I sent you a cable saying . . . I would not call you again for reasons which I would explain later . . . I sent the cable to the Geneva Hotel, Geneva, where you said you would be until the 31st then two days later I got word from the telegraph company that they had been advised by Switzerland that the Geneva Hotel no longer existed!!!
>
> "I just received a letter from Sylvia (de Castellane). She says she saw you in Paris . . . She also tells me that you are very important indeed in Paris nowadays . . . Luckily lately I've managed to send her (Sylvia) $100 a month . . ."

The Hoover report continued with the statement that Kleinschroth was in the German Diplomatic Service and that

---

* Barbara Hutton became a Danish citizen after her marriage.

Sylvia, the Countess Castellane, had received letters from Hutton through an intermediary, the Count de Nava de Tajo of San Sebastiàn, Spain, father of the Grant-Hutton protégé, Count Cassina.

Barbara's pleas failed. Despite every effort made by von Kleinschroth, von Cramm was not excused and served on the Russian front and North Africa as a common enlisted man, not as severe a fate as punishment in a concentration camp, but certainly a degrading assignment for so big a tennis star and public idol. He remained in disgrace with Hitler.

Who leaked Barbara Hutton's secret correspondence, apparently sent through diplomatic pouches, to J. Edgar Hoover? Was it an FBI plant on her staff, or was it Cary Grant himself? The answer is unknown. Further FBI reports failed to name the informant.

At the end of September, Cary had a series of meetings over lunch and dinner with Frank Capra, who was preparing the screen version of the popular stage play *Arsenic and Old Lace*. He agreed to go ahead on condition that the central role of the manically energetic Mortimer Brewster, scion of a crazy family, including two murderous aunts and an uncle who thought he was President Teddy Roosevelt, was much enlarged and improved. Cary was pleased to learn that Jean Adair, who had been so kind to him in 1922, in Rochester, NY, when she had appeared with him and the Pender troupe and had nursed him through his bout of rheumatic fever, would be playing one of the aunts. It was always good to catch up with old vaudevillians, and Jean Adair, like Josephine Hull, who played her sister, was a most accomplished performer. As preparations for the picture began on October 6, Cary and Barbara entertained Lord and Lady Mountbatten, who were visiting the film colony. A week later, the couple once more left for Mexico City on urgent business; Barbara was again attempting to reach Germany and knew that her telephone and mail were being intercepted. Meanwhile, in great haste, *Arsenic and Old Lace* was being rewritten to Cary's specifications.

Oddly enough, his version, put together with Capra and the writers, was an ironical comment on his own peculiarly unsatisfactory private life. The story took place on Mortimer Brewster's wedding-night when the fool seems to be thwarted at every turn from getting into bed with his wife, played by Priscilla Lane.

Shooting began on October 20. Capra had decided to make the film in sequence, which put considerable strain on the studio resources. Cary was testy throughout the filming, very unhappy with the set of the Brewster house near Brooklyn Bridge, and complained constantly about it. He changed the lamps, the furniture, the curtains, fussed over the clothes of the entire cast and had a stand-up quarrel with his old friend and former lover Orry-Kelly, who had done the costumes. He was annoyed to find Orry-Kelly on the picture, because he was busy burying his New York past. He told anyone who would listen that he would have much preferred to appear in a film version of Noël Coward's play *Blithe Spirit* as the newly married husband who is visited by the spirit of his dead spouse, a story strongly reminiscent of *My Favorite Wife*. He was also talking about appearing in *Saratoga Trunk*, from the novel by Edna Ferber, for Howard Hawks.

Cary divided his salary for *Arsenic and Old Lace* between the United Service Organization, British War Relief and the Red Cross. This arguably generous gesture was interpreted by many as an attempt to save on taxes since Cary's income had already reached astronomical proportions and was being taxed at some eighty-five per cent. The Treasury took exception to the fact that after he had made the gift he tried to withdraw part of it and give it to the slush fund for British ambulances and other war-associated groups in Hollywood. He was forbidden to make the change, and in fact the Treasury memoranda rather heavily implied that he was seeking to overcome his tax problems in the manner referred to.

On December 3, Cary at last relented and gave Barbara a large diamond engagement ring. The announcement of their forthcoming marriage was underplayed; the reason may have been that at the last minute Barbara was compelled to bribe the German Government of Denmark to finalise her divorce from Count Reventlow. It cannot have been convenient for her that Reventlow was believed to be guilty of subversive Nazi activities during his marriage to her and that he was under constant surveillance.

On Sunday, December 7, the Japanese bombed the American fleet and military and Naval installations at Pearl Harbor. The cast of *Arsenic and Old Lace* assembled the following morning in a grim mood, but schedules were schedules and Jack Warner insisted they proceed with the work. Everyone had to concentrate under the excessively overdone direction of Capra; it is possible that the strained mood of much of the film is due to the fact that everyone who made it was depressed, concerned and fretful over the future. Capra had already been enlisted in the Army, and while production continued he was informed he must report to Washington as soon as possible. Despite that instruction, he ran considerably over schedule and budget on the picture, and Jack Warner was not pleased with the results. For various reasons, partly because the stage version was still running in New York, the film was not shown to the public until September 1944. Cary returned to Columbia Studios (which he increasingly disliked) to make *The Talk of the Town* for George Stevens.

It was the tale of Leopold Dilg, an escaped criminal who hides out in the home of a Harvard law professor played by Ronald Colman. The comedy sprang from that irony, and from the peculiar and farcical events that surrounded the housekeeper's (Jean Arthur) emotionally ambiguous relationship with Dilg. Once again, Cary was especially touchy and irritable during the filming. He complained about minutiae of the early-American décor of the charming set of the professor's house, constantly switching chairs around and complaining if the banister rail of the stairs was not sufficiently polished. Although he had respect for Jean Arthur's comedic gifts, he was also afraid of them; at one stage, when Miss Arthur had to follow him down a corridor of the Supreme Court, he was convinced that the crew's laughter was not from his own performance and hers but for hers alone. He misunderstood, and sulked like a child.

At Christmas, when shooting was concluded, at least three weeks late, he provided cast and crew with gift certificates for turkeys, only to realise that he was causing ripples of laughter because it was assumed he was referring to the quality of *The Talk of the Town* itself. No turkey, the film became a critical and commercial success.

That same week, Cary attended a party for King Carol of Rumania and King Carol's mistress, Magda Lupescu, given by Dorothy di Frasso. In a Foreign Activities Correlation report dated December 13, 1941, the Countess was described as "very anti-American, being both pro-Nazi and pro-Fascist". The report continued, "In September 1941, she was in close contact with the Italian minister, Marchetti, and the German minister, von Collenberg." A Naval information file was also sent to the various authorities stating that the Countess "had made about fifteen trips to Italy within the last five years, recently travelling by clipper. She is well acquainted with Mussolini, Ciano and Edda Mussolini." The report continued, "[The Countess] is an aunt of Alessandro di Bugnano, Italian Consul at Pittsburgh until the closing of the Axis consulates in June 1941 . . . [She] is further reported to be an intimate friend of Prince Boncompagni, Italian alien now in custodial detention at Ellis Island, New York, also of Vladimir Behr, suspected Axis agent."

It should be noted that, unlike the FBI, both Foreign Activities Correlation and the Office of Naval Intelligence were careful and meticulous in such reports and did not base their findings upon random statements made by scurrilous gossips. The unsolved mystery is whether Grant was informed of these reports so that he could be wary of what he said to di Frasso and also keep an eye on her.

The new year of 1942 opened with Barbara Hutton's

spectacular party in San Pedro to launch the "Bundles for Bluejackets" campaign, designed to raise money for US and foreign sailors in the Atlantic and Pacific. On January 5, Cary gave one of his biggest parties with Randolph Scott, at their old beach house, to celebrate the opening of the play *The Late Christopher Bean*, in which his favourite stand-in, Malcolm Gray, took the leading role. There was word from Douglas Fairbanks, Jnr., serving aboard a destroyer in freezing waters off Iceland. Jean Dalrymple was in town, full of memories of when she had hired Cary for the Janis Company in 1925. Lord Beaverbrook was also visiting to confer with Korda and Goldwyn on Secret Intelligence matters at the house of the Fox executive Joe Schenck. In February, Cary was passed over as Best Actor at the Academy Awards in favour of Gary Cooper, who had made a splash in the title roll of *Sergeant York*. He was indifferent to this; the Oscars meant nothing to him: he had not attended them hitherto and would not attend them again for some years. In March, Korda left for London on Government business, and Cary continued his Intelligence activities with Samuel Goldwyn. On March 12, he and Barbara had a quarrel: apparently, she was determined to pin him down to marriage, and he was again proving skittish. She flew suddenly to New York, where she had a breakdown, crying almost constantly and taking to her bed. In Hollywood, Cary also had a temporary rift with Randolph Scott, who took off for a long stay in Virginia. It was clear that if Cary did marry Barbara, Scott would finally have to move out. Whether or not that fact was the basis of their difference is unknown.

During April, Cary was conferring with Leo McCarey and the writer Sheridan Gibney on a screenplay entitled *The New Order,* later to be renamed *Once Upon a Honeymoon*, an anti-Nazi adventure story about a couple travelling through occupied Europe before America's entry into the war. It was in many ways reminiscent of Cary's and Phyllis Brooks' journey to the same countries in the summer of 1939. Shooting was delayed while some rewrites of the script took place. One disastrous sequence was left in, inexplicably, with Cary's approval. This showed the couple posing as Jews in order to get into a concentration camp. How Cary could have lent his name to such a scene is beyond comprehension. It was oafish, vulgar and stupid, and reflected Leo McCarey's incipient anti-Semitism and total failure to understand the real purpose of World War II.

As always, events piled up, relationships became more complex, and he lived on several levels at once. Clifford Odets returned from New York and began writing a script based upon the life of George Gershwin, a project of Cary's original mentor, Jesse L. Lasky. Odets was determined that Cary should play Gershwin, who had been a friend of Cary's in the 1930s. Grant would have been ideally cast, but unfortunately, the director, Irving Rapper, who had been born in England, felt that Cary was insufficiently American for someone so quintessentially American as the composer, and, in a decision he regrets today, ruled Cary out. But that decision was not taken until a year afterwards.

While Cary was meeting with Odets to discuss the interpretation of the role, he met a young and attractive man named Milton Holmes, with whom he would sometimes play tennis at the Beverly Hills Tennis Club. Holmes showed him an original story entitled *Bundles for Freedom*, the story of a gangster and draft-dodger who is reformed by the love of a good woman. Cary was fascinated by the story and pulled a string at RKO that resulted in the fortunate twenty-one-year-old tennis-court keeper getting the then colossal sum of $30,000 for his efforts, plus $500 a week on a ten-week guarantee. Just a few days earlier, Holmes had had to borrow ten dollars from George Cukor in order to afford some food.

Holmes worked on the script with Adrian Scott, a left-wing writer who would subsequently be blacklisted in the purges of 1952, while, simultaneously, Sheridan Gibney was at work on *Once Upon A Honeymoon*. Meanwhile, Cary and Barbara Hutton began investing in land developments in Acapulco, correctly foreseeing that it would one day be a resort. In 1942, Acapulco was little more than a fishing village in the magnificent setting of a huge, crescent-moon beach and flanking mountains. Perhaps annoyed by Cary's role in the hated British Secret Intelligence Service, with which he was supposed to be cooperating, J. Edgar Hoover sent a memorandum to Assistant Secretary of State Adolf A. Berle on April 6, 1942, which read as follows:

> As of possible interest to you, information has been received from a reliable, confidential source to the effect that William Randolph Hearst, Cary Grant, the screen actor, and Barbara Hutton, the heiress, have all become interested in the potentialities of Acapulco, Mexico, as a tourist resort and have made investments in land developments at that place.
>
> It will be recalled that a large real estate allotment is presently being developed at Acapulco by an American named Glenn Pullen. Pullen has been associated in this enterprise with Wolf Schoenbrun, a naturalized American of German origin, and the firm is known as the Fraccionadora de Acapulco S.A.A.

This report was also sent by Hoover to Nelson Rockefeller, Co-ordinator of Inter-American Affairs; to the Co-ordinator of Information; to the Board of Economic Warfare; to the Director of Naval Intelligence and to the Chief of the Military Intelligence Service.

More seriously, Hoover and his Mexican staff were continuing to investigate Dorothy di Frasso and her association with Barbara Hutton, Cary Grant and others. Frederick B. Lyons, Assistant Chief, Division of Foreign Activity Correlation, who worked directly under Berle in this Secret Intelligence branch, appointed Washington, DC, lawyer Joseph B. Keenan to investigate the Countess in Mexico City. Keenan was unable to leave until July 25, but in the meantime put feelers out in the Mexican capital. A Dr.

Bonotto, formerly authorised by the Italian Government to supply it with the explosive device in which Bugsy Siegel had an investment, was now busy trying to sell the same explosive to the US War Department. This characteristic example of cheek was to enrich Dorothy di Frasso further. She also entered into partnership with Senator Robert R. Reynolds, of the Reynolds tobacco family, who was Senator for North Carolina.

Reynolds had been a key figure in the appeasement policy that had kept America out of World War II until Pearl Harbor. Di Frasso's correspondence and telephone calls with Reynolds were carefully monitored; she was caught up with him in a business that involved making extracts of shark liver, and was also investing in the peanut business with questionable individuals, including Ben Smith, the Wall Street plunger, who in 1942 had met with Joseph Kennedy and Field Marshal Goering in an attempt to make a negotiated peace between Britain and Germany. This circle of dubious acquaintances was scarcely encouraging to Adolf A. Berle, and the investigation into the Countess and her circle continued unabated. However, no aspersions were cast on Cary and it is possible that Foreign Activities Correlation was using him as a source of information.

That spring, the surveillance on Barbara Hutton was still unrelenting, and J. Edgar Hoover was keeping Berle informed about her activities, at the same time as she was seeing Cary almost every night. Her letters were intercepted, supplied to Hoover from what he described, in a memorandum to Berle dated March 20, 1942, as "a strictly confidential source". The memorandum read as follows:

This source is advised that the writer [Dr. Heinrich Kleinschroth], who was a famous German tennis star twenty-odd years ago, enclosed a letter to the addressee from one "G" [code name for Gottfried von Cramm], who seems to have been the addressee's lover and with whom the addressee has been carrying on a correspondence for some time. The letter states as follows:

"Your letters and your love for him mean his only happiness and his whole life. If ever you should decide to change your life so that it would mean the end of 'G's' dreams and hopes, don't let him know it before the end of the war, because it would make him too unhappy and he would suffer terribly."

In the enclosed note, "G" writes:

"During all the twelve months [referring to 1941–2] I have received the most lovely letters from you. Henry [referring to the writer, whose first name is Henry] promised me to send you a cable as soon as possible, give you my love, and tell you the new address under which you can go on writing to me. Though I'll have to live in a more primitive way for a couple of weeks now, there will be no danger for me. If you should get a letter, written with a pencil, from me, don't think I have become lazy. I will then have no ink at my disposal."

The writer in his letter states:

"I have seen 'G' quite often. He left yesterday for a kind of inspection trip and will be back in a couple of weeks. Nothing to worry about, darling."

The confidential source has advised that in his opinion the writer is in some sort of confidential German Government service, inasmuch as in his letter he states: "You can always write to me Palace Hotel, Madrid, or to the Hotel de Paris at Monte Carlo, or to a friend of mine, c/o Mr. Marc Bloch, 4 rue de l'Ancien Port, Geneva, Switzerland."

The confidential source has also advised that the Palace Hotel in Madrid has often been described by American correspondents as the chief hangout of secret and open German agents in Madrid. The fact that the writer travels a great deal in Europe and has permanent addresses in three cities indicates that he is secretly or openly in the service of the German Government.

At the same time, Cary and Barbara's close friend and protégé Count Vejarano y Cassina continued to be under constant investigation by Berle and Foreign Activity Correlation. Memoranda flew to and fro in the State Department, many of them emanating from Visa Division chief, Fletcher Warren. It was determined that Cassina was receiving much correspondence from his father via the New York shipping company of Garcia and Diaz, which was believed to be the front organisation for the extremist Fascist political movement known as Falangism. The theatrical producer Gilbert Miller, a friend of Barbara Hutton through his wife, Kitty Bache, and an associate, both sponsors of Cassina's visa, were being investigated for illegal currency transactions. Thus, on every side, while seeming to be leading a bland and comfortable life in the oasis of Hollywood in the middle of World War II, Cary Grant was hemmed in by every imaginable form of intrigue.

And he was also filming some additional scenes for the recently completed *The Talk of the Town*, and discussing with RKO the possibility of Rita Hayworth appearing with him in the film of *Bundles for Freedom*. Hayworth herself was embroiled in all manner of intrigue behind the scenes: her husband Edward Judson was involved in mysterious business activities that some considered criminal, while, according to the famous Red Light Bandit Caryl Chessman, she was indulging in an affair with him, risking her career and perhaps her life because of the involvement. In June, Cary received excellent news: King George VI had knighted Alexander Korda for his special undercover war work as well as for his propaganda films designed to assist the Anglo-American cause against the Axis. Merle Oberon was granted the privilege of standing next to her husband at the ceremony at Buckingham Palace, a sure acknowledgment that she also had risked her life in the cause of freedom. It would be five years before Cary was honoured for his war work.

Once Upon a Honeymoon was still shooting. Hoping for the role of Gershwin, Cary played the composer's works constantly on the piano in his dressing-room and even studied rare recordings of Gershwin's speech, so that he could match the vocal patterns. Unknown to the world, he also volunteered for service in the Royal Navy. The work he was doing as an Intelligence agent evidently didn't satisfy him, and he wanted to see action. He was smarting from what Douglas Fairbanks, Jnr., has described as widespread criticism of his failure to enter the war. The Admiralty in London was prepared to accept Cary as a Naval rating on a hostilities-only engagement, subject to his being able to satisfy medical standards. However, a series of memoranda, now lodged in the files of the Public Record Office in London, makes clear that he was felt to be of more value where he was. D. L. Stewart of the Foreign Office wrote in minutes that "The position of BSS [British Security Service] in the USA has not been finally settled in detail." In the same memorandum he added, referring to Cary and the actors Richard Ainley and Ian Hunter, "[They] are very successful . . . and there seems no reason to alter our decision that they should stay." Another reason for having them remain was that it was important for British types to be represented by Britons on the screen, and that British performers in American films helped to assure good dollar earnings. Furthermore, the men mentioned were virtually useless from a military point of view. The Foreign Office overruled the Admiralty in the matter, but as it turned out, both Richard Ainley and Ian Hunter returned to England the following year, and Ainley soon lost an arm in military service. Cary remained, to continue his liaison work with Korda, Coward, and the Goldwyns.

It was clear that, in view of the decision not to enlist him, it would be necessary to secure him an unofficial position which would allow him to travel to Europe without attracting particular suspicion. Through Edith Gwynn, Wilkerson planted the statement, in the *Hollywood Reporter* dated June 18, that Cary would soon be "getting US Army papers" but would be "given leave to finish *Once Upon a Honeymoon*." A further statement on July 6 added: "Grant took a physical and as soon as he's finished *Once Upon a Honeymoon*, he will be a lieutenant in the US Air Force." The contradiction contained in these two announcements of course struck nobody, used as they were to the random items to be found in typical Hollywood gossip columns. Cary was still careful not to expose his work. It was probably a relief to him when Edward Ashley, the British character actor, did not approach him to join a special investigative unit entitled Allied Artists, which operated up and down the California coast. He was pleased to note that Freddie Brisson was now a lieutenant in the US Army, involved in cadet procurement. Urged by Cary, Barbara Hutton was offering her Regent's Park mansion, Winfield House, to the British Government. Because of the suspicion surrounding her, and the fear that she might have German connections, the offer was refused, whereupon, at Cary's suggestion, she gave the use of the house to the anti-aircraft defence brigades of London as a headquarters and dormitory combined.

After many delays, Cary and Barbara were at last married on July 8, 1942, at Frank Vincent's Lake Arrowhead summer residence. Shortly before, Cary had legally altered his name from Archibald Leach and become an American citizen. He and Barbara signed documents waiving all interest in each other's property for the future. This was the agreement that had so greatly distressed Phyllis Brooks' mother.

The service lasted only six minutes. The US Army Air Corps ace and Flying Parson, the Reverend H. Paul Romeis of the Lutheran Church of San Bernardino, read the wedding-service. Frank Vincent was best man, and Mrs. Madeline Hazeltine, the wife of a sculptor friend, was matron of honour. Other witnesses were Cary's long-term secretary and former fellow vaudevillian, Frank Horn, William Robertson, a friend of Barbara's, and Barbara's former governess Mademoiselle Toquet. Ironically, in view of the fact that Cary was making *Once Upon a Honeymoon*, the couple did not have a honeymoon. Cary had to report to work the following morning. Although columnist Sheila

Graham wrote, two days later, that she had overheard Cary on the set saying that the wedding-night was the best night of his life, some friends of Barbara insist that the marriage was not consummated.

Just days later, Cary's close friend and fellow British agent Reginald Gardiner announced his engagement to the beautiful White Russian, Nadia Petrova. Cary and Barbara were overjoyed. *Once Upon a Honeymoon* dragged on. Barbara became restless and irritable because Cary would come home late at night after a gruelling shoot, almost too exhausted even to speak. When she had friends over, to keep her company, he would sometimes disappear upstairs, too tired to make small talk and uninterested in the doings of the very rich. Cary was bored by the array of exiled European petty royalty that filled Barbara's drawing-room; she in turn had little in common with his film friends, who talked of nothing except contracts and deals and money and movies. The couple found common ground only in the work they were doing for war relief. Whether pricked by her reputation as a possible Nazi sympathiser or not, Barbara felt strongly, under Cary's influence, that she should give as much as she could to British War Relief, while he served with such figures as Binnie Barnes and Ronald Colman on the British War Relief Society committee sending seed packets to the National Allotments Society for Great Britain. In one of her rare public appearances, Barbara joined Cary for the August 29 première of *The Talk of the Town* to benefit the Hollywood Canteen, followed by a party given by Canteen President Bette Davis at Ciro's. In an attempt to improve their relationship, the couple flew to San Francisco in September, where they saw and were captivated by the young Dorothy McGuire in the play *Claudia*. Cary talked to Twentieth Century-Fox President Darryl F. Zanuck, successfully urging him to cast the unknown McGuire rather than Gene Tierney in the movie version.

Preparations for *Bundles for Freedom* began seriously that autumn, as Cary and Barbara moved into Westridge

House, the Douglas Fairbanks estate, at 1515 Amalfi Drive. It was situated in the Pacific Palisades, with a sweeping view of the ocean. It had five bedroom suites, a massive hallway, a cavernous drawing-room, tennis courts, a large swimming-pool and a sauna bath. There was an Oriental garden and a servants' cottage. But so large was the household employed by the Grants that they had to rent adjoining houses to accommodate the staff. There were about twenty-eight servants, sometimes augmented to over thirty. All were under the control of a butler and a housekeeper. The Swedish butler, Eric Gosta, also acted as a bodyguard. There were footmen in livery, upstairs and downstairs maids, a valet, special security guards, for Cary, two gardeners, a masseur and personal trainer and Barbara's live-in companion, Mademoiselle Germaine (Ticki) Toquet.

On November 1, 1942, *Bundles for Freedom*, renamed *From Here to Victory*, and later to be entitled *Mr. Lucky*, began shooting. It was a fascinating movie, filled with echoes of Cary's life, which suggests that he must have had a major hand in the all-too-revealing script. The character of the gangster draft-dodger who uses a dead man's 4F card to escape enlistment, seemed to be a compendium in equal parts of what his enemies thought Cary Grant was, and of Bugsy Siegel. The gambling scenes evoked Bugsy's activities in Nevada while the war relief organisation, on which the quintessentially English Gladys Cooper served as a major committee member, was clearly modelled on the almost identical organisation supported by Cary and Barbara in Hollywood. Moreover, there were curious parallels with unfavourable comments on Cary's private life. As if to support those in Hollywood who cast aspersions on his masculinity, he was shown as awkwardly tackling the task of learning to knit sweaters and socks for the Army by an ebullient war relief committee member, Florence Bates. In one comic sequence, he knits away furiously while a row of highly suspicious men watched him through a window, his embarrassment increasing by the minute. "What will they think of you?" his henchman asks him. In another sequence, the frosty committee girl, played by Laraine Day, after endless delays finally takes the matter in hand and kisses him. He responds by withdrawing awkwardly. She asks him whether he enjoyed it. He replies that he isn't sure. Few male performers would have dared risk such a scene; much to the relief of his fans, at a later stage in the action he announces, after a second kiss, that he does enjoy it this time.

Two further scenes he influenced can only strike chords in followers of Cary Grant's career. The first had him using rhyming slang, a typical Cockney activity. At one stage, he refers to "a lady from Bristol" which means pistol, announcing that this is in his pocket. Could any "in" joke go further? In the film's most remarkable episode, he is discovered in the Maryland country estate of Laraine Day's grandfather, played by Henry Stephenson, who would later repeat the role almost identically in Cary's film *Night and Day*. He talks of his miserable, poverty-stricken childhood with an intensity and passion he had not equalled on the screen. His face grew gaunt and drawn, his eyes sharp with pain. He mentioned running away from home, altering the date to the age of nine. Then he launched upon a speech condemning the very rich and their follies, a speech which he could have delivered to Barbara Hutton, and probably did deliver, two or three times a week. Unfortunately, the purport of the speech became a prime factor in the condemnation of co-writer Adrian Scott during the blacklist era: it was taken as Communist propaganda, and Cary seems to have done nothing to quell this false judgment. By 1952, he would be committed to the Cold War against Communism.

Mr. Lucky ran into trouble with industry censors. From the beginning, it had been disliked by Ulric Bell, former executive director of the Fight for Freedom group, who was now representative of the Office of War Information's Overseas Branch. Bell felt that the movie would be damaging to US prestige overseas and that it failed to show that every sector of the American public was playing its part in the war. He hated the draft-dodging theme, quite misunderstanding it, and sought the banning of the film abroad. He wanted it to be forbidden an export licence.

The warm reviews for the picture the following year deactivated Bell and the Motion Picture Production Code Administration under Joseph Green made arrangements for an export licence to be granted. But the film remained controversial. It was argued over for years to come.

During the shooting, Barbara Hutton took her son Lance to the studio to see Cary work. She had never seen Cary Grant make a film before. She seemed bored by the long hours of preparation for shots that lasted only a few minutes, and left quickly in the early afternoon, never to return. She looked drawn, suggesting late-night quarrels, or at least insomnia, when she and Cary attended the wedding of Reggie and Nadia Gardiner on December 6, the anniversary of the eve of Pearl Harbor. Ida Lupino was matron of honour, Freddie Brisson in uniform was there with Rosalind Russell, and among the other guests were the Goldwyns, the Selznicks, the Herbert Marshalls, Claudette Colbert and her husband Dr. Joel Pressman. At Christmas, columnists were told by Cary's press agent that he would soon be leaving to entertain the troops.

That autumn and winter of 1942, Cary became a true father to Lance Reventlow. His frustrated need to be a parent, constantly eating into his mind, was at least partially fulfilled in this happy relationship. Lance had name-tags reading Lance Grant sewn into his clothing and Cary gave him several thousand dollars, stuffed into one of the suitcases in his bedroom. Cary and Barbara gave the boy Cartier cufflinks, tie clips and jewelled dinner-jacket studs. Lance was not an easy child. A restless, miserable pupil at school he was torn between Barbara and his father, who was living at the Huntington Hotel in Pasadena. He shocked everyone by using numerous four-letter words and he was spoiled rotten. According to C. David Heymann in his biography of Hutton, *Poor Little Rich Girl*, there were odd events at the Huntington when Lance was there with the Count and his wife Peggy. A Miss Grant (no relation) was engaged as a governess for the boy; she had a habit of stripping him bare, standing him in the bathtub and beating him when he couldn't remember the Lord's Prayer. Barbara herself was changeable in her attitude towards her son, and this was troublesome to Cary. As if imitating his stepfather's involvement in Secret Intelligence, Lance devised a code, possibly with Cary's help, in which he would talk with his mother from the Huntington Hotel so that Reventlow, who was listening in to his calls on an extension line, would not know what was being discussed. At one stage, according to Heymann, Peggy Reventlow discovered a written code and showed it to her husband. It consisted of dots, dashes and circles. Reventlow steamed open a letter Lance sent to Barbara. When the Count read the first lines, they decoded as, "To hell with my father. I hope he dies." Replying to this deeply felt message, Barbara wrote, "You must write me some more like that." And she added, almost giving her husband's game away, "General [Cary Grant] sends his best love."

More serious matters were afoot. Cary made some very serious mistakes. He hired Count Vejarano y Cassina to teach him and Barbara Spanish; undoubtedly, Cary would need the language for any Intelligence activities in Mexico. He also arranged a screen test for Cassina. This was a failure, but soon afterwards Cary got him a job with Columbia Pictures, handling translations into Latin American languages. Cassina supplied Spanish soundtracks for films sent south of the border which parodied or attacked the Nazis for whom he worked. Among these movies was *Once Upon a Honeymoon*. Even now, Cary was not alerted by J. Edgar Hoover or the FBI to the fact that he was aiding and abetting a Nazi agent.

How can one explain this? According to Ernest Cuneo, who was the special liaison between President Roosevelt, Hoover and Berle in matters of Secret Intelligence:

Hoover hated Stephenson. He detested having his territory invaded by a foreign Intelligence organization. It would please him if one of Stephenson's people such as Cary Grant (I didn't know about the Grant matter personally) should be in any way embarrassed.

This statement is confirmed by Curt Gentry, author of a book in progress on J. Edgar Hoover, who says: "It's true. The fact that Grant was with British Security Coordination would be sufficient reason for Hoover to want to embarrass him." And embarrass Cary Grant Hoover did. But not for another year.

9

Cary Grant's marriage to Barbara Hutton was in every way unsatisfactory. Binnie Barnes, the well-known British actress who had known Cary since England in the 1920s, observes:

> It wasn't a very happy union. I don't know why they got married at all. He was an impetuous man; he sort of went into hibernation with all of his wives. I think he had a terrible time with most of them, to tell you the truth. I think they all found out after they were married that he was gay.

Cary's extreme tightness with money emerged very strongly during this period. As early as the 1930s, he had begun putting a red mark around the milk bottles in the refrigerator so that he would know if the housekeeper or another member of the staff had drunk any of the milk in his absence. They would then have to replace the milk out of their own pockets. He counted the eggs and he also checked every single item in every closet of the house, and even (a habit copied from Rosalind Russell) kept a count of the logs in the garage. He was endlessly nervous that the petrol in his car might have been syphoned off. He hated sending out furniture covers or curtains to the cleaners. He would not allow his clothes to go to even the cheapest Chinese laundry in down-town Los Angeles, but instead would roll up his sleeves and wash them himself, afraid that one of the staff would ruin them. If a shirt or jacket finally wore out, he would clip off the buttons with a pair of nail scissors and save them. Every time he played a phonograph record, he meticulously dusted it, and he checked the needle almost every day of the week. He would invite people out to dinner in a fashionable restaurant and then insist that the bill be divided between his guests, not equally but according to the exact amount each one owed.

If he saw an electric light burning in the daytime or unnecessarily at night, or in a closet, he would not only turn it off, but would determine who was responsible for the blunder in power saving and dock their pay. Barbara Hutton paid black-market prices for rationed shoes or foods that were in short supply. Cary refused to deal with black-marketeers. In a conversation with the author C. David Heymann, Dudley Walker, his valet, added some other details to the litany of stinginess. Cary hated each member of the staff to have his own copy of the newspaper delivered to the door, and he restricted the household to one copy a day. If anybody wanted to read the paper, they had to go out and buy it. At Christmas, Barbara would be lavishly generous, handing the staff gifts of $400 watches and presenting the maids with designer jewellery. She handed over her used dresses, sometimes worn only once, to a maid she particularly liked. But when Barbara handed Dudley Walker a set of expensive cufflinks, Cary grabbed them and put them in his pocket and handed Walker a cheap pair instead. They had been given to Cary by Bugsy Siegel. Walker added:

> He would sit at dinner and eat and put his fingers in his mouth and suck his fingers. He would eat very heavily, and Barbara would barely touch her food. And he was a bad drinker. He would really get nasty and cold. He would become sadistic. He could be a terrible bastard, that one.

Barbara Hutton plunged deeper and deeper into headaches and depression, and began drinking heavily. When Cary locked the alcohol away in a place she couldn't find it, she was so desperate for something to drink that she threw down half a bottle of white vinegar. She was also on drugs. Separately housed in her own bedroom, she would not sleep with Cary, and there was no indication that he was particularly anxious to remedy the situation.

Cary broke the monotony by appearing with the comedian Alan Carney in January 1943, doing impromptu skits at the Hollywood Canteen that convulsed audiences of servicemen. Noël Coward was in town again, on his way to special assignments in Latin America, and ironically Cary's Spanish lessons with Count Cassina no doubt proved helpful when Coward sent messages in that language from Mexico and south of Panama. In early February, Cary renewed an earlier friendship with the veteran vaudevillian Don Barclay, who had proved to be so helpful to him when his career was falling apart in the mid-1920s. He never forgot that Barclay had urged him to leave the crumbling world of vaudeville and make his début on a legitimate stage, and he put together an Army camp show with Barclay, in which Noël Coward also took a hand. The intention was to travel to an obscure part of America, Louisiana bayou country, breaking off the tour to make a secret trip to England. Unfortunately, the *Hollywood Reporter* yet again exposed his intention in a column item dated February 8; as a result, he had to be extremely careful to conceal the precise date on which he would leave for London by bomber. His movements at the time are still classified under the British Official Secrets Act, but his former assistant, Ray Austin, remembers the tentative statements that Cary made to him about the trip:

He told me about the spy thing. Cloak-and-dagger stuff. Cary went to Switzerland, I think, he and another actor.* They went [to Europe] and brought back a lot of information in their personal clothing. Maybe they brought back film, he never went into great detail. Goldwyn sent

* Don Barclay.

him to Switzerland. Goldwyn was the head of the spy ring [in Hollywood]. Cary went into Europe under Nazi domination, and he could have been put away for it. He said it paid its dividends ... that he was rather like Raffles in the old book and movie about the safe-cracker. He had to learn to crack safes, to get information. The government owed him so much that strings were pulled for him in an incident involving a sailor ...

To what incident was Austin referring? A curious episode, confirmed by Austin and other close associates of Grant, in which, at some stage just before his trip to Europe, he was arrested in a men's lavatory for a sexual act with a young man. Somewhere between the department store where the incident took place and the police precinct, a response from headquarters to the radio message from the police-car caused the two arresting officers to make a diversion to a certain address. Grant was dropped off, and another actor, who was paid a substantial sum to be a substitute, was arrested in his place. Finger-printed and docketed, the man was released soon afterwards, on the understandable grounds that there was insufficient evidence to convict him. An almost identical episode would take place involving Howard Hughes nine years later.

Cary was back in Hollywood in May, to appear on a radio broadcast of *The Talk of the Town* for the "Lux Radio Theater", no doubt combining his appearance with a report to deMille. A recorded War Bond speech he apparently made in Europe had been broadcast on April 26. On May 24, he appeared in the patriotic Air Force broadcast *Island in the Sky* as Major Robert Scott, and on May 31 he was on *Where From Here?*, another important patriotic programme. With Cary's encouragement, Barbara gave several hundred thousand dollars to the Free French, to help in the fight against the Germans, a sum which greatly assisted the young underground guerrillas in both Vichy and occupied France. He himself contributed heavily to the Free French while continuing to cut corners at home. After considerable nagging, he managed to free himself temporarily of his binding Columbia contract, using his own Frank Vincent agency to twist the arm of boss Harry Cohn.

He decided to make *Destination Tokyo*, from an excellent script by the writer Delmer Daves, and another of the writers doomed to be blacklisted in the 1950s, Albert Maltz. The producer was the pushy, energetic and manically productive Jerry Wald; Daves directed. Daves was a fascinating individual: scientist, geologist, crystallographer, photographer of ancient American settlements and townships, an authority on the history of the West, and an expert in dozens of other fields unrelated to the movies. Huge, with a massive head and giant shoulders, Daves was equipped with a booming speaking voice and a genial but domineering manner that fascinated everyone who met him. He was a master technician at film making, and he personally supervised the submarine sets for this story of a sub-captain and crew heading for Japan through dangerous, enemy-haunted waters in the midst of the Pacific War. John Garfield, then at the height of his career, Alan Hale, and Dane Clark were among the co-stars.

According to Ray Austin, Cary left for the Pacific region at about this time, his appearances with Don Barclay on the war front used as a cover to pick up information. Also, the fact that he was planning to do *Destination Tokyo* could have been used as another excuse for some diligent reporter to get onto him. But his movements were never made public, not even in the pages of the *Reporter*. Apparently William R. Wilkerson and his wife had finally learned their lesson in the matter of secrecy.

Destination Tokyo began shooting on June 21, 1943. Grant had just returned with Barbara Hutton from a week at Lake Arrowhead, presumably making an effort to save their already crumbling marriage. According to his usual custom, Cary thoroughly inspected every inch of the submarine, and for once did not find the set wanting. Manically set upon punctuality, which was his creed, he was very annoyed when an actor was late a couple of times. He and the rest of the crew banged on gongs and on submarine piping when the actor turned up, red-faced and furious at the gag, unable to appreciate the humour of it. It was a gruelling shoot. Cary's nerves began to fray as the extreme authenticity of the set proved to be a burden after all. It was done almost to the exact scale of a submarine itself, cramped, filled with equipment, and made of actual steel, not painted wood. The cubicles used for cabins, the engine-room, battery-room and cramped officer quarters of the USS *Copperfin* were stiflingly hot under the burning studio sun-arc-lights, trained relentlessly on the cast by cinematographer Burt Glennon. Cary and John Garfield sweated so much that they had to have thirty changes of uniform ready at any given moment; there was always the fear that the make-up would run down their faces and ruin their carefully starched Navy shirts. In scenes in which the submarine was swamped, water bursting through the hatch and sweeping through the machinery of the conning tower, Cary and the rest of the cast were drenched to the skin again and again, when the timing of the shot was thrown off by the force of the dump tanks. The submarine interior was mounted on rockers, which imitated the movement of a heavy ocean swell. Some of the minor members of the cast got seasick, and Garfield complained of vertigo. Utterly professional as always, Cary fought his way through the work, only occasionally cracking up in an uncontrolled brainstorm of rage when he could take the strain no longer. He told the studio publicist for the wire services, "We spend most of our time in this show 150 feet or more under water and there are no women. Take seventy-five men out on a 300-foot craft for two months without women and you can bet it's serious."

The actor Dane Clark recalls:

Working with Grant was a great pleasure. He was the most knowledgeable man I have ever met in this business. He was aware of every value, every detail on the set. I recall one day when we were shooting on Stage Twenty-

One, shots of the submarine about to leave San Francisco Bay on its perilous journey to Japan.

He continued:

> We were all aboard the sub. It seemed that there were about a thousand lights overhead, flooding us. As Cary got into the shot, he suddenly said to Delmer Daves, "There's a light missing up there. I'm not getting it!" Some members of the crew laughed: how could anyone see an arc-light from that position when there were so many hundreds of others. "We'll try to find out," Daves said. Members of the crew went up into the flies and were amazed to discover that one small light was not functioning. We all applauded and continued with the work. Amazing!

Despite protestations from Jack Warner, shooting was broken off for a couple of hours on June 26 when Cary celebrated the first anniversary of his US citizenship and said, in a speech delivered on the set, that it was his gravest disappointment that the British Government, followed by the US Navy Department in Washington, would not allow him to be in the real man's Navy. He received a round of applause.

Shooting of *Destination Tokyo* continued for eleven painful weeks. There were threats against the production when an obscure writer charged the studio with plagiarism. There were also several interruptions when technical problems with throttles and wheels and levers forced the exasperated director to suspend shooting for a day. Cary tried to relax by showing John Garfield pictures of himself in the Pender troupe as a knockabout clown and stilt-walker. He told Garfield, "I was sixteen then and pretty cocky. This is harder. I can't keep my mind on all these technical things. It's hard to remember technical words while I'm pulling levers and twirling knobs. This picture is making a blackboard actor out of me."

Whether it did or not, *Destination Tokyo* provided Cary with one of his best parts. And, during the shooting, there was talk of his making another film for Warner, on the life of Cole Porter, which Hal Wallis had bought as an independent production for $300,000. Cary knew Porter well; he was fond of his music and frequently would sing his songs at parties including "You're the Top", "Miss Otis Regrets", and "I've Got You Under My Skin". Grant was also friendly with Porter's talented boon companion, the bearded actor Monty Woolley, and was very interested in playing the part, but correctly apprehensive that the film would have to be almost totally fabricated since Porter's private life as a homosexual could not even be suggested on the screen.

Contradictory as always, Cary showed great generosity on July 12, 1943, when he gave Barbara Hutton an eighteen-carat diamond ring to try to cheer her up. She was overjoyed, but soon afterwards plunged again into one of her morose moods. Count Reventlow was still fighting her over the custody periods in which she was allowed to have access to Lance, and before long she would have to face a horrifying kidnap. She was bored and restless during the long weeks of shooting *Destination Tokyo*. Cary would come home, again his great strength depleted after the devastating, seemingly endless hours of work that continued all the way up to midnight and beyond. Devoid of much inner life, kind and outgoing, but uncomfortable with herself and convinced she was unattractive, Barbara would stare moodily into mirrors, savagely upset when someone would compare her unthinkingly with an actress whose looks she disliked. When the critic compounded the felony by saying such words as, "You'd know I was lying if I said you looked like Lana Turner," she would sink into an abnormal depression and begin to hate herself. Many would have shaken off the harmless insult with a shrug. But her self-consciousness and easily affected ego drove her into herself and made her virtually impossible to talk to. Her insecurity was in a different way as deep as Cary's; they were uniquely ill-suited to give each other peace of mind. No matter how often people would tell her she was pretty, she refused to believe it, just as he (incredibly) would refuse to believe those who called him handsome.

On July 17, Cary appeared at a special gala for the men of the Army Air Force of Gardner Field at the Masquer's Club in Hollywood. As a gag, Frank Vincent walked in with him in a wedding-dress, disguised as Barbara Hutton, carrying an exact replica of the bridal bouquet. Barbara was not amused: she hated inklings of Cary's bisexuality. Just three days earlier, their anniversary had been drab, uncelebrated and not even mentioned by Cary.

On rare occasions, Barbara would go out to nightclubs, but always without Cary. On August 1, she turned up with, of all people, Randolph Scott, as well as with Lady Korda and her notorious cousin Jimmy Donahue, at the Mocambo nightclub. As if to annoy Barbara deliberately, Cary turned up in drag as part of a gag routine on Orson Welles' Magic Show on August 5.

The long-drawn-out shooting of *Destination Tokyo* at last ended in September. An odd episode occurred shortly afterwards, in which a woman in New York who had the walls of her house lined with photographs of Grant claimed to be his sister. He angrily rejected this assertion, and there the matter should have lain, except for the fact that the gossip columnists tried to make something of the story. He threatened a legal action, and at last the matter was closed.

Simultaneously, Cary and Barbara made their first appearance together in months at Ciro's with Bugsy Siegel and his recently established mistress, Virginia Hill. This seemed to be a direct snub to Dorothy di Frasso, who was back in Mexico City wheeling and dealing and whom Bugsy had brutally jilted a few months earlier. Virginia and Bugsy made a striking team; both were handsome, charismatic, exciting, and dangerous. They moved from one location to another as they pursued their fiercely intense relationship: from the Château Marmont to the Town House, to Falcon Lair (Rudolph Valentino's former home) and houses in

Coldwater Canyon and North Linden Drive, seeing Cary constantly. Virginia's jewellery, furs and gowns cost her over $400,000 a year. She had a hundred pairs of shoes and a dozen mink coats, as well as other furs. Even in the middle of the war, her sportswear was flown in by some mysterious influence from London. Her bright red Cadillac convertible was one of the sights of Hollywood. Siegel's ill-gotten gains also bought her a mansion at Miami Beach formerly owned by William Randolph Hearst.

The price she paid for all the luxury was constant fear. She and Bugsy were certain that sooner or later they would be in grave danger from the Mob members they had crossed. They had a twenty-four-hour guard on all their properties, and hidden cameras in their houses that would record the arrival of unwanted guests, as well as complicated burglar-alarm systems triggered off by photo-electric cells. According to Siegel's biographer, Dean Jennings, the nefarious pair accumulated as much as $5 million from illegal gambling, paid killings and fixed races during a two-year period. Yet their profligacy and lethal activities seemed not in the least to worry their circle of friends headed by Cary and Barbara Grant, George Raft, and Mark Hellinger, the famous, fast-talking roughneck reporter-turned-producer and former writer. Cary spent more time with this remarkable pair than almost anyone else. He also saw a great deal of Don Barclay, and on October 11 saw him off to the South Seas with actor Joel McCrea.

Cary began work that autumn on a film entitled *Curly*, later to be renamed *Once Upon A Time*, in which he played a theatrical producer who becomes interested in a young boy's caterpillar. The creature dances to the tune of "Yes Sir, That's My Baby" and the producer decides that this remarkable insect should become a major star. Alexander Hall, whom Cary remembered with pleasure from Paramount at the start of his career, was assigned to direct.

Cary was unhappy about the choice of the attractive and talented Janet Blair as his co-star, despite the fact that she was a close friend of his partner Frank Vincent, and, as a

Vincent client was in fact his own, but Vincent had over-ruled him. She recalls that he was charming at first; she confesses, "I felt almost faint when I saw him as we started work," but adds:

> He had fought Harry Cohn over my being cast because I was so much younger. There would be too much contrast. There was a kissing scene between us he insisted be cut out. Sometimes he wouldn't communicate with me at all, just stare into space. He would be cold and distant and then even rude; he would walk past me without saying a word. He was deeply preoccupied with his problems with Barbara Hutton.
>
> Sometimes he was skittish, jolly, happy and cute, and he would do all sorts of funny things at the piano. (He was) incredibly limber. Then at the end he gave bottles of brandy to the cast and crew and I wasn't included. I didn't like brandy but it was hurtful. He didn't even shake my hand or say goodbye. I thought of barging into his dressing-room to talk to him, but finally I just slipped away. It was painful.

Ted Donaldson was the touching, winsome young boy in the film. As he had to Lance Reventlow, Cary became a surrogate father to this accomplished young actor. The agent Edith Van Cleve, who discovered Marlon Brando, also discovered Donaldson. In one of his rare gentle moods, the studio chief Harry Cohn himself supervised Donaldson's test and, despite the fact that the boy was sick with flu, coughing and sneezing, sensibly gave him the role.

Then Donaldson had his dramatic test with Cary. He remembers that Cary spoke to him warmly, introducing himself and talking to Donaldson as though he were an adult:

> He made everything easy for me. He had an innate graciousness. When we started shooting, he greeted me cheerily every day, always saying something amusing to

put me at ease. He loved games and riddles. I loved them too, and we would have so much fun together. He loved the current hit of that time, "Marezeedoats" with the line "and dozee doats and little lambsidivy". He loved it because it was so silly. It appealed to that wonderful, boyish side of him which of course was part of his great charm.

He was so effusive and outgoing that I seldom saw the more reflective, private, withdrawn and serious Cary Grant. But I do remember once when we were sitting waiting while the cameraman, Franz Planer, who was very, very meticulous, was taking his usual two hours to light the set. Suddenly, Grant leaned forward on his forearms and began to talk about Lance. "You know, I have a son," he said. And he added that he didn't see the boy very much, and regretted it. I could see the regret in his face. He wasn't joking now. He didn't deal with that regret in a humorous way. I was very moved. It was a loving moment, his talking like this to a ten-year-old boy. I think he had developed an affection for me. I certainly developed enormous affection and love for him. I wanted to help him. But how could a ten-year-old boy help Cary Grant?

Donaldson remembers that Barbara Hutton came to the set one day and sat on a couch. She was polite, but cold, or at least so she seemed to Donaldson. He didn't understand her shyness. He had no rapport with her, but his rapport with Cary deepened every day. Donaldson was having some difficulties with his father during the making of the film. They had an argument during the shooting. At one stage, his father raised his hand to him, threatening him. This unpleasant situation drew him even closer to Cary, who, by contrast, was never anything but kind.

There was a difficult sequence in the film, which came towards the end of shooting. Flynn, played by Cary, has to sell Curly the caterpillar for a trivial sum in order to rescue himself from bankruptcy. Donaldson has to struggle with

Cary, and Cary slaps him. The child lost his sense of being
in a film and felt the terror he had experienced when his
own father raised his hand to strike him. As Cary advanced
for the blow across the face, Donaldson ignored the director's instructions and shrank, turning away so that Cary's
hand descended on his neck. Although naturally Cary did
not deliver the blow in full, he was afraid, given his extraordinary strength and the great size and power of his hands,
that he might kill the boy. The director became more and
more frustrated as, even after eleven takes, the scene could
not be concluded. Finally, Donaldson at last forced himself
to hold his head in position and Cary struck it, just hard
enough for Donaldson to burst into tears. The effect was
stunning. For years afterwards, Donaldson was haunted by
that moment, agonising over the reason he had been unable
to play the scene.

The relationship between this thirty-nine-year-old man
and this talented child was one of the most remarkable in
Cary's life. As a result, the film was moving and disturbing
far beyond what its somewhat absurd theme would suggest.

One evening, when Cary returned home from the studio
too exhausted to have dinner and was sharing a plate of
scrambled eggs with Barbara in an upstairs drawing-room,
there was an unexpected ring at the doorbell. The butler,
Eric Gosta, informed Cary that Captain Rand of the US
Army, who was involved in intelligence work and acted as
a liaison for Cary in the European war theatre, had arrived
with two other Army men. Cary walked down stairs with
Barbara to see Rand and his companion officers standing
at attention and saluting. The three men took out a rolled
Stars-and-Stripes flag and unfurled it, presenting it to Cary.
He burst into tears. It was the Army's way of thanking him
for his work as a special agent, giver of funds for the war
effort, and champion entertainer of the troops. During
the shooting, Cary was made to realise how deeply the
American troops loved and respected him for his war efforts. Soldiers in the Aleutians sent him, on November 1, a
map, in needlepoint, of Alaska which they had made,

showing every small village in relief on the surface. On October 27, the incorrigible *Hollywood Reporter* announced: "Cary Grant is doing a wonderful constructive job in connection with the war effort on which he wants no publicity – and about which we wish we could shout here."

In November, Cary turned up at a farewell party for Phyllis Brooks, who was on her way to Australia to entertain the troops. He himself had plans to make another trip overseas after Christmas. He appeared with Laraine Day at a meeting of the Victory Committee to raise funds for improved food for the GIs, and, on December 10, bought a block of seats for the première of the film *Madame Curie*, a benefit for the same committee.

That day, Jacob L. Fuller, special agent of the FBI in New York City, arrested Count Cassina at Barbara's Sutton Place apartment in New York City and charged him with espionage. This was almost as great a shock to Cary as his own arrest almost exactly a year earlier. He and Barbara were panic-stricken. Informed by Los Angeles FBI agent, Richard B. Hood, that Cassina was a suspected Nazi spy, the Grants called Barbara's uncle, Joseph E. Davies, one of the most prominent attorneys in the United States, and the former Ambassador to the Soviet Union, whose *Mission To Moscow* had been a successful book. Davies refused to take the case. He knew how dangerous defending such an individual would be in terms of his career as a patriotic diplomat. Cary and Barbara now turned to a young, up-and-coming lawyer, Milton S. Gould, today one of the leading Manhattan figures of the bar.

Gould, who was still building his reputation, decided that he would take the case, even though his commitment to the anti-Nazi cause was in every way American. He still remembers Cary Grant's "frantic tones on the telephone from Los Angeles, begging me to protect his and Barbara's reputation". By skilful negotiation, Gould managed to reduce the charge (by plea bargaining) from espionage, which would mean death by execution, to the lesser offence of being an unregistered agent for Germany. This was possible because Cassina was a citizen of Spain, and thus technically neutral. Gould remembers that five days before Christmas he advised his terrified young client to plead guilty. The Grants were not present at the brief New York hearing and by considerable effort their publicists managed to keep their names out of the press. Among those who testified to Cassina's employment at Columbia Pictures through Cary Grant's influence was Columbia attorney Irving Morass. Two of Cassina's fellow workers also provided depositions. The story of Cassina's involvement with the enemy came out: his being hired by German agents in Biarritz, his attempts to determine pro- or anti-Nazi activities on the East and West Coasts of the United States, his knowledge of the Errol Flynn–Nazi connection, and the circle of friends whom he milked for information. However, in his confession he did not indicate that he had in any way guessed that Cary Grant was a British secret agent, nor was there any evidence that he gave away Cary's movements, or put him into any danger.

It was fortunate for the Grants that the forces of protection for the rich and powerful were as strong as they were in 1943. Had it been known that they, however innocently, befriended a Nazi spy in time of war, and that they were paying a substantial sum to defend that spy, Cary's reputation could have been severely damaged, and Barbara's as well.

The Grants were forced to continue their social activities as though nothing had happened. Two days before Christmas, Cary was among the first to congratulate Randolph Scott, who had finally moved out of the Santa Monica beach house and announced his engagement to the heiress Patricia Stillman at a party at his house next to the Los Angeles Country Club. Scott and Miss Stillman were present when the Grants threw an open house on Christmas Day and Barbara gave Cary a painting by Diego Rivera.

On December 27, Cassina entered a guilty plea in the New York Federal Court and was sentenced by Federal

Judge John W. Clancy for a year and a day at Danbury, Connecticut Prison Farm. Three months later, he swore out a statement about Errol Flynn to William H. Naylor, special agent, and to C. Dallas Mobley, also of the FBI. The statement was that while in Berlin, in June 1937, reporting on his activities in the Spanish Civil War, he had been to the Spanish Embassy to pay his respects to the diplomatic attaché of General Franco, his friend Antonio Vargas. Vargas introduced Cassina to Errol Flynn's German associate Dr. Hermann Erben. Vargas had on his desk a tall pile of photographs that Erben had just brought in which showed the gun emplacements and other installations of the anti-Franco loyalist troops, and Flynn was standing next to them. Erben had already taken one set of the pictures to the Berlin headquarters of the Abwehr (Military Intelligence). Subsequently, the Austrian journalist Rudolph Stoiber discovered from internal evidence of Erben's diaries and letters that Flynn had personally taken thirteen reels of film of the loyalist installations and given them to the Franco spy, Bradish Johnson, at a meeting at the Plaza Athénée Hotel in Paris. As it turned out, Cassina would spend less than the term of his sentence in jail and was deported to Portugal in March 1945.

The fact that Cassina knew about Flynn's Nazi connections indicates that he may well have told Cary Grant about them. Hence the fact that Grant was able to discuss the matter with Joseph Longstreth at the party at Constance Bennett's house in 1941.

It was a painful way to start the year 1944. Cary was under a cloud of depression, and no doubt there were repercussions in Whitehall because it was known that he had been duped. He cancelled plans for another trip to Europe, possibly because he was deactivated and disciplined by MI6 at the time. Meanwhile, Brian Donlevy, a client of Cary's Frank Vincent Agency, had joined such figures as Eddie Albert and Rochelle Hudson and Greta Garbo as a secret agent. Cary was testy, uncomfortable and hard to get on with that winter. He was vexed also by the many problems of Howard Hughes, who was in touch with him constantly on the matter of his latest obsession: a new flying boat, the HK-1.

Suffering from the after-effects of a crash in which his mechanic had died, Hughes was now more eccentric and neurotic that ever, besieging everyone he knew with phone calls at all hours of the night and letting out a stream of anguished invective in his unique, sharp, high-pitched bat's squeak of a voice.

Perhaps because of the stress he was under, Cary had a violent quarrel with his old friend Orry-Kelly, who at that time left Warner Brothers, apparently because Cary had used his influence with Jack Warner to make sure that Kelly did not design the clothes for the proposed film of Cole Porter's life which was now being discussed with Grant as its star. At the same time, Cary was deep in meetings with Clifford Odets, discussing a new picture, *None But the Lonely Heart*, which Odets had written and would direct. It was based upon a novel written in Cockney slang by Richard Llewellyn, author of *How Green Was My Valley*.

It was the story of a young man in London during the Depression. Odets and Cary worked together on the dialogue, ensuring the accuracy of the Cockney dialect which Llewellyn had sometimes misrepresented. Ernie Mott, the anti-hero, was a ne'er-do-well, an unemployed nobody who had long since deserted his mother. He returns to her reluctantly since he has nowhere else to live except her cramped house in the slums and discovers that she has cancer, which draws him closer to her.

It goes without saying that the story was close to Cary's heart. He saw much of himself in the character as developed by Odets: a man obstreperous, cocky and self-confident on the surface, but underneath tense, unhappy, tortured by his inadequacies, filled with hidden guilts and ambivalent in his outlook on everything, including people.

Odets cast Ethel Barrymore as Mrs. Mott. Cary had not seen her since the 1920s, when Orry-Kelly had been her leading designer. With her huge, dark, liquid eyes, beautifully formed features and deep, throbbing voice with a catch in it, she was ideal for the role. She had not made a film in eleven years, not since the controversial *Rasputin and the Empress* in which she had played the Czarina of Russia. She felt more comfortable in the theatre, and had made a big impression in *The Corn Is Green*, which later became a memorable vehicle for Bette Davis. George Coulouris, once a member of Orson Welles' Mercury theatre company, was chosen to play the slimy East-End villain who threatens the well-being of the Motts. He had come directly from a triumph in Lillian Hellman's *Watch On the Rhine*.

Odets and Cary continued the rapport that had marked their friendship from the beginning. As they began work on the film at RKO Studios in March, the work was never less than pleasing for both men. At last Cary felt he had broken with the antic comedies of which he had grown tired. He would now be taken seriously as an actor in what was a deeply tragic role. Jane Wyatt, who appeared in the movie as a struggling cellist, remembered the intensity and concentration that existed on the set, but she also recalled that, after a sequence, Cary would do handstands and cartwheels, recalling his old vaudeville days, using this form of release to break the excruciating tension of acting out so much of his early life.

On March 16, Odets wrote to a friend, "Directing a picture is really a labor [but it] is lightened by a talented actor like Cary Grant, not to mention Miss Barrymore . . ." In a separate, undated note he wrote, "Cary Grant is the hero of a Conrad novel: Lord Jim, etc." He was referring to Cary's capacity to detach himself from his surroundings, to find an island in himself away from the pain of existence. Like Lord Jim, he had managed to commandeer his own special territory and no matter how vulnerable he might be (and he was especially vulnerable during the making of *None But the Lonely Heart*) he could set up the defences and push back the jungle.

He had other ways to relax though: turning up at the

Show-Shop theatre to do a magic act with John Calvert. Cary performed a Houdini trunk trick, climbing into a large locked metal box after being tied hand and foot and escaping within seconds to loud applause.

But this was only a brief break in the tortured, if rewarding, job of making *None But the Lonely Heart*. And he had another cross to bear: also in March, after obtaining a divorce under mysterious circumstances from Marion du-Pont, who was now living with a member of her horse-breeding staff, Randolph Scott married Patricia Stillman. *None But the Lonely Heart* continued every day and night of the week including Sundays. The atmosphere created by the director began to weigh on Cary's spirits. He advised Odets on the sets, ensuring that the dimensions matched exactly those of sitting-rooms and bedrooms he had inhabited. He asked for ceilings, made of muslin, to emphasise the claustrophobic character of life in the East End. The narrow street, with its semi-detached houses and its railway bridge in the background crossed by steam trains, was a marvel of the designer's art. In the ugly, cluttered dining area where Ernie eats his meals with his stricken mother, the décor is so authentic that the viewer has the illusion of eavesdropping on the characters. The most remarkable sequence, shot on the last day, proved to be an endurance test for both Cary Grant and Miss Barrymore. Mrs. Mott is dying in a prison hospital; the pain of the cancer is now unendurable and all that is left to her is her love for her son. Penniless, deceived by gangsters, finding his mother in this horrifying predicament, Mott is desolate. As he hugs his mother, they burst into helpless tears. It was Cary Grant's finest moment on the screen. And it was also Miss Barrymore's. Neither performer would ever match that moment of transcendent beauty and terror. It was cathartic and shattering, and Odets' direction had a sensitivity and delicacy virtually unmatched in American cinema.

By a sad coincidence, that perhaps may have helped the intensity of the scene, a close friend of Cary's and Ethel Barrymore's died that same week: Myron Selznick, the

brilliant brother of David O. Selznick and the most important agent in Hollywood. Shooting was broken off while
director and principals went to a funeral that even by
Hollywood standards was unusually ostentatious and was
attended by virtually every prominent figure of the industry
in town. A columnist significantly noted: "Now that Myron
is gone, Cary Grant is the best agent in Hollywood."
Most people thought it was a gag, including Cary's own
distinguished clients.

The Grants turned up with Garbo at a huge party on
May 4, 1944, given by Lady Mendl in honour of the
celebrated clothing designer Mainboucher, and other guests
included Dorothy di Frasso and Bugsy Siegel. It was a
brief respite, followed by Cary's appearances in more radio
productions, several of them with Don Barclay, who had
returned from the tour, with Joel McCrea, of the South
Pacific. Cary rejoiced in Barclay's company, reminiscing
and laughing as they talked about the old days.

Barbara was frequently ill that spring, her relationship
with Cary in serious trouble. Even the persuasive and
charming Clifton Webb could not induce her to come to
one of his famous parties on May 22 in honour of his
mother Mabel, nor to Cobina Wright's affair for the Webbs
at which Judy Garland sang. Barbara did turn up briefly
with Cary, a few days after *None But the Lonely Heart*
concluded shooting, at the Birmingham Hospital for
Wounded Veterans, to present a cheque to the administrat-
ive officials, but she soon shut herself away again. It seemed
that the marriage was coming to an end, when, suddenly,
a crisis arose binding the unhappy couple temporarily
together. Count Reventlow refused to yield Lance up in
June, and Barbara began fighting him in court. She lost a
round of the custody battle and was compelled to pay $1
million to Reventlow to retrieve her son. Cary himself
delivered the money and picked up the boy in Pasadena.

In the early part of August, Cary disappeared to an
apartment in Beverly Hills, only returning to Barbara's
house on August 22 to attend a party for the producer,

David Hempstead. His mood had been lightened somewhat by the encouraging word of the Allied victories against the Germans in Europe and he was temporarily reconciled with Barbara, only to break the relationship off again later the same month. His moods changed from day to day. He found consolation in the successful first preview of *None But the Lonely Heart*. "Cary Grant is actually off his handsome head with delight," Odets wrote to his secretary in New York on August 7. He would be nominated for an Academy Award for the film the following year and would reap some of his most excellent reviews. Yet the film's bleak realism ensured it a choppy passage at the box-office. It was not what audiences were looking for in time of war, and not even the Grant name could save it.

Plans for the biographical film of Cole Porter began to accelerate in September, but Cary kept edging away from the project, uncertain if he could commit himself to it in his present tortured state of mind. On the one hand, he wanted to escape from the constrictions of Columbia, a studio he now detested, on the other, he was uneasy about portraying dishonestly an artist he knew and admired. The first-draft screenplay he was asked to consider seemed so utterly contrived and false that it did not even adhere to the available public record of the rise and triumph of the genius of the American musical theatre. The almost incomparable galaxy of songs and stars that made up Porter's life would of course lend itself ideally to the deluxe Hollywood treatment, but, fresh from his experience with Odets, Cary wanted depth and richness and moving intensity in the treatment of Cole Porter's character, even though its most essential ingredient, his homosexuality, would have to be omitted.

On November 7, columnists were saying that Cary Grant might not make *Night and Day*, now the official title for the movie, at all. When he made an appearance at the Birmingham Hospital, this time without Barbara, on November 15, he declined to discuss the film even with the patients.

He and Barbara Hutton returned Westridge House to Douglas and Mary Lee Fairbanks, who had returned to Los Angeles, on November 15. Lady Fairbanks recalls that the beautiful Japanese garden she had helped to design had been replaced with a potato patch where Mrs. Grant had been endeavouring to raise the vegetables for the war effort. Although the house was immaculately neat (due, she feels, to Cary Grant rather than to Barbara Hutton), she was appalled to discover that Mrs. Grant's obsession with keeping the house temperature at eighty degrees during summer and winter had caused some warping and also some cracking of the painted or enamelled surfaces of antique furniture.

The Grants rented a mansion in Bellagio Road. It was a big white elephant of a place, huge, daunting and lacking in warmth. With all its structural problems and its colossal size it came between the couple as they struggled to save their depressing relationship. Barbara flung herself into the extensive redecoration and then lost interest completely and stopped working on the house, becoming morose and distant again. On November 30, Cary, perhaps influenced by his unhappy circumstances, gave a convincing performance as a tormented, haunted near-psychopath in Cornell Woolrich's *The Black Curtain*, for Roma Wine Company's CBS radio series *Suspense*. He played the role with brooding force, suggesting a spirit in purgatory. He looked thin, gaunt and depressed wherever he went, whether it was at a loan drive, an Elsa Maxwell party or a Purple Heart veterans' get-together at the Bel Air Hotel. Always a determined achiever, Cary hated to admit that he had made a complete botch of his marriage. He felt he had failed Barbara, though it would probably be more accurate to say that she had failed him.

On November 26, Steve Trilling, the Warner Brothers chief of production, who had taken over the reins of *Night and Day* from the recently departed Hal Wallis, called Frank Vincent to urge him to have Cary sign the contract for the film. Vincent told Trilling that because of Cary's mental condition Cary would not be able to make any picture for an indefinite time. It might be six months before he could even consider working. Vincent knew that the director Michael Curtiz and his writers were at the Waldorf Towers in New York toiling with Cole Porter on the script and he was aware that aspects of the screenplay were tailored to Cary's personality. But he also felt that Jack Warner should "look elsewhere" for his casting, and that Cary's "mind should be straightened out", because he was "so low", before any consideration of the matter should be entertained.

There is no question that, as Frank Vincent's secret partner, Cary was the true author of this refusal. But Jack Warner stood firm. And so did Cole Porter, who would have nobody else play him.

Barbara had flown that week to San Francisco, where she was holidaying with Gene Tierney. Grant begged her to return and Miss Tierney interceded on his behalf, but the effort at this new reconciliation was doomed. Although Barbara did return to Bellagio Road, she stayed only a few days before she moved out. Frederick Brisson and Rosalind Russell tried to patch the broken relationship together one more time. Miss Russell wrote in her memoirs:

[The Grants] wound up sleeping in Freddie's room at our house, and Freddie moved in with me. Next morning Freddie went back to his own room to get a pair of socks and saw Barbara alone in the bed. When he went into his bathroom, there was Cary asleep on the floor. Stepping over him, Freddie picked up a toothbrush and came back to me. "I think we've got trouble again," he said.

On February 26, the couple announced to the press that they were going to divorce. Cary's nomination for the Academy Award came two weeks later. He lost to Bing Crosby, who had achieved a great success in *Going My Way*. But Ethel Barrymore received the award as best supporting actress.

Depressed because he felt that he should not have been

overlooked, but still not taking the Academy Awards seriously (he did not even attend the ceremony), Cary forced himself to sign the contract for *Night and Day* in April. He went in for colour photo tests; he had never appeared in Technicolor before. The make-up irritated his skin and made him more on edge than ever. He was difficult with the make-up staff, and felt no rapport with the Hungarian director Michael Curtiz. The script was rewritten daily as he fussed over every line of dialogue and insisted that he be allowed to supervise both male and female costumes, sets, and even the selection of the cast. He was determined to have Porter's best friend, Monty Woolley, playing himself in the picture, and he succeeded in overriding Jack Warner's puerile objections to the casting. He firmly approved the beautiful Canadian actress Alexis Smith as Porter's wife, Linda. Statuesque, tall and imposing, Miss Smith had been born lucky: discovered while at Los Angeles City College by a Warner Brothers talent agent, she had, after only two pictures, co-starred with Errol Flynn in the patriotic Air Force movie *Dive Bomber*. She had been outstanding in *The Constant Nymph*, in *Conflict*, and as a patroness of George Gershwin in *Rhapsody in Blue*. Her flawless looks, charm and perfect elocution earned her almost immediate stardom, although today she regards herself as no more than a Warner Brothers contract player with little position and no influence.

The picture at last began shooting on June 14, 1945, on a replica of the New Haven, Connecticut railway-station built on the Warner Brothers backlot. Grant complained all day long about the dialogue, which he had already approved, grumbling about how bad it was, how poorly written, and what a "lousy characterisation" it gave him. Jane Wyman, Mrs. Ronald Reagan, was unsettled by his behaviour during this scene she shot with him. It had to be completely redone with new dialogue; again and again, Miss Wyman, in her heavy period dress, in record heat, had to climb onto the train until she was exhausted. Ironically there was also a snow scene and the ice-machine and generators broke down. Everyone went home in a bad temper, most notably Cary Grant.

There then followed some sequences in Cole Porter's Indiana home. Cary had cast Henry Stephenson, whom he had liked so much during *Mr. Lucky*, in an almost identical role as a crusty grandfather, and he enjoyed playing the scenes with Stephenson. But Selena Royle, cast as his mother, was very ill during the sequences, with a kidney infection and a temperature of 101 degrees, and she had to be virtually written out of the script, with scenes endlessly reconstructed around her.

During one of those sequences, Alexis Smith had the pleasant assignment of kissing Cary Grant under the mistletoe. She says:

Just a short time before, I had been seeing Cary at Saturday matinées in Hollywood with my girlfriends. Now all of a sudden I was actually kissing him! I completely forgot all my lines and didn't know what I was doing for several minutes. Can anyone blame me? I've never been so flustered in my life!

"[Cary] was a perfectionist . . . he agonised many times over something I might consider incidental," Miss Smith recalls. "It didn't help that he kept changing the dialogue, and that the other performers and I had to memorise different coloured pages of script every day." There would be meetings in dressing-rooms when Michael Curtiz would pull out huge cardboard boxes filled with red, yellow, pink, blue and green pages, sifting through them in an effort to find a version that would work.

Cary was fretful over a sequence set in Kensington Gardens, London, when Cole Porter re-encounters his future wife, who is taking care of a bunch of children. Porter assumes the children are hers; the gag was excessively overdone and Cary rewrote it several times, the players returning to their dressing-rooms, and then re-emerging for another stab at the action. During another sequence in a theatre during a performance of one of Porter's musical shows, the director told Miss Smith to link arms with Cary to express her pleasure at the performance. She followed the instruction; her arms were bare. Suddenly, Cary drew back as though stung, snapping angrily, "Do you have body make-up on?" She replied that she did. And he said, sharply, "This is a Savile Row suit, and it's the war, and I can't replace it. If it gets covered in body make-up it will be ruined." Exasperated, Michael Curtiz shrugged and the arm-linking gesture was dropped.

Then Cary shouted at Curtiz, "Do you see these cuffs? There's a quarter of an inch showing. It should be an eighth of an inch!" In despair, Curtiz summoned the wardrobe staff as Cary returned to his dressing-room, irritably removing his shirt and refusing to continue until it had been adjusted. "At the time I thought it was silly," Miss Smith says. But she adds:

> That kind of perfectionist attitude was indicative of his work. I would rather have him be fussy about a quarter of an inch on a cuff and give the performance he did, because it was that care and attention that carried him through everything he did. His *acting* wasn't an eighth of an inch off.

Alexis Smith was intimidated by Cary in many ways. She felt paranoid about the constant reshooting, wondering if it was her fault, and knowing that she wasn't on a par with him as a performer. She points out that one of the reasons Cary was unhappy with the film was that he had just been working with Clifford Odets and suddenly he had to deal with lines that were virtually meaningless, and delivered on coloured pages out of cardboard boxes.

There were more problems on the picture. Monty Woolley, whose skilled comedy playing was so crucial to the overall success of the work, was suffering from a severe bladder problem which may have been cancerous. He had to be filled with drugs, and sometimes failed to turn up at rehearsals. Cary warned Curtiz that if he continued pushing Woolley, the actor would very possibly die. Some of Woolley's scenes had to be rushed through so that he could get to a hospital for a very serious operation.

The cameraman Bert Glennon walked off the movie when he overheard Curtiz criticising his daily rushes. He was replaced by William V. Skall, also experienced in colour cinematography, but Skall took ill and was replaced in turn by Peverell Marley. The scene of Porter's grandfather's death was reshot again and again. Cary disliked the way he was photographed, complaining that he looked more deathly ill than Henry Stephenson was supposed to look. Cary hated the frosted window in the scene, grumbling that the frost should be on the outside and not the inside. Curtiz tried to explain that the only way to photograph the window was to fake this effect, but Cary insisted there would have been central-heating in the Porter family home in Indiana, and that frost could not possibly have formed on the inside of a pane. He at last won the argument.

On July 2, Monty Woolley was in the hospital in great pain, and Cary twice insisted that the shooting end early so that he could visit him. There was another row on July 11 during the filming of an outdoor scene at Yale when the students joined Porter to sing in a group. Curtiz lined up the young men along with Cary's stand-in, Mel Merrihugh. Cary began to conduct the student choir, then suddenly announced that he detested the whole set-up and did not feel that Cole Porter should be portrayed on the screen as a cheer-leader. Curtiz reminded him that he had already agreed to the sequence as written in the script. Cary announced he would play the entire scene with his back to the camera, and he did.

By July 13, Curtiz was depressed and irritable, screaming at his favourite prop man, the British World War I veteran "Limey" Plews, because he dared not scream at Cary. So desperate was the situation by mid-July that Cary, studio boss Steve Trilling, Michael Curtiz and the writers met at the Brown Derby restaurant on Vine Street and sat there until the early hours of the morning trying to pull the entire project together. Later, a hospital scene in France had to be changed from beginning to end because Cary hated the set and insisted, over the protests of the art director, John Hughes, that it was inaccurate. On July 21, he suddenly declared that over 130 soldiers in the hospital were incorrectly uniformed. Milo Anderson, the experienced costume designer, was furious when he was told to redress every single extra from head to foot. Alexis Smith remembers that there were aspects of the World War I scenes that also struck her as absurd:

> Cary was composing the song "Night and Day". He was sitting at the piano in the hospital and rain was dripping down, inspiring a line in the verse. I had to stand there as an ideal woman looking at him lovingly. It was so funny, because there I was as his romantic inspiration and I was wearing this terrible nurse's uniform and heavy white regulation Army shoes! I couldn't stop laughing. Cary didn't see the joke.

By August 3, Eric Stacey, the production manager, was writing in his daily memorandum, "It's a wonder some of us don't go nuts!"

On August 18, after two solid weeks of fussing and picking over the script, there was a sequence supposedly at a Long Island mansion in which Cole Porter performed "You're the Top" with a small band that included Mel Tormé on drums. Cary was appalled to see the young boys and girls of the chorus incorrectly dressed for an out-of-door rehearsal, and they had to go back and be newly costumed to his specifications.

On the 21st, Cary walked onto the set of a five-and-dime store music counter at which he and Ginny Sims were supposed to be selling sheet music. The moment he looked around he flew into a rage and announced that he couldn't possibly work on the set because he was married to the Woolworth heiress and everyone would think he was trying to promote her family business. Moreover, he said, everything on the set was wrong, including the clothes worn by the people in the store, which were totally out of period; the shop itself looked like one that was contemporary with the year in which he was making the film. The frantic Michael Curtiz had to close down shooting for the day while Cary instructed John Hughes in the correct form of a cheap store between the wars.

Complaining loudly that the public address system used to summon people to the telephone, and the exhaust fans which droned and whirred irritatingly, made it impossible for him to work, he walked off the set on September 1. He was even more cantankerous four days later, when he played a sequence in a theatre box with an eight-year-old boy who played the son of Dorothy Malone and Donald Woods in the story. He objected to the child's lines, and suddenly announced that the child must be dropped from the story completely and sent home. The boy screamed, burst into tears, and ran off the set. Cary seemed unaware of the extreme cruelty of his action.

The same day, Eric Stacey wrote, "I don't think there is a set in this picture that hasn't been changed by Cary, and it has cost this studio a terrific amount of money." Six days later, a truss was loosened mysteriously on a large arc-lamp which crashed onto the stage, missing Cary by inches.

The same day, a summit meeting was called in Jack Warner's office to discuss the remaining scenes. Cary refused to appear. He was called repeatedly until ten p.m., and still did not turn up. He refused to post-record a scene in a New York taxi cab, which had been spoiled by noise, and was on edge again when Jane Wyman, who looked worn down from all the pressure, announced that some scenes would have to be rearranged to allow her to begin work on *The Yearling* at MGM.

On September 29, Cary had a head-on collision with Curtiz, as at the last minute he had decided to introduce his favourite studio hot-dog stall into a London scene where it had no business to be. Curtiz protested against this, probably on the grounds that after all of Cary's emphasis on realism it was absurd to have a hot-dog stall in 1930s England. But Cary was adamant that the stall's owner, Willy King, should be in the film. Curtiz screamed furiously at the mixer and the boom-boy with words intended for Cary. At that moment, the entire crew and cast booed the director, an unprecedented episode in Hollywood film making. Curtiz said he was going home and that Cary could direct the picture. It was only when Jack Warner turned up in the middle of this crisis that Curtiz was persuaded to continue the shooting, now at least twenty days behind schedule.

10

The ordeal went on. At home, Cary was impossible to live with, his mind deeply disturbed and seared with frustration and annoyance. Barbara Hutton filed suit for divorce right in the middle of production, on July 11; she told reporters that their last reconciliation had shown that they could not live together as man and wife. Now she had moved out, Grant told Louella Parsons:

> I feel badly that we couldn't make a go of our marriage. I honestly tried and I believe Barbara did too. Her ideas and mine were different. She was brought up in Europe and, well, I like [going] to prize fights [with] my gang. Barbara's friends were mostly continental titled people. She is a wonderful woman, kind and sweet, and I have only the best thoughts and wishes for her happiness.

Two days after that, on July 13, Cary was shocked to learn that Count Reventlow had absconded with Lance, now aged nine, to Canada, after failing to succeed in getting full custody of the boy on the grounds that Barbara was an unfit mother. Cary shared Barbara's extreme distress at the news. This matter unsettled him even further, and, despite the fact that he was annoyed with Barbara, chiefly over the divorce, he promised to help her in this disagreeable struggle for Lance yet again. Grant was furious when instead of standing firm with him in the fight, Barbara moved to New York, where she became involved with the infamous adventurer, crook and Nazi collaborator, Freddie McEvoy, Errol Flynn's closest friend. This lean and handsome athlete was a spiritual twin of Errol Flynn, already involved with him in gun, drug and tungsten smuggling. He ran a human stud farm, in which he sold handsome and virile young men to wealthy women in marriage.

Even the end of World War II following the bombing of Hiroshima and Nagasaki, in the middle of making *Night and Day*, seemed not to appease Cary's tortured nature. As if he did not have enough crushing burdens, he had agreed to make a very ambitious film that was to follow *Night and Day* almost at once. The film was Alfred Hitchcock's *Notorious*, which yet again had intriguing parallels with his own life. He had succeeded in turning the script of *Night and Day* into what was virtually his autobiography; in its final form it was the vibrantly directed story of an emotionally cold, work-obsessed and utterly detached genius whose wife is a permanent grass widow, isolated from him by his obsessive pursuit of a career. Similarly, Cary had exerted influence upon Clifford Odets and Ben Hecht, both of whom had worked at great length on the script of the new film. The picture had been under discussion for just over a year, as a project of David O. Selznick's based remotely on a short story entitled *The Song of the Dragon* by John Taintor Foote which had appeared in the *Saturday Evening Post* for November 1921. The plot concerns a German-American girl, Alicia Huberman, whose father has been apprehended as a Nazi agent. She is used by an FBI spy in Rio to infiltrate a circle of German industrialists in exile who are planning to develop uranium from mines in the nearby mountains in order to start a third world war. Because of the recent American attack on Hiroshima and Nagasaki, uranium was very much in the news. When it was discovered that Cary was to star in the film as the spy, the FBI began to take a special interest in it. J. Edgar Hoover had not forgiven him for his role with British Security Co-ordination on FBI territory. Now the fact that he would be playing an FBI agent in the film greatly annoyed Hoover. For a time, the project hung in the balance; Hitchcock thought that the reason for the problem and for the FBI agent's constant surveillance of him was that the use of uranium in a film story was a breach of security. It was only through the efforts of Selznick, who sold the property to RKO, but still maintained an interest in it, that the FBI was placated to the point that Motion Picture Production Code chief Joseph Breen was told he could approve the script.

Cary wanted Ethel Barrymore to play the mother of the Nazi villain, Alexander Sebastian, whom Alicia Huberman was to seduce into marriage. But Miss Barrymore was back on the stage, capitalising on her recent Academy Award, and declined the part. Instead, Leopoldine Konstantin was chosen. She had been the star of the Max Reinhardt production of *Sumurun* in Berlin, and had been acting in New York when Cary was there as a seven-year-old child. Claude Rains was the ideal choice for Alex Sebastian and Ingrid Bergman was cast as Alicia Huberman. There were parallels with her own life as well: she had been a Nazi sympathiser before World War II, and had been observed heiling Hitler, but had been wooed away from the Nazi philosophy and had become a patriot. Like Alicia, she was promiscuous, despite the fact that she was married and had a child. During the shooting, she was involved with Larry Adler, the noted harmonica virtuoso. Her life was complicated as she commuted between Larry Adler's home and her own, turning up at Hitchcock's dinner parties with her lover in defiance of the columnists. At the same time, tortured by her own inability to stick to one man, she contrived to date the eminent young photographer Robert Capa. She had no attraction to Cary nor he to her. Even though the film contained some of the most intense sequences of kissing and embracing ever filmed, there was no sexual chemistry between the stars.

It was extraordinary for Cary to be acting out his real-life role as a spy on the screen. There was a parallel in the action to his friend Reginald Gardiner's affair with the suspected German agent, Hilda Krüger, in order to determine her activities. In an early aeroplane scene, Devlin, the

FBI man played by Cary, tells Alicia that her father has committed suicide in prison in Miami, by taking a poison pill. The Nazi collaborator Charles Bedaux, a friend of Barbara Hutton's, had also poisoned himself in a Miami jail after being arrested for treason.

Notorious illuminated an aspect of Cary's character. At the beginning, he says, "I've always been scared of women." Even when Devlin kisses Alicia Huberman it is either to inveigle her into a plot that would involve her sexual betrayal of him, or to cover up when they are discovered by her husband spying in the wine-cellar where the bottles contain the precious uranium. Having scarcely protested, and indeed, aided the precipitation of a beautiful woman into bed and marriage with an unattractive man she detests, Devlin criticises her for what was in fact his own moral failure. His possessiveness, sexual ambiguity and deep-seated guilt and fear are from beginning to end Cary Grant's own.

As for Hitchcock, he was virtually a sexual neuter, who once bragged to the Italian journalist Oriana Falacci that he had only once experienced sex, and that was because his wife Alma had declared that she wanted a child. The film, in his own words to Charles Higham, was, "a voyeur experience. The audience became one person, sharing a room with Cary Grant and Ingrid Bergman in a ménage à trois." The director dwelt with lip-smacking emphasis on the couple's long, clinging kisses, as they discussed cooking and washing-up, a typical joke of the director's at the expense of human folly. Nothing could be less erotic than the famous scene in which Grant and Bergman embrace on a balcony overlooking Copacabana Beach, and then, pressed close to each other and whispering, move through shadows and light into the softly glowing apartment. In an additional joke, Hitchcock makes sure this protracted lovemaking is not followed by any suggestion of inter-course; the audience is left frustrated along with the charac-ters as Devlin, in what can only be described as a direct jibe at Cary's private life, walks out on Alicia at the crucial moment, leaving her with the sole consolation of a wine bottle.

Unlike *Night and Day, Notorious* went smoothly, the director's habit of pre-planning every sequence down to the tiniest detail resulting in a film which resembled the inside of a Rolex watch. It was the most perfectly formed and exquisitely timed of movies, revealing the director's talent at its peak. The scenes between Alex Sebastian and his mother could easily have been expositions of conventional villainy, but the strong hint of incest, the mother fiercely jealous of Alicia, wearing a pierced heart brooch during a critical confrontation with her son, carried a powerful charge. The performances of Rains and Konstantin were excellent, extracting every last drop of subtle menace from the cunningly written roles. *Notorious* was destined to be one of Cary Grant's greatest successes, and remains arguably his most enjoyable dramatic film. And in another tiny touch, Sir Charles Mendl, mentor of Count Cassina and British special agent, turned up at the beginning as a wealthy old yachtsman, trying to lure Alicia into a voyage to Cuba.

During the shooting of *Notorious*, Cary was dating the beautiful, blonde and ambitious twenty-two-year-old, Betty Hensel, who had been born in St. Louis and whose parents had been sponsors of the municipal opera in which Cary had appeared in 1931. Miss Hensel, who strongly resembled Phyllis Brooks, was well-to-do in her own right, undemanding, but delighted to be received in the highest levels of Hollywood society as Cary Grant's girlfriend. In March, she had been scheduled to marry Lieutenant Henry William Dodge, Jnr., of New York City in San Francisco, but had cancelled the wedding at the last minute following a nervous collapse during which she announced feebly to her parents that she couldn't proceed because she loved Cary Grant.

Possibly in order to irritate her and Cary, Barbara suddenly turned up in Hollywood at the time, not with Freddie McEvoy, but with the handsome actor Philip Reed. Cary hated Barbara's interest in Reed, and, quite irrationally, charged him with breaking up the marriage that had in fact long since ended. As it turned out, Barbara's incapacity to sustain any sort of relationship doomed her affair with Reed from the beginning. And besides, she was even more obsessed with Baron Gottfried von Cramm now that the war was over. She wanted to make sure that he was not in any trouble in Germany and that full note would be taken by the occupying forces of the fact that he had been in prison and forced to serve in the Army on the Russian front. She succeeded in using her influence on his behalf. At the same time, at Cary's suggestion, Barbara had finally given Winfield House, her home in Regent's Park, to the British Government. The arrangements were concluded late that autumn, and by December letters of gratitude were pouring in from dozens, led by President Harry S. Truman and Acting Secretary of State Dean Acheson. The transfer was completed at Christmas.

Cary's close friends Bugsy Siegel and Virginia Hill were secretly married in Mexico. Only Dorothy di Frasso, Cary, Barbara Hutton and a handful of others knew the truth. Cary and Betty Hensel flew to Las Vegas following a party given by the Randolph Scotts. Bugsy was opening the Flamingo Hotel, in league with his Mob connections. At the last minute, Cary returned to Los Angeles without attending the opening, at which only George Raft, Charles Coburn, George Sanders, Jimmy Durante and Sonny Tufts were present of the Hollywood contingent. The reason is probably that there had been warnings of possible violence during the opening, and that Cary didn't want to expose Betty Hensel to any danger. Instead, he and Betty turned up at a party given by Edith Gwynn in Hollywood. They didn't like it, and walked out, with the result that neither was mentioned in the *Reporter* for almost exactly a month.

Meanwhile, Cary continued his friendship with Howard Hughes. By now, the FBI had opened a voluminous file on Hughes in which Cary was frequently mentioned as the closest of his innermost circle. While Hughes conducted a lengthy liaison with the actress Yvonne De Carlo, and with a less well-known player named Faith Domergue, agents checked on his hotel and apartment assignments with these and other women, trying unsuccessfully to determine anything untoward that might result from these harmless affairs.

J. Edgar Hoover was also concerned that Hughes had obtained large quantities of raw film stock for *The Outlaw* through the black market, and more importantly he focused upon Hughes' special relationship with Bugsy Siegel. Hughes was in partnership with Siegel in the founding of Las Vegas as a crime and gambling centre, and had a hand in the Flamingo Hotel. At the same time, another of Cary's friends and supporters was being investigated for his association with Siegel: William R. Wilkerson, who was also a partner of Siegel in that same hotel.

Cary's continuing association with these individuals was of interest to Hoover. Hughes was busy that December drumming up a salacious publicity campaign for *The Outlaw*, in which Jane Russell displayed her heroic breasts in camera shots that gave considerable pause for thought. He was also continuing to work night and day on his Spruce Goose, which Cary was invited to see in its vast hangar.

Meanwhile, Hughes invited a large number of stars and film producers to accompany him on the inaugural flight to New York of his masterpiece: the Constellation aircraft on which he had been working through much of World War II. Several executives, including Louis B. Mayer, Darryl F. Zanuck and Jack Warner declined the invitation because they knew that Hughes was in trouble with Washington and that his aide and pimp Johnny Meyer was also under intensive investigation. However, quite rashly, Cary Grant accepted the invitation, probably because of the exciting idea of the trip and because (no small consideration in his case) it was free of charge. Bugsy Siegel declined to go because he was tied up with severe problems in Las Vegas. He was bothered by threats from rival Mobsters who resented his activities; he had opened the Flamingo Hotel too early, and had overextended his budget so severely that he could not sustain initial losses of over $300,000 at the gambling tables. He was hard-put to it to pay the $4 million in architects' and builders' bills that he owed. Despite the fact that he had jilted Dorothy di Frasso, she turned up and offered him whatever help she could. But she herself was no longer wealthy, and was unable to bail him out.

The Constellation flight left from Los Angeles at midnight on February 14, 1946. Forty of Hughes' best friends were able to make the trip, including Johnny Maschio and Constance Moore, Edward G. Robinson, Alfred Hitchcock, Linda Darnell, William Powell, Paulette Goddard, Janet Blair and Celeste Holm. Cary had had a major quarrel with Betty Hensel, and had decided to use the trip as an opportunity to get away from her for a time. Johnny Maschio was the genial host, plying the passengers with lavish amounts of food and drink. The atmosphere was uproarious, and at one stage, when the windscreen misted over, Hughes jokingly wiped off the condensation with a cloth soaked in vodka. Cary was the only passenger Hughes allowed in the cockpit. In New York, Cary checked into the Sherry-Netherland Hotel with the other guests, and the elaborate wining and dining went on. FBI agents kept a constant watch on the hotel, observing the comings and goings of Hughes' group, which flew back to Los Angeles two weeks later. Upon their return, with Cary's friend Count Bernadotte of Sweden and Governor M. C. Wallgren added to the passenger list, Cary joined up with Jimmy Stewart to throw an immense party at the Clover Club for Hughes and Johnny Meyer at which Bugsy Siegel was present. Among the guests were the Cornel Wildes, Linda Darnell, Connie Moore, Johnny Maschio and Teresa Wright.

In April, Cary flew to London, where he had meetings with Alexander Korda to discuss a production company that Cary and Korda would be forming to produce films of quality, including *The Third Man*. But there is no evidence that this plan actually had any foundation in reality. It is more likely that London Films was still being used as a cover for the Secret Intelligence Service, still under the control of Sir Stewart Menzies, assisted by his special deputy Major-General John Alexander Sinclair. As Anthony Cave Brown wrote in his book *C: The Secret Life of Sir Stewart Menzies*: "By early 1946, 'C' had reformed the Service to reflect his belief that the only potential enemy was Russia. Nazism was so dead that it seemed it had never existed."

The activities of the Secret Intelligence Service in Europe became especially valuable because the OSS under General William Donovan had disintegrated completely, and the CIA was about to be formed. It was a watershed period and the FBI was not empowered to fill the gap by operating in Continental Europe. Thus, Menzies had virtually sole responsibility for setting up anti-Soviet operations in Europe. There is no proof, in view of the continued classification of the Grant files in London, but there is certainly circumstantial evidence to suggest that Cary did not discontinue his work for British Security Co-ordination at home and abroad under Sir William Stephenson. Korda positively continued his own activities, transposing his whole organisation into an anti-Soviet network. Cary arrived in London at this crucial time and he also had another reason for being there. That May he received the King's Medal for Service in the Cause of Freedom, an award which, according to the historian at MI6, Nigel West, was customarily given to individuals who had performed special Intelligence services for the Allied Governments. This award was never made public.

When Cary returned to New York, his reservations at the Sherry-Netherland were made by Johnny Meyer on behalf of Howard Hughes. Hughes had been living with Lana Turner in a suite at the hotel. Cary arrived on May 5. Two days later, Hughes and Meyer returned from Louisville, where they had been attending the Kentucky Derby, to join up with Cary and Miss Turner for several dinners and small parties. The FBI followed all concerned every minute and bugged their suites. At the same time, in the full glare of publicity, the Senate investigations continued.

A motley collection of actresses, clerks, and small-time hangers-on was interrogated while Cary, Hughes, Meyer and Lana stayed on at the Sherry-Netherland. Cary spent a good deal of time in New York that week with Virginia Cherrill, still Countess of Jersey, who was in town on her way to Hollywood. He returned home to see the finished cut of *Night and Day*, which he disliked, but was surprised to find that Cole and Linda Porter thoroughly enjoyed, probably because it whitewashed their lives. In the third week of May, Cary agreed to make *The Bishop's Wife*, to be produced by Sam Goldwyn; he would play the bishop, who, much troubled over the building of a new cathedral in a small American town, is visited by a polished gentleman stranger who turns out to be an angel in human disguise. While Cary waited for some revisions to the screenplay, Count Bernadotte stayed with him at his house on Beverly Grove Drive, for the second time in less than a year. Bernadotte had a special role in the international Allied Intelligence Network against the Soviets. He had played a part in the negotiations through the Red Cross that terminated the war. Bernadotte had no interest in the film industry or in film people and it is highly likely that his purpose in coming to Los Angeles was to confer with Cary in the matter of the problems that would arise in that immediate post-war period.

Cary spent the summer of 1946 at his house on Beverly Grove Drive. His relationship with Betty Hensel was unstable, a succession of arguments and reconciliations. He still remained close to Randolph Scott, and he was still fond of Barbara Hutton, following with great interest her present life in Tangiers, and her increasingly complicated relationships, not only with Freddie McEvoy but also with McEvoy's protégé, Prince Igor Troubetzkoy. Soon, Barbara would reward McEvoy with $100,000 for setting her up with Troubetzkoy, a smooth, athletically built Don Juan who used his title to seduce various susceptible women.

On June 17, Cary refused the leading role in *The*

Hucksters, a story of the advertising business in Manhattan, suggesting to his friend Clark Gable that Gable should play the part instead. Gable did; at the same time, with *The Bishop's Wife* still not satisfactorily scripted, Grant somehow got talked into doing a feeble romantic comedy, *The Bachelor and the Bobbysoxer*, written by Sidney Sheldon, in order to work out his old RKO contract. He would play a painter, involved in violent incidents in which he is wrongly suspected of criminal tendencies; a teenager, to be played by Shirley Temple, falls in love with him. He was not happy with the selection of a contract director, Irving Reis, a favourite of studio chief Dore Schary, to handle the project, and would have preferred Leo McCarey or even H. C. Potter.

The Bachelor and the Bobbysoxer began shooting on July 15. Characteristically, Cary introduced into it elements of his own childhood which included the mention of his old art teacher and the incident of alleged stealing.

The shooting of *The Bachelor and the Bobbysoxer* was uncomfortable. Although Cary had always admired Miss Temple, especially in the films in which she appeared with Phyllis Brooks, and although he was glad to be working with Myrna Loy again after more than a decade (she played a judge in the film), he could not tolerate Irving Reis. Miss Loy recalled:

> When I asked Irving to redo my first scene twice, Cary got his back up and left the set to phone Dore [Schary]. "What's going on here?" he said. "You've got a director down here who doesn't know what he's doing, and Myrna's getting away with murder!" Dore came down to the set and Irving walked out.

Writing in his memoirs, *Heyday*, Schary commented:

> Irving Reis . . . was a mercurial young man who did not respond too well under pressure, and one day he blew up and left the stage. I took over for him and directed some scenes with Cary, and Myrna. After a few days

ABOVE: Archie, aged seven, making one of his first stage appearances.

A rare photograph of Archie appearing at the St Louis Opera House.

BELOW: Cary and Randolph Scott.

Cary and Virginia Cherrill, the first Mrs Grant, seen leaving a Hollywood party.

Phyllis Brooks (Brooksie), perhaps Cary's greatest love.

Cary and Katharine Hepburn took the lead roles in a number of romantic comedies including *Sylvia Scarlett* (1936) and *Bringing Up Baby* (1938). They are seen here in *The Philadelphia Story*.

With Barbara Hutton, his second wife, on their wedding day.

With Ann Sheridan in *I Was a Male War Bride* (1949).

Betsy Drake starred with Cary in *Every Girl Should Be Married* (1948) and became his third wife a year later.

Cary worked with Alfred Hitchcock, ABOVE LEFT, on several
occasions, and their films together include, ABOVE RIGHT,
Suspicion (1941) and, BELOW, *Notorious* (1946) with
Ingrid Bergman.

With Sophia Loren
on location for
*The Pride and the
Passion* (1957).

Dyan Cannon,
the fourth Mrs
Cary Grant.

Cary with his fifth wife, the former Barbara Harris.

A snap shot of Cary with his beloved daughter, Jennifer, born in 1966.

One of Cary's most treasured moments – the award of an honorary Oscar.

Irving returned, permitting us to establish a *modus vivendi* in which I could work closely with the actors while he worked on camera set-ups and movement. This arrangement satisfied Cary, who had found Irving too complicated a director.

Sidney Sheldon confirms the misery of making what was supposed to be a light-hearted comedy. Miss Loy recalls that Cary was in a stage of "jitters", nervous and uncomfortable during much of the shooting, and that he was subjected to questioning by the FBI's Richard Hood on the whole Hughes–Siegel–Meyer complex of activities in Las Vegas. Only the presence of Don Barclay on the set seemed to soothe him, but then he received an unpleasant shock. Frank Vincent, his devoted partner and friend for over twenty years, died suddenly of a heart attack at the age of sixty-one. Furthermore, Howard Hughes was involved in a near-fatal accident during the shooting, which distressed Cary severely. Flustered by his problems with the authorities, Hughes had poured himself into the final construction and test flight of his XF-II airplane. On July 7, he set out on his pioneer flight in the aircraft, inviting his new girlfriend, Jean Peters, to watch the flight. He took off from Culver City and circled around Hughes Field. But at 5,000 feet, he began losing altitude and realised there was no way that he could maintain the XF-II in the air. He was appalled to see that Beverly Hills was suddenly looming underneath him, and he began to plunge towards the Los Angeles Country Club. Instead of hitting the clubhouse, he crashed into 803 North Linden Drive, which, by a curious coincidence, was next door to Virginia Hill's home. He ploughed into the second floor, the right wing of his plane smashed into the neighbouring house. Then his craft skidded to a halt at 808 North Whittier. Both plane and house burst into flames. Fortunately, the owner, Lieutenant Colonel Charles E. Meyer, was in Europe. But Hughes was severely injured. Seven ribs were broken, his nose was fractured, his scalp was cut open and he was severely burned. His left lung collapsed, his right lung was damaged and his heart had been thrust aside in the chest cavity.

Cary rushed from the set of *The Bachelor and the Bobby-soxer* to his beloved friend; only Jean Peters, Lana Turner and Errol Flynn, of the Hollywood community, were permitted to join Cary at the bedside. Investigations showed that the problem was with the right rear propeller, which, according to Hughes' biographers Donald L. Barlett and James B. Steele, "had lost oil, reversed pitch, and created a drag on the right side of the airplane". The investigating board also determined that Hughes was in error himself. He had not used a radio frequency authorised for the XF-II, had not understood the emergency operating procedures for the propellers, and had not properly retracted the landing-gear. Hughes' recovery late that July and early August of 1946 was painfully slow. The visits to Hughes' sickbed during the convalescent period were harrowing to Cary. Hughes was screaming with pain, and his doctor had to fill him with morphine to appease him. He talked to Cary of their taking a trip to Mexico together when he was better. Of all the people he knew, Cary was still the closest to him. It is not surprising that Cary found it almost impossible, even given his professionalism, to act his way through the trivial and mindless situations of *The Bachelor and the Bobbysoxer*. Moreover, he and Betty Hensel were still in trouble. He lent Hughes the Beverly Grove Drive house and moved into a small, four-room house nearby, ceaselessly calling Hughes to see how he was getting on.

The Bachelor and the Bobbysoxer at last came to an end. These were grievous times for Cary, and he was more dissatisfied and restless than ever, tortured over Hughes' condition, worried about the danger of Bugsy Siegel, harassed by Dorothy di Frasso's appearances at his house to complain of the situation with Siegel, on edge because of the FBI pursuit of him, and vexed by the fact that the sudden decision to make *The Bishop's Wife* that winter removed all hope he might have had of going to Europe to work with Korda and Sir Stewart Menzies.

11

After an uninspiring Christmas, relieved only by visits to nightclubs to see Jimmy Durante and Don Barclay in performance, Cary took off on a much-delayed flight with Howard Hughes. Hughes was now almost fully recovered from his accident, but his mind had been affected, and from then on he would become increasingly erratic and strange. He developed his celebrated fear of being touched, wearing white gloves everywhere and having his food tested as though he were a member of the court of the Borgias. He flew Cary without a crew in a B-23 bomber to New York in January while some last-minute adjustments to the script of *The Bishop's Wife* were being made. Hughes had to appear before representatives of the still-continuing investigative committee; he and Grant flew on to Washington, DC, where Hughes would plead his case with Lieutenant General Ira C. Eaker, Deputy Commanding General of the Air Force. Commanding General Carl Spaatz listened to Hughes and authorised him to make another test flight of the XF-II. However, there was nothing the two leaders of the Air Force could do about the still highly adverse position the special committee was taking on Hughes' activities.

On the flight back to Los Angeles, Cary and Hughes were reported missing. They had made radio contact with Indianapolis Airport, but no further word had been heard from them for several hours. Announcements flashed over the radio and wire services that the two men were believed to be dead. The truth was that they had simply decided to slip out of contact and take off to Nogales, Arizona, and then to Mexico City, apparently using their influence with the local air controllers not to report their whereabouts. Cary Grant walked into a lobby of the Reforma Hotel in Mexico City in order to read the headline, SENORS GRANT AND HUGHES ARE BELIEVED TO BE DEAD. Cary called Betty Hensel and his friends in Hollywood, and laughingly assured them that, as with Mark Twain, reports of his death were "greatly exaggerated".

The two men returned to Hollywood. Hughes left for Washington yet another time to testify before the committee, while Cary began work on *The Bishop's Wife*. He co-starred with his friend David Niven, who played the angel in the story to Cary's befuddled, irritable bishop. Niven had been bereaved the previous May by the death of his wife Primula, a young and beautiful British girl, who had opened the wrong door during a game of hide-and-seek at the home of Tyrone and Annabella Power and had plunged to her death down steps that led to the stone floor of a cellar. She was only twenty-six. Niven had not recovered from the shock. He was depressed and out of sorts during the shooting, and Cary was not happy with his role. The director, William A. Seiter, was working at a sluggish, almost funereal pace, and Samuel Goldwyn was disappointed with the dailies. After three weeks of desultory shooting, Goldwyn decided to scrap the existing footage. He called up the trusted, warmly good-natured German-American director Henry Koster, who had made his name with the charming, *gemütlich* Deanna Durbin pictures. Goldwyn showed Koster the scenes that had been shot and told him that he was going to have Robert Sherwood's screenplay rewritten by Leonardo Bercovici. Cary would now play the angel and David Niven the bishop. Koster saw at once that this decision should have been made from the beginning. He remembered:

I met with Cary Grant, whom I admired all my life, and who was the best comedy leading man in the world. He was very upset. He thought the part of the bishop which he had been playing was much better than the part of the angel, because the angel was simply a straight-forward, very self-assured man, while the bishop would be comically befuddled, one of Cary's specialities. He was annoyed because Goldwyn was forcing him to play this other part. Cary wanted to resign; he told Goldwyn he wanted the part for which he was signed. Goldwyn told him that only Goldwyn could decide what Cary would play. This created great friction.

Koster met the actors each morning before they were made up; he sat with them on the set with the cameraman, Gregg Toland, next to him, and rehearsed the entire sequence so that everyone was prepared. Then he had the actors go into make-up and costume and return, with a clear idea of how the scene was going to be played. Cary did not mind this approach, even though, by now, he was bored with the whole project. He liked Koster, but again and again he still felt at odds with the material. He was so irritated by a scene involving an ancient Roman coin that he simply picked up the coin and began to walk off the set. Koster asked him where he was going. He replied that he couldn't play the scene. He was sweating; his face was moist because he was so tense. Koster tried repeatedly to have him do the scene. Cary insisted that the angel would not do what the script made him do. It took a whole day before a compromise was reached.

There were other problems: there was a scene in which Cary and Loretta Young, who played the bishop's wife, were supposed to be gazing at each other, the tenderness between them and a sense of communion without physical passion very essential to the mood of the film. Neither actor had objected to being shot in profile. Now they did. Cary said he looked better from his left side, and Miss Young said that she also looked better from that side. In despair, Koster said, "How can I direct what is in essence a love scene if both of you are looking the same way?" The stars shrugged and looked at Koster. Finally, Koster reworked the sequence so that Miss Young walked to a window and looked out, and Cary stepped up behind her and put his hands on her shoulders and gazed past her head into the night.

Koster remembered:

Sam Goldwyn used to come in early to see the rushes. He called me to his office. He said, "What is this, Cary and Loretta looking out the window? That isn't the way the scene was scripted. They're supposed to be gazing into each other's eyes." I told him what had happened. He came down to the set. He was very annoyed with Cary and Loretta, but he let the scene go in as I had shot it. And he told them as he walked back to his office, "From now on both of you guys get only half your salary if I can only use half your faces."

The truth was, of course, that both stars photographed perfectly from any angle. There was also a problem with a scene in which the angel and the bishop's wife go skating. Although both performers could skate a little, the sequence called for great expertise on the rink. After searching for every possible solution, Koster put masks on the stunt doubles; even seeing the picture today, it is impossible to tell the difference. Cary was annoyed about this, feeling that he could easily have mastered the technique of figure skating in no time at all. But Goldwyn was adamant that he must not risk an injury, and he sulked even more.

Koster adds:

When Cary did a scene, any scene, I knew he was miserable, that he didn't want to play the character at all. This is the worst thing that can happen to a director, to work with an actor who doesn't want to play a part and is contractually forced to do it. David Niven was no more pleased than Cary.

During the shooting in the winter months of early 1947, Cary did his best to break up the tension and monotony of the work. He turned up at a party given by his old friends and fellow special agents, Ralph and Carmel Meyers Blum, for the newly-weds Van Johnson and Evie (formerly Mrs. Keenan) Wynn. He delighted the guests by playing a record he had made at home of "One For My Baby", in which he entertainingly imitated a heavy-weight torch singer grinding out the lines in his characteristic nasal Cockney until everyone was convulsed with laughter. He presented the record to his friend Anita Colby while Binnie Barnes, Charles and Pat Boyer, and Mr. and Mrs. Dana Andrews applauded.

On February 18, Cary let slip to the *Hollywood Reporter* that he was now "officially" his own agent. He was also representing Edward G. Robinson, Rosalind Russell and Joel McCrea until all three were able to find other representation, but, for some reason, the general public never found this out.* The Ralph Blums gave yet another party on February 21, at which Cary was seen tenderly playing what one columnist described as "a right good, soft, hot piano for the benefit of Virginia Cherrill Jersey" and others, including his dear friends from the 1920s, George Burns and Gracie Allen, and Joan Crawford and Virginia Mayo. The party was in honour of Cary's friend Gardner (Mike) Cowles, publisher of *Look* magazine, and his bride Fleur. He was also at a soirée given by the prominent writer Leonard Spiegelgass, in honour of the British playwright Ronald Millar. Loretta Young was there along with producer Hal Wallis, who was dating the Australian actress Ann Richards. Miss Young was already telling people that she wasn't happy working with Cary, because of his fussiness over the sets in *The Bishop's Wife*. In a later interview, she complained that he had held up the day's work grumbling over the absence of frost on a window, a complaint reminiscent of the one he made during the filming of *Night and Day*.

He was seen dating actress Peggy Cummins and partying

* Outside Hollywood, the *Reporter* was strictly a trade publication.

at the singer Ginny Simms' house with Howard Hughes on April Fool's Day (he again played piano). He very seldom saw Betty Hensel and he was without her at a do given by Howard Hughes on May 6. A few days later, he had a violent quarrel with her and they broke up for the last time. Edith Gwynn reported in her column, "We've observed that they sure seem to have a deadening effect on each other." During the making of the picture, Cary received notice of a similar award to that which he had received from King George VI earlier, and a medal in France. The exact nature of these last awards, listed in the British Foreign Office indexes, was apparently for distinguished services to the Allies.

The Bishop's Wife finally wound up shooting in early June. On June 20, Cary received a phone call. He was told that Bugsy Siegel had been shot at his house on North Linden Drive in Beverly Hills. The circumstances were gruesome. Siegel and his friend Al Smiley were sitting in the living-room in the early morning hours discussing the new edition of the *Los Angeles Times*, which in those days could be bought at midnight. A car drove up and parked at the kerb next to Al Smiley's Cadillac. A man got out. He took a .30-30 carbine revolver with a silencer and, fixing the back of Bugsy's head in the sights, fired directly through the glass window past the drawn curtain. The bullet smashed into Bugsy's skull and blew his right eye fifteen feet away into the dining-room. The second bullet struck Siegel in the back of the neck and exited, burning its way through Al Smiley's coat sleeve. A third bullet also ripped through Siegel's neck, striking the painting of an English duchess on the wall and yet another slug crashed into a nude figure by Bacchus on the piano.

Luckily Virginia Hill was in Paris. Her brother Chick ran down the stairs, and the horrified Al Smiley turned out the lights. When Chick turned them on again, Smiley was cowering in the fireplace. Chick ran to the safe and took out Virginia's $100,000 worth of jewels, while his girlfriend called the police. He dropped the jewels in the laundry chute, letting them lie in the dirty laundry until the police were gone.

Cary was among the handful of friends whom Chick Hill called. Wisely, Cary did not turn up at North Linden Drive and stayed out of the publicity, as did Howard Hughes, whose refusal to help Siegel out of his financial predicament undoubtedly played a major role in Siegel's death. Siegel had been unable to meet his heavy debts to the Mob. A few days later, gangster Lucky Luciano, from the safety of Rome (Italy had no extradition treaty with the United States), took credit for the killing.

Soon afterwards, Virginia Hill returned to the United States, following a suicide attempt at the Ritz in Paris. She attempted suicide again at a Miami Beach hotel, but recovered to spend the rest of her life in terror.

Perhaps wisely, Cary left for London in July, driving east in his first cross-country journey by car since 1932. While in London, he again conferred with Alexander Korda, on a picture to be entitled *The Devil's Delight*, which Carol Reed would direct and in which he would appear as Lucifer in modern clothing. He told a London reporter, "I wasn't happy as an angel. I think I'll be much more at home playing the devil."

Cary visited Elsie Leach, who gave one of her rare interviews to the press, saying, "Archie always was restless, even as a child. He never likes to feel he's tied in any way." During his stay in London, Cary went to see an American play, *Deep Are the Roots*, in which a young American actress, Betsy Drake, was appearing. She was coltish, leggy, with a strangely irregular, but not unattractive face and an exceptionally well modulated, cultivated and expressive speaking voice. She was tomboyish, determined but paradoxically pliant and she walked with a swinging, almost masculine stride.

In late September, when Cary returned to New York aboard the *Queen Mary*, he was intrigued to learn that Miss Drake was also on board. She was even more intrigued to learn that he was a passenger. For years, she had been deeply attracted to his presence on the screen and was very anxious to meet him.

Betsy Drake was born in Paris on September 11, 1923. Her parents had separated when she was in her teens, and the broken home had made her wary, hypersensitive and nervous. Life in the tenement district of Manhattan had been gruelling and depressing; she had become obsessed with the idea of escaping from her environment in the only way she thought possible, as an actress. She was not very well suited to her profession: her figure was uninspiring and her features not very photogenic. She was awkward, shy, and her habit of standing splay-footed was not particularly appealing. Somehow, she contrived to get obscure jobs as a model with the Conover Agency and for the Montgomery Ward catalogue. She was hired as stage-manager for a production of the play *Only the Heart*, but ran down the curtain by accident in the middle of a scene and was dismissed in tears. Director Herman Shumlin took pity on her and introduced her to Hal Wallis, who gave her a screen test. He was interested in her playing a blind English girl in the movie *I Walk Alone*, which included Lizabeth Scott and Kirk Douglas. Wallis was pleased with her convincing impersonation of blindness, and put her under contract. But when she came to Hollywood, he wrote her character out of the script and left her idle for months. When he offered to renew her contract she declined and she did a cold reading for *Deep Are the Roots* and was cast over many well-known actresses for the London production.

Merle Oberon was aboard the *Queen Mary*, accompanied by Dorothy di Frasso. Divorced from Korda, she had just finished shooting *Berlin Express*, which Cary had turned down, and was recovering from an unsatisfactory romantic liaison with Robert Ryan. She was also accompanied on the ship by her new lover, Lucien Ballard, the cameraman. Cary was having tea with Elizabeth Taylor in the ship's lounge when he noticed Betsy Drake going to the telephone. He followed her, pretending to be making a call in the adjoining booth. As she came out, the ship was caught by a heavy wave; she stumbled and Cary caught her before she fell. Commenting on this, Cary said later, "I think Betsy was using a bit of coquetry." She blushed and pulled away and ran out of the lounge.

Next day, Cary was walking with Merle Oberon on the deck and saw Betsy. He asked Merle to arrange an introduction. Astonished that Cary would require one, the romantic Miss Oberon complied and invited the two of them to a buffet lunch and they became strongly attracted to each other. Cary was impressed with Miss Drake's intelligence, her knowledge of many subjects, especially psychology, and her interest in hypnotism, which also fascinated him. He assumed the role of authoritative film star, deciding that he could help Miss Drake in her career, and using this in order to fascinate her. But from the beginning, it was noted by friends that their relationship was more like that of brother and sister than that of lovers.

In New York, Cary announced that he would speak to Dore Schary about obtaining a contract for Miss Drake and would also introduce her to David O. Selznick. They travelled to Los Angeles together. There, Cary was as good as his word. Selznick put Betsy under contract immediately. Whether this was as a favour to Cary or because he saw actual merit in Miss Drake is uncertain, but at the same time he began discussing with RKO executives the idea of loaning her out to that studio. He was already in negotiation about possibly buying RKO outright. Cary did not introduce her at parties at first: he may have been too insecure about their relationship, and uncertain whether this bookish, almost too well-informed and fiercely determined young woman would fit in with his more light-hearted, not learned and superficially cheerful circle of friends.

He was also preoccupied because he was starting work at RKO on *Mr. Blandings Builds His Dream House*, with Myrna Loy and Melvyn Douglas, about a New Yorker seized with a vision of a fancy weekend residence who plunges into a series of comical and grotesque mishaps in the process. Betsy would turn up on the set to watch Cary work, her quizzical, intense stare somewhat irritating Dore Schary and the director, H. C. Potter. The film was bland, harmless, uninspiring; Cary as the harassed advertising executive faced with the problems of a bucolic existence was at his most accomplished, and he concocted some business which involved playing on the matter of transvestism: in an early sequence in a Manhattan apartment, he drags his wife's underwear from a drawer while looking for his missing socks, making questionable jokes about the suitability of such garments for himself, jokes which were improvised on the spot in order to avoid censorship by the ever-vigilant Joe Breen. Cary made arrangements to appear on radio, with George Burns and Gracie Allen, in the Maxwell House Coffee Time Show. Gracie played his secretary in an episode on October 16, in which the amusing Bea Benadaret was a movie columnist interviewing Cary for a magazine. She was based wittily on Louella Parsons. On October 30, he appeared with Hans Conried and Gale Gordon, both of whom he had worked with in his early stage career in New York, in the Maxwell House show, and in a third appearance on November 13, he was in Maxwell House's *Uplift Society*, a parody of social life in Hollywood which he undertook in high spirits.

During the shooting of *Mr. Blandings*, the early days of the witch hunts against alleged Communists in Hollywood were marked by conflicts within the industry. Directors John Huston and William Wyler turned up on the film's set and asked for support from the cast in order to establish a First Amendment Committee which would allow those who had been named in the initial investigations to fight against potential or actual blacklisting. Melvyn Douglas, who, along with his wife, the actress and politician Helen Gahagan, was considerably left of centre, agreed to co-operate with the committee. Miss Loy, who was above reproach politically, was at heart a liberal and was happy to join Douglas in opposition to what she felt was a grave threat to freedom of speech. But Cary refused to have anything to do with the Committee for the First Amendment. Still a staunch Republican, he was committed to the cold war. Although he was opposed to any interferences with personal freedom, he knew that many members of the film industry were, whatever their protests to the contrary, members of the Communist Party. He went a step further. He appeared more than once in secret session before the House Committee on Un-American Activities in later years, probably naming names.* But the hearings' minutes remain closed to this day, suggesting that whatever he said was under special privilege; he was not exposed like such directors as Elia Kazan and such actors as Lee J. Cobb to future calumny for informing on his fellow employees in the film industry.

In the winter of 1947, Howard Hughes, who was still suffering from the barrage of the Senate committees in Washington, took over RKO. Cary talked Hughes into buying the other half of Betsy Drake's contract, and then he talked Dore Schary into agreeing with Hughes that Betsy would be perfect for a comedy that Cary would make for the studio, *Every Girl Should Be Married*. She herself had aspirations to be a dramatic actress, but Cary felt that, with her awkward, appealingly gauche manner and crinkly smile, she would be far better suited to farcical material. By now, she was completely under his spell – or seemed to be. She said later that he controlled everything she did, from the food she ate, to eating it with a knife and fork in the British manner, from the car she drove to the clothes she wore, and even her hairstyles. He was moulding her, slowly but surely, into what he felt to be a desirable and sophisticated woman.

In *Every Girl Should Be Married*, co-written by the director Don Hartman (a specialist in visual and oral gags who had written for Bob Hope and Bing Crosby) and Stephen Morehouse Avery, head of US Military Intelligence in Los Angeles in World War II, Betsy Drake was cast as a department store clerk in a children's wear department who

---

* The late Noah Dietrich confirmed this.

sets her sights on Cary as a paediatrician, Dr. Madison Brown. She researches him thoroughly in order to catch him, finding out about his college background, the food he likes to eat, and even the colour of his underwear. Despite a series of mishaps and roadblocks, she finally captures her prey. The story was a reversal of real-life where Cary researched Betsy Drake.

This picture of single-minded female aggressiveness troubled several critics later on, and since Cary is known to have had a hand in the script, the film may have reflected a deep-seated hostility and fear of women. For all of the strenuous efforts of the director to make the character of Anabel Sims appealing, the result was a movie that could scarcely have been more misogynistic. Cary watched every move Betsy Drake made on the set, endlessly checking her out, imitating her cruelly in scenes, and at times encouraging her mistakenly to imitate Katharine Hepburn by indulging in excessively mannered playing. Betsy seemed to take colour from Cary's own fussiness, and soon afterwards studio publicists would be complaining that, self-conscious over her thinness, she would not pose in a bathing costume for publicity shots.

Once again, Cary was drawn to an extremely sensitive, self-conscious girl with an inferiority complex: Betsy Drake even looked a little like Barbara Hutton. In March 1948, Cary was offered the leading role in the film *A Double Life*, the story of a Shakespearean actor who confuses his part in *Othello* with reality and strangles the actress cast as Desdemona. He turned the role down for two reasons: he was nervous about having to recite Shakespeare in his nasal accent and seemed unwilling to train with a voice coach, and George Cukor, who was assigned to direct the film for Universal, also made it clear that Betsy Drake could not possibly play Desdemona, for which he had the Swedish star Signe Hasso in mind. There was some tension between Cary and Betsy for the first time in April, when he was seen at the Café Gala with, of all people, Betty Hensel. It took much of his diplomacy and skill to overcome Betsy's concern. He announced to the press that he was determined to appear in the role of Morris Townsend, the shallow and heartless seducer who pursues the unattractive heiress in William Wyler's proposed version of Henry James' *Washington Square*. At forty-four, he was of course far too old for the part, which went to Montgomery Clift. He was disappointed; he had always wanted to work with Wyler, whose masterpiece *The Best Years Of Our Lives* he had admired.

On April 12, 1948, Virginia Cherrill married the former World War II airman Florian Martini. She had obtained her divorce from the Earl of Jersey two years before. Her ardent Polish husband had met her in Liverpool in 1947 and had pursued her all the way to Los Angeles, where she had come to visit her mother. Cary did not attend the wedding or send a gift.

The situation at RKO was chaotic. Howard Hughes never appeared at the studio, preferring to conduct his business from a separate address. He seemed to regard running RKO as a hobby, a secondary occupation and an example of total self-indulgence. Schary wanted to make a film called *Battleground**, in which Cary would appear, but Hughes was totally opposed to it, hating the idea of a war picture and convinced that no one would go to see it. He was still lingering at Cary's house on Beverly Grove Drive, living without furnishings, except for two chairs and a sofa and a mattress instead of a bed in the master bedroom. When Schary arrived for painful, long-drawn-out conferences with Hughes on studio policy, he found, in his own words, that "there wasn't a paper, a cigarette, a flower, a match, a picture, a magazine . . ." He blocked Schary at every turn. Schary himself was also making painful trips to Washington to appear before the House Un-American Activities Committee.

Every effort was made by committee chairman J. Parnell Thomas to discredit Schary, who by 1948 was under a

---

* Later transferred to MGM.

cloud. Yet Schary was able to continue functioning because the committee was unable to prove anything against him. Hughes shared Cary's right-wing position in the matter, and Schary was released from RKO that summer of 1948. The situation was extremely difficult, and Cary was aware that Hughes was daily becoming more eccentric and impossible to deal with.

Cary broke, albeit amiably, his contract with Hughes and signed a contract with Twentieth Century-Fox. As we know he showed his devotion to his Jewish origins by giving a cheque for $10,000 to the United Jewish Appeal on June 8, in the name of his "dead Jewish mother". Nobody picked up the fact that Elsie Leach, the mother the world accepted in that role, was both alive and a Gentile.

Cary and Betsy Drake left for Europe on August 26. He was to make *I Was a Male War Bride* for Howard Hawks from a script by Charles Lederer, nephew of his old friend Marion Davies, Leonard Spiegelgass and Hagar Wilde. Ann Sheridan would be his co-star. He would play a French Army captain, Henri Rochard, who is unable to obtain entry to the United States after World War II except under the heading of war bride. According to Hawks, Grant was apparently pleased to note that much of his performance would be spent in drag, with a large, dark-brown wig cut in page-boy style.

En route to Germany, Cary had long discussions with Howard Hawks at Shepperton Studios. He acted out a scene in his WAC uniform, but Hawks, always cold, hard and detached, though with a wry, sharp sense of humour, was not amused. He told Cary to set aside his effeminate gestures; he must not pretend to be a woman, but must walk and talk like a man. Cary protested that this was ridiculous: no one could possibly mistake an aggressively male figure in a skirt; much of the comedy sprang from the misunderstanding, and this approach would destroy the movie. Hawks won. His macho hang-up about homosexuality was such that he would not tolerate even an inkling of gay behaviour on any of his sets, even when, as in this instance, the script unquestionably called for it. As for Cary, he knew that his large female audience so completely believed in him as a sex symbol that no matter what he did he would run no risk of undermining his reputation.

England was suffering from post-war austerity, although Cary and Betsy were scarcely aware of it, housed as they were at an apartment in Grosvenor Square. They met Ann Sheridan for many pleasant dinners and lunches, immediately drawn to her warm, outgoing good nature. The three of them needed to keep their spirits up: the weather was depressingly dark and rainy. When they reached Heidelberg, via Paris, the weather was worse than ever. Ann Sheridan was distraught because her luggage and that of her secretary had been removed by customs officials at the French–German border while Miss Sheridan was asleep in her compartment. She was accused of smuggling, and it took considerable effort for Twentieth Century-Fox to prove that she had been mistaken for another passenger. One of the earliest days of work, in driving rain, involved Miss Sheridan driving a motorcycle with Cary as her sidecar passenger. She had assumed a double would be used, but Hawks, tough as always, told her she must master the thirty-four-horsepower, 800-pound contraption herself. She was petrified. To make her feel more comfortable, Cary helped former German paratrooper Hans Seidel to train her. At last, Ann took Cary for his first rehearsal drive. But she was hysterical, shaken badly by the jolting and vibration, and to her horror ran over a goose. Upset by the blood, she burst into tears. As she continued though, the sight of Cary bumping up and down in the sidecar made her burst into laughter. She began to relax and enjoy the experience.

Working in Germany was difficult. Not only was the weather cold and depressing, it was almost impossible to get a decent meal and the hotel in Heidelberg was inferior. Conditions were no better in Zuzenhausen, a fifteenth-century village with tiny, winding cobbled streets and stone houses. The cast, Cary included, had to eat meals off tin plates, and, when the make-up man suddenly disappeared, they had to paint their own faces. Betsy tried to cook for Cary on a hot plate in their room, but the result was hopeless; she burned the food and her attempts at omelettes were disastrous. At weekends, in desperation, Cary and Betsy took local planes across the border into Switzerland or to Strasbourg in France, where they could at last indulge in expensive good food, especially Cary's favourite pâté de foie gras. It was difficult to return on Mondays to recommence the unpleasant job of making the picture, especially in a country whose people sustained many bitter resentments against Americans. Ann Sheridan was Cary's chief consolation; no matter how unpleasant the conditions, she was eternally joyful, spunky, and full of life.

But Cary apparently either ate some contaminated food, or perhaps indulged in an unfortunate romantic adventure, because in late October, after about a month of shooting, he began to experience symptoms of infectious hepatitis. He felt ill, lost much of his energy and his appetite, and was frequently sick. When the doctor pressed the area of the liver, he felt pain in his abdomen. He began to have attacks of vomiting and diarrhoea, and went into hospital for a series of tests. The doctors found that his lymph nodes were enlarged and that he had developed antibodies. He insisted with great courage on continuing work. There was a scene in which he had to ride into a haystack on a motorcycle; it was suffocating in there, and he began to feel faint. When the crew pulled him out, he was breathing with difficulty and his skin had a yellowish tinge. He asked if he could be rushed to London, where he could get the best care. Hawks agreed; he went for tests at a Harley Street specialist's, and the picture closed down. Then Hawks fell ill with an outbreak of hives all over his body that was probably caused by nervous stress.

Betsy nursed Cary through several weeks of illness. An old friend, Pamela Churchill, who had been married to Winston Churchill's son Randolph, insisted that Cary move into her apartment, where she could help take care of him with the aid of day and night nurses. Betsy Drake was supposed to return to Hollywood before Christmas, to star in a film which Cary had more or less forced Twentieth Century-Fox to make for her. He had insisted the studio buy for her the 1931 stage success *The Band Wagon*, co-written by Howard Dietz and Arthur Schwartz. In the film script by Jay Dratler and others, a fallen film star finds an obscure young girl and pushes her into success on the stage. Under his tutelage, she learns to sing and dance; the story resembled *A Star Is Born* and *Citizen Kane*. William Powell was to play the fallen film idol (a part originally written for Clifton Webb), and Betsy Drake the ambitious girl who turns out to be his daughter.

Betsy hadn't wanted to make the film. She had hated herself in *Every Girl Should Be Married* and was so shocked by her appearance on the screen, and what she felt to be her terrible acting, that, after the first private preview, she had told Cary she wanted only to return to New York and the stage. She was convinced she wasn't photogenic and now she was going to play in a picture that called for her to sing and dance. She could do neither; she was bright and knew instinctively that the result of making the film would be public humiliation. But she was so anxious to please Cary, and perhaps so afraid of his extraordinary will and his temper if crossed, that she fell victim to his ambitions for her and agreed to go ahead with the project.

She returned to Los Angeles with a heavy spirit, not at all happy about leaving Cary behind in London when he was so unwell. He followed her later on a Dutch ship, the *Volendam*, through the Panama Canal. Meanwhile, at the outset of 1949, she began shooting *The Band Wagon*, retitled *Dancing In the Dark*. Incredibly, in view of Cary's dislike of him, and the unfortunate circumstances of making *The Bachelor and the Bobbysoxer*, the ex-vaudevillian producer, George Jessel, chose Irving Reis to direct the film. It takes no feat of the imagination to visualise Cary's fury and Betsy's despair at this selection. Moreover, Jessel, an ex-friend of the studio chief, Darryl F. Zanuck, had wanted either June Haver or Carole Landis to star in the film; both were capable of singing and dancing and were gorgeous, voluptuous women of the kind Jessel favoured.

Furious at being forced to use Betsy Drake, Jessel set about humiliating her with extraordinary cruelty from the beginning. He ordered the dance director Seymour Felix to push Betsy relentlessly through various dance routines which she broke off finally in tears of hopeless disappointment. There was no way she could reach Cary on his ship to tell him what she was going through. For long periods he was out of reach of all communication. There was a line in the script, "I walk like a duck," which she refused to speak. So many people had told her that was one of her problems. Her self-consciousness over her splay-footed perambulations reached a peak. Jessel came on the set and insisted she speak the line. She still would not. That night, she appeared with Jessel on Louella Parsons' radio show. Jessel turned on her in fury and told her she was acting unprofessionally and disgracefully by not following the script. To Louella's astonishment, Betsy, in an unprecedented burst of rage, condemned Jessel out of hand. There had never been an incident like this, in which two guests on a radio show tore at each other while the host sat helplessly by, making a feeble attempt to referee. And those who heard the broadcast were amazed to discover that the mousey Betsy Drake could be very dangerous when crossed. She had a steel will underneath all her seeming weakness and subservience, and the horrible experience of making *Dancing In the Dark* slowly but surely hardened her.

After weeks of monotonous voyaging, Cary arrived in Los Angeles on April 7. He was some thirty pounds lighter, his skin still a yellowish shade under the tan. He looked terrible and Betsy, worn out by the long and depressing filming of *Dancing In the Dark*, was herself unwell. She told him of her ordeal, but there was little he could do at this stage. Later that year, and early the next, the cruel reviews poured in, critics stating repeatedly that it was shocking to think that Twentieth Century-Fox, which had

Betty Grable and June Haver under contract, would have chosen to cast in a musical an actress who was uniquely incapable of performing in one. Almost every time a column item appeared on the film there was another vicious and heartless stab at the unfortunate actress. The critiques only confirmed what Betsy had thought about herself.

Understandably, Cary and Betsy withdrew from the Hollywood scene. They declined invitations to parties and tried to make a life together at her apartment and his house. Betsy in some ways grated on his nerves: she was untidy and clumsy, and Cary as always was fanatically neat. She was an obsessive reader, who would pile books up everywhere, even on her bed and in the back of her car. Books meant nothing to him; his interests remained chiefly in the field of old-time vaudeville, and his friends from the old days annoyed Betsy as much as they had annoyed Barbara Hutton. It was almost wilfully perverse of him to have entered into a relationship with a woman with whom he had almost nothing in common. What could they talk about in the evenings? Virtually nothing. The pairing of a tortured, disturbed, but elegant and graceful matinée idol and a self-conscious introspective bluestocking seemed doomed to failure from the beginning.

Nineteen forty-nine was in many ways a dreary year. *I Was a Male War Bride* was recommenced that summer with scenes that had been shot in Germany more or less efficiently matched up with new studio work. But the spirit had temporarily gone out of Cary; he had lost interest in the picture, and the well-known weakening and depressive effects of hepatitis weighed him down. He tried to cheer himself up by appearing in a radio series, starting on July 1, of *Mr. Blandings Builds His Dream House*. His friend and director H. C. Potter was a guest on the programme discussing the theme with Cary before the studio audience. Frances Robinson played the Myrna Loy role of Jim Blandings' wife and later Betsy took it over, and also, surprisingly, contributed several scripts. In the second half of 1949, following a week of tests at Johns Hopkins Hospital in Baltimore, Cary began to improve. He gave up trying to run the remnants of the Frank Vincent Agency and his own career, and signed with MCA on August 5. That relieved him of much pressure, and his enthusiasm returned. From complaining about Betsy's obsession with books, he even started to examine them, discovering that her serendipitous mind had its own appeal. He would pick up a volume on spiders or on astronomy or mysticism and begin dipping into it, expertly seizing on elements in it without the bother of reading the work as a whole. He stored up all kinds of odd, entertaining information, and instead of resenting her superior intelligence he started to appreciate the fact that Betsy had a wide-ranging number of interests. Bit by bit, she began to gain, if not an upper hand, certainly an almost equal one. She was earning his respect at last.

A new friendship was formed in 1949. The couple got to know the handsome and dashing, fiery and opinionated young star Stewart Granger, who had made a great success in such entertaining films as *The Man in Grey, Caesar and Cleopatra*, and *Saraband For Dead Lovers*. He had just come to the United States to make *King Solomon's Mines*, a romantic story of adventure set in Africa.

Granger says:

> I was fitting clothes for *King Solomon's Mines* and was testing for the leading role in *Quo Vadis*, a part which later went to Robert Taylor. As I entered the MGM commissary, Cary was paying his bill. He gave me a warm smile. He said, without any preamble, "Would you like to come and have lunch with me?" I knew he was sexually attracted to me. He never laid a hand on me. But I knew.

Instead of lunching in the commissary each day, Granger was surprised to find himself having his meals at Cary's house. He mentioned the severe rationing of post-war England, of which, of course, Cary was aware. He asked, naïvely, how much butter, sugar, beef, lamb, bacon and eggs he would be allowed in the United States. Cary laughingly informed him there was no such thing as rationing in America, and hadn't been, except in a very minimal sense, during World War II. Cary drove the bedazzled Granger to Farmer's Market, where the produce was piled high, and stood by grinning while Granger snapped up all those goods that were rationed in England. Despite the fact that the Beverly Hills Hotel offered fine cuisine, Granger stored these newly acquired treasures in the refrigerator in his suite as though they were diamonds from Tiffany's.

Granger remembers how Betsy Drake was always concocting extremely complicated dishes for dinner from a variety of gourmet cookbooks.* When all three went out to dinner, sometimes with Granger's girlfriend Jean Simmons and with another friend, the twenty-three-year-old actor Richard Anderson, Cary showed his tightness with money. Granger recalls:

> One evening, as we finished dinner, I called for the check. Cary demurred. I insisted; but he wouldn't take no for an answer. He took up the check himself. I thought, "These stories about him are wrong. He's going to pay."
>
> He examined the check carefully. And then, instead of taking out the money, he said to me, "Well, you had the wine and such-and-such a dish," trying to figure what my separate payment would be. I was furious, and I dragged the check out of his hand and paid for everyone. He was furious. Very upset indeed.

Later, when Granger became engaged to Jean Simmons, he told Cary he was looking for a diamond engagement ring. Cary took him to the safe in his house. Granger was astonished to find that the safe was:

full of the damnedest things you've ever seen in your life:

---

* Hitchcock told Charles Higham that he satirised Betsy's culinary mishaps in his film *Frenzy* (1972).

diamond cufflinks, diamond rings, gold cigarette cases
. . . all sorts of things. He had one diamond ring which
he was prepared to sell me himself! It was a four-carat
ring, and I wanted a six- to eight-carat. He would have
sold it to me for what he paid for it. He wasn't trying to
make money off it. As it turned out, he introduced me
to the diamond merchant who sold me the size of ring I
wanted. But it had a big flaw, or rather a chasm. I should
have bought Cary's ring. It was beautiful.

Towards the end of 1949, Betsy Drake appeared in *The
Second Woman* at United Artists. It was a thriller about an
architect, played by Robert Young, whose Rebecca-like first
wife has died, and whose presence haunts his second wife,
played by Miss Drake. The architect's life is threatened, his
favourite horse is killed, his rose-bushes are poisoned and
his favourite painting defaced. It was not a satisfactory film.
Robert Young was struggling with a drinking problem, and
Betsy was disturbed by the sequence involving a horse: she
had a terror of them. Yet at the time, Cary suddenly
discovered a long-lost interest in riding and began trying,
without success, to overcome Betsy's fears.

The couple decided after much discussion and argument
that they should be married that December. Together, they
had a tendency to over-intellectualise and discuss things
too much. And this in itself complicated their feelings for
each other and delayed the wedding. They were both so
insecure, and then there was the fact, hidden by her on
studio orders, that Betsy had been married before. She
had had a disastrous marital relationship with a poor and
struggling young actor with whom she had shared a coldwater apartment in Manhattan, and was afraid of being
hurt again.

12

Even before *The Second Woman* was completed, Betsy began shooting a comedy, *Pretty Baby*, at Warners. She was cast as a young woman in an advertising agency who, in order to get ahead, pretends to have a child which she names after her boss, played by Edmund Gwenn. The comedy sprang from her attempts to conceal the fact that the doll she carried around with her in the streets and subways and offices of New York was not a real infant.

She broke off shooting for two days at Christmas to fly with Cary in a plane piloted by Howard Hughes to Phoenix, Arizona, where the simple wedding-ceremony took place at the desert home of Mr. and Mrs. Sterling Hebbard; Hebbard was an old friend of Cary's lawyer Will Hinckle and rich in Arizona real-estate. The Reverend Stanley M. Smith presided. Hughes was best man and Betsy had no bridesmaid, an indication of how remote the couple had become from all Cary's friends in Hollywood. Test pilot C. A. Shoop and Phoenix attorney Richard Mason were witnesses. As with the marriage to Barbara Hutton, there was no honeymoon. Nor did the couple even stay at the house that night. Hughes flew them back to Los Angeles, and next day Betsy Drake appeared with her fake baby in a scene shot on a subway train during the rush hour.

Ten days later, Cary began work at MGM on Richard Brooks' *Crisis*. The tough, skilful Brooks, who would soon be a close friend, had made his mark with the admirable screenplay of *Crossfire*, based upon his novel, *The Brick Foxhole*. The story had been altered from a homosexual theme to the more acceptable one of anti-Semitism in the

Army. Brooks, having written a fine script for John Huston's film *Key Largo*, signed a contract with Metro as writer-director. However, his first two scripts were directed and rewritten by other people, and he was about to quit because the terms of his contract had not been satisfied. He was at work on *Crisis* when he went to the racetrack on a Saturday and was introduced to Cary, whose passion for horse-racing had begun in the 1930s. Cary mistook Brooks for Jack Webb, later famous for his television series *Dragnet*. When Brooks identified himself, Cary said he was enjoying reading the *Crisis* screenplay. He was thinking about making the picture.

Brooks told him that he was determined to direct the script himself. Cary asked him, "How do you get along with people?" Brooks replied, "I don't know." And Cary said, characteristically, "Well, I guess what you don't know about directing, I do."

Cary liked Brooks at once: the man was honest, straightforward and decent, and he had the look of someone who could direct a picture well. Cary went to Dore Schary, the MGM boss, saying that he wouldn't make the picture unless Brooks directed it. That settled the matter. Cary was cast as Dr. Eugene Ferguson, a brain surgeon who is kidnapped while on vacation in an unnamed South American country and is forced to perform a dangerous and difficult operation on a Juan Peron-like dictator, Raoul Ferrago, played by José Ferrer. Ferguson is told by a rival junta to kill the dictator, but instead he saves the man's life. The story of medical conscience versus political ethics was an interesting one, and was intelligently developed by Brooks. Nancy Davis, later Mrs. Ronald Reagan, was supposed to play the role of the doctor's wife. But Dore Schary was not pleased with the choice and decided to cast Paula Raymond instead. In a letter to Roy Moseley, Reagan has stated how grateful he was to Cary for his kindness and support to Nancy, wanting her to have the part and soothing her spirits when she lost it. The former President wrote: "Cary took her to lunch at the studio cafeteria and very kindly talked away her disappointment and complimented her on her acting. He told her she did something [on the screen] many actors didn't know how to do. She *listened* to the other actor."

The shooting was marred by violent arguments. According to Richard Brooks, the cameraman, Ray June, who had for years wanted to be a director, insisted on usurping Brooks' powers. On the first day of shooting, there was a cumbersome, difficult crane shot, with the camera mounted on a wheeled crane travelling on metal tracks. Brooks was nervous that June would defy him in the composition of the shot by moving the crane in an unauthorised direction. He walked beside the crane, monitoring June. Then, whether accidentally or deliberately, a member of the crew pushed the crane over Brooks' feet. Cary shouted to the man, "You ran over his foot! Take him to a hospital." Brooks said, "The hospital is next to the funeral parlour on the lot. If I leave this stage for five minutes, there'll be another director on this movie." Cary replied, "There is *not* going to be another director. I want you to go there, because first of all, the insurance people will require it. Second, you probably broke some toes, and you'd better get them attended to. And thirdly, if they throw you off the movie, I'll walk." All through the conversation, Brooks was hopping on one foot and there was blood all over his shoe, but amazingly nothing was broken. His foot was bandaged, it was dunked in an ice-bucket back on the sound stage and he continued till the end of the day.

Cary was in a nervous mood as *Crisis* began. Perhaps because of the strain of beginning his third marriage, perhaps because Betsy was having her own problems at Warner, he began drinking, more heavily than he had in years, and he twice smashed his car in collisions in Beverly Hills. Now he had to go to work in a cab. He was in danger of losing his licence, but strings were pulled and it was not suspended. Paula Raymond, his leading lady, reports that shooting *Crisis* was an ordeal for all concerned.

This was Richard Brooks' first assignment as a director, and he knew nothing about the camera. He was having people go off screen to the right and coming back on the right, and this wasn't the correct way to direct. He was so frustrated, and I could understand why, he screamed at everyone; he even screamed at me. I would tell him to calm down. He screamed at the grips, the cameraman, the electricians. He might have been forgiven, except that he never screamed at Cary Grant. That was much resented. Brooks was a darling guy; I understood that with all that massive responsibility he had to react the way he did.

Cary celebrated his forty-sixth birthday on the set. He was shown cutting the cake with Paula Raymond. The caption in one magazine read, "Paula: When you invited me up for a piece, I thought . . ." Cary was furious, outraged. He wanted to sue the magazine, because he felt that the caption, which was harmless enough, suggested that there was an affair between them, and Betsy Drake would be upset. Paula Raymond couldn't believe he would react in this manner and refused to join Cary in the suit. When he phoned her to ask her, she said, "Cary, how can you sue a sense of humour?" He snapped, "Goodbye," and hung up. He did not forgive her.

Cary had little political rapport with José Ferrer, who had been decidedly left-wing in politics and who would soon name many names to the House Un-American Activities Committee in an attempt to clean up his political record, but he enjoyed working with him. Richard Brooks remembers, "Cary and José would often improvise, come up with touches to enhance the scenes. They were inventor actors. They managed to create the impression of normal or haphazard dialogue through their skilful handling of my lines." However, Ferrer's intensely anti-Fascist views gave an added edge to his portrayal of the Peron-like central figure. Betsy's problems at Warner continued. She was much disliked there: as early as December 5, twenty days before her wedding, the studio's legal chief, Roy Obringer, and the production chief Steve Trilling, were discussing her difficult behaviour in memoranda. Trilling noted that Betsy was "trying to throw her weight around, possibly supported by Grant", and later there were some troublesome days of shooting in which she was unfairly blamed for the problems. She hated film making more and more. And the contrived humours of *Pretty Baby*, the humdrum directing of Bretaigne Windust and the uninspiring presence of her fellow actors, Jack Carson and Dennis Morgan, left her frustrated and irritable. The truth was that not only did she lack the timing, skill and colouring necessary for high-comedy acting, but the routine films she was appearing in were an insult to her intelligence. The hard-working troupers who played with her sensed her superiority complex and resented it. It wasn't her fault that in every sense, both as Mrs. Cary Grant and as a would-be star, she was miscast.

Towards the end of *Crisis*, Cary fell ill with a recurrence of hepatitis. He apparently hadn't followed the rules of abstinence from alcohol and modest intakes of fatty foods. The shooting ended on June 15. It had been strenuous as Cary had had to learn the techniques of surgical procedure for the grim operating-room sequences. He had studied with a surgeon at night, attended operations, and interviewed nursing staff (ironically, since he was in hospital himself from June 17 for two weeks). The result was one of his most authentic and carefully moulded performances.

On August 1, Howard Hughes offered Cary a property he had recently bought, the Terence Rattigan play *O Mistress Mine*, which had been a vehicle for Alfred Lunt and Lynn Fontanne on the stage. Hughes wanted Cary to play the part of a British cabinet minister in charge of munitions during the London Blitz. But Cary hesitated; he was sick, bored, fatigued and he was not anxious to work. Hughes was unable to talk him into proceeding. At the same time, Cary's plans to work with Alexander Korda were finally and irrevocably called off. He and Betsy Drake remained in almost complete isolation. "We never saw them," his close friend Johnny Maschio says. "They gave no parties.

And Cary and she just never went out. We never knew why. None of us in Cary's circle ever got to know Betsy Drake."

During that period Richard Brooks often went to the house to visit Cary and Betsy. When Brooks made his film *Elmer Gantry*, many years later, Cary (who had studied the subject) would prove to be extremely helpful on the subject of evangelism, and Brooks to this day is everlastingly grateful to him.

That August, the seemingly interminable matter of investigations into Hughes continued in Washington. Hughes would overreact to the charges made, and call Cary at all hours of the day or night to discuss them. He had established a code name, Kato, which those in his immediate circle were to use if they wished to reach him urgently and much of Cary's time was spent trying to soothe Hughes' nerves.

In December 1950, Howard Hughes flew Cary, Stewart Granger and Jean Simmons to Tucson, where Granger and Simmons were married.

Depressed by the reviews of her first two movies, Betsy Drake continued to talk about leaving the screen. Meantime, Cary began work on his second film for Twentieth Century-Fox, *People Will Talk*. Few films were more accurately named, since the script by the director Joseph L. Mankiewicz was among the most prolix on record. The characters were always delivering speeches of a highly verbose and pretentious character.

Cary played Noah Praetorius, an obstetrician, who falls in love with an unmarried woman who is about to have a baby and has tried to commit suicide. It is easy to see how Cary would be drawn to such a story in view of his own history. The premise provided a springboard for a comedy-drama in which the crusading doctor fights against the repressive attitudes, prejudices and traditions of a university medical school. The implicit critique of the establishment appealed to Cary, who disliked the complacency and inefficiency of conventional medicine and embraced homeopathy.

There was another parallel between the story and real

life. Although Cary had shied away from any involvement in critiques of Joe McCarthy, and although he remained opposed to Communism and had named names, he now became disturbed by the invasions of privacy, prejudicial charges, and disruption of family life, of the House Un--American Activities Committee. Mankiewicz used the film as a platform to criticise these matters. Betsy Drake, with her intellectual interests, also approved the script, and it was a disappointment to her that Jeanne Crain, and not she, was cast as Annabel Higgins, the pregnant woman in the story.

Betsy Drake filled her spare time writing more scripts for the *Mr. Blandings Builds His Dream House* radio series and then, thanks to Cary, took over as co-star. It says much for her determination that she was able to master the specialised craft of radio drama and, of course, her short-comings as a screen actress were not so evident in her radio performances. Her greatest asset, seldom commented on at the time, was her husky but resonant and expressive speaking voice, which was notably revealed in a fine and harrowing version of Alfred Hitchcock's thriller about a mass murderer, *Shadow of a Doubt*. She spoke the part with considerably more expertise than the rather shallow and uninteresting (and vocally thin) Teresa Wright had done in the film version. By contrast Cary was unsatisfactory in the central role of Uncle Charlie, and in fact his vocal inadequacies were sharply exposed by radio. His limited range of voice and his habit of gabbling his lines in strangely exaggerated Cockney ruined the authenticity of his performance on the non-visual medium.

He was not much more effective in the CBS version of *My Favorite Wife* that also came out at the time. Cary was now among the highest paid of all Hollywood stars, earning $300,000 for *People Will Talk*. Meanwhile, Betsy remained unemployed and unbankable in films, disappointed that she had been shelved by the industry. The only way to save her film career was for Cary to co-star with her.

Betsy was concerned with the problems of homeless

children and would one day specialise in them as a psychiatrist and would write a novel about the unhappy offspring of divided parents. She became interested in appearing with Cary in *Room For One More*, adapted from a book she liked by Anna Perrott Rose. She would play Anna Rose, a naïve, outgoing girl who, along with various human or animal waifs and strays, adopts an unwanted daughter of divorced parents, gradually weaning her away from her mistrustful and unhappy attitude to life. Later, she also adopts a handicapped boy. Cary would play "Poppy" Rose, Anna's much-embattled husband. In view of the character of the film, and the evident sincerity with which the Grants embarked on it, it is curious to reflect that they themselves did not adopt children. Such an adoption would have cemented their marriage, and perhaps given them the fulfilment they failed to find in each other. Whatever the reasons, and they may only have been dislike of responsibility and fear of being tied down, the Grants remained childless even in the adoptive sense of the word.

Room For One More started on August 16, 1951, and ended on October 18. At the end-of-shooting party, Cary said to the co-author of the script, Melville Shavelson, "So this picture cost four mil. It's not much of a movie, but it's something I wanted to do for me and Betsy." Shavelson comments: "He wanted to change the image of Cary Grant, from the ultra-sophisticated, too-rich-whatever, to a family man, which he always wanted to be." Years later, Shavelson would renew his working relationship with Cary under very different, and quite disturbing, circumstances.

In November, the magazine *Motion Picture* published damaging statements against several stars. These were unfounded: Cesar Romero, Joseph Cotten and Dinah Shore were charged with having black ancestry and Scott Brady and Dan Dailey were accused of being drunks. It was also said, absurdly, that "Jimmy Stewart didn't get married for so long because he was the type of male with no great interest in the opposite sex . . ." Nothing could have been further from the truth: despite his skinny, drawn-out appearance and apparent lack of physical strength, Stewart was probably the best-known and most coveted Casanova in Hollywood, at least in his younger days. The article went on, referring to certain stars' lack of interest in women, "Cary Grant heard this one about himself, too, although no one who knows Cary can exactly figure out why." Surprisingly, none of the victims of this piece sued the magazine. And Mike Connolly of the *Hollywood Reporter* compounded the felony by reprinting the piece in a condensed form.

At the end of 1951, Cary once again united with Howard Hawks; the occasion was a film entitled *Darling, I Am Growing Younger*, which was to become the entertaining *Monkey Business*. The screenplay was written by Ben Hecht, whose impassioned support of the recently formed state of Israel had drawn Cary's financial and personal backing, Cary's old friend Charles Lederer, Marion Davies' nephew, and I. A. L. Diamond, later the excellent co-author of scripts with Billy Wilder.

Monkey Business was a daring farce, made in defiance of the Motion Picture Code. Cary played Professor Barnaby Fulton, a research chemist working on a formula to revitalise the exhausted tissues of the human body. Applying the formula, he renders himself young again, along with his wife, played by Ginger Rogers, and several other individuals in his clinic. Grant's performance foreshadowed his later interest in rejuvenation. He had seldom been better; his manic playing of a now "teenaged" academic, jazzing around, contained more than a hint of his own middle-aged distaste at the mindless enthusiasms of adolescents. The script exposed the foolishness of 1950s American popular culture, which was sweeping post-war Europe. The film satirised the American obsession with youthfulness, showing the absurdity of impossibly trying to preserve it. Grant's acting was effortlessly assured, carefully stylised and timed.

Neither *People Will Talk, Room For One More*, nor *Monkey Business* succeeded at the box-office, and Cary Grant began to feel that his time in films had passed. He was out of step with the 1950s; he had no rapport with new idols of the screen such as James Dean and Marlon Brando. Years later, he said to an interviewer, "That was the period of blue jeans, dope addicts, and Method, and nobody cared about comedy at all." It wasn't true, of course: several comedies of the period were successful, but *Monkey Business* was altogether too sophisticated and satirical a work to appeal to the mass public. It exposed too much; it didn't pander to mass tastes.

Cary poured much of his frustration into a renewed foster-fatherhood: Lance Reventlow, now a good-looking sixteen-year-old, returned to Hollywood with his mother, and Cary found a home for them in Beverly Hills. The house had belonged to Irene Mayer Selznick, who had moved to New York following the great success of her production of *A Streetcar Named Desire*. Cary loved the boy, and the feeling was returned. He helped him with his schooling, assisted him in problems with his fellow pupils, sat up late at night tutoring him for exams, and encouraged him to develop his athletic skills.

In a last-ditch effort to find a popular comedy, Cary embarked on *Dream Wife*, for MGM, with Dore Schary as producer and Sidney Sheldon as director, with a script by Sheldon and two other writers. Cary would play Clemson Reade, a businessman married to a State Department official whose concern over an oil crisis threatens the marriage. The comedy sprang from Reade's interest in an attractive Bukistan princess, who is a specialist in the techniques of pleasing men.

Cary was not well when he began making the picture. Sheldon recalls that he had had yet another recurrence of hepatitis, and was thin, drawn, and pale, with a yellowish cast to his skin, but he refused to wear make-up. He fought with Sheldon from morning to night. When he saw the set of a Bukistan palace, he snapped at the writer-director, "If I had known that set was going to look like this, I never would have agreed to make the picture." When a tiny scene was changed, he snarled, again, that if he had known the alteration would be made, he wouldn't have done *Dream Wife*. He was angry when Sheldon forbade him to kick a little boy in an airport who was bothering him. "I told Cary, 'You can't do that,' " Sheldon says. " 'The audience will hate you.' He replied, 'Well, I want to do it.' And he did it. I wasn't even watching him, because I knew I wouldn't use the scene. And then we got into an argument because I wasn't watching him do it."

In another sequence, in which Cary was discussing the oil crisis with Deborah Kerr, playing his wife, he spoke the lines with such excessively solemn emphasis that both Miss Kerr and Sheldon burst out laughing. Time and again, the scene was attempted and then ruined because they could not stop themselves from bursting into peals of merriment. A love scene with Deborah Kerr bored Cary so much that he raised and lowered his eyebrows like Groucho Marx. Sheldon begged him not to grimace. Cary promised he would co-operate and then repeated the mannerism. When Sheldon laughed uncontrollably, Cary turned around and said to him, "Sidney, if you're going to do that, I can't go on with the scene." Sheldon says the scene was dropped.

Grant's fussiness was displayed again and again. He objected even to such details as the type of collar he wore and when Walter Pidgeon appeared in a suit of the same cut and colour as his own, he announced that he would change into another, holding up shooting for hours. He had, of course, already arranged for Pidgeon to wear the duplicate suit.

During the making of *Dream Wife*, Betsy Drake began hypnotising Cary, to cure him of smoking and other habits that she disliked. Melville Shavelson remembered that Betsy made a recording on tape in which she said, over and over again, "Cary Grant, you are the greatest actor in the world. Cary Grant, you are the greatest actor in the world. Cary Grant, you are the greatest actor in the world. Cary Grant, you have nothing to worry about. Cary Grant, stop worrying," over and over again. By building his ego, Betsy obtained at last a degree of power in the relationship. Cary said later: "Betsy planted a post-hypnotic suggestion that I would stop smoking. We went to sleep, and the next morning when I reached for a cigarette, just as I always did, I instantly felt nauseated. I didn't take another one that day, and I haven't since."

Although he was cured of smoking, Cary was not much happier, and he and Betsy decided to have a holiday. Early in 1952, weary of Hollywood and feeling that the future offered little, Cary sailed with her on a long freighter trip to the Orient. In Tokyo, he announced at a press conference on February 6, 1953, that he was annoyed by the treatment of Charlie Chaplin, who had been accused of being a Communist and was forbidden by the US Department of Justice to return to America. The next day he and Betsy left for Hong Kong.

During Cary's absence, a shocking incident occurred in Hollywood. According to one of Howard Hughes' aides and closest friends, Hughes was arrested in a Hollywood motel, where the manager had burst into his room and found him in bed with a young male prostitute. He was brought into the local precinct, finger-printed and held in a cell for further questioning. Hughes' aide says: "It could have been the end of Howard's career. But somehow the whole thing was dropped. It was never investigated further; there is no telling how much money changed hands, it could have been as much as a million." Hughes, still predominantly heterosexual, continued to indulge in reckless adventures of this kind, apparently certain that he could buy off anyone who might possibly threaten to expose him.

On the Grants' return to Hollywood, Cary was offered the starring role of Norman Maine, the drunken, fading actor who adopts a young and struggling singer, in George Cukor's remake of *A Star is Born*. The script was written by Cary's old friend from his New York days, Moss Hart, who had Cary in mind. Hart had tried to persuade him to appear in his 1946 version of Laura Z. Hobson's bestselling novel, *Gentlemen's Agreement*, but Cary had refused the role of a magazine reporter who poses as a Jew to expose anti-Semitism in American society on the grounds that he was not only Jewish himself but looked Jewish, and that therefore the audience would not accept him in the part. Hart had not resented this decision, understanding the basis of it very well, and instead the role had gone to the admirable Gregory Peck.

Hart had rewritten the original Alan Campbell–Dorothy Parker script of *A Star is Born* with many characteristics of Cary: his early drinking, a feature of the original character of Maine, was counterbalanced by the comic elements and the bitter humour of Cary's nature, and the matinée idol once played by Fredric March had now become a more complex character, moody, introspective, filled with anger and seized by fits of depression. Cary may have recognised too much of himself in the character Hart had so sharply drawn. George Cukor, witty and opinionated, invited Cary to his house several times to read the part in his ornamental garden, while Katharine Hepburn and Greta Garbo swam in the pool at the same time. Cary was characteristically skittish, changing his mind almost from hour to hour, but it is doubtful that he ever seriously entertained the idea of playing in the picture. The film emerged as Cukor's masterpiece, with James Mason as Norman Maine and Judy Garland in the performance of her career as the up-and-coming Vicki Lester.

During Cary's and Betsy's Far Eastern journey, on a brief stop in Hong Kong, Alfred Hitchcock had flown a script to them, with an urgent request that Cary respond quickly. The screenplay was by John Michael Hayes, and was based upon a novel by David Dodge. The title was *To Catch a Thief*. In view of Cary's dismissal from Fairfield Grade and Secondary School for theft, it is possible that this was one of Hitchcock's sadistic little jokes. *To Catch a Thief* was the story of John Robie, known as the Cat, a reformed jewel thief living in comfortable retirement on the Riviera. A series of burglaries takes place in Cannes, many of them carrying the Cat trademark of John Robie. In an attempt to clear his name, and capture the real criminal, Robie meets and falls in love with the wealthy heiress Frances Stevens.

This slight, not particularly intriguing, tale was enlivened by Hayes with much suggestive, witty and provocative dialogue, and offered Grant an ideal role as a debonair, cultivated and sophisticated crook who is untroubled by moral considerations and enjoys a hedonistic existence in the South of France. But Cary did not respond at once to Hitchcock's suggestion that he appear in the film, dodging immediate commitment with his usual coyness. During the period of his return to Hollywood, he had successive discussions on the matter with Paramount executives and with Hitchcock himself and for a time seemed to be leaning more towards doing a musical with Vera-Ellen.

Then, out of the blue, a tragic event temporarily removed all thoughts of making the film from his mind: he had been troubled for some time by the declining health of Dorothy di Frasso, whose extravagance had finally consumed her personal fortune, and she was worried by her accountants' reports, afraid that she might eventually have to sell her $350,000 worth of jewellery in order to give herself an income. (From an inheritance of $12 million, she was now worth less than $20,000.) She had never fully recovered from the death of Bugsy Siegel, and she was depressed over losing Gary Cooper who had briefly gone back to her. She developed a coronary condition that made her greatly aware of her mortality, and she was warned that under no circumstances must she drink another drop of alcohol as long as she lived, or indulge her appetite for rich food, or even have affairs with younger men. She complained to Cary and other friends that she was forced to live rather like "a turnip".

Even walking up stairs was forbidden to her. But nothing would stop the ebullient Countess going to parties night after night, against doctors' orders. Cary begged her to take things more easily. When she learned that Marlene Dietrich, a close friend, was to open in her one-woman stage show at the Sands Hotel in Las Vegas at the outset of 1954, she insisted upon going. Cary talked her out of taking the plane, so she took the more restful eight-hour train journey instead. He saw her off at the depot, then flew, without Betsy, to Las Vegas to keep watch over her and make sure that she didn't exert herself.

The Countess led the applause at Marlene's first night. She, Cary, Clifton Webb and other friends stayed at the home of Tom Douglas, show producer for El Rancho Vegas. The group attended a big party at El Rancho and another, next night, at the Sands where Dorothy collapsed after leaving the ladies' room. Gasping, she urged Marlene to give her her six pellets of nitroglycerine. She said to Cary, "You know, darling, I am going to die." He did his best to reassure her. Cary insisted she return to Los Angeles immediately, to her doctor. According to some reports, he drove her to the train; according to others, he accompanied her on the journey, along with Clifton Webb, the three taking adjoining compartments. Cary had already called her chiropractor Ruth B. Elwell in Encino, to urge her to give Dorothy treatment. The Countess boarded the train with luggage containing two pearl necklaces, two emerald hat-pins, a pair of diamond earrings, ruby clips, and gold compacts, the whole valued at almost a quarter of a million dollars. She hugged her mink coat about her, telling Clifton Webb she felt unnaturally cold, as though death were creeping up on her already. She lay down in her compartment under an expensive ermine wrap. As the train rolled through Pomona on its way to Los Angeles, Webb came in to wake her up, and was horrified to discover that she was dead. Cary insisted on accompanying the coffin to New York for burial in the Taylor family plot, and he and Betsy sat up all night, as Dorothy had wished, with other friends on the eve of the coffin's departure, paying tribute, in laughter and tears, to Dorothy's much loved memory. Cary and Betsy told the *Hollywood Reporter*'s Mike Connolly, "We did it because we remembered how much Dorothy hated being alone."

Perhaps to quell his grief, to find escape in an attractive

and undemanding project, Cary at last accepted Hitch-cock's long-standing invitation to make *To Catch a Thief*. The picture would start shooting on May 1 in Cannes; he and Betsy, who had now reached a watershed in a relationship marked by quarrels, would welcome the chance to spend the spring and summer weeks in the South of France. Cary's vanity was touched when Hitchcock told him he would be doing many of his own stunts, including running across roof-tops, and that he would be displaying his physique in swimming-trunks in several scenes. Although he told reporters he did nothing to get fit for the film, this was typical of his irreverent attitude to the press. He began to train, starting each day with push-ups (he could still manage twenty at a go), swimming laps in his pool, fast-walking and stretching and toning with a personal trainer. The result was that he rapidly lost a burgeoning double chin and suspicious signs of extra flesh at his waist-line – the dread of most leading men past forty. And even his hair needed little touching up with dye, attractively flecked as it was with hints of grey, and showing not an inkling of thinning.

While he was looking forward to this new experience, Cary was struck another blow. In his second bereavement in two months, he learned in late February of the sudden death of Bette, the former Mrs. Clifford Odets. He had grown very fond of her, and had much regretted the divorce. Beautiful, talented, and only twenty-four, she had had an abortive career as an actress, handicapped by her hyper-sensitive and easily unsettled nature. Someone had given her children two parakeets and she had grown fond of the birds, fondling their feathers. Suddenly, she came down with a severe fever and a stomach upset, and within a matter of days she was dead. Her condition was diagnosed as psittacosis, or parrot fever, a rare malady contracted from feathers. Cary wrote to Odets on February 26, 1954, explaining that he would have telephoned but that Odets must have had many matters needing his attention. Cary went on to say:

There's an unreality, delusion of disbelief, an incredulity that affects — perhaps even protects — the feelings of each of us when we lose, and miss, someone who has shared our emotions and thoughts, yet none of us can know the extent of another's inconsolability or the degree of his sadness . . .

Cary added that he was sending the note "as I would reach out a hand, to bring you sympathy and affection, dear friend". This heartfelt communication exactly expressed the more sensitive and considerate side of the actor's complex nature.

Cary and Betsy left for New York, sailing two weeks later than originally planned, on May 15, on the ill-fated *Andrea Doria* for Cherbourg. In Paris, at the Ritz, they met the Hitchcocks, and all four flew to Nice; they transferred to the Hotel Carlton at Cannes, where they were joined ten days later by Grace Kelly, who was cast as the wealthy and attractive Frances Stevens. Cary had enthusiastically agreed to Grace Kelly's selection as his leading lady. Impressed by her discipline, looks and poise, he had admired her in *Fourteen Hours* and in *High Noon*. When MGM proved reluctant to lend her out to Hitchcock, he is believed to have pulled strings behind the scenes to influence the studio to relent.

Cary and Betsy were delighted with Grace. Although she was exhausted from shooting a film about emerald mining, *Green Fire*, she was unfailingly charming, lacking in star temperament, and letter-perfect. Hitchcock, often testy, was greatly mollified by her and Cary, by the Carlton cuisine, and by visits to the Moulin des Mougins, a three-star restaurant only a short drive from the city. Good company, good food and fine wine were among the few palliatives that could soothe Hitchcock's savage brow. A sure sign that he was happy was when he would run his hands over his ample stomach and his face would flush deeply and he would blink heavily from his fleshy eye sockets.

Making *To Catch a Thief* was one of the most pleasant experiences of Cary Grant's life; James Spada, Grace Kelly's biographer, recalled that the Grants, the Hitchcocks, Grace and her lover Oleg Cassini would dine in the evening and at weekends in a variety of excellent small restaurants or would have a flutter at the local casinos. In a foreshadowing of the future, Grace became fascinated by Monaco, and in one sequence with Cary, Prince Rainier's palace is shown in the background of the shot. Many times Cary was impressed by her cool professionalism. In one sequence, the script had John Robie grappling with Frances Stevens and pushing her up against a wall. Cary's hands were so powerful that Grace had to massage her wrists, her face twisted in pain, between shots. But she never showed the slightest hint of complaint as she returned to play the sequence again and again.

There was one moment when Cary almost lost his façade of composure. Grace was a notoriously bad driver, and the twisting, tortuous roads of the three Corniches were hazardous to all but the most expert motorists. There was no way to fake or double her at the wheel; Hitchcock took a deep breath and instructed her to drive rapidly round the bends, with a sheer drop below and Cary in the passenger seat. In no time at all, Cary began to panic. He begged her to be more careful, but twice she nearly carried him over the edge. The second-unit director screamed to her to stop, and she did, with a grinding of brakes, on the edge of a precipice. It was a disturbing forewarning of her death in 1982 at the wheel of her own car.

A friendship formed between the Grants and Grace which would not be broken. Cary always admired control and excellence of deportment almost more than anything else. Grace personified both, and, with her gentle, considerate nature, she was a true friend.

To Catch a Thief was much liked by audiences. The reviews were good, the combination of the stars irresistible. Neither had looked as glamorous or performed with greater polish or more perfect timing. The director handled the superficial, glitzy material with impeccable skill.

In the wake of a disastrous *Room For One More, Monkey Business* and *Dream Wife*, Cary had felt his career was at an end. *To Catch a Thief* restored his confidence in himself and made him feel he could continue as an actor. But ironically, as so often happens in major careers, he followed this shrewd choice of subject with a blunder. He elected to appear in *The Pride and the Passion*, for the producer-director Stanley Kramer, the script of which had been written by Edna and Edward Anhalt based on the novel *The Gun* by C. S. Forester.

13

The Pride and the Passion would be ready for shooting in April 1956. Stanley Kramer, who had made his name as Hollywood's foremost liberal producer, spent many weeks in Spain laying the groundwork for this top-heavy, elephantine epic. Cary would play the role of a British Naval officer during the Napoleonic Wars who has to protect an enormous Spanish cannon from French seizure. Peace-loving, the officer wants only to obtain possession of the cannon and transport it to a safe place. But he encounters the passionate and committed Miguel, a Spanish guerrilla leader who is determined to have the cannon dragged across many miles of difficult terrain and aim it at the French garrison at Avila. Much of the story involved a gruelling cross-country journey followed by a spectacular siege.

It had taken considerable powers of persuasion for the determined Kramer to convince Cary that he should undertake the film. Cary decided to go ahead, despite his Cockney accent, when C. S. Forester, who had written the *Hornblower* series of books, told him he would be perfect in the part of the hero. Meanwhile, Cary, in Hollywood, had many meetings with Clifford Odets to discuss doing Thomas Mann's *Joseph and His Brethren* for Jerry Wald at Columbia (Odets commented in his diary on Cary's "evasive, non-committal commitment ... strange 'flirting'", and nothing came of this).

Cary was also juggling with another Odets project. He had discovered in the newspapers the story of Edgar Fassberg of Brooklyn, a suicide, who had been found in a hotel-room in Baltimore. When police questioned his widow, she told them that she had known him as Edward James Phillips, and had thought him to be a Brigadier-General in the Army Reserve, assigned as a pathologist at Governor's Island. She was horrified to learn that he had had at least eighteen aliases and had lived several lives at once. Cary sent a note to Odets on March 1, saying, *inter alia*, "Was it HIS body that was found? Perhaps he hid behind someone else even then . . . his final triumph." Cary was drawn to the idea of a life lived in deception, akin to his own.

At the same time he was flirting with the Thomas Mann subject, Cary was talking more seriously with his friend, the writer-director Melville Shavelson, about a story Betsy Drake had written, recounting the adventures of a couple living on a houseboat. Yet again, the material concerned adopting children. Cary was delighted with her script, seeing in it an opportunity for him to co-star with her again. He took the screenplay to Shavelson and Shavelson's partner, Jack Rose, at Paramount studios. One of the reasons he wanted them to film *Houseboat* was that he had liked their newly completed *The Seven Little Foys*, starring Bob Hope. It was based upon Eddie Foy's memoirs of the adventures of the celebrated vaudeville family act of the first two decades of the century, which had, of course, appeared with young Archie Leach in more than one theatre in the provinces.

Shavelson recalls that neither he nor his partner thought much of the scenario, finding it dull and lightweight. However, when Cary told him and Rose that Betsy Drake had written it, they felt compelled to lie that they loved it.

The truth was that they would have been quite happy to have worked with Cary Grant on any project, even the story of the world's last flea-circus proprietor, or of a man who built the Empire State Building out of matchsticks. At a second meeting with Cary, they asked him how much money Betsy would want to co-star. The question was accompanied by a sinking feeling: much as they liked her, they knew that she had no pull at the box-office. He told them she would want $30,000, a not inconsiderable sum at the time. They agreed, provided that Paramount agreed with the figure.*

Cary told Shavelson and Rose: "You must understand this: I will not commit to make the picture until the studio buys the story, because I don't want Betsy to know that they didn't buy it because they wanted it for itself, but only because I would agree to star in it."

This put the two men in an impossible position. After all, the truth was that no one would buy the story unless Cary Grant went with it. But in order to preserve a cordial relationship with Cary, they went to see the Paramount boss D. A. Duran, whom they called familiarly the "Tower of Jello" because of his alleged dislike of making decisions. He told them, "Okay. *Houseboat* isn't very good. How can we commit to this project and agree to buy the story and hire Betsy Drake to appear in it without knowing whether we'll get Cary Grant?" Shavelson reassured Duran that Cary would definitely do the picture; he just didn't want Betsy to know the manner in which the project had been put together. But Duran had his doubts.

Just as Cary was about to leave for Spain to make *The Pride and the Passion*, Duran turned up at the airport and cornered him, saying, without any beating about the bush, "Cary, unless you sign the contract, and make a commitment, we're going to tell Betsy everything." Cary panicked; reluctantly, he was forced to agree. As he flushed with irritation and anger, Duran, who was certainly not the "Tower of Jello" on this occasion, took the contract out of his pocket and handed it to Cary, who signed it in desperate haste before Betsy turned up to see him off.

Cary registered at the Castellana Hilton in Madrid, for meetings with Stanley Kramer. Sophia Loren had been cast opposite him in the picture. She was to play a passionate girl, Joanna, who falls in love with Cary's British Naval

---

* Cary had resumed his original role as agent, handling Betsy as his only client.

officer. Cary had not wanted her; he was interested in having Ava Gardner act the role. However, Stanley Kramer believed that this virtually unknown actress, whom he had admired in the film *Woman of the River*, was the only possible choice for the part. Cary remained sceptical; Miss Loren, who was sensitive and vulnerable despite her headstrong ambition and drive, was all too harshly aware of his attitude towards her when she appeared at the cocktail party at the Ritz designed to launch the production. It was a big affair, crowded with paparazzi and attended by many of the society figures of Madrid.

Perhaps because of his lack of interest in meeting Miss Loren, Cary broke his usual rule of punctuality and arrived over an hour late. Frank Sinatra, cast as the guerrilla fighter Miguel, upstaged him by turning up after an hour and a half. Cary deliberately failed to recognise Miss Loren's name, mixing her up with Gina Lollobrigida as he said, "How do you do, Miss Lolloloren, or is it Lorenigida? I can never get these Italian actresses' names straight." But he didn't talk to Miss Loren in a condescending or deliberately wounding manner. He spoke to her teasingly, lightheartedly, and as he explored her eyes he saw at once the strong virtues of her personality. She was scarcely able to absorb the fact that she was actually talking to him.

The shooting began. It was arduous for all concerned. The first scenes were of the retreat of the Spanish Army, shot not far from Madrid, followed by days in Segovia. Cary's health suddenly and unexpectedly collapsed. He had yet another recurrence of hepatitis, and he seemed to have acquired another virus, probably because of his weakened liver, that laid him low. Many scenes had to be shot around him. Yet he failed to send for Betsy, who heard of his condition with concern. According to Melville Shavelson, Cary had become romantically interested in a young male Spaniard and their relationship continued throughout the shooting. He recovered gradually, joining the gruelling cross-country trek in his heavy period uniform. He was reliable as always, uncomplaining and supportive of Stanley

Kramer. But he had little rapport with Frank Sinatra, who was bizarrely miscast as the revolutionary-minded peasant, Miguel.

Sinatra was at his worst, repeatedly displaying his volatile temperament, much to everyone's annoyance. He insisted on calling Cary "Mother Cary", a directly insulting reference to his homosexuality, refused to drive in a Mercedes with a chauffeur, and insisted his Thunderbird be flown in from Hollywood, a request that was finally refused, and he threatened to urinate on Kramer if the director would not get him back to his hotel before midnight. He also charged hundreds of dollars to the company for calls to his bookie in Chicago, and allowed his girlfriend, Peggy Connolly, to charge all her clothing and jewellery to the studio.

Stanley Kramer remembers that Sinatra "had an eye on Sophia, maybe not actually, but jokingly":

> Frank always said, in the vernacular which Sophia didn't understand, "Sophia, you're going to get yours." It was pretty obvious what he meant. He meant she was going to get Frank Sinatra.
>
> Finally, Sophia asked someone, "What means this, 'get yours'?" and they explained to her. We were shooting at night, and called a dinner break at midnight. I remember tables were set out under a big tent because it had begun to rain. Sinatra had had a few drinks, and he yelled out, "Sophia, you're going to get yours!" Now she was ready for him, and she stood up and said, "Not from you, you Italian son of a bitch!"

Sinatra screamed constantly about the primitive conditions of work, threatened to walk off the picture, refused to rehearse, wouldn't wait around while shots were being set up, and created so much tension that several people were ready to beat him up. Cary hated this unprofessional behaviour. He tended to ignore the temperamental star, and instead focused upon Sophia Loren. Betsy, reading the gossip items in Hollywood, must have suffered intensely.

Despite the fact that Sophia was dating the Italian producer Carlo Ponti, and was close to becoming engaged to him, she couldn't resist Cary Grant. He began using her as a kind of psychiatrist, talking of the fact that, in her own words, "he had never had a really sustained relationship in his life". He displayed his self-doubts, probably revealing to her his sexual problems. She knew that he wanted to be open and honest with her, and yet "not make himself vulnerable. Of course, one cannot have it both ways." She reported in her memoirs that as he grew to trust her, he no longer bothered wearing his mask; she was referring to his false image, so carefully sustained, of unequivocal masculinity and strong emotional security. They compared notes on their unhappy childhoods, and they visited small romantic restaurants in the hills, listening to the guitars, and the high, piercing sounds of the flamenco singers. And, Miss Loren declared, they fell in love.

It wasn't easy for him to be involved with a woman who was already apparently committed to another man. But Carlo Ponti was married with children. Miss Loren's mother had warned her that if she waited for Carlo to be free in a Roman Catholic country which didn't recognise divorce she would wind up "an old maid lighting candles". Cary assured her (fortunately, Betsy Drake didn't hear about this) that he would obtain a divorce and marry her immediately if she were ready.

There is no evidence that the relationship between Cary and Sophia Loren was consummated. The candles and the flamencos and the flower-scented evenings in obscure hide-aways went on and on, the discussions consumingly focusing on Cary's emotional problems, but there seems to have been no personal liaison. However, he offered her the starring role in *Houseboat*, thus ruthlessly ditching Betsy. She accepted, not knowing Betsy had been cast. Stanley Kramer comments:

I have no idea whether Cary and Sophia had a [physical] affair. It is true he was taken with her, but she, of course, already was tied to Carlo Ponti. She was pretty matter-of-fact about it. I guess she'd been approached by many men in her time, God knows. There was something almost boyish about him in his attitude toward her. In his insecurities, whatever they were, vis-à-vis this sex symbol. Certainly, they were friendly; he was wonderfully courteous and gallant as he always tried to be. I don't think anyone took the situation between Cary and Sophia seriously. Ponti always loomed on the horizon; he visited us often. I never heard him make any objection about Cary. He was an older man, was kind of Sophia's mentor, discoverer, sponsor. Love can be many things, and who can say whether one person loves another?

Cary wined and dined Sophia often on balconied overhanging restaurants all over Spain. She had a sense of humour, and she treated the whole thing lightly. And I suppose she must have known he was a married man. Of course, she had a lot of pride. Anybody from bare beginnings who raised herself to her position would have pride.

In his novel *Lualda,* Melville Shavelson, who is anxious to point out that the central figure of an ambitious Italian actress is not based on Miss Loren, portrayed Bart Howard, described as "America's Number One screen lover, who offered to make Lualda an international superstar in return for her making him a man". Shavelson confirms that the portrait was based upon Cary Grant. Bart Howard, handsome, the idol of millions of women, is a secret homosexual, privately insecure and nervous, forced to "make love to women when the whole sex repulsed him". Howard confesses to Lualda that he is gay, and that his emotional condition is the cause of his extreme state of stress and temper tantrums. At one stage, Howard (a direct reference to Cary's sessions in hypnosis with Betsy Drake) explains to Lualda how easily anything can be learned while one is asleep. Lualda snaps at him, "Then why don't you learn how to fuck girls?" He replies, "I've tried. You'd think being able to have such complete control over my body would be enough. But you see, that's where the God you mentioned has been able to laugh at me. He put the control of *that* function not in the body, but in the mind. Sex is a mental process."

The laborious shooting continued. Betsy finally did come to Spain, only to find an appalling situation. There seemed to be no hope for her marriage now. Everyone was talking about the situation between Cary and his female co-star. She felt humiliated, a not unfamiliar sensation for this star-crossed young woman. Even though Cary was not sexually involved with Miss Loren, Betsy can only have been depressed and shocked by his seeming indifference to her happiness in continuing to see the Italian actress even after she had arrived.

Stanley Kramer recalls that Frank Sinatra's behaviour grew even worse as the shooting went on. To this day, Kramer remembers Cary's extraordinary skill in dealing with the situation:

> I think Grant felt that what Sinatra [was doing] was unreasonable and not professional. Sinatra left the picture. It was six weeks before completion. He simply told me, "I have a lawyer and you have a lawyer," and that he had to leave. I pleaded with him because the six weeks concerned revolved around him, but to no avail. Finally, I made a deal with his attorney, Martin Gang, to finish the film in California on a stage with fake palm trees.
>
> Cary made superb efforts to fill the gap. Nothing was too difficult: he played close-ups that were supposed to be with Frank with coats on hangers, put himself out no end, and acted as a professional from beginning to end, for which I was everlastingly grateful. I've never forgotten him for it. But he couldn't save the picture.

Kramer recalls that some of Cary's work in the film was physically dangerous: at one point, he was caught helping to push the cannon on a steep hill, and it rolled down the slope, dragging him on a cable. But he took the risk in his stride.

Cary grew tired of the interminable production. He said to Kramer, "Let's give up and go home." And Kramer remembered that he was tempted. Although doubles were used for some shots, in others Cary had to fall into mud, wade through a swirling river, and struggle up the side of a flint-strewn hill. At the end of the day's work, he would ignore Betsy Drake and take off to a rendezvous with Sophia Loren. Towards the end of shooting, they were in Avila; he proposed marriage at a restaurant one night, romantically accompanied by a half-moon shining through a window and the echo of a flamenco from the valley below. Miss Loren was dumbstruck. She told him she didn't dare to respond, that she still needed time—to go back to her own environment and to be able to make up her mind away from the magic of the Spanish nights.

Cary accepted her hesitation. By now, Betsy Grant had understandably had enough. She joined the *Andrea Doria*, the vessel that had taken her and Cary to England in happier days. With her she had almost a quarter of a million dollars' worth of jewellery Cary had given her, and the manuscript of a novel, of a semi-autobiographical character, which was locked in the ship's safe. She was seen by few passengers on the Atlantic crossing.

On July 25, 1956, the ship was on the last leg of the voyage, sailing towards New York harbour. A dance was in progress in the first-class saloon. Never fond of social life, Betsy had gone to bed early in her boat-deck cabin, to enjoy a book and relax. She was packed for arrival, and her luggage was ready to be placed in the corridor outside.

It was shortly after eleven p.m. when she heard a strange grinding sound, which made the ship shudder from stem to stern. The *Andrea Doria* lurched, and, as Betsy looked out of the porthole, she saw a burst of mysterious multi-coloured lights in the dense ocean fog. There was a scream of torn steel and the cry of someone in pain. The lights of another vessel gleamed through the darkness. There was no alarm, and Betsy couldn't determine what had happened. No one answered the telephone when she picked it up.

Throwing on a life-jacket, she ran out into the corridor. The ship was listing badly. People were running about, panic-stricken and screaming. There was smoke all around, and the smell of oil. She could not get to her jewellery or manuscript and no one, neither crew nor passenger, seemed to have the slightest idea what had taken place. Betsy followed instructions and went to a lifeboat station, which had been set at the time of the boat drill on the first day of sailing.

As she made her way to one of the few usable lifeboats, struggling along the sloping decks, Betsy was surrounded by hysterical passengers. At last, she found the boats, but it had been impossible to launch them with the passengers aboard, and they were dropped into the water. She had to slide down a rope to safety; the small craft was rowed out into the turbulent sea. Her ordeal ended when she was rescued and taken aboard another ship, the *Ile de France*, for transportation to New York.

It was not until the early morning hours that she at last learned what had happened. The *Andrea Doria* had collided with the Swedish ship *Stockholm*, whose heavy steel bow had ripped the Italian vessel apart. Many died; but one survivor, a small girl, was flung from the tortured metal of what had been her cabin onto the *Stockholm* itself, surviving this astonishing transition. She was found clinging on to an autograph book which, by coincidence, contained one of Cary Grant's.

News of the mishap reached Cary in Madrid. He waited through a day and night of anxiety for word of Betsy, but she was unable to get through to him on the *Ile de France*'s overcrowded ship-to-shore telephone system. When at last she spoke to him from New York, following a cable she had managed to get out through Western Union, he cried out with relief and gratitude. The day before, Sophia Loren had just turned down his proposal of marriage, and he must have felt his only hope now lay in returning to Betsy. Yet there is no indication that his wife's rescue drove him closer to her.

The Pride and the Passion turned out to be a disaster. Stanley Kramer is the first to admit this, though he does not only blame Sinatra's unprofessional behaviour for the fiasco. He retains his admiration for Cary and regards him as the finest of his professional associates. When he made the picture *Ship of Fools*, in 1965, he wanted Cary to play the difficult role of the ship's physician; a tortured, miserable alcoholic. It would have been a complete change of course in Grant's career, but Cary, despite Kramer's promise to rewrite the role for him, decided against it.

Betsy had a consolation prize. In the wake of her ordeal, she found herself suddenly given back the co-starring role in *Houseboat*. When Melville Shavelson told Cary that the revised screenplay of that film was almost finished, Cary said he no longer wanted Sophia Loren to appear in it. This was bewildering to Shavelson, who had assured Paramount that Miss Loren would be the co-star. Cary was full of vengeance because Miss Loren had refused to leave Carlo Ponti for him.

In the meantime, Cary was to make another film before *Houseboat*, under a long-standing arrangement with Twentieth Century-Fox: *An Affair to Remember*, with Deborah Kerr, which would start shooting in early 1957. Cary's old friend and colleague, Leo McCarey, was signed to direct this remake of McCarey's own *Love Affair*, directed at Columbia in 1938, when Cary was under contract to that studio. The stars then had been Charles Boyer and Irene Dunne. It was the poignant romantic fairy tale of a couple who meet aboard a ship, fall in love, but are unable to consummate their relationship because of difficulties involving their separate backgrounds. Jerry Wald was the ebullient producer. His decision to make the picture reflected Cary's desire to return to the make-believe world of 1930s romantic comedy-dramas. In yet another parallel between real life and the screen, the new script for the picture, written by

Delmer Daves and McCarey, called for an Italian vessel as the setting: a ship similar to the *Andrea Doria*.

On the first day of shooting, Cary typically made a scene, objecting to the buttons on the Naval officers' uniforms, and refused to continue work until they were corrected. He made trouble every day for everyone, still frustrated and angry over Sophia Loren's rejection of him.

Paramount, behind Cary's back, had contracted Sophia Loren to make the film. The contract he had signed so hastily at the airport when he was on his way to Europe to make *The Pride and the Passion* had been ingeniously worded so that he had no right of choice of co-star. Melville Shavelson had the unpleasant task of informing Cary that Sophia had been cast. Once again, the unfortunate Betsy Drake was out of a job and humiliated. She would have to face the ordeal of seeing her husband's former lover play the role which she herself had created, in a film for which she had supplied the original story, speaking lines which were an adaptation of her own.

She was distraught. As for Cary, there is no describing his fury. Shavelson recalls, "He offered Paramount two pictures free if they would pay off Sophia's contract. They refused." Cary fumed, screamed, but it was useless. He was forced to make a film with a woman who had rejected him and Miss Loren was compelled by the contract signed in Spain that followed Cary's offer to appear in a film with a man she no longer wanted to see.

When Sophia Loren and Carlo Ponti arrived in Hollywood and checked into the Bel Air Hotel, Carlo Ponti was feeling annoyed. He knew that Cary Grant was far more handsome than he and that, as a fat, unattractive man, he could not possibly compete with the idol of millions of women. There was always the danger that the futile, asexual, but still threatening, liaison with Cary Grant might resume. In a desperate effort to soothe everyone, to try to begin the picture in some kind of harmony, Shavelson invited Loren and Ponti and the Grants to his house for a discussion. The conversation was understandably strained.

The only thing that was made clear was that Loren and Ponti were obtaining the necessary papers to get married in Mexico following a Mexican divorce of Ponti from his present wife.

The shooting of *Houseboat* began on August 8, 1957. The same day, Cary irritably turned down an offer to appear with Frank Sinatra and Shirley MacLaine in *Can-Can*. At first, Cary was so edgy that it was almost impossible for him to play the light comedy scenes. Then, in the absence of Ponti from the set, and in the constant presence of his voluptuous co-star, he resumed his earlier feelings for her and decided once more that only she could unlock his sexual problems and make a complete man of him. He went to see her in her dressing-room to make peace. She was prepared to accept his apology for his behaviour in trying to drop her from *Houseboat*, and, in the interest of dignity and making a picture together, shook hands with him. Sophia would have been happy to have left the matter there. But then, to her horror, Cary again proposed that she should leave Ponti once and for all and marry him. The shock was intense, she was utterly committed to Ponti, and must have known that there was no security in a future with Cary, that his bisexuality and overall sexual insecurity would make her life a torment, and that his challenge to her to cure him was no basis for a proposal. As she told more than one reporter, she felt much safer with an ugly, fat man (she seems to have overlooked the brutal insult to Ponti), her implication being that many women would chase Cary Grant, but almost none would chase Carlo Ponti.

In this ghastly circumstance, *Houseboat* continued. Cary refused to take no for an answer. Shavelson recalls that Sophia would come to him in tears, crying, "This man is married. Now he's starting again with me. He doesn't know that Italian girls are different and I am looking for a proper husband, not a glamour man." Shavelson did his best to soothe her disordered nerves. Cary was by now completely out of control. He went to see Carlo Ponti and offered to do four movies for him for virtually nothing (an assurance of several million dollars in profits) if Ponti would give Sophia up for good. Disgusted, feeling that Cary was less than a man, Ponti refused.

After that, Shavelson says, "It was murder on the set. Cary made things very, very difficult for everybody because he was in such a bad temper, having to kiss, to hold, to play love scenes with a woman who not only had turned him down but was living with her lover." Cary complained about the daily rushes. He hated the very good camera work of veteran Harry Stradling. He charged Stradling with making him look as though he had a double chin. He forced the ailing cameraman to climb up ladders to shoot him from above, so that a shadow would fall and conceal the fleshiness under his jaw. For all his careful exercise programme and his attention to diet, middle age was finally catching up with him.

Charles Rosher, a great cinematographer and close friend of Stradling's, heard about this needless cruelty to Stradling, making him risk a heart attack by climbing perilously to the top of the sound stage to satisfy a star's vanity, and he was furious. As Cary came out of his dressing-room one morning, the powerfully built Rosher blocked his path, grabbed his fleshy jowls in both hands and screamed into his face, "Why don't you get rid of this shit so Harry can photograph you?" Cary flushed, turned on his heel, and slammed into his dressing-room. He didn't come out for the rest of the day.

He exploded again during a sequence in which he was dancing with the actress Martha Hyer. Just as Alexis Smith had annoyed him on *Night and Day* because of her dark body make-up, so Miss Hyer angered him. The heavy tan foundation on her arms came off on his tuxedo, and he screamed and walked off the set. He refused to continue until it had been removed. He was even angrier when Sophia Loren used body make-up. She was already dark-skinned, her exquisite olive colouring the result of her Italian origins. But she held to the old lower-class Italian canard that a deep suntan was proof of great wealth. Because her character, the daughter of a famous conductor, was supposed to be rich, she was determined to have a more spectacular tan than Cary Grant. She kept adding more and more make-up until she looked virtually black.

Cary took over the direction, giving orders to both Miss Loren and the child members of the cast. He screamed at Martha Hyer. Determined to destroy Sophia Loren, he accused her of having an affair with the handsome actor, Harry Guardino, and sent a detective to spy on the actor's house. There was no basis for his suspicion; Miss Loren was incapable of being unfaithful to Ponti. But even when the detective reported that Guardino was having an affair with another woman, Cary wasn't satisfied. He called the man a liar, fired him and hired another private eye, who issued an identical report. Cary sulked.

Guardino, who had been a fan of Cary Grant, soon learned that Cary was having him spied on. He had to go on the set and play scenes with Cary, concealing his fury.

All through the shooting of *Houseboat*, Betsy Drake seemed to accept what would have driven most women from a man for good. Possibly, the glamour of being Mrs. Cary Grant, and a residual fondness for him that persisted through every conceivable kind of humiliation held her to him. And it was during *Houseboat* that they began to experiment with lysergic acid, or LSD.

It is possible that Cary may have been aware of LSD as the so-called "Truth Drug" employed by both British and American military intelligence men in order to obtain information from prisoners. The effect of lysergic acid was to remove inhibitions and to release the unconscious mind; the drug was used in cases of sexual impotence. It had a deeper and more lasting effect than hypnosis, emphasising every aspect of the human mind to an extraordinary degree. The good and bad elements in the psyche were unleashed, in sessions that made the subject see colours and smell scents in a way that was not possible in normal conditions.

The memory chain was opened up, often with painful consequences.

This was a severe challenge, and on top of it the LSD patient has to deal with marvellous or horrifying hallucinations. Acid, as LSD became popularly known, can cause an individual to walk into his own bathroom and suddenly see violent streaks of colour in the basin, a flushing lavatory like Niagara Falls, a face in a mirror that turns into that of a gila monster, a vision of oneself as a baby or an old, dying human being, a magnificently formed athlete or a cripple. The patient can become violently hysterical or rigidly catatonic. For some people, the experience of LSD produced nausea, terror and despair. For others, it brought exhilaration, visions of transcendent beauty, and the confidence to deal with anything. Cary Grant went into LSD treatments to overcome his constant self-doubts, his characteristic actor's feeling of unworthiness, of being less than a man, the pain of human relationships and the tormenting memories of his childhood.

He wanted to be the impossible: an average, "normal", uncomplicated human being who could experience simple happiness. But the fairy-godmothers who had bestowed upon him his many gifts exacted the familiar price of depriving him of the very things he wanted most. His actor's egomania would not tolerate such misjudgment on the part of the guardians and fates. He wanted it all: money, success, looks, and, more than that, the ability to enjoy day-to-day living without complications and without conflicting thoughts, the ability to relax, the ability to love and be loved, which of course starts with loving oneself. And for all his efforts, for all the roller-coaster rides of acid treatments, there were no signs that his wishes were to be fulfilled.

He underwent carefully guided treatments with two of the leading proselytisers of the new cure-all: Dr. Mortimer Hartmann and Dr. Oscar Janiger. He conferred with Aldous Huxley, one of the self-appointed shamans of mescalin, and he soon encountered the ineffable Timothy Leary, whose conversion to this use of the drug eventually gained him international notoriety as the idol of millions of students.

Leary recalls that Cary had been involved with LSD for five years before Leary became the chief glorifier of the drug. He met Cary through a mutual friend, Virginia Dennison, a student and teacher in the Ramakrishna Vedanta group, of which Huxley and Christopher Isherwood were adherents. Miss Dennison had taught Cary yoga. Leary was in San Francisco with his girlfriend, Peggy Hitchcock, and Cary invited the couple to lunch at his office. Leary says: "It was a thrill because it was the first time I'd been in a movie studio. Cary Grant was always my idol. When I was young I modelled myself on him; I'm very pleased, I think I made a wise choice. Cary was eager to meet me."

Later, Cary told Leary how he discovered a love for Elsie Leach for the first time because of LSD; the drug enabled him to knit up some ravelled threads of his life. Over the years, Cary saw a good deal of Leary: he was helpful to the younger man, giving him advice on many things, including film making, in which Leary wanted to be involved. He questioned Leary closely when he started a training centre for the use of psychedelic drugs in Mexico, and Cary wanted to visit Leary there, but the Mexican Government closed the centre down. Leary insists:

The joke of all this is that, in a sense, Cary Grant got me into psychedelic experiences.* I was a psychologist, from Harvard, when I heard about Cary Grant getting into [LSD]. That struck me very much; that attracted my attention. I had been very much against the use of drugs before that; I had written books on the subject, because I felt that doctors shooting patients up and giving them pills was making them into an assembly-line cure. I knew that truth drugs were being used by the CIA and the KGB, and that LSD was being used in chemical warfare, so I was much against it. Cary changed my views. He converted me.

* It was generally claimed that the reverse was true.

Cary began telling anyone who would listen that he was gaining strength through his treatments; he was finding happiness for the first time in his life. He would turn up on Saturday afternoons at the offices of Dr. Hartmann and Dr. Arthur Chandler, stretch out on a couch with an eye shield, block his ears with wax, and revisit his past while music was played in the near-darkness. He wrote later: "I passed through changing seas of horrifying and happy thoughts, through a montage of intense love and hate, reassembling, through terrifying depths of dark despair replaced by heaven-like religious symbolism." In another place he would also write:

> I had to forgive my parents for what they didn't know and love them for what they did pass down – how to brush my teeth, how to comb my hair, how to be polite, that sort of thing. Things were being discharged. The experience was just like being born for the first time; I imagined all the blood and urine, and I emerged with the first flush of birth. It was absolute release. You are still able to feed yourself, of course, drive your car, that kind of thing, but you've lost a lot of the tension.

He added that all human beings were "unconsciously holding their anuses". In one LSD dream, he defecated all over the psychiatrist's office rug. In another dream, he became an enormous penis, shooting off from earth like a spaceship. He realised that in his earlier days he had despised himself. Betsy Drake also went on record on LSD. She wrote, "You learn to die under [it]. You face up to all the urges in you – love, sex, jealousy, the wish to kill. Freud is the road-map."

Cary had several further discussions with Timothy Leary. Leary says:

> He took me aside and started pouring out things to me . . . The LSD experience is a life-changing experience. Today, people are cool, they don't talk about it. But in

the sixties, with everyone running around, taking off their clothes and saying they'd found God, and John Lennon eating LSD like popcorn, people talked about it a lot. Actors are insatiable neurotics. Actors depend upon getting love all the time. And after all, Cary was the focus of a hundred million women lusting after him. You couldn't expect him to be like the guy next-door; he was carrying the weight and freight of the world's fantasies. LSD helped him with his burdens. And he was always charming, professional, courteous, open and helpful. I remember he said, referring to his Universal cottage, "What do you think of this bungalow? Would it be a good place to have LSD?" I replied, "Well, I always like to have a fireplace [during the experience]." He said, "Well, I'm going to call the studio right now and have them put a fireplace in." That was typical of him.

Leary comments further upon other reasons why Cary needed LSD:

All actors are impossibly sensitive and impossibly questioning. If the phone doesn't ring every minute they're worried nobody loves them anymore. This is not a neurosis that normal people have. I don't mean to say that you can equate this neurosis with the kind of self-questioning of a man like Cary.

In the midst of meetings with Leary, the psychedelic nightmares and happy dreams, the visions of defecation and masturbation, Cary Grant continued to act out the bland, meaningless humours of *Houseboat*. He broke off shooting once or twice, first to have a meeting with Alfred Hitchcock, at which he stated that if Jimmy Stewart were unavailable for the film *From Amongst the Dead*, later called *Vertigo*, he was ready and willing to play the part of the obsessive hero.

Towards the end of shooting, Sophia Loren, yielding to Carlo Ponti's entreaties, was married to him by proxy in

Mexico, two men standing in for them before a judge. Cary was desolate at the news. The day he heard it he had to appear in the wedding scene in the picture, walking up to the altar with Sophia Loren. The sequence was tormenting for both of them.

Much to everyone's relief, *Houseboat* was at last finished, and Cary accepted the leading role in *Indiscreet*, a romantic comedy to be made by Warner Brothers in London. Stanley Donen would direct from a screenplay by Norman Krasna, based on Krasna's play *Kind Sir*; Cary's co-star would be Ingrid Bergman.

Before shooting began, Cary and Betsy flew to England to spend a few days with the author Fleur Cowles; Fleur wanted Cary and Betsy to spend Christmas with her, but they had decided to accept an invitation from Aristotle Onassis to stay with him on his yacht in the South of France.

In London, in November, Cary acquired a new assistant, a burly twenty-one-year-old Englishman named Ray Austin, who also was chauffeur and secretary for Betsy; she was shooting the comedy *Next to No Time*, with Kenneth More. Austin drove her each day from her hotel to the studio.

One evening, Cary, Ray and some friends were sitting at the back of a coffee bar on Park Lane, enjoying cappuccinos, when two men and a young woman appeared in the doorway and, much to Cary's annoyance, spotted him and came over to the table. The girl asked him for his autograph. Cary hated the custom of autograph hunting, feeling it was a subhuman activity. Like so many stars, he failed to realise that fans made up the bulk of his audience.

He refused the girl saying, as politely as he could, "Please, if you start doing this, everybody in here will want my autograph." One of the two men accompanying her viciously insulted Cary because of his lack of co-operation. Cary, Ray and their party stood up to leave. The man blocked Cary's way, looking menacing.

Austin told Cary to step back and struck the man across the face. When Cary reached the street he immediately thanked Austin and told him he would be hiring him at once.

Cary liked Austin very much. The young man was intelligent, charming, and reliable; he was not homosexual, and thus provided a good cover for Cary (a gay assistant would have instantly drawn untoward gossip). As a Cockney, whose accent was similar to Cary's, Austin liked panto-mimes and the music-hall tradition, and Cary again assumed a Professor Higgins role in a younger person's life. He began training Austin to modify his accent, to talk more slowly and not to swallow his words as so many English people do. Austin says:

> I told him I was proud of my accent. He said that no one in America would understand me. So I gradually began to adapt my speaking until I finally sounded exactly like him! When we were alone together in the car, we would sing old Cockney songs. We would enjoy such things as sausage and mash, fish and chips and kippers.

Ray, then and later, would drive Cary to Bristol to see Elsie Leach. Cary would never say, "It's time we went to see my mother." He would just say, "Let's go to Bristol." Austin would leave Cary at the door of Elsie's house, with instructions to pick him up two hours later. He would wait until the front door opened and Cary walked in and then would drive down the road and park just around the corner, checking from time to time to see if Cary had come out. Austin knew Cary would never stay in the house for the full two hours, even though he had the best intentions. The visits were those of a loving son, but it was difficult to stretch out conversation when Elsie had no interest in show business and had nothing whatsoever in common with her son.

On one occasion, Cary and Ray carried a portable tele-vision set into the house, but Elsie said she had no interest in owning it. Disappointed, Cary was nonplussed when a few days later Elsie decided she did want the set after all. This unpredictability was difficult for him.

Once or twice, Austin stayed with Cary during the visit. He was a witness of the halting, painful communion between them. He says: "There were a few introductory remarks, empty and of no consequence, and then Cary would ask Elsie if she needed anything. She would shake her head, and then there was nothing left for them to say." Austin adds:

> He desperately wanted to say more to her, but there was no conversation possible. She would just answer yes or no, and that was it. She wouldn't even go out with us, nor did she like Cary's fame. She could never think of him as, or call him anything but, Archie. She didn't even want to see any of his films.

Austin soon found out that Cary was bisexual. He says, "Cary was gay, but nothing that would ever disturb anyone at all. Cary would purposely play being gay, way over the top." At a party, there would be some attractive women with their husbands, and Cary, according to Austin, would deliberately make a great fuss over the husbands until they were uncomfortable, sensing something untoward. Later, he would telephone the husband and invite himself over. Suspicious he might be homosexual, they would tell him they would be at the office that night, but that he could visit the wife instead. When people would say to the husbands, "How could you leave Cary Grant with that gorgeous wife of yours?" they would reply, "Don't worry, he's gay. Didn't you know?" And the wife concerned was sleeping with Cary.

Ray Austin was attracted to Betsy Drake. He found her wistful, delicate charm appealing. At first he suppressed his feelings because of his respect for her and Cary. He always called her Mrs. Grant.

14

Indiscreet began shooting in October. Donen's direction was polished; Cary's role as Philip Adams was another in his gallery of romantic deceivers: Adams tells the women he dates that he is married to a Roman Catholic who will not grant him a divorce. He becomes jealous of a butler-chauffeur when he sees the man with Anna Kalman, who is in love with him, in her bedroom. It would not be very long before Cary became equally suspicious of his own chauffeur, Ray Austin, vis-à-vis Betsy Drake.

Ingrid Bergman, cast as Kalman, flew into London in icy November weather to begin wardrobe fittings and photographic tests. She was already in the headlines because her widely publicised scandalous marriage to Roberto Rossellini was in difficulties. She was suspicious of Rossellini's relationship with another woman, and he, in turn, was consumed with jealousy because of her interest in another man, the Swedish producer, Lars Schmidt. Both partners were in financial trouble, and her five-year-old daughter, Isabella, had just gone through a difficult appendectomy. Ingrid had also had a dramatic reunion with her other daughter Pia Lindström, the child of a previous marriage, whom she had not seen for many years.

When Bergman arrived at the airport, Cary and Stanley Donen were there to meet her. Reporters swept down on her, demanding to know what was going on between her and Rossellini, and seeking details of her children. As Bergman tried to deal with the gruelling questions, Cary interjected, "Why don't you talk to me? My troubles are far more interesting!" Generously, for her nature was generous,

Miss Bergman assumed that Cary's interruption was intended to protect her from too many personal questions. But when they got into the limousine that was to convey her to the Connaught Hotel, where Cary and Betsy were staying, Cary, instead of asking her about her problematical affairs in a sensitive and friendly way, and inquiring after Pia Lindström, Isabella, and her other children, talked non-stop about his LSD treatments and "serious conflicts" from beginning to end of the journey. Ingrid tried not to sigh with boredom.

The weather worsened. Betsy kept hypnotising Cary repeatedly so that he would not catch influenza, as he had the idea that if the mind was sufficiently positive and composed, viruses would have no chance to strike. Absurd though this was, he was almost the only member of the cast who remained healthy from beginning to end of the shooting.

The rain was cold and persistent and accompanied by a bitter wind. Betsy was restless and uncomfortable in the Connaught suite, irritated by the imitation antique furniture. Fighting off 'flu, Donen struggled into work, but others caught the virus from him and were sent to bed. Margaret Johnston, an admired Australian actress who played a major supporting role in the film, was opinionated and aggressive, and failed to agree with Donen on anything. She did the unthinkable and actually left the picture. It had to be started all over again with the charming Phyllis Calvert. Then, on the day she signed the contract, Miss Calvert's bookseller husband, Peter Murray Hill, died suddenly. There were further delays as a result, but with great professionalism and courage Miss Calvert, to save Warner Brothers money, went to work. It says much for her that there is no trace of her distress visible on the screen. She gave an expertly light and graceful performance.

A heavy yellow sulphur fog descended on London at the beginning of December. Day after day, Ray Austin had to drive Cary through the swirling, toxic near-darkness to the studio, with his fog headlights on, and almost no visibility, while Betsy remained marooned at the Connaught.

The cameraman, Frederick A. Young, fell ill, also from Asian 'flu, and Max Greene (Mutz Grünbaum) took over. Then the editor, assistant cameraman and wardrobe mistress were also unwell. And sometimes work was delayed by heavy snow.

During the shooting, Cary formed a closer friendship with Ingrid Bergman. He had grown to understand her extraordinary qualities as an actress; however he was not in tune with her lover, Lars Schmidt, whose imposing form seemed to be omnipresent during the production. But in general, though at times he was testy over Schmidt's visits to the set, preferring to work without an audience, Cary did not provide his usual number of problems on the production. He was impressed by the impeccable design and by Donen's tasteful, accomplished handling of the action. And he felt more confident with British film craftsmen than with those in Hollywood.

Ray Austin recalls the curious behaviour of Cary during the last week of shooting. He and Betsy moved from the Connaught Hotel to 9 Brompton Square, to escape the unwanted attentions of press and fans alike. Cary would go to newspaper libraries, public libraries, and anywhere else where publications were stored, even to Bristol at weekends, to explore the indexes for any references to Archie Leach, and then, with a razor blade, cut out the appropriate articles and destroy them. He couldn't bear anything in print that referred to his former persona.

Austin adds:

Sometimes he would go off walking on his own in London. My instructions were that, if I dropped him at the corner of the Embankment, I would wait by the telephone, and then, after a period of one or two hours, according to what we set, pick him up again. Often, this was on the Thames embankment. I had to sit by the phone because I never knew when he would call me. As it turned out, he never did. And I never found out where he went.

At that time, Roy Moseley, a young admirer of Cary's, approached him for an autograph. Cary flew into a temper and, in front of Ray Austin, violently clutched at Moseley's hair, with so much strength that he succeeded in taking out a tuft of it.

Seeing Moseley's discomfiture, Cary realised the seriousness of what he had done and yelled at the young man to come into the Brompton Square house. There, he lectured him furiously for fifteen minutes on the foolishness of seeking autographs of stars, and advised him to do something better with his life, including learning languages, in particular Hebrew. By now, Cary had calmed down somewhat and realised that Moseley would "let him off" once he had supplied the requested signature. Cary willingly gave the autograph with a sigh of relief. Outside the house, as he left, Moseley laughed uproariously with Austin over the incident.

The picture stopped production for the week of Christmas to allow everyone a break. This was a custom almost never followed in Hollywood at the time, when only Christmas Day itself would be taken off. Ingrid Bergman flew to Rome to spend a week with her family. Cary and Betsy paid a quick visit to Fleur Cowles and her husband in Sussex, and then flew via Nice to Cannes to spend the rest of the holiday with Aristotle Onassis on his yacht. They both ate far too much of the superb food served aboard, and Cary gained weight. Members of the international set arrived in droves, bitching, as Betsy Drake later reported in a letter to Clifford Odets, in several languages, a habit which irritated her intensely. She complained about the constant vicious gossip, neither joining in, nor able entirely to ignore it.

Everyone reassembled after New Year's Day. Betsy wrote a long, graphically picturesque letter to Odets on January 9, to which Cary added some handwritten comments. Betsy thanked Odets for his own letters; she described how she and Cary would read them together and apart, and then out loud to each other. She expressed her gratitude to Odets for arranging that his friend, the actress Claire Bloom, visit them. She talked of London lying at the bottom of a "yellow black grey dirty green dead blue fog funnel", how the rain was dirty, making her and Cary sneeze, and how the cold was like that of an old, wet cave, but London was still beautiful, with its parks and squares and crescents, and friendly doors and inviting windows and trees and Rolls-Royces. She wrote of the cosiness of the house despite its shortcomings in décor, of how a brass coal-box reflected "what looks like sunlight on the wall".

Jack Warner was in London to see forty-five minutes of *Indiscreet*. Dapper and suntanned, with slicked-down, dyed-black hair and a well-tailored blue yachting blazer, Warner was his usual self, alive with mischievous humour, self-confidently delivering witless remarks, and behaving very much as he had done as a young man on the vaudeville stage. Cary and he always got along very well. Warner had been annoyed with Cary for not accepting the role of Norman Maine in *A Star is Born*, but, in the wake of James Mason's excellent performance, had forgiven him, and they were good friends again. The studio chief was on his way to the South of France, to win and lose several fortunes at the gambling tables.

To console himself for the weather and the long-drawn-out days of shooting, Cary exchanged the dove-grey Rolls-Royce he owned for a black-and-tan Silver Wraith, with CG1 on the plates. It was put on the production account and would be sold when his services were concluded. However, he decided to keep the car, transferring the title in it to a third party to save taxes. He could afford it: apart from his existing wealth, he was being paid $25,000 a week for twelve weeks' work on *Indiscreet*.

When shooting ended Cary and Betsy flew to Moscow for a week's vacation.

Betsy remained in England in March and April to make

a film entitled *Intent to Kill*, directed by Jack Cardiff. It was a thriller, set in Montreal, about a murder in a city hospital, in which Betsy played a member of the medical staff. Cary flew back to Hollywood with Ray Austin, who had never been there before. Clifford Odets wrote in his diary on March 8:

> My mysterious friend, Cary Grant, back from Europe. He wants and says we must meet immediately. But it will be weeks before it happens. I wonder what he is so busy with all the time? . . . You never know where he has come from or where he is going, as if he had no home, like a fish in the oceanic night.

During the making of *Indiscreet*, Alfred Hitchcock had completed plans for a new thriller, *North by Northwest*, in which Cary would co-star with Sophia Loren. They had become friendly again; Cary appeared to be resigned to her marriage to Carlo Ponti. Cary would play an advertising executive, Roger Thornhill, who, mistaken for someone else, is kidnapped by a Soviet-controlled espionage ring. It was yet another in his gallery of men who were of confused identity, or whose identities were confused with others'. The story in many ways paralleled that of *The Man Who Never Was*, about an imaginary figure concocted as a decoy by British Intelligence in World War II. It was the kind of plot that was calculated to appeal to Cary Grant immediately. The picture would be shot at Bakersfield, California; Rapid City, South Dakota; New York City and Long Island, starting in the autumn.

Betsy was back in Hollywood in June. She and Cary joined Clifford Odets for dinner at Chasen's on the 24th. Cary's friendship with the playwright was troubled now. Odets had become embittered because Cary would promise to do a picture and then suddenly go cold on it; without Cary as star, it was impossible for Odets to obtain a commitment from a studio to allow him to direct.

By the late summer, Betsy and Cary, who were arguing

over everything, had separated. Yet, so paradoxical was their relationship, that even while they were discussing property settlements he was still acting as her agent, attempting to get her new film roles. He did not succeed: she had made very little impression in *Next to No Time* and *Intent to Kill*, which were released within a few days of each other in July.

Odets summed up much about the Grants when he learned of their separation. He wrote in his diary:

> They made . . . an unwritten and unspoken (indeed unconscious!) pact of invalidism, of not living fully together and not really disarranging or disturbing each other inwardly, or making demands in true depth or dimension. This was living by a negative, by default. Their common life was oiled by good manners and politeness, by a style of breeding, true affection, by reticence and even some diffidence, not to say characteristic embarrassments and unease. Candor was not present and real relatedness was bypassed for small common enthusiasms and fads. Also by commonly held prejudices. What each wanted was supposed to be understood by RADAR, never directly.

Odets summed up Betsy Drake:

> She was early rigidly held up to standards of behaviour and affection. She stammers, feels deficient and inadequate, and she marries Cary Grant, who has so many empty standards. She believes, finally, only in manners and good taste and makes *no human** demands. She goes to nostrums.

As soon as Betsy moved out of their home Cary fretted at her departure. Like so many people, he could not live with, or without, a partner. He began discussing Betsy obsessively with friends such as Melville Shavelson, telling him, during

* Odets' italics.

296

one *tête-à-tête*, "If you want to know why I married Betsy, she was the only woman who could hypnotise me." He relied very heavily on Austin for friendship and psychological support.

By now, Cary was happily settled at MCA-Universal, persuaded to settle there by the genial studio chief, Edward R. Muhl, who recalls:

We all liked Cary very much. But most of the time we had a devil of a time coming to terms with him, getting him to say "yes" to anything. He was very cautious, very thoughtful, he wanted to review everything, and, of course, one would go mildly mad wondering why he wouldn't say yes.

Muhl reports that there was no official contract with Cary at the studio. Each deal for a picture was made separately, and each had different terms. Cary enjoyed the university-campus-like atmosphere of the studio, with the executives housed in bungalows, one of which was given to Cary as his office. Rabbits and cats ran around wild in the grass and bushes outside the bungalows, and, Muhl says:

When Cary saw the bunnies grazing on the grass and nobody chasing them or rounding them up and sending them off the lot, I think he must have felt, "These people can't be all bad." We liked him resident there, because one could go by and say, "Morning, Cary," or one could just drop in to his bungalow with the words, "I have a script here, I just wish you'd give me your expert advice as a comedy man," and he'd say, "Well, yes, if you'd give me a little time I'd be glad to read it." He always responded, even on scripts of films other than his own. Sometimes he lived in the bungalow at night.

Another reason that Cary liked MCA-Universal so well was that Muhl made a unique arrangement with him whereby he would get three-quarters of the profits of a picture, in return for taking a fairly modest $100,000 up front. After a certain number of years, the picture's rights would fully revert to him, and he would soon set up a separate production unit with Stanley Donen as an effective tax shelter, and they would make more than one good film together. Muhl says, "It was still a very good deal for us. Cary's name ensured very high grosses, and while he made an enormous amount of money from the arrangement, so did we." However, several members of the Universal executive board gave Muhl an extremely hard time over the deal, which remains an historic one in Hollywood history.

Shooting of *North by Northwest* began, with Eva Marie Saint replacing Sophia Loren; there had been alleged contractual problems, and Miss Saint was all too clearly aware she was a replacement. She acted, very intelligently, the part of an American double-agent who becomes romantically involved with Cary Grant's Roger Thornhill after (in a reversal of the situation in *Notorious*) sending the man she already is attracted to into a situation of mortal danger. Hitchcock and Cary Grant knew that such situations were commonplace in cold or hot wars, and one can scarcely doubt that Cary, with his Intelligence background, had himself been involved in similar situations.

Filming started in Manhattan, in the lobby of the Plaza Hotel. Cary had to get out of an elevator with a group of women, and two crooks who were following him. Ray Austin was present during the scene. Hitchcock was heard to observe as Cary walked across the lobby with Austin, "Here comes Mr. Grant and his man."

Austin says:

Twenty years later, I was at Universal Studios. I called Hitchcock's name when I saw him filming a sequence. He ignored me. So I went to his office, and he said, "Lord love a duck. What are you doing here?" He added that he had been watching my career (I was a director by

then). And, as we sat down and talked, he said, right out
of the blue, "I owe you an apology. I always thought you
and Cary were . . . you know."

A famous sequence was shot at Bakersfield in the first week
of October 1958. Roger Thornhill has been lured to an
obscure destination in a remote cornfield in Illinois. Cars
pass; a bus stops and goes. The sky is a hard, blank blue;
the road is dusty and endless. Suddenly, Thornhill becomes
aware of the buzz of a crop-dusting plane. Someone points
out that the plane is dusting crops where there are none.
Soon, Thornhill realises that the mysterious group determined to kill him has manned the crop-duster with a
machine-gunner. He narrowly escapes death when the
crop-duster's pilot slams his plane into a truck.

The sequence had been carefully planned on the
drawing-board. There was nothing Hitchcock liked better
than to see perfectly groomed stars dishevelled, and he
looked pleased when Cary was forced to crawl on his
hands and knees in the dust, ruining his beautifully tailored
pale-grey business suit. But Cary didn't quite achieve the
look of absolute terror Hitchcock required. Suddenly, as
he crouched down, Cary saw a tarantula crawling across
his hand. He screamed like a frightened child. Hitchcock
made sure the cameras were turning. The scream was not
recorded, but the expression of horror was. It would have
been typical of Hitchcock to have planted the spider. Every
inch of the ground had been checked, on Cary's nervous
instructions, for any sign of insect life.

During the shooting, Cary became friendly with Martin
Landau, who played Leonard, the gay killer sidekick of the
villain played by James Mason. Landau recalls a curious
incident during the shooting. Hitchcock wanted him to be
better dressed than Cary, a tall order, and took the actor
to Quintino, Cary's tailor, ordering several suits made
for him, sometimes in duplicate because they would be
damaged in a scene of violent struggle, and they must
always look elegant. Hitchcock was using Landau's clothing

symbolically, in order to show him that he was menacing and dominant.

For a sequence being shot at Chicago's railway-station, Hitchcock wanted Landau to turn up ahead of time so that the director could make sure his suit was perfect. Landau arriving, hung back, concerned that he might be seen in a large crowd scene in which he was not supposed to be present. Suddenly, somebody tapped him on the shoulder. He determined later that the man was Ray Austin.

Austin said, "Excuse me. Mr. Grant would like to know where you got that suit." Landau was astonished by this question, delivered in a Cockney accent by somebody he had never met. Then he replied, "Why does Mr. Grant want to know?" Austin answered, "Only two tailors in the world could make a suit like that: one's in Hong Kong and one's in Beverly Hills." Landau said, "I would suggest that Mr. Grant discuss the matter with Mr. Hitchcock."

It is possible that Cary finally acquired the suits, because they were in wardrobe and Landau was not allowed to keep them. Both men were similarly built, although Cary was broader; both were somewhat round-shouldered, though Cary's problem was less obvious on the screen. Landau says, "Grant actually did have curvature. The suits compensated for it."

He remembers that, during the shooting, Cary would look at his clothes and say, "We're about the same size, aren't we? Let me try your suit on," or, "You don't have anything in your contract about keeping these, do you?" Despite all his wealth, Cary was looking for free use of the beautifully tailored clothes.

At a later date, Landau asked Quintino about Cary. The tailor told Landau that Cary measured his lapels with a ruler and if there was a fraction of an inch between the angle of the cut and the lapel, even as little as a millimetre, it had to be corrected. Quintino told Landau he had never had a customer so fussy.

Landau recalls another episode during the filming at Mount Rushmore. He says:

The tourists were there to see the famous carved heads of the presidents on the mountain face. They found us shooting and besieged Cary for autographs. He charged twenty-five cents for each autographed picture! He would give the money to the Actors Fund. He collected something like forty or fifty dollars that day. We were lunching in the cafeteria, all of us, when an old woman with blue hair appeared. She said, "Mr. Grant, I've been a fan of yours for years." And she asked him for his autograph.

Cary replied, "For twenty-five cents you can have it. And for fifty cents I'll bite it in your neck." Eva Marie Saint exploded, coughing out a full mouthful of coffee. Hitchcock didn't bat an eyelash. The woman was shocked out of her mind!

Late one morning, Landau walked in and Cary Grant was missing. He had been in his dressing-room earlier, entertaining Richard Brooks, who was preparing *Elmer Gantry*. A call was put through to Cary's house. Asked why he was not present for the day's work, he replied, "If you look at the appropriate clause in my contract, it says that my mobile dressing-room has to be a precise number of feet from the set, and it isn't". It had proved impossible to lodge it in its usual place because it would be seen in the wide-angle shots of the villain's living-room. It was not until the production manager found a solution, and the dressing-room was wheeled into place just inches out of camera range, that Cary was satisfied.

In a fight scene on Mount Rushmore, Landau had, on Hitchcock's instructions, to press his foot hard on Cary's hand as Cary clung to a stone face. Landau says:

Cary was anxious. Nervous. He said, very politely, "I'll be indebted to you if you don't actually step on my hand, but instead fake it, Martin." I decided to pull his leg. I told him, "I'm from the Actors Studio. I'm a Method actor. I have to actually step on your hand, very hard. I hope you'll forgive me." Now he was really nervous. He said to me, "Oh no, you won't." I replied, "Yes, I will. You'll never play the piano again. You'll never play the guitar again . . ." Of course, when it came to it, I didn't put pressure on the hand and nobody knew the difference.

Cary fretted over Landau's smoking during the production, telling him he could rid himself of the habit through hypnosis. On the other hand, Cary could be remarkably unfussy. Landau remembers standing in a small airport, waiting to take off in bad weather over the Black Hills of Dakota. Somebody was heard to say, "Do you think we'll make it?" And Landau replied, "Jesus, is there any doubt?" He went over to Cary saying anxiously, "They're talking about whether this bloody thing can get off the ground." Cary was utterly calm. He told the nervous actor, "It'll be all right. The pilot has a wife and family." They boarded the aeroplane, and Cary, saying, "I'll wake up when I get to Los Angeles," fell asleep. Looking at his slumbering form, Landau felt reassured and lost his fear.

Landau remembers that Cary consulted with Hitchcock through much of the shooting. There was a sequence in which Roger Thornhill creates a commotion in an auction-room. Cary helped Hitchcock choreograph all the movements, assisting the director in executing the complicated sequence, which had already been prepared on the drawing-board.

Cary was on his best behaviour during the making of *North by Northwest*. His respect for Hitchcock was so complete that he knew every set was perfect and that such sequences as the auction scene, when Roger Thornhill deliberately disrupts Sotheby's in order to engineer his own arrest and escape his pursuers, would become classics. He proved to be as athletic as ever at the age of fifty-five. Although the big final sequence on Mount Rushmore could not be done on the actual site (Hitchcock told Charles Higham, "They objected to a chase sequence up the nostrils of Lincoln's nose. Maybe they were afraid he would sneeze at this desecration of the shrine of democracy?"), enormous replicas of Gutzon Borglum's presidential heads were built on the sound stage and involved a good deal of hazardous clambering about. Although publicity stated there was no safety net, the insurance company undoubtedly would have demanded it; be that as it may, Cary could easily have twisted an ankle or bruised an elbow and held up production for days. He went through the experience unscathed.

Cary was at his most handsome and best in the picture, playing scene after scene with wit, charm and verve. He was especially good in the opening episode when Thornhill is kidnapped in the Plaza Oak Room, and admirable in the scenes on the train in which his complicated relationship with Eva Marie Saint's Eve Kendall begins. He conspired with Hitchcock to introduce all kinds of personal touches in the picture: at one stage, he uses his own favourite motto, "Think thin"; at another, he produces a matchbox with the initials R.O.T. on it. Asked by Eve Kendall what the "O" stands for, Thornhill replies, "Nothing." This was a dig at David O. Selznick. Another gag is that Thornhill's mother Clara, played by Jessie Royce Landis, is almost exactly the same age as her son. Hitchcock loved to play this kind of joke on an audience, relying on Grant's athletic youthfulness to carry it off. There is also a strong homosexual undertext in the film; the relationship between the Soviet agent Phillip Van Damm (James Mason) and his evil familiar, Leonard (Landau), is quite overt. In one sequence, Leonard tells Van Damm that his suspicions of Eve Kendall are based upon "a woman's intuition". Van Damm replies, "I believe you're jealous. I'm very touched." One wouldn't put it past Hitchcock to have inserted these sly references as a secret joke against his star.

Both *Indiscreet* and *North by Northwest* were enormous and deserved successes at the box-office, and were almost uniformly admired by critics. Cary took a holiday in Key West at the end of shooting. When he returned to Hollywood, he and Betsy patched up their broken relationship and she moved back into his houses. It was a truce, rather than a restored marriage, because each was lonely and lost. There was talk, at the outset of the year, of Cary filming *Beloved Infidel*, from Sheila Graham's book about her relationship with F. Scott Fitzgerald, but nothing came of this, and Gregory Peck assumed the role. Instead, Cary agreed to make *Operation Petticoat*, to be directed by Blake Edwards from a screenplay by Stanley Shapiro and Maurice Richlin, at MCA-Universal. He would be back in a submarine again, sixteen years after *Destination Tokyo*, playing the skipper, who is determined to raise a badly damaged submarine sunk by Japanese torpedo planes off the coast of the Philippines during World War II. Cary was attracted to the role of Captain Sherman, which gave him an opportunity for the kind of dead-pan, befuddled, punch-bag character he had played in *Arsenic and Old Lace*, combined with the looks and manner of Captain Cassidy in *Destination Tokyo*. He was delighted when it was agreed by the studio that the film would be shot in pleasant winter weather in his now beloved Key West in February.

Cary was troubled at the time by the many problems, both personal and professional, of Howard Hughes; although Hughes' biographers, Donald L. Barlett and James B. Steele, claim that Hughes was without a single friend at the time, that is not true. Not only was Noah Dietrich still close to him, but he also had the constant support of Cary, as well as half a dozen other intimate associates. He was living at the Beverly Hills Hotel, in Bungalow Four, while Jean Peters occupied Bungalow Nineteen. Barlett and Steele report that he had leased several other bungalows to house his personal staff, including one for cooks and waiters, one for messengers, doormen, and gofers (known as the "third man detail"), and one for storing the Poland Water, which was the only kind he would drink, as well as enormous piles of boxes of Kleenex. Cary, on visiting Hughes, found that he had reached an extraordinary degree of eccentricity, living on a diet that consisted largely of milk, Hershey bars with almonds, pecan nuts and the inevitable Poland Water.

Sometimes, when Cary arrived at the hotel, Hughes was completely naked.

Suddenly, Hughes left the hotel and moved into the Nosseck private screening-room on Sunset Boulevard, where he lived like an animal. He would urinate on the expensively carpeted floor, or all over the bathroom, and when the janitors tried to clean up the toilet, he would lock the door on them, pushing them out with violent threats. He would not allow anyone else to use the bathroom, even the security guards, and, according to his associate Ron Kistler, told the Los Angeles police to "Piss in your milk cartons!" Then, without warning, he moved back into the hotel, having kept Bungalow Four fully paid for the whole time.

Cary found him in a state of nervous breakdown, hysterical, screaming and still urinating all over the floor. He continued to squat in the living-room, staring blankly as countless films were unreeled on a screen. He was surrounded by enormous piles of newspapers, through which Cary and other visitors had to pick their way as though through a labyrinth. Fastidious Cary, who hated even an inkling of dandruff on a shoulder, or a hint of body odour in a servant, must have been appalled by the filth he witnessed, but, ever loyal, and still loving Hughes, though not in a sexual sense, he put up with everything.

Hughes made Cary painfully aware of his financial problems. Despite Hughes' apparent near-insanity, he never lost his obsession with money and how to improve his holdings.

Cary flew to Key West with the problem of Hughes still not entirely resolved. He had just had a strong difference of opinion with Clifford Odets, and an entry in Odets' diary gives a picture of this. The date is February 23, 1959: "Dinner – Cary Grant – six-thirty. Went to Cary's house. Angry. He euphoric."

Odets' secretary of the time writes:

I believe it was on this occasion that Mr. Odets told me he was really angry with Cary Grant's attitude. Cary

Grant was in bed (where, I'm sure you know, he often transacted his business, ate his meals, etc.), and Mr. Odets had expected to firm up plans for a movie. As I understood it, Grant had been vague and evasive and simply wouldn't commit himself. Mr. Odets finally told Mr. Grant he was tired of his pussyfooting around.

While filming aboard a borrowed US Navy submarine at Key West in March, Cary had an interesting visitor. Joe Hyams was a tough, skilful Hollywood insider reporter, former lover of Ava Gardner, close friend of Humphrey Bogart, and powerful through his widely admired column. With his hooded eyes, piercingly observant stare, tense, watchful manner and lean, whipcord physique, he was something to behold. People either loved him or hated him; very few had the temerity to refuse him an interview.

Cary agreed to see him, to discuss his whole career for a series of articles that would appear in the New York *Herald Tribune*. Seemingly hypnotised, Cary, who was accustomed to talking skilful balderdash to most journalists, for whom he had little time, opened himself up to Hyams as he had never opened up before. He described his experiences with LSD, saying, according to Hyams:

Now I know that I hurt every woman I loved. I was an utter fake, a self-opinionated bore, a know-all who knew very little. Once you realise that you have all things inside you, love and hate alike, and you learn to accept them, then you can use your love to exhaust your hate. That power is inside you, but it can be assimilated into your power to love. You can relax. And you can do more than you ever dreamed you could do. I found I was hiding behind all kinds of defences, hypocrisies and vanities. I had to get rid of them layer by layer. That moment when your conscious meets your subconscious is a hell of a wrench. You feel the whole top of your head is lifting off . . . There was one day, after weeks of treatment, that

I did see the light. Now, for the first time in my life, I am truly, deeply and honestly happy.

He told Hyams that in his early days he had despised himself, but only when he admitted that fact to himself did he begin to change. He said he was a bad-tempered man but hid it – a bare-faced lie Hyams had no way of seeing through. Ignoring his physical cruelty to Virginia Cherrill, he said, "I was very aggressive, but without the courage to be physically aggressive." He said he did not intend to foul up any more lives; he could be a good husband now, because his attitude towards women had changed. Yet he failed to explain why he had, just two weeks before, again left Betsy Drake high and dry, and, why, despite her loyalty to him, he was already preparing the groundwork for a divorce. He added as a footnote the curious fact that he wore women's nylon panties, adding hastily that the reason was they were easy to drip-dry when one was travelling.

Hyams was excited by these revelations, but Cary asked him not to publish them, at least for the time being. Yet, with his typical perversity, his love of mischief, Cary gave exactly the same interview to the London *Daily Mirror*'s Lionel Crane, and Crane published it.

As Hyams returned to Hollywood, feeling somewhat frustrated, Cary proceeded with *Operation Petticoat*; he had an affair with the actress, Madlyn Rhue, on location. He returned home, looking fit and relaxed, after twelve weeks of uncomplicated, pleasant shooting. One night, he went to the theatre in Hollywood, and noted that Betsy Drake was present in the stalls, not far away, with another man. By coincidence, Joe Hyams was seated next to him. Cary remarked on Betsy's good looks. Hyams asked him how he felt about her dating another man. Cary remarked with a smile, "Betsy would be incapable of being unfaithful. None of my wives have been unfaithful; neither have I. This has never been a problem."

Hyams wrote a series of articles on Cary for the *Herald Tribune*. The newspaper editor was delighted with these revealing pieces, and there was a splashy announcement in the paper that they were about to appear. Cary was horrified at what he took to be a breach of his arrangement with Hyams, despite the fact that he had himself already given much of the material to Lionel Crane. He picked up a phone and called Hyams, demanding that he cancel the series instantly. Hyams told him it was out of the question; there was no way he could interfere with the newspaper's course of action. Still angrier, Cary told him he would have to find a way. Hyams repeated that he could not stop the articles, and Cary's fury rose to a pitch of mania. He told Hyams that unless the series was put to an end, he would discredit Hyams by saying he had never seen him. Hyams told Cary that was absurd, but Cary snapped, "It's your word against mine! And you know who they'll believe!"

Cary slammed the phone down. He immediately called his lawyer, Stanley Fox. In turn, Fox called Hyams and demanded that not a word appear. Hyams refused to co-operate. Fox charged Hyams with making the series up or pirating it and told him that Cary had declared he hadn't seen Hyams in two years.

Hyams reminded Fox that he had met Cary in Key West. And that they had just run into each other at the theatre. Cary phoned Louella Parsons and even his old enemy Hedda Hopper, again denying he had seen Hyams, this time in "many months". Louella wrote in her column that Hyams had made the whole series of interviews up, and Hyams reported in his memoirs:

I was a nervous wreck . . . running between the bathroom and the office. My stomach was churning and I couldn't keep my food down. Most of the people who called me were well-meaning friends. They sounded amused at the controversy and impressed with the articles, but I felt that they too thought I made them up. Cary had been right; when it was his word against mine, no one would believe me, not even my friends.

Cary's influence spread everywhere. Stars who had promised to see Hyams for interviews backed away. His son Jay was bullied at school, where his contemporaries called him "a liar's kid". The matter blew up into a giant controversy. Newspaper after newspaper, magazine after magazine, influenced by Cary's continuing hysterical phone calls, refused to believe Hyams. Proud and stubborn, Hyams was so angry at their disbelief that he wouldn't even condescend to arrange a press conference and play his taped interviews with Grant. This was a serious mistake.

Determined to obtain revenge, Hyams began to do some detective work, and discovered that Cary had a reason for cancelling the series, a reason that had little or nothing to do with his self-protective love of privacy. He had signed a contract with *Look* magazine to write a piece about LSD and its effects on him. Once Hyams found that out, he was furious, and filed suit against Cary for slander, asking $500,000 in damages. He forced Louella Parsons to retract her statements against him under threat of a lawsuit. Universal Studios yielded up a photograph of him with Cary on the deck of the submarine during the shooting of *Operation Petticoat*.

This surely was sufficient evidence that Cary was lying. But even when Hyams' lawyer Arthur Crowley advised Stanley Fox that this piece of crucial evidence had surfaced, Cary rashly refused to drop the case. Fox subjected Hyams to many hours of deposition testimony, and the following curious exchange took place:

HYAMS: I chose not to say that Cary wore women's panties.
FOX: Why?
HYAMS: If I wrote it, some people might think he was unmasculine.

Hyams produced the Key West tapes. Fox did not respond to this conclusive evidence.

Now it was time for Cary to give his deposition to the

relentless Crowley. And typically, Cary panicked at the thought of this. Although Hyams insists that he never found an inkling of Cary Grant's bisexuality, and therefore would not have instructed Crowley to expose Cary, and although it is doubtful that Hyams would have been ruthless enough to bare Cary's mental disturbances and constant addiction to lying, Cary could not have known this degree of blindness and tact in his shrewd and hard-bitten opponent. He was deeply afraid. Up to the last minute, hardly able to sleep, his alleged happiness as described to Hyams totally dissolved in a daze of anxiety, terror and self-hatred. He still seemed to want to risk the ultimate exposure. But then, he finally realised he dared not. Stanley Fox offered Hyams a compromise. Cary would drop the lawsuit, and would work with Hyams on an autobiography, which Hyams would actually write but which Cary would sign and authorise. Clearly, Cary thought he could hoodwink Hyams, who was unequivocally masculine, and hide the painful truth of his life from him. Hyams could keep all the money.

Hyams was uncertain whether anything would come of this, but he wanted to avoid a protracted lawsuit. It is unfortunate in many ways that he did not have the nerve, and perhaps the capital resources, to proceed with this onerous case. By doing so, he would have removed every last vestige of suspicion about his motives and actions; although he saw himself as vindicated, Cary's fans probably did not agree.

Hyams was not particularly impressed by the so-called settlement. He knew Cary Grant well enough by now to know that he might dodge his responsibility and give a meaningless interview. When he arrived at Cary's office at Universal, Cary, with expertly disarming stage-management, one of his specialities, did not greet the embattled journalist in a business suit, neatly bespectacled in horn rims behind a massive desk, the manner in which most guests were received, but instead, covered only by a towel over his loins, lay flat on his back on a massage table. As though nothing had happened, he was cordial, and his secretary brought Hyams a Coca-Cola. Cary announced, with total falsehood, that he did no exercise, thought thin, and had willed his teeth not to decay. Certainly, he was in excellent condition, thanks to countless massages and male beauty treatments, a meticulously watched diet and frequent swims in his pool. These latter, and stretching exercises learned long ago in vaudeville, he kept from Hyams, so that he would seem to be a miracle man, his firm muscles and flat stomach evidence of some kind of mystical self-control rather than of the gruelling effort it took to preserve them.

Hyams began to make a series of tape-recordings. Gradually, his feelings of bitterness and resentment faded, swept away by Cary's carefully applied charm. Cary skilfully reworked the truth, omitting his childhood journey to New York, rearranging facts very much as he had done for the last forty years, carefully avoiding any discussion of Virginia Cherrill, not mentioning his war work, skating past Barbara Hutton, and saying little of consequence about his marriage to Betsy Drake. Hyams did his usual expert job on the series, and, by prearrangement, handed them to Cary to check. Characteristically, Cary rewrote them, and, with extraordinary modesty, Hyams accepted his version as an improvement.

For months, into 1960, Cary devoted many spare moments to working on the series. It was his way of getting the best of the bargain, and it is surprising that Hyams took a long time to realise he had been duped. Finally, Cary messengered the finished result to Hyams and it was sent to the *Ladies' Home Journal* under the by-line "By Cary Grant as told to Joe Hyams". Hyams was paid $125,000 for the series. Short of money, heavily in debt, he needed cash to support his wife and son, and accepted what some writers might have thought was a humiliating arrangement: the publication of a piece that was unchecked for accuracy, suffused with its real author's self-protective fantasies, and, though ably written, quite lacking in self-analysis or incisiveness. *Ladies' Home Journal* was of course delighted to have Cary's own story. They fixed up the erratic punctuation and spelling, and Hyams sent the final edited draft to Cary, who again, with shocking unpredictability, reversed his stand and demanded that the articles not be run. Hyams was appalled. He saw $125,000 going down the drain.

At the last minute, however, Cary relented. He turned up at the *Home Journal* for lunch with the editors, delivering a speech at the executive dining-room table, which was crowded with every female member of the staff, others filling the room and the corridor outside. He announced that he wanted his grammar, spelling and punctuation restored to their original form, no matter how clumsy they might seem. The magazine had to run the piece exactly the way it was written or not at all. Laughing, the editors agreed.

Hyams was advised. Then came another catch. Hyams had neglected to mention to Cary that he had been paid $125,000. When Cary found out, he was drastically upset. He wanted a share of the money. Hyams asked Stanley Fox how much. The reply was that Cary wanted a new Rolls-Royce. A Rolls in 1960 cost $22,000. Hyams' lawyer said he would be insane to give Grant any money at all, but with astonishing generosity, Hyams, who needed every penny for his family, gave the multi-millionaire star the $22,000. And there the matter ended, except that the editors of the *Ladies' Home Journal* corrected the spelling and grammar after all. Cary was furious.

In the meantime, Cary was in trouble with another prominent columnist. Hedda Hopper had disliked him for years, and now she conducted a secret campaign against him. Since she could not explicitly state her suspicions about his sexual ambiguity in print, she began attacking magazine editors when they wrote of his romantic affairs with women. In an extraordinary letter to Mike Cowles, of *Look* magazine, dated August 31, 1959, she had written: ". . . The article you ran on Cary Grant was the damnedest mishmash I have ever read. Whom does he think he is fooling?

This will probably surprise you: he started with the boys and now he has gone back to them."

Referring to a man who was very close to Cary, Miss Hopper added: "Grant introduced him to his social friends, and now Cary is using a lot of pretty girls to cover up. I used to like him, but no more."

15

Ray Austin recalls an extraordinary incident that took place that year. He flew with Cary to Las Vegas, where they went to see several shows. Cary received a message that someone wanted to see him, and he told Austin to hire a car. Austin picked up an expensive vehicle, but Cary told him to return it and get a humble Chevrolet. He wouldn't explain why.

They took off. Cary refused to say where they were going, but as they neared the Desert Inn he told Austin to park at the rear laundry exit. As they drew up Cary said, "Stay out of the way. I'm meeting Howard Hughes." The exit-door opened, and a figure appeared. Cary got out of the car and walked over to Hughes, who stood there, holding the door open. They looked at each other for a few minutes, saying nothing. Austin couldn't help watching them, deeply fascinated by this silent communion.

After a few minutes, while Hughes still held the door, Cary beckoned Austin over and introduced him to the billionaire. Forgetting that Hughes refused to shake hands with anyone, Austin reached out with his own. Hughes withdrew; then Austin remembered.

Hughes said to Austin, "You look after Cary, do you?" Austin replied, "Yes, as much as I can," and Hughes said, "Good. Look after him. I had to see him."

Austin returned to the Chevrolet* and, looking back, saw that Cary had already finished his brief meeting with Hughes and was following him to the car. Hughes slipped back into the hotel, the emergency door closing behind him.

---

* Hughes always drove Chevrolets.

314

Today, Austin realises that Cary only went to Las Vegas for the one meeting. "I think Howard Hughes just wanted to look at Cary one more time," Austin says. This example of intense feeling between the two men was, of course (though Austin couldn't possibly have known it), typical of their entire relationship.

It was not long before Cary's friendship with Austin ended. Betsy Drake was living alone, separated from Cary at the time, yet Cary would visit her, not necessarily seeking a reconciliation, but perhaps worried that she would, once she divorced him, make excessive demands on his finances. He was paying her a fairly modest separation income. Austin found that, as time went on, he was more and more drawn to Betsy. Ashamed and embarrassed because of her marital status, he was still fascinated by her. He says:

> I fell in love with her. We would walk and talk together. I wanted to get rid of all the other silly things in my life. I used to lie to her as well when I was with other women. But she really liked me. In the end she found out that I was a Romeo. That upset her and she dropped me.

Cary became convinced the couple was having an affair. With his customary jealous possessiveness, demonstrated again and again in his life, he flew into a violent temper and dismissed Austin from his service. He never forgave him, and never spoke to him again. Austin was, he says, so depressed that he was driven to attempt suicide. He was rescued just in time.

Soon afterwards Cary received an offer to go to England, and Betsy accompanied him, allaying any stories of adultery in the press. The project that took Cary there was *The Grass is Greener*, to be made under his new Universal agreement (he never had a formal contract) which would grant him a percentage of the profits.* Stanley Donen

---

* The considerable success of *Operation Petticoat* added substantially to his personal fortune.

would produce and direct, from a screenplay by Hugh and Margaret Williams, based upon their successful West End comedy. Cary's old friend Noël Coward would supply the music and lyrics, and, another link with the past, the setting was Osterley Park, ancestral home of Virginia Cherrill's former husband the Earl of Jersey; she had lived there for many years. Studio work would be done at Shepperton.

Originally, Kay Kendall, the charming British actress who had made a strong impression in the comedy *Genevieve*, and was Rex Harrison's wife, was supposed to play the leading role of the Countess Hilary, wife of the landowner Victor, Earl of Rhyall, in the story. The Earl would be played by Harrison. But Miss Kendall was stricken with leukaemia, and died before she could embark on the role. Harrison naturally withdrew, leaving the part clear for Cary. Ingrid Bergman wanted to play the Countess, but Deborah Kerr called Cary and said, "What about me?" He decided at once to accept her instead; Miss Bergman was furious. Cary had originally been selected to play Charles Delacro, an American millionaire, who falls in love with the Countess. Robert Mitchum assumed that part, and Jean Simmons was also cast in the picture.

The film was shot in the summer of 1960. All except two days of work were hampered by rain. Cary walked through the role, playing easily but without much enthusiasm, the material being quite artificial and uninspiring. Jean Simmons' presence in the cast was awkward, because she was involved in a messy separation from Stewart Granger, Cary's old friend. However, the cast tried to make the best of a bad job, meeting sometimes in the evenings to discuss such intriguing trivia as the fact that the house was supposedly haunted by a Lady Caroline Woods, who was said to have thrown herself from a window to her death in a wedding-gown because King William IV had rejected her. This spooky nonsense at least kept the cast reasonably entertained.

During the filming, Cary met and was strongly attracted to Alma Cogan, who was twenty-eight at the time. She was one of England's most successful recording artists, a successful variety performer who had been a joint headliner at the London Palladium. She was busty and tall, with masses of dark hair and warm, dark eyes. She was not beautiful, but she was very attractive, and had a quality of sexual voluptuousness.

She shared Cary's love of music-halls and pantomimes, and she had a broad, down-to-earth, brassy sense of humour combined with an odd aloofness towards most people that exactly matched his own. Their relationship developed rapidly, despite the fact that Betsy Drake was in London with Cary, staying at the Connaught. Suzy, the society reporter, wrote in her column:

> Cary . . . holding hands with Alma Cogan, is quoted as saying, "She's the sweetest girl in the world. She has brains, talent, a sense of humour and a wonderful sense of understanding. She's such wonderful company." Cary has neglected to mention whether his third wife Betsy thinks Alma is wonderful, too.

At the same time, Louella Parsons was mentioning that Cary had been seeing Jackie Chan, former girlfriend of Anthony Armstrong-Jones. ("Cary, my informant tells me, is completely fascinated with the tiny Oriental beauty, and they make quite a picture.")

During the shooting of *The Grass is Greener*, Cary became friendly with a talented young actor in the cast, Moray Watson, and told him of his Jewishness. He complained about the dialogue, feeling that he was called upon to deliver too many long speeches, and confessing to Watson that he had great difficulty in learning chunks of indigestible text.

Cary opened his heart to Watson on the subject of his marriage to Betsy Drake. Watson recalls:

> One day, Cary said Betsy was coming over. I said, "Oh, good, are you looking forward to seeing her?" He replied,

"Yes, I'm looking forward to seeing her, very much indeed. But as soon as she gets here, I shall look forward to her going away again." That was typical of him. He did need her, and yet he didn't; he had too much independence. He was obviously not a happy man, nor was he relaxed. He could never make up his mind about anything.

Watson asked Cary whether he was at all happy. Cary replied, not convincing Watson, "Oh, yes, I suppose I've had quite a good life, looking back." Watson went on, "Are you at your happiest like this, when you're making a film?" Cary replied, "No, no, no. I'm at my happiest when I am perhaps with one other person, maybe two other people, and I'm in the hills in California."

Watson recalls some of the problems during the production: Cary was restless over the numerous takes called for by Stanley Donen, sometimes as many as thirty; Deborah Kerr failed to communicate with Cary, and at times, Watson observed, they were rude to each other. He was exceptionally fretful when visitors to the set, or even crew members, got into his line of vision, and he used to insist that all the rehearsals be conducted in a studio from which all personnel except the actors and the director concerned with a scene were banished.

At times, Cary would usurp Donen's privileges and announce after, say, a twenty-seventh take, "Let's print that one." According to Watson, he wasn't concerned whether Deborah Kerr was at her best in the take. Neither he nor Donen ever consulted her when they made the selection of the take they would use.

Jean Simmons was not too comfortable with Cary either; he was distant towards her throughout the shooting, never referring back to their earlier friendship when she was married to Stewart Granger. And Cary had nothing in common with Robert Mitchum, who ambled about the set looking terrible after a late night, his eyes baggy, but gave an effortless performance, his professionalism concealed in the appearance of total casualness. Cary had always worked with gruelling intensity on perfecting his scenes, and, anxiously, was always first on the set. Mitchum would arrive at the exact moment a scene began, appear to do absolutely nothing in the way of acting, and upstage everyone in the process.

Watson remembers that Cary invited him to lunch one day, and that Cary ate nothing but eggs and bacon. The eggs were poached, not fried. He did not even treat the young actor to such inexpensive repasts in the canteen; instead, he asked for separate bills. At one stage, he asked Watson what films he had done. Watson replied that he appeared mainly in the theatre and Cary commented, "God, that's brave of you. I wouldn't have the nerve. You can face a thousand people a night, live? I would never dare do that."

Cary confessed to Watson that he was winding down his career. When the character could no longer get the girl without looking embarrassing because of his age, he would quit. Nor would he dream of becoming a character actor like the grizzled old C. Aubrey Smith. "I'll always want to be the hero," Cary said.

Watson hated going to the day's rushes to see himself walking and talking on the screen. He told Cary this, and said he had been looking at himself the night before and was convinced he had been overacting. He asked Cary about playing in films: what was Cary's technical approach? Cary replied, "My idea of film acting is that if you and I are having a conversation, and the camera's peeping through the keyhole at us, it's natural; it's just you and me and there happens to be a camera somewhere hiding." In other words, acting in pictures was like being eavesdropped upon . . . by millions.

The troubles with Deborah Kerr went on to the last day of shooting. Finally, Miss Kerr called Watson aside and said, "Cary's different. He's just not the man he was when I knew him before. He was fun then, and amusing, and fast, and funny, and professional, and always knew his lines, and was cooperative, and there was total give and take. That all seems gone now. It's very sad." The truth was that Cary no longer felt a rapport with Miss Kerr; she had become a part, for him, of his entire feeling of dissatisfaction with *The Grass is Greener*.

Cary lingered on in London, continuing his affair with Alma Cogan,* and separating again from Betsy Drake, who told a reporter, "My marriage was lived on Cary's terms, really. It was terribly frustrating to be married to him . . ." Betsy returned to Hollywood, but arrived at the airport to greet Cary when he returned. During November, Cary was mentioned frequently in the columns because of his alleged relationship with the actress Ziva Rodann. He was supposed to have given Miss Rodann a bracelet, inscribed with the words: "To Ziva, the only one who really knew. Love, Cary." Knew what? several reporters asked Miss Rodann. She replied in each case, "It's an inside joke strictly between Cary and me. It wouldn't make sense to anyone else." Asked about Betsy Drake, Miss Rodann replied to a *Photoplay* magazine writer: "Cary and I never talk about Betsy. I know she is very much in love with him, and I admire her intelligence although I have never met her. No one will ever hear any details from me, even if Cary should stop dating me tomorrow."

That December, he and Betsy, living together again in Hollywood, heard appalling news. They had always been close to the actress Patricia Neal and her husband, author Roald Dahl, and on December 5, Betsy received a horrifying phone call. She was told of a ghastly accident that had occurred to the Dahls' baby son. The nursemaid had been wheeling the child across a New York street when a taxi crashed into the pram and carried it forty feet, crushing the child's head against a truck. Cary and Betsy flew to New York to be at Patricia's side, then returned, reunited, to Hollywood.

On December 21, 1960, Ziva Rodann, wearing the brace-

---

* Who died tragically of cancer at 34.

let Cary had given her, drove him to the Los Angeles Airport for a flight to London. Betsy, who had gone ahead, picked him up at Heathrow and Austin drove them to the Connaught. Almost immediately, and no doubt to Betsy's distress, Cary again began dating Alma Cogan. He accompanied her to a performance of *Humpty-Dumpty*, a popular pantomime that year, starring Harry Secombe and Alfred Marks.

Cary was delighted to note that Humpty-Dumpty was played by Sammy Curtis, his old friend from the early days of the Pender Troupe. Humpty-Dumpty fell off the wall at the end of the first act; thus, Sammy Curtis went home at the intermission, a midget stand-in taking the bows at the end in Humpty-Dumpty's costume and egg-shaped head. Cary ran into Roy Moseley after the show and asked him where Curtis was. He wanted to renew their friendship. He told Moseley how delighted he was that Humpty-Dumpty, throwing snowballs at the audience, had aimed most of them at him and Alma. Cary told Roy that when he and Sammy were in the Pender Troupe, because Sammy was only five feet three, they were known as "The Long and the Short of It". Roy told Curtis that Cary Grant had come backstage to meet him and was sorry to have missed him, and Sammy reminisced to Moseley about their friendship.

At the time, Cary yet again assumed the role of surrogate father in respect of Clifford Odets' son Walt and daughter Nora. Walt Odets writes:

Cary regularly gave us Christmas and birthday presents, and treated with that generous charm for which he seems famous. He would take me clothes shopping several times at Carroll's on Santa Monica Boulevard in Beverly Hills. I recall his expressing some disapproval of my father's rather intellectual, New York style of dress – baggy woolens mostly – and wanted to provide a better influence. He told me that he knew about clothes because his father had been a tailor [sic]. And I also recall his saying, en route to Carroll's in his Rolls-Royce, that the car and the clothes were important to him because he had grown up in such poverty. I remember him as quite honest and direct about such things.

He arrived at our house once during the day, quite elegantly dressed, but with bare feet in his black, tasseled loafers. I asked him why he was not wearing socks. He said he was more comfortable without them, and took one shoe off, showing me how they were specially lined in soft leather and constructed with hidden stitching so that he could wear them without abrading his feet.

Walt Odets remembers feeling an easiness and acceptance with Cary which his very critical father never gave him. On one occasion, Cary gave Walt an expensive telescope, and Clifford Odets made what Walt describes as "a stink" about it. Odets, Snr., felt that to deserve such an instrument the recipient should be seriously interested in astronomy. He gave Walt a serious lecture about that. Walt Odets adds:

Later, when Cary was at the house, I mentioned this rebuke to him in front of my father. Cary said, "But really, Clifford, why can't the boy just have fun with it?" My father didn't argue the point. This was a relatively common event in my childhood, for my father was filled with a lot of serious expectations and didn't like other people intervening when he was trying to communicate them to me.

In Hollywood, early in 1961, separated yet again from Betsy, Cary was watching television as he would do before retiring at around nine thirty or ten p.m., alone in his house in Beverly Hills. He saw an episode of an uninspired television series in which he noted the presence of an un-usual, rather striking girl in her early twenties. She had a mass of honey-blonde hair tumbling over her eyes, a tiny button nose, staring eyes, thick lips, and a very large bust – a little too large for her height of five feet five. On the plump side, she certainly wasn't pretty. But Cary was immediately aware of her sexuality, the warmth of her laughter, the sensual way she moved her body, and the way she had of throwing back her head and tossing her mane of hair in a manner that must have reminded him of Phyllis Brooks. He quickly found out who she was. Although very young, she was already a veteran of television. Her name was Dyan Cannon.

Born Samille Dyan Friesen in Tacoma, Washington, in 1939, she was the half-Jewish daughter of an insurance executive. She had made her way to Hollywood with a combination of chutzpah, driving energy, brash good humour and down-to-earth common sense. A good, sincere but not brilliant actress, she was earthy, identifiable by many women, and she had a streak of coarseness that for some men added to her appeal. She seemed to promise a slangy companionship which they didn't always find among women, and her face, for all its irregularity, and lack of conventional prettiness, was made for the cameras. She toiled through almost 250 TV shows, including *Playhouse 90, Gunsmoke, 77 Sunset Strip, Bat Masterson, Highway Patrol,* and *Have Gun Will Travel.* She had just finished shooting a gangster picture, *The Rise and Fall of Legs Diamond.*

Obsessive as ever, Cary, like his associate Alfred Hitchcock, who behaved similarly in the matter of Tippi Hedren, called everyone imaginable to find out where Dyan Cannon was, and discovered to his annoyance that she was in Rome. He made it known to her agent that he wanted her to test for a part in a picture that in fact didn't exist. When she received word that the great Cary Grant wanted her for a part, she showed her good Jewish common sense – she asked whether the fare would be paid. When told that it would not, because of Cary's legendary meanness, she stayed where she was.

It was only when she had completed work on an obscure film that she returned to America and went to see Cary at Universal. She made the screen test, suspecting the real reason she had been asked there, but became frightened, perhaps sensing that for all his charm, Cary was essentially self-absorbed, and that to become involved with him might lead to disaster. Again and again, he would ask her to dinner, and again and again she would break the date. Sometimes she would even make the date and not turn up, which exasperated the ever-punctilious Grant. Of course, calculating or not, her behaviour increased his interest. She told the author Henry Gris (Coronet, March 1971):

> Ours was a Pygmalion–Galatea relationship. I was like a sponge. I soaked up everything. I did anything he said, but, then, Cary has an incredible mind and I was very, very naïve. He wanted me to accept his beliefs, and I came to accept them as gospel truth. Until the rebel in me finally began to say, Oh, no, that doesn't make sense. That's not good for me.

In the meantime, Cary again continued to see Betsy Drake. It was as though he was determined to avoid commitment, to be, skittish as ever, seemingly bent on having an affair with Dyan Cannon without any responsibility towards her. This must have irritated both women. At the same time, he began preparations for a new picture, *That Touch of Mink*, to be co-produced and co-written by Stanley Shapiro, and directed by Delbert Mann. In one of the early days of work, Cary wandered into the office at Universal to talk to Shapiro and tell him about Miss Cannon. Shapiro recalls saying to him, "Cary, why don't you get married and have a baby? Look, you've got all this. What are you going to do with the rest of your life? Have your lawyer drive you to the studio every day? Have a child. What the heck; why not? It's a great joy, I imagine."

As it happened, Cary had become determined to be the father of a child. He told the Los Angeles film critic Kevin Thomas years later, "Be sure you have a child. No matter how, have a child." He had even decided he would have a Jewish baby, and for a while dated Susan Strasberg, daughter of the acting teacher Lee Strasberg: she recalls that he offered her marriage and security if she would give him a Jewish child. Now, it was clear that he wanted the half-Jewish Dyan to be the mother. But first, like the manic central figure he might have played in Hitchcock's *Vertigo*, he had to remake her, obsessively changing her hairstyle, her make-up, her clothes, her behaviour even, until she should satisfy his requirements, and become the woman he wanted for his wife. How soon their physical relationship began is uncertain, but what is clear is that, despite his frequent cruelty to, and domination of, Miss Cannon, she was unable to break with him. He had a hypnotic influence over her, and even compelled her against her will to undergo LSD treatments, which made her ill and severely affected her sense of well-being.

That Touch of Mink was a foolish, superficial affair about a millionaire bachelor whose Rolls-Royce splashes a small-town girl (Doris Day) on a rainy afternoon in Manhattan. A romance ensues, the situations predictable and uninspired. A few touches reflected Cary's life. In one sequence, he takes Doris Day to what she assumes is a romantic assignation in his apartment. She finds that it is in a building still under construction, the pair spend an antiseptic evening in bare, unpainted rooms. Later, all manner of meaningless events occur to prevent them from marrying and going off to Bermuda for their honeymoon. The peculiar sexlessness of the film, the plastic central performances, were all too typical of Universal films at the time.

Delbert Mann recalls:

I found Cary rather strange. He was always charming: always smiling, warm and witty, and very likable. But I think he knew he was quite close to the end of his career. He was rather bored with acting by now; he was looking forward to not doing it anymore, and it just did not challenge him or excite him. Maybe it was the role; he was playing someone I think essentially rather close to himself; therefore, the role itself didn't offer the kind of stimulation another part might have. His concern seemed more with the physical aspects of the production than with his performance, though in every way he was always totally professional, on time, never caused any problems, knew his lines.

Mann feels that Cary's chief concern was with the paintings which decorated an office set, the clothes and shoes Doris Day wore, and as a result, making *That Touch of Mink* was "not the most comfortable, not the most fun experience I ever had"; he felt, as so many others did, grateful for Cary's warmth and friendliness, and kept asking himself, he remembers, "How can a man be this cheerful all the time? What is it that's going on behind that? There was a wall there that I never could get through and come away saying, 'Yes, I really know Cary Grant.'"

Stanley Shapiro remembers Cary's fanatical emphasis on detail. Convinced that the aforementioned office set supplied by the Universal art department scarcely suggested the opulence of a multi-millionaire, he brought in some paintings he had owned since his marriage to Barbara Hutton and hung them on the walls. Disliking the look of the doorknobs, convinced that they looked cheap, he believed that by putting a spot of black paint in the middle of them they would appear more elegant. At night, after he left the set, Shapiro wiped off the dots with paint remover. Next morning, Cary would arrive, note that they had been erased, take out a tiny brush from his pocket, dip it in paint and replace the dots. Once again, Shapiro would remove them. Finally, Shapiro cracked and said, sharply, "Cary, if you and Doris are on the screen and someone looks past you into the back of the set and sees a dot in the middle of a doorknob, we're paying you too much money." Cary laughed, but the dots went back again.

Delbert Mann remembers the story differently. He recalls that the two large, ornate brass handles on the office double door, contained a jade-coloured stone in the centre about three-quarters of an inch in diameter, so they would not be seen in a long-distance shot. Cary always disliked the colour of jade, and felt that it was inappropriate for the handles. Shooting stopped for two hours while the art department staff came down to discuss the matter. Cary insisted that the doorknobs be replaced. Alexander Golitzen, chief studio art director, announced that he was unable to find anything similar. Meanwhile, the company was kept waiting, at very considerable cost. Finally, Golitzen had the doorknobs painted white. Mann adds:

> I made sure in photographing the picture that we never saw the goddamned door handles, that they were never visible on the screen. That did annoy me. It was such a foolish waste of time and money. I never said anything about it to Cary; I wanted to maintain as comfortable a relationship with him as possible.

An incident during the shooting was reminiscent of another in the making of *The Bishop's Wife*. There was a sequence to be shot in a fake taxi supposedly travelling through the streets of New York, and both Cary and Doris Day insisted they be photographed on the right side of the face. Throughout the shooting, Mann had done his best to accommodate them, by staging each set-up appropriately. But it was difficult to satisfy their requirements because of the nature of the scene in the taxi. Nor, Delbert Mann says, did it matter "one whit who was on the left side or who was on the right side of the cab, since it was a totally static scene covered by several camera angles".

Mann remembers that Cary came on the set first, and said very gently that he wanted his right side shown. The director shrugged and agreed, saying that this could be arranged without any trouble. He reversed the two stand-ins who were sitting in the back of the prop taxi. Satisfied, Cary returned to his dressing-room. But when Doris Day emerged and saw that the stand-ins had been switched, she went back to her own dressing-room and angrily called her husband, Marty Melcher, who was one of the co-producers.

Melcher called Mann, who explained the problem to him. Cary and Melcher joined Miss Day in her dressing-room for a prolonged discussion. Mann had all the stage lights turned off and sat in near-darkness waiting for a decision.

At last, Melcher emerged and requested that Mann join the discussion. Mann refused. "Doris is crying," Melcher told Mann. Mann replied, "I can't help it. It's your problem." Two hours of further talking went on. Finally, Cary walked out of the dressing-room and returned to his own. Melcher told Mann, "Put the stand-ins back in position." Doris Day had won.

This was painful for Cary, but he proved to be both gentleman and professional in the matter. Mann remarked succinctly: "It took another couple of hours for Doris's tears to be dried and for her make-up to be repaired." He adds:

> Cary never mentioned the matter, nor did she. They were quite cheerful and at ease with each other in the doing of the scene. She won the battle. She was the lady, and she was firm-willed. And there is some distinction between her right and left profiles – more so than Cary's.

Delbert Mann reports that he had been accustomed in other pictures to having a certain amount of relaxed, amusing badinage between himself and the players. On his film *Lover Come Back*, with Doris Day, Rock Hudson and Tony Randall, he had had a wonderful time, enjoying many jokes with the star. But working with Cary was different:

> There was not that kind of ease and teasing each other and joking back and forth. Our relationship was pleasant but formal. The toughness I saw in Doris was expressed in her extreme attention to how she looked, which led to that sort of over-gauzed, soft-focus sort of close-up. She was aware of the fact that lines were starting to show, and one can understand that concern, but beyond that she was marvelously witty and gay and fun, and highly

professional. I would say she was more popular with the crew than Cary was . . . not that Cary was in any way disliked. He was jovial and easy, but he didn't bring the kind of totally relaxed sense of fun that Rock brought to the set.

According to the art director Alexander Golitzen, soon after the shooting Cary decided he was bored with the view from his bungalow, which showed nothing more interesting than some bushes. He ordered the art department to make him a *trompe-l'oeil* painting of a pinewood door opening onto a typical English scene of a path going up through a garden to a cloudy grey skyline with patches of pale blue and lambs gambolling on distant hills. The scene was painted perfectly – it seemed. But Cary summoned the whole art department and demanded to know why they had made a serious mistake. They protested that they had not. He pointed to the door. "What's wrong with that?" he said. Several remembered that pinewood doors were not common in England. But that wasn't what he was complaining about. "Do you *see*?" Cary Grant said. "You can't see the sky through that knothole in the door!"

One of the friendships Cary preserved at the time was with his former director Richard Brooks. Brooks was shooting *Elmer Gantry*, from Sinclair Lewis' novel about an evangelist, with Burt Lancaster as the star. Cary had sent Brooks clippings about various evangelists, with notes suggesting an appropriate approach to the story. Brooks would drop over to the house on Beverly Grove Drive, and Cary would provide all kinds of valuable ideas. After *Gantry* was released, they had close discussions on religion; Brooks says:

Cary was of the opinion that everybody should have his own religion and not interfere with anybody else's. My impression is he was not sure about the existence of a God, a formal God as described in the Bible. Yet despite that he felt there was a power on earth which made things

329

cohesive, made everything hang together, and if that was God he understood it. He could not believe in a personalised God because of the injustices he saw around the world. He hated the fact that formal religion caused anger and hatred among people, which annoyed him and hurt him deeply. He took these matters very seriously.

Delbert Mann remembers that after *That Touch of Mink* was completed, he received no feedback from Cary. He says that there was "a sense of relief that the picture was finally over, even though it was a comedy, and right to the end I had felt I should have been having a better time doing it than I did".

In Hollywood that season, Cary enjoyed a much-publicised liaison with Greta Thyssen, the former Miss Denmark. He first noticed her when she walked by his table in a restaurant, and had word sent to her the following day that he would like her to have dinner with him in his office. Beautiful, with masses of gold hair, a wide smile, brilliantly intense eyes and high cheekbones, Miss Thyssen was seen with him everywhere. She made a telling statement to the fan magazine *TV Movie Screen* in August 1963:

> One of the first things he explained to me was his unique philosophy of life. According to him – and this is a viewpoint he expressed over and over again – he has a full right to love all the attractive people he meets. He believes that many people feel this way, but that most are afraid to admit it . . . Maybe he's right. Maybe the only thing different about him is the fact that he dares to admit his feelings. At any rate, that is his theory, and it carries over even to marriage: if people are married, he says, they can still have an attraction to others. What I suppose he actually means is that you can love more than one person at a time . . .

Miss Thyssen continued in the same vein. She remarked that Cary told her often, "I might love you today, but I can make no promises if I find someone as pretty as you tomorrow." She added that one of the reasons they were happy together was because she never made any demands on Cary; he was used to having his own way, and did not appreciate anyone disagreeing with him. She reported his strictness with his staff, demanding they be constantly on their toes and keep everything in immaculate order. Once again, he applied Professor Higgins tactics to her. He told her how to dress and apply make-up, having, on their second date, informed her he hated her use of cosmetics (an echo of his rudeness to Alexis Smith on *Night and Day*, and to Sophia Loren on *Houseboat*). She described, accurately or not, romantic evenings in charming restaurants with strolling violinists, dinners in his huge circular bed, served by a butler on individual trays, followed by wine and coffee. Evenings were spent watching television on an enormous set built into the wall near the bed. Miss Thyssen went a step further: "[Cary] can teach younger men quite a few tricks when it comes to the romance department!"

She described aimless drives in the Rolls-Royce through the Hollywood Hills, towards the beach. Sometimes, she insisted, he would utter such words as, "You have the sexiest-looking body I have ever seen."

Whether this relationship was as romantic as Miss Thyssen claimed is uncertain. What is certain is that it did not last very long. Simultaneously, Cary was living with Dyan Cannon and was still married to Betsy Drake; and at all times he showed signs only of a continuing desire for gratification. His detachment and self-absorption, typical of stars, must have exasperated everyone.

Nineteen sixty-one passed without incident. There were still no indications that Betsy would divorce Cary; in his diary for Thanksgiving Day, November 23, Clifford Odets wrote:

At night I went alone out to Betsy's for . . . dinner. A nice, small group there, an older couple and a younger, both men writers. And Cary with his usual unease — where to put the feet down. His relationship with B[etsy] seems a very strange and tangled one. They live apart and are on the verge of legal divorce, but he spends as much time with her as possible, as if she were home for him. As for her, she seems to be forging ahead from weak member to the stronger, with him somewhat abject and apologetic. What? I don't know.

Odets added the following note:

In one way or another, [Cary] is always trying to *disarm* you. He feels threatened — you may lose your regard, affection or what-not. He is always disarming everyone . . . Later he may take it out on you.

Cary continued to annoy his old friend Odets by showing interest in one of Odets' properties as the basis for a film, and then, when it came down to concentrated discussion, skipping away in an irritating manner.

For some time in 1962, studio boss Edward Muhl tried to convince Cary to make a comedy thriller, *Charade*. Muhl recalls that Cary was very reluctant to agree, because the script called for him to chase a much younger woman. Muhl says:

He was fifty-eight years old at the time, as charming and handsome as ever, but for some reason he thought the screenplay was unseemly. So it was changed, and in the new version the girl was coquettish, leading him on, and he was playing hard-to-get.

Cary went ahead, with one of his favourite actresses, Audrey Hepburn, as co-star. *Charade* was to be shot in Paris, based upon a script by the accomplished Peter Stone. Cary would play Peter Joshua, an American agent living in France who helps an unhappy widow, Regina Lambert, to solve the mystery of her husband's murder. Walter Matthau would play the villain. The director would once again be Stanley Donen.

Cary decided not to stay in a hotel in Paris, but instead, and rather surprisingly, moved into Barbara Hutton's apartment. His British chauffeur Tony Faramus arrived by Channel ferry with the Rolls-Royce. Mona Eldridge, who was Miss Hutton's secretary at the time, recalled in her memoir how, as Cary walked down the long central hall of the apartment with its glass-fronted display cabinets, containing priceless antique figurines, pieces of jade and snuff boxes, he never examined the contents, but instead glanced from right to left to observe his reflection in the mirrored cabinet doors, fussing over his hair, and fretting over his wrinkles.

Miss Eldridge recorded that he was the despair of Barbara Hutton's cook Herminie, who planned elaborate meals for him: he would wind up eating nothing much more substantial than a poached egg, served on a flawless china plate. This was his secret: he refused to do more than the most minimal exercise, but his frugal diet fulfilled his most often repeated personal slogan, "Think Thin".

Miss Eldridge noted that Cary spent much of his time making elaborate decisions to travel all over the world, asking her to make the reservations, and then suddenly cancelling. He promised daily that he would autograph a photograph for Herminie, dazzling her with his smile, but finally failed to fulfil his promise. Although he fascinated both Mona Eldridge and the cook with his constant display of charm, he failed to send a thank-you letter when he left.

Miss Eldridge wrote: "It would appear that [his] bisexuality took the form of alternate preferences. One period of his life it would be men, then he would be heterosexual for several years. I often wondered if he was capable of real, genuine feelings, so obsessed was he with his own public image."

At this time, he was constantly getting in touch with very young women, expressing his love for each, equally, then dropping them with startling swiftness. Ageing, he was apparently trying to bolster his ego. His quirkiness intrigued Mona Eldridge constantly. Although he allegedly disliked reporters, he would, she noted, stare out of his bedroom window day and night to see if there were reporters waiting there, and count them, expressing great pleasure when he found that their number had increased. On a whim, he noted that one was a very pretty, dark girl, and delighted the cub reporter by summoning her to the apartment and giving her an exclusive interview. He was overjoyed as she stared at him with rapture.

Although Audrey Hepburn and her husband Mel Ferrer got along quite well with Cary, they sometimes had their differences. Herbert Sterne, who was in charge of publicity for the film, says:

It was normal for contact sheets of stills, prepared for approval by stars, to include both the male and female lead in a picture. However, both Cary and Audrey wanted separate sheets in which neither one would appear with the other. This was absurd. Cary didn't want Audrey to look as good as he did in the photographs, and Audrey didn't want Cary to look as good as she did. So I said to Stanley Donen, "Let us have two sheets, so each star can kill a still and the other will not know which still they have killed." This went great until my secretary, who was busy kissing Audrey's ass, sneaked out a print which Cary had killed and made sure it was published. Cary came in, very gentlemanly, showed me the newspaper picture, and asked me how did it get out. I said, "I haven't the fuckingest idea." "Well," Cary asked, "how are we going to stop this happening again?" I told him that each negative would go to him and to Audrey, and both would be given a punch to kill what they didn't like. We couldn't find a punch in Paris, so somebody went down and paid all kinds of money and bought punches from the people in the Métro, the Paris subway.

During a scene being shot in a theatre, a chase sequence involving Cary, Audrey, and a demented Walter Matthau, the set was closed; but without warning, Hollis Alpert, the well-known film critic of the *Saturday Review*, turned up.* Herb Sterne begged the stars to allow Alpert on the sound-stage and to give him the VIP treatment, which they did with a supreme effort.

Cary and Audrey worked well together. In a sequence shot among the pillars of the Comédie Française, in which Audrey had to decide whether Cary Grant or Walter Matthau was telling her the truth, Cary and Audrey worked out a series of ballet-like movements to overcome the improbabilities of the scene, giving what could have been a tiresome episode a good deal of visual charm.

A member of the film company staff recalls:

One night, in Paris, I went to a famous gay bar and restaurant. The atmosphere was very highly charged, as it tends to be in such places. It was even more so that night because, to the astonishment of many people there, Cary Grant appeared with a very handsome young man, sat down at a table and had dinner, with every eye in the room on him and his companion! He didn't seem to care.

Despite the gruelling winter weather that season, Cary had good reason to be in high spirits during the shooting of *Charade*. *Operation Petticoat* had earned him at least three million dollars, and the picture would be his property after eight years. It was one of the most commercially successful comedies ever made. *The Grass is Greener* had done slightly less well, but he still benefited from substantial profits it made, and *That Touch of Mink* earned him a fortune. *Charade* would enhance his bank balance still more. It was a pleasant, undemanding film, fairly well directed and well played, especially by the principals.

---

* Alpert says Cary Grant told him of his bisexuality.

In August 1962, Betsy Drake obtained her divorce from Cary. She turned up in a Los Angeles courthouse to tell Judge Edward R. Brand that Cary had left her for long periods, appeared bored with her, preferred watching television to talking to her, and "told me he didn't want to be married". She said, looking tense for a moment, "I still love him very much, I was always in love with him and I still am." Mental cruelty was the grounds for the divorce, which was granted without demur, and the property settlement was reasonable. Grant did not attend the hearing.

In 1963, Clifford Odets was suffering from terminal cancer. Not yet sixty, his career had declined, and his health with it. His disaffection with Cary had increased and he blamed Cary for not picking up his scripts when he had begged Cary either to guarantee an appearance in certain of them or to find a place for them at MCA-Universal. By August, Odets was dying at the Cedars of Lebanon Hospital. Cary arrived with a large bouquet of carnations, but Odets would not see him. Odets was convinced Cary was phony and false; he refused to see him and told the nurse to give the flowers to another patient. It was a painful and unpleasant ending to a friendship that had lasted over twenty years.

Charade had a triumphant opening at Radio City Music-Hall in New York in December; Cary enjoyed standing at the back of the auditorium on the opening night to drink in the audience's laughter. He was already planning another film, *Father Goose*, from a script by Peter Stone.

At Christmas, he put through his customary phone call to Elsie Leach, who was now eighty-six years old. In the previous twelve months, he had made three trips to Bristol to see her, always staying in the Churchill Suite at the Royal Hotel in Bristol. Reporter Henry Gris dropped in for an interview with him at his Beverly Hills home right after the holidays. Gris asked him how he looked so young. That most unhappy, tense, anxious and fanatically obsessive of men fibbed cheerfully: "It's because I am permanently relaxed. I don't like to call this the secret of keeping young, but that's what it amounts to. And I have accomplished this by various means over the years."

Grant revealed that he was still taking LSD regularly. Commenting on the drug's healing properties, he said:

> You have to overcome fears. One fear that lives in every heart, including mine, is the fear of death, but I have conditioned myself to accept it and so reduce even this fear to a minimum. There should be no limit to one's desire to stay alive . . . for a hundred years. And longer. You reassure yourself of that and go on from there. And as long as a man remains a man with an ability to love, he should feel secure . . .

Cary did not, according to statements made later by Dyan Cannon, live up to these precepts in real life. She was living with him at the time at the Beverly Grove Drive house. It was scarcely an accommodating establishment. His miserliness showed in the lack of luxury in his personal environment. There was very little furniture, and some rooms were virtually bare. Venetian blinds were poorly dusted, odd in view of his fanaticism over cleanliness, and, when broken, remained unrepaired for months. Carpets were worn and threadbare. There was no sense of warmth and comfort in the home, which seemed austere and even unpleasant, and few were entertained there.

As Dyan would charge in their divorce hearing in 1967, Cary would "beat me with his fists", and "laugh when I cringed in fear". On one occasion, he locked her in her room. On another, he struck her to the ground because he didn't like her wearing a miniskirt. His relationship with her resembled that with Virginia Cherrill in its brutality and harshness. Yet because he was Cary Grant, and because the couple had many happy times together, Dyan forgave everything.

She took up health foods, homeopathic medicine, hypnotism and almost anything that might possibly help her.

Yet the pain remained, and to this day she is unable to talk about Cary Grant. She once told her friend Corinne Introtter, "My life with Cary was hell. It was like *The Diary of a Mad Housewife*." In that novel and in the film version, the heroine was made to suffer from the insupportably priggish and domineering behaviour of her husband, who constantly and rudely criticised her hair, make-up, clothes, figure, deportment, ability to reason, and common sense. Despite his cruelty to Dyan Cannon, Cary was determined to have a child by her, yet years passed without her becoming pregnant.

Cary became absorbed in *Father Goose*. It was a change of pace for him: the story of a beachcomber, Walter Eckland, living in New Britain during World War II, who is enlisted as a coast-watcher, one of the courageous Australian spies who radioed their reports on Japanese fleet and troop movements. The story contained a distorted echo of the past: Errol Flynn had begun his association with Dr. Hermann Erben in New Britain in 1933 and had volunteered to be a coast-watcher during the 1940s. Fortunately for Australian and American security, he was turned down.

Cary worked on the script with Peter Stone and Frank Tarloff. David Miller, who had handled one of Joan Crawford's best pictures, *Sudden Fear*, was to have directed. Charles Higham visited Cary Grant following one of the production meetings. He noticed the cleanliness, elegance and order of the Grant bungalow. When he arrived, Grant was wearing a grey suit and tie, while everyone around him was in jeans and open checked shirts, and had just finished dictating his correspondence to his secretary, Dorothy Palmer.

Grant explained how the company was working long hours on *Father Goose*, breaking off in the evenings for dinner at Storey's, a nearby restaurant. He said that he was involved in casting the picture, running endless film clips in order to make selections, and the day before he had decided to cast Trevor Howard, whom he had seen in *Outcast of the Islands*, as the taciturn Australian Naval Commander

338

Frank Houghton. He also wanted Leslie Caron as the coast-watcher's girlfriend since Audrey Hepburn had proved to be too busy with another picture. He, himself, was looking forward to being the bearded, grizzled and unkempt beachcomber in the new picture.

The conversation was charmingly inconsequential, bland and superficial, designed to conceal his personality from the most investigative eyes. His glasses were more like props than the real article, almost like stage glasses, and he seemed to be wearing contact lenses. With the curious staring blankness of a ventriloquist's doll, and the perfect razor-cut hair, his face looked steely, hard and secretive.

As his secretary and an assistant disappeared, Grant showed Higham into an inner office, pointing at a yellow Mexican table, relieved by painted flowers. "Kind of gays things up a little," Grant said, with a frank and knowing wink. It was hard to miss the point.

Lunch with the director George Cukor had been set for twelve thirty at his house, and Higham had to interrupt Grant in the middle of a sentence to reveal this, and therefore he had to leave. Grant's face froze for a moment, and it was clear that he was displeased. But he recovered himself and said, with a flashing smile, "It's your loss." Then he lied wittily, perhaps fearing that his remark might be misinterpreted, "Of course, George Cukor is much more important than I am!"

David Miller dropped out of *Father Goose* after many script discussions, and Ralph Nelson, a capable, but not outstanding, middle-of-the-road director, took over. Shooting took place in Ocho Rios, Jamaica, in early 1964. After Cary's return, Dyan Cannon, whom he had asked not to make pictures during their relationship, and who had unwisely given up her screen career for him, was away, touring in the musical *How to Succeed in Business Without Really Trying*. He became lonely at Beverly Grove Drive, and with unusual generosity paid for her to return to him on Sundays from various cities; she would fly back on the Sunday night. This was exhausting and difficult for her, but apparently she couldn't resist him, or even fail to do what he wanted. Enslaved by him, she had lost her willpower.

Cary's life assumed a dull monotony. He arrived very early each day at the studio, where the popular gatemen Chester and Scotty greeted him. Once in his office, he would have a cup of tea, attend to his correspondence and confer with his assistant Fred Clasel, and do the occasional interview. After a light lunch of salad, he always saw his attorney Stanley Fox, and then he would go out onto the veranda of his bungalow and sun himself, wearing a metal face-frame. At weekends, he went to a hacienda he had bought ten years earlier in Palm Springs. He took a close interest in all of his investments, and knew to the last penny where his money was.

In June of 1965, Dyan became pregnant. She was over-joyed. At the same time, she came from a conventional family and couldn't face the idea of bearing a child outside marriage. According to Cary's friend, Binnie Barnes, "When Dyan knew she was pregnant, Cary had to marry her." Delighted though he was, even thrilled at this long-delayed proof of his virility, Cary became characteristically coy again in the wake of the discovery, and it was only after a protracted delay that he decided he would marry Dyan. A delay which caused her a good deal of mental anguish. She told Henry Gris:

I remember my finding out that I was pregnant, and my being so nervous about telling him. I came home and made four tuna-fish sandwiches and ate them all while figuring how to break the news to him. And then he walked into the house, and he knew [the truth] by the look on my face . . . We celebrated that night by going to a ball game . . . He was so frightened, even if he didn't want to show it, and concerned, you know, suddenly, my God, it's happened!

You know, he didn't want to get married because, he thought, if we did it would ruin our relationship. "I can't be married," he said. "I've tried. I ought to know." But

I couldn't understand that, and of course I wanted a child, his child. So, after that he asked me three times. The first time he was so nervous he came down to my house and cracked up his car in the garage.

I said, "Okay, I'll marry you," then nothing happened. So after a while I said to him, "It doesn't look like we are getting married, so I'd better check out." He didn't like that, so he asked me again.

This time, Dyan accepted. Cary had wanted her to meet his mother before he actually proposed and they flew to Bristol. Elsie Leach was in a nursing-home. The first time Cary drove Dyan in the Rolls to the nursing-home, he panicked and decided not to introduce her to Elsie after all. However, she did meet his cousin Eric* and Eric's wife Maggie. She loved them. While he visited Elsie, Dyan told Henry Gris, "I did the town and read books and walked through churches and spent a lot of time with his cousins, who are marvellous."

At last, Dyan met Elsie, who called her Betsy. Dyan said later, "Elsie's incredible, with a psyche that has the strength of a twenty-mule team. We had good times with her, we had fish and chips and drank beer with her. A remarkable woman."

Cary was apprehensive of too much attention before the wedding, so he and Dyan decided to marry in secrecy in Las Vegas. The nuptials took place on July 22, 1965, at the Desert Inn, which Howard Hughes owned. According to some versions, Howard Hughes was present, but this is unlikely. These were years when Cary saw little or nothing of him. The couple flew to London for the honeymoon, and to do some advance promotion for *Father Goose*, and travelled on to Bristol for another visit with Elsie. The paparazzi swarmed into town, besieging the Grants at their hotel, asking such rude and pointed questions as why they

* Not to be confused with Cary's half-brother, Eric Leslie, whom he would not acknowledge at the time.

had not invited her parents to the wedding. Cary became flustered, red-faced and angry at this intrusion into his life. He was furious when reporters tried to worm their way into the hospital and talk to Elsie, and had them thrown out.

Cary had always been very careful not to provoke the press, but on this occasion he antagonised reporters, and for once some of the articles on him were less than flattering. Yet few took the occasion to attack Dyan, and many remarked on her strong, sexy attractiveness. When they returned to Hollywood, the first announcements that the couple were expecting a child appeared.

16

Soon after the wedding, Cary embarked on plans for another picture, *Walk, Don't Run*, a remake of George Stevens' *The More the Merrier*. The light-hearted comedy was set in an overcrowded Tokyo during the 1964 Olympic Games, but unfortunately the new script by Sol Saks was a pale echo of the original, the whimsical humour of which was drawn from the bundling that was necessary in World War II Washington, DC.

That all was not well with the Grants' marriage was made clear when Cary decided to leave for Japan alone. The official reason given was that Dyan was not feeling well enough to make the journey across the Pacific, but the fact of the matter is that she was seen in public, glowing vibrantly, with all of the apparent cheerfulness of an expectant mother; the couple apparently felt they needed to separate for a while to try to iron out their differences. Barely two months after the marriage, in the last week of September 1965, Cary flew with the director Charles Walters to Tokyo, where he joined his co-stars Samantha Eggar and Jim Hutton. The Columbia film was fully backed by Grant's own production company.

Cast and crew were housed at the forbidding, vast, and excessively modern Okura Hotel, with Cary occupying the Imperial Suite. The weather was bad that autumn, and, as in so many other of Cary's pictures, day after day was washed out by rain. Cary seldom emerged from his hotel during the breaks in shooting, only attending one big social function, at the American Embassy; a cocktail party in honour of his friend Senator Ted Kennedy and Kennedy's wife Joan. He saw a good deal of them during their stay.

Much of his time was spent in training in race-walking with Toshio Hosokawa, the Japanese Olympic race-walking coach of 1964. Cary kept up remarkably well with Jim Hutton, the athletic young actor who had spent three months at Terry Hunt's Gymnasium in Hollywood, mastering heel-and-toe walking. Scenes were shot at the Olympic Stadium, in the narrow, winding streets of the Shinjuku district, on the Ginza, with its dazzle of electric signs, in the Happo-En Gardens, and at the Shimbashi Railway Station. Despite the black clouds that filled the sky and the sudden bursts of rain, the gifted cinematographer Harry Stradling of *Suspicion* and *Houseboat*, overcame every technical problem, shooting in the midst of dense crowds in all areas, never allowing anyone to suspect the presence of his hidden cameras. He used food trucks, vans, boarded-up buildings, and disused telephone booths, or even had cameras tucked into the overcoats of the crew, or (for stills) carried by Japanese messenger boys in the baskets of their bicycles. Cary was in a sombre, detached mood during most of the work. He seemed absorbed in it, quite ignoring the countless dubious pleasures that awaited the tourist in the back alleys of the city. Attempts to lure him to a geisha house failed. He apparently needed time to reflect, to be alone and celibate, to feel peace of mind in a strange foreign environment. Few journalists penetrated his privacy in the tourist bus used as his dressing-room.

The other actors were equally preoccupied. Jim Hutton (his son, Timothy Hutton, has stated) was overwhelmed by the idea of working with Cary, hero-worshipping him unabashedly. Hutton was engaged at the time to the attractive Lynn Sofro, and his co-star, Samantha Eggar, was caught up in her marriage to Tom Stern, an independent film producer, and in her new baby son.

Cary took a paternal interest in his fellow actors, monitoring Jim Hutton's tendency to drink too much, helping to supervise his physical training; making Samantha Eggar alter her hairstyle, and redoing her wardrobe. On the occasional evenings when he went out, it was only to visit senior executives of major Japanese companies, who gave official, rather dull parties in his honour. The head of Sony was a fan of his, and invited him several times to his home.

Dyan, her warm and sentimental feelings for Cary overcoming her misgivings, turned up to surprise him on his sixty-second birthday on January 18, 1966. She stayed only briefly but the film's publicity department, in an attempt to build up the importance of the quick stop-over, pretended that she had come to see Cary for several weeks. Shooting finished at the end of January, with Cary in a depressed mood. Jim Hutton recalled that Cary would talk to him for hours about what he wanted for his child and how he hoped to have many more children; becoming a father, he said, was more important to him than anything he had ever done.

When he returned to Los Angeles, Dyan was already eight months pregnant. She had found a bigger house for them, rented from the singer-actor Gordon MacRae. Now that the baby was about to be born, Cary seemed in a better mood; but he was aware that *Walk, Don't Run* was not going to be a successful film, and he was also aware that he had not made a success of his marriage. His moods kept switching from exhilaration and excitement to considerable gloom. He began taking LSD again. These were not happy times, and neither Cary nor Dyan felt inclined to discuss them later.

On February 26, 1966, Dyan went into labour, and Cary drove her to St. John's Hospital in Burbank, which he had settled on after, with his usual obsessiveness, going from hospital to hospital to decide which one should be favoured. He had gone through ward after ward, carefully inspected entrance halls, and insisted upon examining the diet sheets prepared by the resident dieticians. If he could have built a hospital for the occasion himself, he would have done. Once Dyan was installed, he fussed over the décor of the room, the flowers and how they were arranged, the food Dyan was getting, and the cleanliness of every piece of furniture and of the floor. No one would have been surprised if he had taken out a scrubbing brush, soap and a pail, and got down on all fours. Yet, along with his numerous interferences with hospital administration, he was so irresistibly charming in his persistence, and the nurses were so overcome by his presence, that he conquered everyone. Female members of the staff would line up outside the private room just to catch a glimpse of him.

He gave an almost comic performance of an expectant father, pacing up and down outside the delivery room, and peeking into it every few minutes. He was not present at the actual birth, a custom that did not come into general effect until later, but he was under so much stress he might as well have given birth to the baby himself.

It was not an easy delivery, and Dyan was not in the best of health. But the small size of the child was helpful: it was a girl, whom Cary and Dyan immediately named Jennifer. She was only four and a half pounds in weight, and there was some concern about this, but almost immediately the baby was removed from the incubator, she showed her personality: she was winsome and adorable. Cary had never been more jubilant. And yet, such was his nature, he couldn't relax in his new role as father, but became consumed with his greatest obsession. From now on, Jennifer would be virtually his entire life. Since she supplied proof of his manhood, he felt that she was part of him, not just his child, but his *raison d'être* – an extension of his physical being. According to one writer, "He went to his daughter's room at seven thirty each morning to gaze down at her; he supervised the warming of her bottle and the food she would be weaned on; he made certain that he would always be back from working on the editing of *Walk, Don't Run* for her seven o'clock feeding time. Every sound she uttered was tape-recorded and every move she made was photographed either by himself or by photographers he hired." He sent picture after picture to Elsie, not merely showing off his offspring to her, but, quite clearly, telling her, as he would like to shout to gossips, "You see, I'm a normal man after all." There was something verging on the psychopathic about his consuming interest in the baby. The more practical and down-to-earth Dyan, passionately though she loved Jennifer, found his behaviour grating and extreme. It maddened her; and then there were other problems. Dyan's father objected severely to Dyan taking LSD, and arrived unexpectedly, insisting that she stop at once. Cary shouted, "You may be her father, but I'm her husband, and I'm the one she answers to now!" Mr. Friesen replied, "I would tell my next-door neighbour not to take LSD, so why shouldn't I tell my daughter?" Cary continued the argument, and Friesen left. Cary infuriated Dyan by refusing to allow her to take the baby to Seattle to visit her grandparents. The arguments went on and on. Although she had continued to devote most of her time to Jennifer, and the child brought her great happiness, Dyan was utterly miserable with Cary at a time when they should have been bound together by their parenthood. His finicking and fanaticism over the child slowly but surely ground her down. Years later, she told a reporter: "I'm telling you, if I'd stayed in that marriage I'd be dead today. Dead. Dead. Dead. Dead. Really *dead*! In a grave! Dead! I don't want to talk about him. He's a real pain."

Cary cannot be blamed for his behaviour at the time. So hypersensitive a personality, desiring to control every tiny thing in his life, was bound to become consumed with fatherhood. He fussed and fretted over Jennifer's slightest sign of discomfort, and a cough or a sneeze brought him to the verge of hysteria. He would snap at Dyan if he felt she was doing something wrong, and sometimes, with gross unfairness, accuse her of being an unfit mother. The spring of 1966 dragged on in miserable discomfort. Only one relief was offered: Cary found a valuable and likeable new employee, who became one of his most trusted aides and friends.

William D. Weaver was a good-looking, somewhat scholarly twenty-five-year-old Kansan with glasses and thinning fair hair, who had devoted his younger years to assisting his mother with his five brothers and sisters; he had toiled

at night-school for an English degree, and had finally obtained a job with the Atomic Energy Commission. He
applied for the post of secretary to Cary when Cary advertised it through an employment agency. In Weaver's book,
The Private Cary Grant, written with Cary's later close
friend, the multi-millionaire industrialist William Currie
McIntosh, Weaver remembered the circumstances of the
interview. Cary asked Weaver to sit down in a large armchair, placed so that his eye level was below that of Cary's,
as Cary sat at the desk. According to McIntosh, Cary liked
the fact that Weaver had been with the Atomic Energy
Commission, because he was certain that Weaver would
have the capacity to keep a secret, and that therefore he
could keep his many secrets. The existing secretary,
Dorothy, was dislodged, and Weaver took her place.
Warned that Cary would not tolerate the slightest degree
of unpunctuality, he reported to work every day at exactly
nine a.m. He found himself making reservations for Cary
at the Polo Lounge of the Beverly Hills Hotel or the Swedish
restaurant, Scandia; the bungalow became a second home
to him, with its brown leather chairs, spinet, *trompe-l'oeil*
paintings, wedding pictures of Elsie and Elias Leach, and
veranda where Cary tanned himself.

Sometimes, Weaver had to go to the house in Benedict
Canyon, with its swimming-pool and rich groves of trees.
According to Weaver and McIntosh, Cary would sometimes
greet the secretary in his pyjamas, ill-tempered, darkly
brooding, and shouting or screaming at some real or imaginary slight. The authors wrote: "There would be an air
of dither and oppression over the entire household . . ."
The atmosphere was "cheerless, and almost ghostly"; the
recently engaged English butler-chauffeur resembling a figure in a Charles Addams drawing, and the maid, also
English, stealing around silently, almost invisibly, as though
afraid to be seen. So irritated was Cary by his beloved
Jennifer's screams, that the nanny would get very upset if
the child even whimpered.

The quarrels Weaver witnessed between Grant and Dyan

were "a nightmare". Cary proved to be as harshly cruel to Weaver as he was to Dyan. He constantly bitched over his punctuation and spelling, his style of writing, his clothes, and the sort of food he liked. Walking up and down, tense, in his white pyjamas, Grant never ceased to grumble like a fishwife.

Although Cary had given some support to Dyan in her career when she went on the stage in *How to Succeed*, now that she was a mother, he assumed the Victorian attitude that she was never to leave the house. When she announced she was going to an acting class, he ran after her down the entrance hall demanding she stay. She refused to obey him, broke free from his grasp and drove off in a fury. He hid her car-keys twice, forcing her to walk to acting school, obtaining a lift home in the evening. Weaver and McIntosh wrote, "On one momentous occasion, the entire household was galvanized into appalled silence, when, after a row had broken out, Grant pursued his wife into the bathroom, locked the door, and could be heard spanking her. A few minutes later, the bathroom window was flung open and Dyan scrambled through to make her way back down the canyon and into the city."

Despite Cary's many statements that LSD had relaxed him, and changed him from a tormented and tormenting person into a sunny persona not unlike the man millions saw on the screen, it had in fact done nothing of the sort. Friends such as Binnie Barnes and Johnny Maschio and Constance Moore were appalled by Cary's cruelty to Dyan.

Dyan made two trips to New York in 1966. One of these was recalled by Tom Stout, then representative of TWA at Los Angeles Airport. Dyan had decided to take Jennifer to Manhattan. She told Stout that only she and the baby would be travelling. No sooner had Stout seen mother and daughter to the VIP lounge, than he had a message to go to the kerbside, where Cary was in his chauffeur-driven car. Cary told him that he would be going to New York with Dyan and Jennifer, but Stout told Cary that the flight was full. Cary jumped out of the car and ran to the airport, locating the gate number from the monitor screen and dashing to the gate as the passengers boarded, red-faced with fury. Stout was just behind him. Despite the fact that he didn't have a ticket, Cary pushed past the supervisor and forced his way through the plane door, joining the silent and embarrassed Dyan. He shouted, furiously, "I will not leave this plane! I am travelling to New York with my wife and baby!" Both passengers and attendants were stupefied by this announcement. A woman who knew Cary spoiled everything for Dyan by generously offering to give up her seat and take another flight. The last thing Stout saw was Cary flopping into the vacated first-class seat, arguing vigorously with Dyan.

Cary came down to visit the Maschios at their boat moored in Marina del Rey, begging them to help him repair the marriage. He said that Dyan was so sentimental that possibly if they were to invite her to the meeting, she would reconsider. Anxious to help they asked Dyan without telling her Cary would be there. She turned up; Maschio stocked the bar with Dom Perignon, and the food was the best available, but despite the sailing and swimming and sun-bathing, nothing could break the severe tension that existed between the Grants. "It was terribly sad," Constance Moore says.

In a last-ditch effort to save the failing, one-year-old marriage, Cary and Dyan took off to England in August of 1966. They decided to sail on the British P & O—Orient Line supership *Oriana*, a vessel that did service mostly in the Pacific. The voyage would take them via the Panama Canal and the Caribbean to Southampton.

It should have been a straightforward, exciting departure, in which the brass band, the multi-coloured streamers, and the excited, waving crowds would create the idyllic beginning to an escapist adventure at sea. But unhappily, so extreme was Cary's state of neurosis, the entire episode was a torment for all concerned. Among the group who accompanied them to the ship were the Maschios and William Weaver. Constance Moore remembers:

It was very tense when they left. They suddenly fired the nanny at the last minute. And hired another one. Cary had booked four cabins by mistake, one for himself, one for Dyan, one for the nanny and one for Jennifer, who, of course, would have to be in with the nanny. So one cabin went to waste.

Dyan didn't make things any easier by her own agitation. Cary had quite sensibly insisted on having very few suit-cases, realising how restricted the cabin space would be. But Dyan was nervous about the numerous parties that would be taking place on board, from the Captain's soirées to the various festive nights commemorating different countries. As a result, much to Cary's fury, she took with her thirty-six suitcases, like a travelling princess, and thus compelled Grant to enlist not only the Rolls driven by Tony Faramus, but two station-wagons, one driven by Bill Weaver, and the other by a chauffeur, to accommodate them.

When the couple arrived at the pier, hundreds of papa-razzi appeared and annoyed Cary still more. He screamed at Weaver when he dropped Dyan's jewellery-case and it was almost trampled by the scrum of reporters and photographers. Up in the main deck cabin, Cary, in front of Weaver, lashed Dyan with another of his increasingly frequent outbursts, and charged her with ruining the trip by insisting on the thirty-six suitcases. He ripped them open, hurling the clothes and the fifty pairs of shoes she was taking with her all over the state-room. Dyan screamed and burst into tears; Cary ordered Tony Faramus to pile all the excess clothes, in fact all except two suitcases full, into one of the cars and take them home. The wretched voyage did not improve as it went on. The streak of cruelty that had disfigured Grant's relationships with others now emerged most dangerously, and it was clear by the time the couple reached London that there was no hope for the marriage.

Cary turned on the charm for the press in London,

but he was still deeply unhappy, and so was Dyan. They travelled to Bristol, and, following his usual visit to Elsie, who apparently didn't sense the atrocious tension between the Grants, Cary acceded to persistent requests by his half-brother Eric Leslie's family to meet him. Although from time to time he had given assistance, including the sending of Christmas gifts, to Eric Leslie's wife and children, who were named Robert, Melvin, Nicola, Barbara, Betsy and Virginia, he had understandably shown little interest in them. He was annoyed with Eric, whom he in a sense disowned, and saw nothing of him, only yielding to the family's entreaties when they addressed him through his solicitor in London. He probably blamed him for Elsie's years in the asylum.

He met the children at the Clifton Gorge Hotel. Dyan was with him, if only for appearance's sake. The young Leaches sat almost totally silent, gazing at Cary's almost too-immaculately groomed hair, the perfectly tanned and still handsome face, and his impeccable figure: the antithesis of his dark and violent nature. They were overwhelmed by his presence and couldn't think of anything to say. At the end of what must have been a very strange encounter, Cary, with one of those odd bursts of naturalness and generosity which marked his character, offered to drive the whole family home. Embarrassed because they lived in a council house they didn't want him to see, they told him they had some shopping to do, and asked him to drop them off next to a favourite store. They were amazed when he drove them there not in a Rolls-Royce but in an old Austin.

The couple returned miserably to Los Angeles, their marriage physically at an end. Dyan moved into a guest-house in the grounds. The arguments became increasingly more terrible until at last Dyan could endure the situation no longer. She took Jennifer with her and rented a house at Malibu. Even a last-ditch effort to repair matters through a marriage counsellor failed.

Dyan Cannon said later:

The decision to go through with the divorce was the most difficult . . . of my entire life. It took a great deal out of me. I had been hurt and I couldn't understand why. But in order to get myself out of it, I knew I would have to take myself apart and put myself together again, understanding what life is all about. I went to Esalen.

The Esalen Institute was located in Northern California, near Carmel. There, in carefully controlled conditions, people with emotional problems were taught to release their nervous tension and distress in primal therapy techniques, which included wailing and screaming like newborn babies, or going nude, joining with other naked people, sharing baths as children might do. The intention was to tear away the layers of tortured civilisation that encumbered most individuals, their feelings of pressure and stress in modern urban society, and revert to primitive, untrammelled and uncomplicated feelings. It took Dyan some time to feel comfortable with Esalen. She wasn't happy with her own body, and, she said later, felt painfully self-conscious of displaying it in front of men and women.

Gradually though, she did gain strength. Meanwhile, Cary was in an appalling state of nerves. Losing Jennifer even for a day was unbearable for him. He would break down and sob over the loss of the child. As much as anything else, his ego was wounded. He was forced to realise that even he, with all of his wealth and fame, could not control everything and everyone in his life. Dyan generously agreed to allow him visiting rights, so long as they were within reason. Only when he could play with Jennifer, talk to her and dangle her on his knee was Cary able to deal with life. He tried to woo Dyan back with promises, even encouraging her to appear in a play. But his random behaviour never ceased to nag at Dyan, and sometimes she fled to her parents in Seattle, trying to protect Jennifer by introducing her to a normal family home. Unpredictable as ever, Cary suddenly abandoned his visiting rights in April of 1967 and flew to England for yet another visit to Elsie.

He travelled with the MGM producer Ronnie Lubin, who had obtained a story that was a possibility for him, but he did nothing about it. On his return, he had meetings with an old friend, the bland producer/director Mervyn LeRoy, discussing a film about the life of Buffalo Bill. He said to a *New York Times* writer on June 18, "I've thought about Buffalo Bill for a good many years – I saw him perform in person as a kid – and I think his story as William F. Cody, the post-Civil War Indian scout, and, later, as the Wild West performer in circuses – he was an all-around romantic figure – would make a truly great spectacle film." He neglected to note that Buffalo Bill's last appearance in England was before he was born; nothing came of this.

On August 22, 1967, Dyan sued Cary for divorce. She had moved into a house at 620 N. Foothill Road; Cary was living at 2850 Benedict Canyon Drive. She charged him with cruelty, stating that he had treated her in "an inhuman manner". The suit was filed by her attorney, Frank D. Belcher. In it, Dyan estimated Cary's worth at more than $10 million, and his annual income as $500,000. She asked for reasonable support for her and for Jennifer, citing her monthly expenses as $5,470.

There were numerous delays before the next hearing. Cary's state of mind was appalling. He was terrified he would lose Jennifer completely to her mother, and visits to the baby in the wake of Dyan's statements were, of course, severely strained. Cary tried to break the tension that October by making his first release, a two-track record at Columbia Studios at West 52nd Street, New York. One side was a New Year greeting, "Here's To You", by Dick Hazard and Peggy Lee, and the other side was "A Christmas Lullaby". As Dyan grew more and more cheerful, extrovert and happy to be free, Cary became almost suicidally morose. He spent several weeks in New York, part of them in order to be near Jennifer when Dyan took her there. Cary stayed with an old friend, the former Warner Brothers publicist Bob Taplinger, whom he had remembered with pleasure from the old days. Taplinger was a warm and charming companion, and to some extent he assuaged Cary's discomfiture. Taplinger recalled to a journalist that Cary "used to wait at the house all day for word from the nurse as to when he could see (Jennifer) for an hour or two. He wouldn't make plans for doing anything if there was a chance of seeing her." When Dyan opened in a short-lived play in Manhattan (unpredictable as ever, he turned up at her first night), he hung on and on. The effort didn't work. Cary was still in New York by March of 1968, leaving only briefly to attend the World Fair in Montreal.

Dyan's play closed, and she went back to Los Angeles for the next divorce hearing, at which details of the settlement would be discussed. Cary tried to stop the divorce by appeasing her, helping her to reactivate her film career. He successfully persuaded Mike Frankovich to cast her in the comedy *Bob and Carol and Ted and Alice*. She would prove to be a great success in it, and was nominated for an Oscar. On March 12, Cary compulsively set out to follow her. It was a rain-swept, icy night, with a howling wind. Cary took off for Kennedy Airport in a limousine driven by chauffeur Troy L. Lindahl, accompanied by a friend, the Baroness Gratia von Fürstenberg. More than usually restless, he urged the driver to speed up along the Long Island Expressway. It was intensely dark, and the visibility was virtually non-existent.

As Cary peered out into the night, a tractor-trailer pulling a metal platform was struck as it approached from the opposite direction by a large truck. The platform broke loose, jumped the dividing yellow line and smashed head-on into Cary's limousine. Cary blacked out. When he woke, he found himself in very bad shape in St. John's Hospital. Two of his ribs were broken, and he was bruised from head to foot. The Baroness von Fürstenberg had broken a leg, and the driver suffered a broken knee.

Cary, frantic that he could not continue to Los Angeles, where he wanted to see Jennifer, repeatedly struggled out of bed only to be told that he couldn't possibly leave. He called in his lawyers and began a damage suit against the owners of the truck. The insurance companies fought the matter out for years. He complained that he was in hospital in Queens and not Manhattan, but generally he turned on the charm, dazzling the nurses, who, as others had done when Jennifer was born, lined up just to catch a glimpse of him, and used any excuse to attend him personally.

He was in St. John's for seventeen days. He was supposed to leave three days earlier, but he complained of chest pains and the effects of the tubes used for prolonged intravenous feeding and oxygen supplies owing to his badly swollen mouth and nose. He shared a room throughout with the chauffeur, Troy Lindahl, "so that I would have someone to talk to". Throughout the whole of his stay he absurdly assumed the name Count Bezok. George Barrie, President of Fabergé, the giant cosmetics empire was a frequent visitor at the hospital. A multi-millionaire, Barrie was a charming, enormously energetic and hard-driving man whose passionate concern with his low-priced products had helped the company to achieve pre-eminence in the previous decade. Cary met him just before the accident – Barrie was staying with Taplinger, and narrowly avoided being in the crash himself. He had offered to drive Cary, but Cary had refused because of the severe weather; he didn't want Barrie to be inconvenienced.

Taplinger had in mind that Cary and George Barrie should get together. Knowing Cary's power over millions of women, Taplinger realised that if he were to join the board of Fabergé, not only would he benefit from having a new interest in life now that his film career was apparently over, but he would assist Barrie tremendously by making personal appearances in chemists all over the world to discuss Fabergé products with customers in person at the cosmetics counters.

Over the next few months, talks took place between Taplinger and Barrie, and between Taplinger and Cary separately; neither one mentioned the matter to the other until at last Barrie brought them together for a discussion.

Meanwhile, the Grants' divorce hearing had taken place on March 20, the details of it being given to Cary in his hospital bed. Dyan spared a great many of the more unpleasant details in her testimony, but she was quite frank when she stated that Cary drove her to the verge of a nervous breakdown, urged her to take LSD, which she had done only twice, and had been in numerous ways heartless and cruel towards her. She spoke of his jumping up and down on the bed and screaming at the television set during the Academy Awards, making insulting remarks about the winners, and portrayed a man so deeply disturbed that there was some question as to whether he was even fit to be a father. She even described his spanking her, and she repeated earlier charges:

He started to hit me. He screamed. He was laughing as he hit me. He screamed for the help to come and see what he was doing. I was frightened because he was laughing and I went to call the police. He stopped me by pointing out how damaging the publicity would be.

When we were planning our trip to Bristol, he would not let me take Jennifer's baby food. He said the English cows were as good as American ones.

This brought a ripple of amusement in court.

Cary's attorneys produced witnesses, including a Dr. Judd Marmor, who said he had examined Cary psychiatrically and found no evidence of mental damage from LSD, and that in fact the drug had deepened his sense of compassion for people, and his understanding of himself, and "helped cure his shyness and anxiety in dealing with other people". The second psychiatrist testified under oath that he saw no evidence of irrationality, erratic behaviour or incoherence in Cary. The result of the hearing could have been worse, but it was sufficient to cause Cary even more distress. Although the alimony was a comparatively modest $50,000 a year, Cary was only allowed two months out of the year with Jennifer, with specific access by special request, on birthdays and at Christmas.

Brooding constantly, Cary moved back into the Beverly Grove Drive house. Tony Faramus had left the household by now, and Weaver's brother David became the houseman. Grant had failed to keep the Beverly Grove house in adequate condition. Weaver described later how a trellis-work breezeway (covered path), which connected the garage to the main house, had fallen apart, and the screen door had collapsed. Slates were missing from the roof, which leaked severely. When Cary and Weaver tried to make repairs, wind and rain beat against the house, and it was a torment to try to repair the ceiling holes with plastic. Weaver said: "Water stains had pitted the ceiling, where entire patches of plaster sagged dangerously under the weight of water collecting in the eaves. In the bathroom, whenever it rained hard, a rivulet of water streamed down from the central overhead light fitting."

In a bizarrely comic scene, Cary had Weaver place empty jam jars from the larder* and old paint tins from the garage under the ceiling holes; when local authorities arrived and declared the house a disaster area, insisting that Cary have the garden cleared (it was a veritable jungle of weeds), he, with his characteristic stinginess, would do nothing. Because of his fame, the Beverly Hills officials did not force him, but instead delegated Chicano gardeners to undertake the task of cutting away the vegetation. Cary was delighted that he wouldn't have to spend anything.

He was not pleased when he received a stern letter from City Hall, which advised him that he must immediately have the house remodelled or submit to it being declared a condemned property. Very reluctantly, Cary was forced to hire an architect, but he became more and more maddeningly unpredictable as he changed the plans from day to day. Yet again imitating Hollywood in his personal life, he

---

* He forbade the use of the American expression "Butler's Pantry" in the house.

was now, as Weaver observed, Mr. Blandings, building a dream house, constantly in trouble as he tripped over furniture or sliding metal window runners, or so clumsily hammering in a nail that it plunged into his finger. He and Weaver spent days ploughing through old storage boxes, which sat in cardboard mountains everywhere. They were filled with smelly, damp and mouldering books and documents. Among the few items that could be rescued were two valuable Tiepolo drawings, gifts from Barbara Hutton in the 1940s, and a Boudin painting emerged virtually untouched by damp. But many other items were ruined permanently.

Weaver recalled how Cary became obsessed with the positioning of a light socket, changing it again and again until the electricians hired for the job were reduced to exasperation. In an unwanted fit of extravagance, he imported a consignment of earthenware tiles for his new patio. The architects had personally supervised the packing of the tiles in thick bundles of straw, each one numbered for its positioning. On the drive to the house, the trucker accidentally set fire to the straw with his cigarette, and although he managed to put out the flames, he could not prevent the consignment from being rendered pitch-black, scorched beyond retrieval. The whole order had to be repeated.

There was a similar disaster involving the plaster on one wall: it contained too much sand, so that it dried almost immediately and was cracked from top to bottom. The new plumbing failed to work, because brand new pipes, made of copper and carefully insulated, were not properly matched to ancient ones, and there were many leaks. Cary had a dressing-room mirror in his bedroom surrounded by bulbs which were soft, glazed and slightly pink so that they would de-emphasise the lines in his face. He hated and dreaded neon lighting because of its cruelty. Unfortunately, the brackets connecting the frame to the glass were incorrectly screwed in and in the pressure of the summer heat the mirror splintered and blew out.

Cary also ordered plate glass windows for the sitting-room, which would provide a stunning 180-degree view of the city. When it proved impossible to find an American company to take care of the task of making the windows, a French company was approached. But they too proved unequal to the task, and only after some months was an American contractor at last found, who would undertake the job if the window could be supplied in three pieces.

The pieces were fitted expertly into place, with vertical metal dividers. Cary looked at the windows, at the view, and then exploded. Weaver couldn't understand what was wrong. Impatiently, Cary pointed out that the manufacturer's trademark was inscribed with a diamond drill at the bottom left-hand corner. Not a soul would ever notice this or care about it, but Cary had the entire window removed, and sent it back to be redone without the offending logo.

Cary remained reclusive as ever in the late 1960s. He hated to go to parties, and was irritated by the toasts or tributes to ancient celebrities that seemed to turn a changing Hollywood into not much more than a mutual-admiration society. Yet he did not replace a public career or life in society with a particularly profound or meaningful existence. Like his friend Howard Hughes, he enjoyed, if that is the word, an empty life, devoid of intellectual or physical satisfaction, devoid even of an enjoyment of luxury and material pleasures.

He kept in touch with Hughes through the period. Hughes was now almost entirely resident in Las Vegas, his tortured existence no happier than it had been before, deprived now of the healing presence of the brisk and attractive Jean Peters Hughes, who had moved back to California. Hughes' business affairs brought him misery as always. He sat in his suite at the Desert Inn, gauntly naked or dressed in an ancient bathrobe, scribbling endless complicated messages in ballpoint on sheets of lined yellow stationery. He could not distinguish between day and night, lived on tranquillisers and ate only tiny portions of meat with exactly (he counted them) a dozen black-eyed peas. He was involved in the disastrously complex affairs of Air West, planned to buy Paradise Island, a Bahamian resort formerly owned by the Swedish millionaire Axel Wenner-Gren, lost money in various television stations and newspapers, got involved in a takeover bid for ABC Network Television, and in general dithered helplessly whereas before he had dynamically conducted his own destiny. His aide Noah Dietrich told Charles Higham that Hughes found Cary Grant supportive, as he called him from time to time to tell him of his grievous woes. Not least of these was his ill-advised attempted deal with Lockheed in which they would buy the Hughes Aircraft Company in return for Hughes buying 100 Lockheed L-1011s.

Investments in gold and silver, struggles with the law, mix-ups in personnel and strange dealings with Richard Nixon's brother, Francis Donald Nixon, drained Hughes' meagre strength. Like Cary, he obtained no joy from the possession of riches. It would not be an exaggeration to say that both men's lives were quite hellish in the late 1960s.

Cary did find some temporary release from his unhappiness, chiefly in his restricted visits to his beloved Jennifer. But as before, he could not relax even with her, fretting endlessly over her growth, her diet, her health, her well-being, even taking her blood pressure and measuring her, fearful that Dyan was not doing the best for her. And yet, so paradoxical was his nature, he failed to give Dyan sufficient sums of money to ensure that she could provide Jennifer with a magnificent home to live in. His payments were so meagre, despite successive court orders, that by the time Jennifer was four years old, Dyan was forced to live in a mediocre West Hollywood high-rise apartment mostly frequented by visiting New York actors, with a sprinkling of prostitutes and drug addicts.

Cary found escape in evenings at the Magic Castle, an eccentric, neo-Gothic structure above Franklin Avenue in the Hollywood Hills. There, he could escape in joining the friendly brotherhood of magicians who made the Castle their headquarters. He was also attracted by the mere fifty dollars a year it cost to join the Castle, having long since refused to become a member of certain country clubs because of their exorbitant rates.

He befriended a young parking attendant at the Castle, Berri Lee. As with Ted Donaldson and Lance Reventlow years earlier, this was a heterosexual friendship, disinterested, warm, fatherly and considerate. Lee recalls that Cary encouraged him in his budding career as a magician, making a special point of coming to see Lee's magic act.

He helped the young man with his appearances on television shows, and paid for him to fly to New York, where he had an engagement at El Morocco, and where, due to Cary's influence, Liza Minnelli and Pearl Bailey turned up. Lee says:

> . . . He was like a father to me. He treated me that way, I had never had a father. He was a guiding light . . . He would give me advice, tell me what to do and how to deal with things. One time, he invited me to his house for Christmas. The biggest star in the world. I was overcome. He gave me a book called *Stick and Rudder*, which is one of the greatest books on flying. He encouraged me to learn to fly.

Berri Lee describes an ominous incident that occurred at the time, an incident that would soon grow into a larger and more terrifying one:

> We had [a] Christmas dinner on a big table, with a sheet with a hole in it for a tablecloth, and dime-store knives and forks. Against the wall was a stack of paintings, six or eight feet deep, which may have been worth three, four, or five million dollars. He told me that he had been robbed. Everything in the house had been stolen, all his silverware, all his stuff. He pointed out that the reason the paintings had not been lost was that every time the thieves went to pick up some silver, or a TV set, or some insignificant thing, they walked around those millions of

dollars' worth of artwork because they didn't know what it was.

Cary had, apparently, been keeping questionable company. For example, in July, 1969, a wire service report appeared on the desks of certain overseas newspapers. It stated that Cary Grant had been brought in for questioning when the mother of a young man accused Cary of picking up her under-age son in his Rolls-Royce at a Los Angeles motorway junction and making an improper suggestion to him. There was no implication that the young man had responded.

We come now to the most mysterious and puzzling aspect of his entire career, still unsolved and baffling to the biographer. Hard evidence is lacking, but – perhaps because of his persistent use of LSD, which was now illegal, or perhaps because of his penchant for curious nocturnal adventures – Cary had apparently befriended a young man.

According to the late Hollywood producer William Belasco, Cary was visiting the youth on the night of August 9 at a house at 10050 Cielo Drive, a short distance from Cary's own home. The two men were talking in the garden when screams were heard from the main house. Cary fled in the Rolls.

Next morning, Cary learned what he had narrowly escaped. Charles Manson and his gang had burst in and slaughtered the occupants of the main house, including actress Sharon Tate.

Manson said on a Los Angeles TV programme in 1987, "The greatest thrill I ever knew was sleeping in the bed Cary Grant slept in." In his memoirs, published in 1988, Manson describes spending several nights in Cary Grant's bungalow at Universal, apparently during Grant's absence. Manson claimed to have been having an affair with a male member of the studio staff.

Berri Lee describes Cary's terror following the crime. Perhaps he feared that because he was present in the grounds he also would be murdered. Lee says:

The instant the telephone company and utility companies could be reached, he had his phone lines and utilities put underground, so that if somebody came to break into the house, they couldn't cut the power or the telephone. He hadn't forgotten the earlier burglary. He was very worried about Jennifer. He disconnected his telephone and had the number changed. He put $100,000 in a cash account in the bank.

Cary arranged for permanent bodyguards, day and night, for Jennifer, though he still failed to supply her with a luxurious residence. And at the same time, he appeared in court, preventing Dyan from taking Jennifer to Seattle and succeeding in increasing his visiting rights to ninety days a year.

As if he had not had sufficient trouble, he began an awkward affair with a beautiful showgirl named Cynthia Bouron. A close friend of Cynthia Bouron, Marilyn Hinton, described the origins of this unsatisfactory relationship.

Mrs. Hinton recalled that Miss Bouron had at one stage dated Jerry Lewis, who had become strongly attracted to her when she was appearing at the Hotel Fontaineblu at Miami Beach. Exquisitely proportioned, slender but voluptuous, Cynthia Bouron soon drew the attention of Frank Sinatra, who wanted her so badly he begged Jerry Lewis to give her up to him. Sinatra allegedly embarked on a romance with her, and even considered marrying her, but then discovered that she had lied to him on an important particular. She had said that her real name was Bourbon and that she belonged to an American branch of the European royal family of Bourbons. The romance ended.

Without the support of either Lewis or Sinatra, Miss Bouron began to drift into fewer and fewer jobs, and claimed to have been blacklisted. She was working as a waitress when Mrs. Hinton met her and, taking pity on her, supported her. Mrs. Hinton introduced her to Cary Grant, feeling that she would attract him, and Cynthia apparently spent several evenings with him in his suite at the Dunes Hotel in Las Vegas, wearing various sexy evening-gowns, but she told Marilyn nothing came of these romantic encounters of candlelight and champagne.

Cynthia Bouron felt humiliated, and decided to get her revenge on Cary. She went about it in a particularly despicable manner that seems in contradiction to the sensitive and gentle person Marilyn Hinton portrayed. (Mrs. Hinton insisted she knew nothing of Miss Bouron's plan.) The scheme was to become pregnant by another man who somewhat resembled a younger Cary Grant, and then announce that Cary was the father. In view of the fact that he was struggling over visitation rights to Jennifer, and it was essential that he have an impeccable image at the time, and indeed there is no evidence of any love affairs of his at the time, she knew that she could seriously affect him by this vicious deceit.

She conceived in June 1969, two months before the Manson murders and on March 12, 1970, she gave birth to her baby daughter at the Good Samaritan Hospital, Los Angeles, naming the child Stephanie Andrea Grant. The birth certificate carried the name Cary Grant as the father, birthplace England, age sixty-six, present occupation actor and, in a deliberate slap, industry or business: self.

Cary was in the Bahamas, having flown his Fabergé DC3 to Nassau. Joyce Haber, columnist of the *Los Angeles Times*, obtained police records showing that Miss Bouron had been arrested for theft in April 1967, but had been found not guilty. She had been married twice before her present husband and had had two children, one by each of the previous marriages. Friends told Miss Haber that Cynthia Bouron had for some time owned an English collie called Cary, which, some asserted, he had given her.

It is hard to imagine the hypersensitive star's state of mind during those grievous weeks. He had scarcely recovered from the horror of the Manson affair when this new blow struck. The timing was appalling: the following month, he was due to receive an honorary Oscar from the Academy of Motion Picture Arts and Sciences for lifetime achievement. It was more essential than ever that his reputation be unstained on this occasion. He was terrified, not only that he would lose face in the eyes of the public, but that the new special arrangement whereby he was now allowed access to Jennifer on alternate weekends, Monday afternoons, and for one month of the summer holiday would be suspended.

He kept out of Hollywood as much as possible, travelling, visiting his old friend Nöel Coward in Jamaica and flying to Elsie Leach in Bristol. Meanwhile, his friends in Hollywood began investigating Cynthia Bouron further. He discovered more about her murky past: her second husband had been a stuntman, who, in 1966, had murdered Mickey Rooney's wife Barbara and later committed suicide. Cary was determined to prove that the baby was not his. He sought a court order to obtain a blood test, but had to wait for this to be carried out. It was an appalling burden to carry as he prepared for the important night at the Academy. He couldn't sleep and wondered whether he should cancel his appearance, then realised that if he did, it would be worse for him: people would say he was guilty and afraid. And in these excruciating weeks, he was more tortured than ever about the situation with Dyan and Jennifer. Berri Lee recalls:

He would say [in his sadness], "Berri, I have a little place in Connecticut. If everything goes wrong, you and I will go there, and we'll get some girls and just make babies." I'll never forget that. Another of his quotes to me was, "The hand that rocks the cradle fucks the world." He spoke of how mothers "fuck up your mind as a child". We talked about the way mothers screw you around, make you afraid of life, how a lot of men are ruined by their mothers. There was a direct reference to Elsie here.

We never talked about the gay situation. Just things that I saw . . . I think gayness was just another escape, a way out. This was a man who, all his life, had women chasing him, and he never knew whether somebody wanted him or Cary Grant, wanted him for himself, and he was hurt very much by women.

Even in the midst of his crisis over Cynthia Bouron, Cary's bitterness over Dyan was intense. To Lee, he damned women for "being the way they are". Lee shared his feelings: he also loved women, but was frustrated by them. "If things are broken up in a relationship, why can't you just say it's over and try to work it out, instead of a woman coming and just going at you. We were just two unhappy guys, we were going through these things together, and we'd try to give each other advice."

In a wretched mood, Cary stood tearfully on the stage of the Dorothy Chandler Pavilion in Los Angeles on April 7, 1970, to receive his honorary Oscar from his old friend Frank Sinatra.

There was a standing ovation as, his face a sad mask, the star received the award. A montage of his brilliant career from the early Mae West vehicles to *Charade* dazzled and excited the audience. Sinatra said, correctly, "No one has brought more pleasure to more people for so many years . . . nobody has done so many things as well. Cary has so much skill that he makes it all look easy." Then Sinatra read the statuette inscription: "To Cary Grant, for his unique mastery of the art of screen acting, with the respect and affection of his colleagues." In a state of extreme stress, yet deeply moved by the standing ovation, the tortured super-celebrity delivered a brief, expertly phrased speech, mentioning many of his directors and writers, and then adding, "This is a collaborative medium. We all need each other . . . Probably no greater honour can come to a man than the respect of his colleagues." If Cynthia Bouron had appeared at that moment, she would probably have been lynched. Ironically, that same evening, Dyan Cannon narrowly lost the Academy Award as Best Supporting Actress for her vivid comedy playing in *Bob and Carol and Ted and Alice*. They barely acknowledged each other in the crowd.

17

By 1970, Cary was firmly established as a member of the board of Fabergé. He received a nominal salary of only $25,000 a year, but the perquisites were extraordinary. He was given continuous use of the penthouse at the Hotel Warwick in New York City: magnificently furnished and oak-beamed, it had once been the home of his old friend Marion Davies, who had owned the hotel. In addition to the company DC3 available for his private use, he also had access to a G2, a jet which had won an industrial prize for the best private jet-plane in the nation; the aircraft was furnished with a day-bed, comfortable seats and armchairs, and a bar, and there was room for eleven passengers and a steward. He also had the use of a Convair, a propeller plane. Cary, who hated travelling in commercial planes because of the cramped space even in first class, and the attention he attracted throughout the flight with people constantly walking up and down to talk to him, relished the privacy and comfort of these private conveyances.

At that time, Cary obtained permission to redecorate the DC3 whose cabin was described by Weaver as, "rather like a small bungalow, with an ash dining table and four chocolate-brown swivel chairs, a collection of bright yellow armchairs . . . and two sofas, in tomato red and green". There was also a bar, and a piano at which Cary would sit, singing old music-hall songs. He decorated the bulkheads with pictures of Jennifer at play, and was able to use the DC3 for holiday trips, or to go to San Francisco for lunch or to New York for dinner. By now, he had reached that height of eminence at which almost nothing is paid for.

He flung himself into promoting Fabergé's inexpensive perfume lines with all the obsessive energy that had marked his life to date, expounding the product's merits; he was now a super-salesman, maddened by the thought that some other line might compete successfully with what he now regarded as his own. He would turn up unannounced in various chemists or department stores across America, throwing the staff and management into a state of near hysteria because they were not ready for his arrival and had made no arrangements for a special promotion featuring him. The instant he turned up at a cosmetics counter, a crowd formed and virtually every other counter in that part of the store was deserted. By snapping up all the Fabergé lines fans were able to get a close look at their idol. There is no calculating how many products he managed to sell as a result of his impromptu appearances. He covered as many as 300 such stores between 1969 and 1971.

Cary would have long discussions with the managers about what they felt were their needs. He would attend sales conferences, discuss arrangements with buyers, and meet individual salesmen.

Cary remained concerned about the matter of Cynthia Bouron. According to Marilyn Hinton, he engaged a private detective, who made his way into Cynthia's apartment (she was no longer living with Mrs. Hinton) and, in a scene reminiscent of *Rosemary's Baby*, examined the child in the cradle and discovered the girl did not resemble Cary. When Miss Bouron was summoned to appear in court for a blood test, no doubt apprised by Cary's lawyers of this discovery, she understandably failed to appear. Her ending was tragic. Two years later, in 1973, she was found dead in her car in a San Fernando Valley parking lot, according to press reports beaten to death, according to Marilyn Hinton severed limb from limb. The murderer was never found.

The custody battles over Jennifer continued throughout 1971 and 1972 as Cary travelled ceaselessly throughout the United States and Europe, vigorously selling Fabergé products, even in Iron Curtain countries. Once again, one can only be baffled by the contradictions in his character, since these expensive trips effectively deprived him of sufficient periods with Jennifer even at a time when he was struggling for added days with her and alleged that his reasons for cancelling certain official engagements, including tributes to personal friends in show business, were because he could not bear to be separated from his daughter. It seems that he used Jennifer as an excuse to avoid social engagements without revealing the pixieish, mercurial character, and unstable approach to life that actually caused these evasions.

Howard Hughes remained, as always, a close friend. Cary's frequent visits to Las Vegas were to keep in touch with him, even though on many occasions he could only speak to him on the telephone. When Hughes was living at the Britannia Beach Hotel on Paradise Island in the Bahamas, Cary could be found in that region more frequently than was called for by his normal schedule.

On December 7, 1971, he shared Hughes' shock when an announcement was made in the press. The McGraw-Hill Publishing Company had bought world rights to a book which was supposed to be a Hughes autobiography as told to the American novelist Clifford Irving. McGraw-Hill sent out a press release accompanying the announcement, which quoted Hughes as saying, "I believe that more lies have been printed and told about me than about any living man – therefore it was my purpose to write a book which would set the record straight." Whether Hughes personally called Cary on the matter is unknown, but it is certain that Noah Dietrich told Hughes and Cary was informed of the situation.* Cary knew that Hughes could never have written his memoirs, nor could he have authorised a biography of any sort. The Hughes Tool Company issued a statement that denounced the memoir as a hoax. McGraw-Hill and *Life* magazine, which had the serialisation rights, stood firmly behind Irving. At McGraw-Hill's request,

---

* Dietrich discussed the matter with Charles Higham in 1972.

Irving supplied the publisher with a document allegedly written by Hughes, and confirmed by handwriting experts, stating that the manuscript was genuine.

Cary was in acute distress over the matter. He had dreaded something of the sort would happen to him and urged Hughes to come out of his cocoon of silence and obscurity and make a public denial of the matter. Since it would be difficult for Hughes to face the press, Cary suggested (according to Noah Dietrich) that he should give a telephone interview to seven selected reporters, who would be gathered at the Sheraton-Universal Hotel in Burbank, California, from his suite at the Britannia Beach Hotel. All seven were known to Hughes personally; he agreed.

The telephone press conference was held on January 7, 1972. Surprisingly, except for one or two mistakes, Hughes responded well to the interview, and proved that, despite his uncertain state of health and extreme eccentricity, his mind was almost unimpaired. Cary remained supportive of his old friend, suggesting that Clifford Irving's movements on the days he was supposed to have been interviewing Hughes be checked out; one idea he had was that, when Irving went to a library that required a signature on an entry form, the dates of his appearance at the library could be checked. One of Hughes' aircraft designers, Ted Carpentier, remembers that, upon checking certain entry forms, he found Irving was in a library and not in a place where he was supposed to have been interviewing the tycoon. Within a month, Irving admitted guilt. The following year, in 1973, Hughes moved to London.

In the early 1970s, Cary became involved with a British photographer-writer named Maureen Donaldson. Small, blonde, with a round, cheerful, healthy face, a spunky, vital manner, and a great deal of charm, Miss Donaldson fascinated him. Susceptible to admiration, like so many film stars, he was flattered by the fact that she hung on his every word. By 1972, their relationship had deepened, according to her, into a serious love affair. When she told him that she had been a nanny, he apparently thought she might make a good step-mother for Jennifer. And they had their British background in common, a shared sense of humour and Maureen enjoyed Cary's continuing fondness for performing music-hall songs.

Unlike Dyan Cannon, Maureen didn't fight Cary when he objected to her wearing shorts or jeans, T-shirts and sweaters. He worked hard on moulding her into an elegant young woman. Once more, his paternal instincts were at work: Maureen was not yet thirty. During their relationship he continued seeing other young women. She was probably under the impression he was devoting himself exclusively to her. She was sensible enough to know that Jennifer came first in his life, that she could never usurp the child's place in his affections. Cary rewarded her for her thoughtfulness: he gave her, with uncharacteristic generosity, a Bill Blass wardrobe and a $1,000 Cartier Tank watch.

Their life during those periods when Cary was not travelling for Fabergé was unexciting. They spent most of their time at the Benedict Canyon house, sitting around and talking desultorily; in the evenings, they ate a gourmet TV-dinner while watching vintage Hollywood classics on the outsized television set. Very occasionally, they would dine out; when Cary acquired a house near Dyan's at Malibu, so that he could spy on Jennifer, they dropped in to the exotic Polynesian restaurant Tonga Lei, or sometimes, during the winter months, they dined at Chasen's in Beverly Hills, where Cary had an account and didn't have to produce cash to pay the bill.*

They saw very few people, and appeared to be totally involved with each other. The relationship continued into 1977. Miss Donaldson said to journalists that Cary didn't ill-treat her as he had his wives. Others disagreed. She insisted he showed the sensitivity towards her that he had shown to Phyllis Brooks in the 1930s; when she had a jaw

---

* On one occasion, he invited eight to dinner and split the bill eight ways.

infection, and had to undergo surgery at UCLA Medical Center, she said he checked into the hospital itself, as he had done when Jennifer was born, and nursed Maureen during her convalescence at his house. Although she didn't live with him, she moved into his house during illnesses, and he attended to her day and night. When her parents arrived from London, he made sure they had a good time.

Meanwhile, Cary formed another friendship. In 1970, the rich William Currie McIntosh interested Cary in a new investment and promotional adventure: Cary would lend his name and support to a property development on the banks of the Shannon and Fergus rivers, close to Ireland's Shannon Airport. This would be ideal for retired Americans who could obtain comfortable, not over-large houses, in a handsome rural setting; many of these prospective purchasers would, it was expected, be of Irish descent, who wanted to return to their ancestors' native soil for their final years.

Cary, who had always had a fondness for Ireland, and had visited it during his Fabergé promotions, saw potential in this project, which became known as Shannonside. Surprisingly, he handed McIntosh a $10,000 cheque as a first investment. Then, following a visit to Elsie Leach in Bristol, Cary met McIntosh at Heathrow Airport and flew to Ireland. They moved into the elegant Dromoland Castle Hotel, and Cary surveyed the territory. He was impressed: the scenery had a soft, dark-green Irish beauty, with splendid views of the Atlantic. Cary at once became obsessed with Shannonside.

He became a director of the company in September 1971, and consulted constantly with McIntosh and the architects on building just over 2,000 dwellings to the tune of $30 million. So proprietorial was he, so consumed, McIntosh reported in his book, with a conviction that he alone was the champion of Shannonside, that he even objected violently when Jack Lemmon invested $20,000 in the scheme, but McIntosh hung on to the Lemmon investment.

Again in a contradiction of his apparent concern over

being with Jennifer every minute he could, Cary absented himself from California repeatedly, making numerous flights with McIntosh to check out the new development. He fussed over the plumbing, the electricity and took an inordinate amount of interest in roof-tiling and insulation. He even allowed himself to walk around with members of the press, showing them how wonderful everything was, and a film to be made under McIntosh's supervision, in which he was seen boasting about Shannonside while walking the length and breadth of the development.

In 1973, Cary was granted a plot on which to build his own home. He consulted with an architect on the design, excluding a dining-room because he loved to eat in the bedroom, creating a special area for Jennifer to live in, and making sure that there was a Colonial-style veranda overlooking the river and extending to the full length of the house.

According to McIntosh, Cary thought of Jennifer constantly during these trips, buying her gifts and writing letters to her almost every day, containing jokes, puzzles and conundrums. He always enjoyed going with McIntosh to London, where he again stayed at the Connaught. He made a shrewd deal with Sir Charles Abrahams, the jovial chairman of Aquascutum, in which he would wear Aquascutum suits on well-photographed public occasions and in return Abrahams would allow him substantial discounts. He still freeloaded everywhere: Fabergé covered most of his hotel and meal bills, the Shannonside directors paid others, and often managements would waive his restaurant charges because of the customers he attracted when it slipped out on the grapevine that he would be in a particular place on a particular night.

There were signs that Cary was beginning to show his age. Though he had no apparent neurological disorder, his once meticulous, carefully controlled behaviour dissolved during travel. He became absent-minded, and would become excessively flustered as he searched for a pair of spectacles that were actually sitting on his nose, documents that had slipped down the side of his seat, or luggage receipts that had become mysteriously detached from his ticket and couldn't be located – this on the rare occasions when he used commercial aircraft.

Cary had a strange, brief unhappy relationship at the outset of the 1970s with the beautiful widow and second wife of a prominent Hollywood agent-turned-producer. The sensitive widow had first met Cary in 1969 in Palm Springs. She shared his love of privacy and dislike of social events and crowds. They made a trip to Paris, with William Weaver, in which Cary was at his best; but, like so many women before her, she found that Cary was not as deeply committed to her as she was to him. Hypersensitive, she would cry often, sometimes walk out on Cary and then come back under great stress, complaining, unlike Maureen Donaldson, when he would leave her behind for his extended trips to London and Ireland. On one occasion, she became so distraught at Cary leaving her to go to New York that she collapsed; William and David Weaver, fearing that she was dying of a heart attack, tried desperately to revive her, without success. They called the paramedics.

The ambulance drive to the hospital was a nightmare, and the driver was so flustered that he turned into a motorway exit lane, almost colliding with approaching traffic. Greeted by hysterical motorists, he was finally able to leave it, by which time she appeared to be dying. At the hospital, she was given oxygen, but only a tracheotomy saved her life. Perhaps mistaking her sudden onset of illness for the sort of fake suicide he had attempted in the 1930s, Cary, according to Weaver, "adamantly refused to go near the hospital. He wouldn't even send her flowers, informing her with wicked humour on the phone that the flowers would deprive her of what little oxygen she had." She finished with Cary soon afterwards, and finally made a happy marriage. By now, Cary's attitude to her was one of total and cruel contempt.

Cary suffered two bereavements in the early 1970s: in

July 1972, Lance Reventlow, whom he had continued to see over the years, and to whom he was still somewhat of a surrogate father, crashed in his single-engine plane in a violent electrical storm. There was an unseemly squabble over the remains: Barbara Hutton, who was by now a complete nervous wreck, was determined that her son be buried in the Woolworth crypt, but Reventlow's wife Cheryl was determined that Lance be cremated, his ashes scattered at Aspen, Colorado. Grant supported Cheryl in the matter. He refused to allow Barbara Hutton to have her wish, and with Weaver he attended an elaborate memorial service at Aspen.

The other, more serious bereavement happened in January 1973. Weaver received a phone call at the Benedict Canyon house from Cary's cousin Margaret, wife of Eric Leach, to say that Elsie was dead. Weaver beckoned Cary to come to the telephone, but Cary would not. He looked dazed but not grief-stricken and seemed unable to deal with the several questions Margaret raised and Weaver passed on to him. She naturally wanted to make preparations for a funeral, and to know whether he wanted to authorise a specific service or bouquet of flowers for the church. But, according to Weaver, he only kept saying that her death was not to be made public, an absurdity in the circumstances. He made the extraordinary statement, "No hearse. Can't we have a cart?" He ruled out any kind of a service.

Understandably, Margaret preferred to ignore his requests, and herself provided the money for the funeral. Cary flew with Weaver to London and thence to Bristol to attend the service and make the slow walk through fog and drizzle to the cemetery. The plain pinewood coffin carried not a single flower. Apart from Cary and Weaver, only Margaret and Eric Leach were present. Weaver recalled, "As the coffin was lowered into the ground, Grant leaned over, took from Margaret's hands the single rose she was carrying, and laid it on the lid." At tea afterwards, in Margaret and Eric Leach's sitting-room, Cary did not appear to be grieving. He spoke of his father with affection, but said little or nothing about Elsie. William McIntosh comments:

> I have always felt that Cary's visits to Elsie were carried out, not so much from a deep sensitivity or love of her, but because he knew the world was watching him and his image would be affected if he did not keep going to Bristol. There was no real rapport between them, none of the love of a son for his mother. Weaver and I knew there was something deep and dark in the relationship with her at the outside of his life, but not what it was. Elsie didn't know Cary was her son; sometimes, she didn't recognise him; she was uncomfortable at being called his mother. I doubted if she really *was* his mother.

Elsie, who was always uninterested in having much money, died with pathetically little. She had steadfastly refused to let Cary bring her to Hollywood or make her rich and remained stubbornly independent and uninterested in his film career till the end. And, if truth be told, that hard, unyielding woman showed very little gratitude to him for his constant flights to Bristol. Perhaps, sharply observant, she sensed that his visits were dutiful rather than inspired by intense affection, and that very often he just fitted in those visits with trips to Shannonside or to London for shopping. The sheer absence of friends of any age at the funeral has to be an indication of her inability to attract a circle of loving and devoted people who would genuinely mourn her when she died. Nostalgia had softened Cary's memories of his father, whose philandering had made him neglectful and who had so casually handed him over to a vaudeville troupe at the age of six. He seldom spoke of Elsie Leach again.

In the mid-1970s, Cary formed a friendship with the gifted vocal impressionist Rich Little. He was enchanted with Little's appearances in Las Vegas, and invaded the comedian's dressing-room after a show, astonishing Little's wife and sister, who did a double-take when they saw him bursting out with child-like enthusiasm, saying, "Do you realise what you do? For just an hour you let people forget all their troubles, you let them remember all those great stars and great pictures! It's a wonderful gift to be able to do that! You don't realise how many people you have made happy. You should be proud of it!"

For several years, Cary closely followed Little's career. Sometimes, the two friends would fly together on one of Cary's Fabergé planes. Little, a committed film buff, wanted to discuss films, but Cary would reply: "Let's talk about the real things in life: nature, music, that kind of thing. I don't want to talk about my movies because they aren't worth talking about."

Little adds:

And then about ten minutes later the conversation would swing around and we would be talking about one of his movies. And suddenly he'd stop and say, "I don't want to talk about my movies anymore." The pictures he would talk the most about were the Hitchcocks. He had a great respect for Hitch.

Little recalls that he delighted in pretending to be Cary Grant when booking various hotels. He would say that he had been in Africa and had picked up a couple of animals, an orangutan and a cheetah, and that the creatures were with them, and would need a room each. He was testing Cary's fame and influence.

Rich Little says:

There was always a long pause after I made the request in Cary's voice. One time, when I used the request at the MGM Grand Hotel, I remember the clerk saying, "No problem at all, Sir." Then I added, "Well, *we* have a little problem. How are we going to get the animals up to the rooms?" "Good point, Sir," the clerk replied.

I said, as Cary, "We don't want to disrupt everyone in

the casino. How about we dress the orangutan up as a woman, and put her in a wheelchair, and just smuggle her in that way." And then I would go on and suggest how the cheetah might be smuggled in. I kept going. I said, "Maybe we could arrange for some bananas for the monkey. We could use the shower rail for a swing for him." And the man replied, "I don't know how many bananas we can get, but I'll check with the kitchen." It was a long time before I put the guy out of his misery and told him it was a put-on. Cary always came totally unglued when I told him the story. He just didn't realise how famous he was.

Little remembers that when he travelled, he would use his Cary Grant voice to get food quickly:

The guy who brought the food was greeted by my manager, who would sign the check while I was in the bedroom saying through the door in Cary's voice, "Thank you very much. I really appreciate it. I'm in a big, big hurry." The waiter would reply, "No problem, Mr. Grant. Any time. Anything you want, Sir." And "Cary" would say, "Really, it's very sweet of you." These sorts of scenes would go on into the 1980s.

Cary's relationship with Maureen Donaldson began to decline in the mid-1970s. A witness of this deterioration was Tim Barry, tennis pro to the stars. He recalls that, in late 1974, he was enjoying a drink at a bar in Malibu with his close friend, the South African pro Dean Graham, when an attractive girl walked in. She had an English accent, and started saying how horribly her boyfriend was treating her, that he was an older man. She grumbled constantly, at last announcing that her name was Maureen Donaldson.

As the evening progressed, she told Barry and Graham that her lover's name was Cary Grant. Barry said, rather rudely, "You've got to be joking. What would Cary Grant be doing with you?" She replied, "It's true. I live with him

in Beverly Hills, and he gives me an apartment of my own."
She talked about their touch-and-go, relationship, and that
they had been together for a few years. According to Barry,
Dean Graham dated her briefly.

About three months after his meeting with Maureen
Donaldson, Barry received a telephone call from Cary
Grant's manager Don Carey to say that Mr. Grant would
like Jennifer to have some tennis lessons. Barry was delighted. He still remembers the time, four p.m., when a
large blue car stopped at the Malibu tennis court and five
people stepped out: Don Carey; a maid; Jennifer, who was
now about eleven years old, looking beautiful; her closest
friend, Lisa Lennon; and finally Cary himself. Barry's knees
were shaking (he was in his twenties, and just out of UCLA)
at the prospect of meeting "the idol of everybody's lifetime".
Feeling numb, he shook Cary's hand, realising that he
would be put to the surpreme test of making a good tennis
player out of Jennifer. To add to his extreme nervousness
and discomfort, he observed that Cary had brought a
camera to film Jennifer at her lesson. Barry recalls:

> I said (to myself), "Oh, my God, there's enough pressure
> on me as it is. Here I'm going to be teaching Cary Grant's
> daughter, and on film!" It was too uncomfortable to
> think about. Jennifer was nervous herself. I could tell she
> wasn't comfortable at the thought of everybody in the
> world watching her learn tennis, and her father himself
> was making her nervous.

Feeling exceedingly tense, Barry began the process of whip-
ping Jennifer into shape. He worked very hard on her
backhand, overhead drive and the other strokes, painfully
conscious of Cary's constant presence with the camera,
supervising everything he did. As if he were not in sufficient
state of tension already, he also had to deal with Dyan's
frequent visits to the court. She, of course, like Cary, was
just a few feet away in her beach house.

Dyan would turn up, on the Mondays when Cary was

allowed access to Jennifer, according to Barry because she needed to ask something of Jennifer. Both Barry and Jennifer would jump as Dyan would suddenly scream out her daughter's name to come off the court and talk to her. "She would not confront Cary face to face," Tim Barry says.

He remembers that Cary was delighted with Jennifer's progress, and confided that he had always wanted to play tennis but never had the time. This was true; studio publicity shots of him wielding a racket were all fakes. But he did try and bat balls around between camera shots. Barry was surprised that Cary was already showing signs of old age by muttering to himself or gazing transfixed at Jennifer in a manner that surpassed that of even the most devoted parent.

Barry says that Jennifer was as devoted to Cary as he was to her. But then some embarrassing incidents took place: Cary would bring onto the court a friend, not someone he was involved with, and they would carry on in a fake-effeminate way that deeply embarrassed Jennifer.

Maureen Donaldson turned up for lessons later which were also paid for by Cary. Cary wanted Maureen to be a tennis partner for Jennifer, joining her with Don and a male friend in mixed doubles. Maureen remembered her previous meeting with Barry and Dean Graham at the bar, and, as her lessons continued, talked more and more about the difficulties in her relationship with Gary. Barry alleges:

> He had treated her so cruelly. It came out that he had been sleeping with men. I didn't want to get into the juicy details. I would just kind of pat her on the shoulder. And I'd say, as I patted her on the shoulder, "Okay, let's get on with the tennis lesson, okay?" She said, "Sometimes he can be so nice, and other times a devil." She was very distressed. He would yell and call her terrible things. He would get mad at her, she said. It caused her to go out and leave him at night. It was very painful.

Sometimes, Barry recalls, Jennifer would take lessons at a different time from Maureen, but occasionally Cary would get his wish and they would train simultaneously. Jennifer and Maureen liked each other tremendously. And both Cary and Maureen worked hard to keep the stresses and miseries of their relationship from Jennifer at her tender age.

Shortly before Christmas, 1974, Jennifer brought Tim Barry a package in Christmas paper. It was marked "From Cary to Tim". He opened it excitedly, to find that it contained a Fabergé gift package with Brut cologne. Barry was tickled pink, quite overlooking the fact that Cary was giving out his own free samples as presents.

Jennifer became very friendly with Tim Barry as time went on, and as she at last became proficient at tennis, began confiding in him. Barry says: "She told me how uncomfortable it was when Cary's gay-acting friend was around and the two of them would be carrying on like a couple of girls. She knew her father was gay. But she still loved him."

Finally, Jennifer changed schools and couldn't get out to Malibu on Mondays. She wanted to train at night, but Tim Barry didn't have a lighted court he could use, so he says, "We all just parted. And Maureen just faded out of the picture. I always felt stupid not having gotten an autographed picture."

As if his life were not complicated enough in the mid-1970s, Cary became embroiled in yet another love affair. This new relationship proved to be as ill-fated as any of the others and, of all of them, was probably the worst. Victoria Morgan was a ravishingly beautiful, dark-haired girl with an exquisitely proportioned figure. Her sensual lips suggested all manner of erotic possibilities, and her expression was at once inviting, decadent, and suggestive of potential danger. She was born in 1952, the child of a disastrous marriage between a US Air Force man turned Texas department store executive and a British war bride. After the divorce, marked with violent recriminations on both sides, Vicki's mother was remarried to a tool-and-die maker, Ralph Laney. The family settled in a low-class district south of Pomona, California, but Vicki's stepfather died in 1961. Her mother went to work as a cafeteria attendant and Vicki became the target of passionate attention from virtually every boy in her class. She became pregnant by a good-looking youth at school, and was abandoned. In a Los Angeles maternity home, at the age of sixteen, she gave birth to her son Todd in January 1969. She struggled to obtain work as a model, but rapidly discovered that Los Angeles was filled with beautiful girls and that the competition was severe. In desperation, she married a clothing wholesaler, Earle Lamm, in Las Vegas, and moved with him into a plush apartment in West Hollywood. The marriage failed to work. While walking along Sunset Boulevard one day, she was picked up by the multi-millionaire department store owner, Alfred Bloomingdale, who was married to Betsy, a close friend of the Reagans.

He used the line that he wanted Vicki to work with his daughter to improve her tennis. According to Miss Morgan, Bloomingdale confirmed the invitation by putting a cheque for $8,000 in her hand.

He began pursuing her relentlessly and they met constantly at the Old World restaurant on Sunset. Bloomingdale, who was pushing sixty, was besotted with the young girl. For years, he had been a glutton for sex, visiting bordellos to beat women violently. He had to pay blackmail money to protect his reputation.

Bloomingdale made it clear to Vicki that she would have to submit to S&M scenes. She had to watch while he lashed two women's naked buttocks, then he spanked her violently. Soon, she became his victim, paid well in order to satisfy his sadistic impulses. In 1971, she became pregnant with Bloomingdale's child but submitted to his demand that she have an abortion. By now, she was trapped in a relationship with him that was poisonous, mutually destructive, and potentially very dangerous.

In 1972, Bloomingdale discovered that he had cancer of the larynx and underwent extensive cobalt treatments. But despite his appalling health, the result of years of neglect, he still continued his cruel and drastic treatment of the unhappy girl. She plagued him with requests that she might be helped towards a career as a Hollywood actress. Her magnificent looks, only slightly affected by her atrocious lifestyle, might have helped, but she had no acting ability. Bloomingdale did what he could. He introduced her to Cary's old friend, the producer-director Mervyn LeRoy, whom Cary visited one day when Vicki Morgan was there. Cary was fascinated. In many ways the girl resembled Phyllis Brooks, with a touch of Dyan Cannon. He asked her whether she was an actress and suggested that he might be able to help her. Though he was still involved with Maureen Donaldson, he began to take Vicki out to various restaurants, and then at last, risking Bloomingdale's intense displeasure, since Bloomingdale felt he owned her, she moved into Cary's Malibu beach house. She was excited, she told her friend Ann Louise Bardach, who later co-wrote her biography, at the thought of having the affair with Cary. Miss Bardach recalls that Vicki knew of Cary's bisexuality, but her speciality was gays. She loved to prove that there was no man who wasn't at least something of a man, and wouldn't respond to her physical beauty. But like others before her, she was disappointed.

Instead of taking her to bed, as almost every other man, including several homosexuals, had done, he simply suggested she sleep in the guest room. According to another friend, Vicki wore negligées, pyjamas, or even walked nude through the house, trying to excite Cary; every effort failed. His motivation seems incomprehensible; he would have had to lie to Maureen Donaldson about his whereabouts at weekends, not easy in the circumstances, since Miss Donaldson was a shrewd and sophisticated girl, and he would also have to make sure that the press never got wind of the situation. There seemed to be no advantage in it for him: Bloomingdale might easily have found out and caused severe problems, especially in view of his noted violent rages and sadistic behaviour. It was as though he wanted to torture this captive bedroom bombshell, humiliating her because she could not sexually attract the most desirable of men.

The perverted relationship, devoid of meaning or substance, dragged on for much of a year. Cary was as stern with her as he was with other women when it came to the subject of dress. She had to put on heavy jewellery and magnificent gowns to satisfy him, yet he seldom paid for these; Bloomingdale was customarily paying her accounts.

There was little or no advantage for Vicki Morgan herself in this empty liaison with Grant, except, as Miss Bardach points out, in trying to overcome his seeming sexual reluctance. Meanwhile, she continued her ugly relationship with Bloomingdale; and her attempts at being an actress, studying with Lee Strasberg, came to nothing.

Finally, and we have to take Vicki Morgan's word for this, Cary at last consummated their relationship. But he only went to bed with her once, and she, disappointed, and realising that he would never pay her money, not even for costume jewellery, left him in a state of extreme disillusionment. By 1976, he had also parted from Maureen Donaldson, who understandably had had enough. It was tragic that, at this time of his life, he had not found a woman of sufficient stature, background, position and intelligence to marry and find happiness with in his last years.

Vicki Morgan's death was horrifying. On July 7, 1983, Marvin Pancoast, a thirty-three-year-old man with a police record, turned up at the North Hollywood police precinct and announced that he had killed her in a Colfax Avenue apartment. Her death sparked off a scandalous story that involved alleged tapes of her lovemaking with prominent political figures, and revealed a whole life of sordid, sleazy activities leading to near-terminal depression. Bloomingdale had died of cancer, his grave marked with Vicki's calling card and a newspaper photograph with a scrawled message from her. According to Joyce Milton and Ann Louise Bardach, co-authors of *Vicki*, their biography of Miss Morgan, "His family . . . buried [Bloomingdale] hastily in a wooden coffin, before the news of his death became public knowledge." There is one element missing in this unhappy story. Is it possible that Cary, who cruelly mistreated women when the darker side of his nature took over, simply enjoyed Vicki's company because he could beat her without the responsibility of making love to her? Perhaps it was a way of releasing his frustrated needs without actually hurting Maureen Donaldson physically. One hopes that that is true.

In the midst of this squalid misadventure, Cary continued to conduct somewhat of a public career. He gave interviews to the press commenting, in a direct contradiction of his personal behaviour, about the sweetness and loveliness of women, pontificating about mother love and family unity. In May 1973, he turned up at the Fabergé Straw Hat awards in New York, appearing with Helen Hayes, of whom he asked why they had never made a picture together. She replied, with a characteristic roguish wink, "I'm ready any time you are, Cary!" He embraced this remarkable actress who, although over eighty, retained a coy, youthful flirtatiousness and charm. He returned for the awards in successive years. In June 1975, he put on a tremendous act at the ceremony, which honoured his old friend Rosalind Russell: he deliberately mixed up his introduction cards, dropped his glasses, and did a drunk act, then quipped, as he read out the name of one of the performers, "It says here that Helen Gallagher was born dancing. Rough on her mother, wasn't it?" Handing Dortha Duckworth the Best Supporting Actress award, he joked, "She should get another reward for resisting the efforts to get her to change her name," and when Danny Aiello, voted Most Promising Actor, thanked his wife and four children, Cary brought a gale of laughter as he said, "Everybody should have a hobby!" This new role as Bob Hope-like jokester was in typical contradiction with his troubled private life.

Cary suffered a number of major and minor blows in the 1970s. His beloved Shannonside project, into which he had poured so much passion and enthusiasm, and which had involved him in seemingly countless trips across the Irish Channel, floundered and finally collapsed. According to William Currie McIntosh, the first inklings of trouble appeared in early 1974. McIntosh, Grant and their partners had relied heavily upon Associated Mortgage Investors, known as AMI, a US company which was supposed to have invested $6 million in Shannonside. AMI itself ran into difficulties, and in the last analysis was unable to provide the necessary sums. William McIntosh also blames "a self-styled environmentalist" for some of the problems.

Cary first received news of the problem in the most unexpected and unpleasant way, when Lawrence Crowley, the British Official Receiver in Bankruptcy, wrote to him asking him whether he would wish to supply particulars of any claim against the consortium. He called McIntosh immediately, and McIntosh was obliged to tell him the truth.

Cary lost a mere $10,000 in the project, but Jack Lemmon and McIntosh lost a great deal more. It was typical of Cary's tightness with money that he would no longer consider living in Ireland, because the bargain townhouse he had been promised was no longer available. He could have afforded a mansion, or a castle if he wished; he chose to possess neither.

Cary suffered much because of Howard Hughes' decline of health in the 1970s. Hughes' biographers Donald L. Barlett and James B. Steele, in their book *Empire*, gruesomely related his friend's condition by 1975. A malignant tumour grew out of the left side of his scalp; his teeth were too loose to be able to chew food and many were eaten away by decay. He weighed only 100 pounds, and his limbs were covered in needle marks. He had a peptic ulcer, his urinary tract was partly blocked, his prostate gland was enormously enlarged and his kidneys were shrinking. Despite the existence of four physicians on his permanent pay-roll, none seemed able to assist him in his appalling condition.

It is not known whether Cary visited Hughes at the time.

It is probable that Hughes, given his atrocious appearance, kept him at a distance. McIntosh recalls only two encounters between Cary and Hughes in the 1970s. The first was in Las Vegas, at the Desert Inn, just before Hughes' drastic final deterioriation. McIntosh says:

> Howard had long, long grey hair and long, dirty fingernails and was unbearably thin. Cary was full of compassion for him. He didn't stay long. Just as we were leaving, the police arrived. Hughes was being accused of being responsible for a murder. I never heard any more about that. I won't say any more; it's too dangerous to discuss.

The other occasion, and this was not a face-to-face meeting, was at the Inn on the Park in London. McIntosh recalls:

> Howard had hidden cameras monitoring the corridor outside his suite to see who was coming. Cary knew that Howard watched anxiously all the time. As we walked past, he waved to the camera, with great warmth and cheerfulness, so Howard would know he was in the hotel.

By the summer of 1975, though, Hughes was dying. There was a long struggle between his associates and heirs over the will and the overall disposition of the estate. He moved to Freeport in the Bahamas, and then, falsely informed that codeine was not available in the islands (and he was addicted to it) he was flown, in February 1976, to Acapulco and the garish excesses of the Princess Hotel. He stopped eating, and even refused water. Shifted to Houston, Texas, he at last died. He left Cary nothing in his will, which was fought over with great bitterness in the months to come. Cary received news of his death with great sadness. A part of his life was gone forever.

But Cary saw another of his former lovers from time to time: despite the fact that Randolph Scott was happily married, he apparently preserved a sentimental feeling for

Cary and a former maître d' at the Beverly Hillcrest Hotel remembers that, in the 1970s, Cary and Scott would turn up late at night, after the other diners had gone, and, in the near darkness of their table at the back of the restaurant, these two old men would surreptitiously be holding hands.

He heard from other flames: Virginia Cherrill recalls that she spoke to Cary soon after his mother's death, to tell him that a mutual friend, a girl named Troy Sondheim, was dying of cancer and wanted to see him. Virginia had obtained Cary's number from the former agent Minna Wallis and after some difficulty, she reached him at the Inn on the Park.

He called her back from Bristol, where he had been settling up some of Elsie's affairs. She asked if he would be coming to New York, and he said he would. But when he got to the hospital, to see Troy Sondheim, Troy panicked at the last minute and refused to let him in because she looked so terrible: she had lost her hair from the radiation treatments.

Soon after, back in California, Cary called Virginia at her home in Santa Barbara, where she was happily married to her third husband. He said he wanted to bring Jennifer to her to show her off. Virginia said she would be delighted. Why didn't he drive up? He said he wanted to come in the Fabergé plane, and would she mind? She said she would, as she didn't want to have photographers and press taking a picture of her with him at the airport, which they always covered for celebrity visitors. Virginia didn't want it to be in the papers that he had brought his daughter by his fourth wife to see his first. He was furious, snapping at her, in a reminiscence of his old, bad behaviour towards her, "You always were a bitch!" They didn't speak again.

Barbara Hutton was as anorexic as Howard Hughes, suffering from declining health in the wake of her beloved son's death. She would turn up, always spectral in black, at dinner parties, complaining about the food and charging the host with poisoning her soup. She threatened people with lawsuits who said that she had once introduced into her system a tapeworm in order to get thin and it had finally eaten her away. This ridiculous story was particularly favoured by Truman Capote. She would call Cary at all hours of the night, shouting bitterly that those around her were trying to kill her and were keeping her locked up in her suite at the Beverly Wilshire Hotel. In 1979, she died of a merciful heart attack, wasted away to a skeleton and no longer knowing her own name.

Betsy Drake was made of sterner stuff. Her work as an actress long over, she took up a career as a psychotherapist, specialising in disturbed children and adolescents; she led psychodrama groups at UCLA, where she had a position. She published a well-received novel and occasionally spoke with Cary on the telephone. Phyllis Brooks was living comfortably in New England, having married a close friend and associate of President John F. Kennedy; she was the mother of an attractive family that inherited her perfect looks and charm. Mary Brian had married the film editor George Tomasini, who had handled many Hitchcock films including Cary's own *North by Northwest*. She saw Cary occasionally at social events. However, Sophia Loren and Cary were violently in conflict over her memoirs, written with A. E. Hotchner, in which she described her romantic relationship with him in terms more appropriate to a fairy tale than to any known reality. He objected to her having written about their relationship at all, even though she was extraordinarily protective, sympathetic and flattering. If she could be accused of anything, it was of giving the impression that the liaison meant a great deal more than in fact it really did.

As for Dyan Cannon, her struggles with Cary over Jennifer never abated. They constantly battled over the court order that Jennifer must be restricted to the United States, Canada, England, France and Mexico, and that the parents must not harass or annoy each other. The child, remaining surprisingly normal despite her disrupted life, spent, as an example, July of 1973 with Cary in Westhampton, Long Island, after being with Dyan in Montreal during the shooting of Dyan's first picture as a director, *Child Under A Leaf*. Cary managed to block Dyan from taking Jennifer to Tunisia that August. He showered Jennifer with gifts; yet her most prized possession was a horse, given to her by Marje Everett of Hollywood Park Racetrack. Some of Jennifer's happiest days were with her father at the races; Cary had become more and more deeply obsessed with racing in his seventies.

He was involved in various forms of litigation in that decade: in one case suing Twentieth Century-Fox for $1 million for splicing scenes from *Monkey Business*, his co-starring vehicle with Ginger Rogers, into the semi-documentary *Marilyn*, an account of the career of Marilyn Monroe. He was only awarded $10, a humiliating result which he bravely described as "a moral victory". In 1975, he was elected to the board of MGM, where he had made one of his favourite pictures, *The Philadelphia Story*. He proved to be a skilful and dedicated board member, not merely a figurehead. There was the irresistible attraction of many perquisites, influences and benefits that went with the position.

Nineteen seventy-six brought a death and a new and extraordinary relationship. A final link with his childhood snapped when his half-brother Eric Leach died of cancer on November 23. That same year, Cary was in London, staying not at his old haunts the Connaught and the Inn on the Park, but, for a change, at the Royal Lancaster Hotel in Bayswater. He liked the hotel, and he very much liked the public relations woman there, who assisted him during a Fabergé trade show. Her name was Barbara Harris. In her twenties, she was of medium height, dark, slender, and athletic, with beautifully chiselled features and intelligent, sharp eyes. She exuded efficiency, coolness, a degree of culture and an open, uncomplicated friendliness. He was amused by the fact that she would drive him around town to interviews or meetings in a Mini, to enter which he had to almost bend double, and he loved the fact that she didn't treat him like a film star. He told her colleague in public

relations, Sally Bulloch, that he very much liked her expertise.

Cary enjoyed driving with Barbara through small English
villages and imbibing glasses of beer in pubs. He liked
visiting her parents, retired Tanganyika public servants, at
their Devon farm, and although Barbara was far removed
from his usual physical type, Cary found in her a true,
unambitious and unchallenging friend. In his seventies,
friendship was more important to him than anything else.
After the wearying experiences with Dyan and with Vicki
Morgan, he longed for a safe harbour.

Yet even then, he was not destined to enjoy complete
happiness. His recent refusal to exercise, beyond some
morning stretches, had finally taken their toll. His well-
developed physique, the result of years of acrobatics, had
remained with him at an extraordinarily late age, provoking
much envious admiration from friends. But he had made a
fatal mistake: he had forgotten that although it is difficult,
given a careful diet, to lose the muscularity of a pure
mesomorph, even athletes can suffer in old age if they do
not maintain aerobic activity. His heart was weakened by
sheer lack of exercise and his cardio-vascular problems
became increasingly severe: he was suffering from high
blood pressure. At last, even his powerful muscles began to
soften because he failed to tighten them with weights.

In 1979 he was deeply saddened by the brutal assassin-
ation of his old friend, Lord Louis Mountbatten, by the
Irish Republican Army, and burst into tears at the funeral
service in Westminster Abbey. Much admired by the Royal
Family, he attended a special reception following the funeral, to be greeted with enthusiasm by the Queen and the
Duke of Edinburgh.

He was upset by news that NBC was going to film Sophia
Loren's memoirs and made an effort to stop it. Finally, he
agreed to allow John Gavin, whom he much admired and
liked, and had seen a good deal of in his years at MCA-
Universal, to portray him, in return for the sum of $250,000
paid by the studio.

There was more serious trouble with NBC, in November 1980. Chevy Chase appeared as a guest on Tom Snyder's popular *Tomorrow* show and Cary, who admired Chase, appreciating the style of his bumptious comedy routines, made a special point of watching that night. He was horrified when, after Snyder asked Chase what he felt about Cary Grant, Chase said, "He really was a great physical comic, and I understand he was a homo — What a gal!" Chase accompanied the statement, delivered in a lisping, effeminate voice, with a limp-wristed gesture.* Cary exploded, called his lawyer in the middle of the night, and slapped a $10-million slander suit on Chase.

Chase's agent, Jasper Vance, said that Chase would not respond. And, sensibly, Cary failed to pursue the suit; it could have led him into a disastrous situation. More than one friend recommended that he present whatever money he gained from the suit to gay liberation, and, in a characteristic switch, he laughingly agreed. Chase finally commented, "I shouldn't have said that, because it's been such a pain in the neck."

By 1980, Barbara Harris was living with Cary at his homes in Benedict Canyon and Malibu. Breaking, for the first time, the secret that she was leaving London to join him, she said to her colleague Sally Bulloch, "I only hope I can stop smoking!" Cary refused to have smokers in his presence. Jennifer adored Barbara, and the feeling was mutual. Barbara's English coolness, her lack of neuroses or strong emotionalism, and her dislike of theatricality all suited Cary ideally. Although he may have disconcerted her by giving more than one interview at the time stating that he had made a failure of marriages and would never marry again, he at last began saying to journalists that he wanted Barbara to be "the lady of my manor".

She humoured him in his desire to live to be over a hundred. When a journalist friend of his arrived from

---

* In another version, friends called Cary the morning after the broadcast to tell him about it as he had been asleep when it was aired.

Russia with a formula of fresh honey and walnuts to be eaten every morning for longevity and sexual prowess, he happily devoured the harmless concoction every morning. He longed for more children. In the wake of the fracas with Chevy Chase, he apparently had no leanings any more towards homosexuality. And it is reasonably certain that Barbara Harris never accepted that aspect of his past history.

He now entered the only really happy time of his life. Dyan Cannon had grown more mellow, and now that Jennifer was well into her teens, with a strong and well-balanced personality of her own, the extreme tensions between her parents lessened. It seemed time to marry, to consolidate his joy at last. On April 15, 1981, Cary and Barbara's wedding at last took place. The location was in the living-room of the Beverly Grove Drive house, with Jennifer, Mr. and Mrs. Stanley Fox, and two members of the domestic staff as witnesses. They were guests ten days later at the 25th wedding anniversary party of Princess Grace and Prince Rainier, with Frank Sinatra as host.

On December 6, 1981, Cary joined Count Basie, Helen Hayes, Jerome Robbins and Rudolph Serkin as recipients of the Kennedy Center Awards in Washington, DC. President Reagan wrote to Roy Moseley that "We are both grateful that he was one of the Medal winners in the Kennedy Center Honors Awards during our time here." Among those present at the gala reception at the White House were Cary's old friend Audrey Hepburn, James Stewart, still close, and Victor Borge, on whom Cary doted. Humorist Art Buchwald brought the house down when he said, "Mr. President, if you hadn't gone into politics you might be sitting in the seat where Cary Grant is now – and Al Haig would be sitting in yours." This was a proud moment for the Grants. He looked marvellous: still several years younger than the other figures being honoured.

In May 1982, Cary was named Man of the Year by the New York Friars Club in New York's Waldorf-Astoria Hotel and raised a quarter of a million dollars for charity.

Although Cary disliked dinners honouring him, wishing he could spend his time in peace in Los Angeles, he was overjoyed by the presence of George Burns, from whom, he felt, he had learned, in the 1920s, all of his comedy timing. Burns made him burst out laughing when he said, "I was introduced to Cary by Abraham Lincoln's widow." Rich Little broke him up completely as he recreated Cary's Cockney dialogue in *Gunga Din*. Tony Bennett sang "It Amazes Me", Cary's favourite song, and Peggy Lee, with heartfelt enthusiasm, delivered "Mr. Wonderful" directly to his face. Sinatra was in his best form, inimitably delivering Sammy Cahn's "The Most Fabulous Man in the World", a reworking of a Rodgers and Hart number. Cary was so moved by the entire evening that tears streamed down his face as he walked to the podium, saying ruefully, with a smile that would have melted lead, "To indulge in one's emotions is a privilege allowed to the elderly." He abandoned most of his prepared speech, talking simply and touchingly of his gratitude for the admiration of his peers.

There were two more shocking bereavements that year. It was one of the burdens of his old age that so many of the nearest and dearest passed away. He had long suffered the agonising final illness of Ingrid Bergman who, with great courage, had battled against breast cancer. The growth had metastasised, and she had called to tell him the news. At an American Film Institute Life Achievement Award banquet for Alfred Hitchcock, which Cary had come to reluctantly because of a bad cold, she had moved him deeply by giving a Yale key, a souvenir of their film *Notorious*, to Hitchcock. An even greater shock was in store that September: Princess Grace, whom Cary had never ceased to admire and love, had set out to drive from her mountain residence to Monaco along the twisting Grande Corniche when she suffered a stroke, lost control of her Rover, and crashed to her death over a wall. This second grief following Miss Bergman's death just a few weeks earlier was intolerable. Cary was in agony as he and Barbara flew to Monaco to the funeral and did their best to console the devastated

Prince Rainier. As the service in the cathedral ended, Cary's face suddenly looked shockingly old. Barbara had to raise him from his seat, as he seemed unable to stand. But he never lost his dignity in the face of the crowd and the photographers. A trifle unsteady, he made his way to the waiting car and then he broke into helpless tears.

He himself had never been much of a driver and he was drastically concerned that Jennifer might suffer a similar mishap. He begged her not to drive the Honda he had given her for her sixteenth birthday, the first date at which she could legally drive. But in discussions with Dyan Cannon, that brought him closer to his former wife than he had been for years, it was agreed that Jennifer could drive.

In 1983, he set off on a world cruise with Barbara aboard the elegant Royal Viking *Sky*. Both *To Catch a Thief* and *Charade* were shown while the couple was on board. Crew members recall that they were totally happy and relaxed, mingling not only with the passengers but with the crew, appearing at a table in the dining-room with broad smiles, accepting questions from passengers and enjoying the company of the Norwegian captain and officers. It was an ideal opportunity to get away from everything and everyone.

The experience of giving question-and-answer sessions on board, something Cary had long avoided (Joan Crawford and Bette Davis were among those stars who enjoyed such sessions in their old age), prompted him to start a whole new career as a one-man performer with a presentation entitled "A Conversation With Cary Grant". It was a way of getting in touch with his public, and something to do; like many in retirement, he was beginning to be bored and fretful and sensed that he was getting out of touch. He also felt that it would be a chance of seeing parts of America he had never seen. In Schenectady, New York, he delighted a large crowd at Proctor's theatre, giving quick and intelligent replies to questions while seated on a backless stool on stage for ninety minutes. Dressed with his customary elegance in a black tuxedo, he was occasionally provocative, as when somebody asked him about Mae West. He commented: "I don't have a fond memory of her. She did her own thing to the detriment of everyone around her. I don't admire superficiality." For the most part, though, his comments were sweetly innocuous, and none had the temerity to ask him about inconvenient matters. The ovation was prolonged; all ages were there.

It was always a strain for him to attend the Academy Awards, but Cary, as an elder statesman of the industry, felt that it was a social obligation to appear. Timothy Hutton recalls an incident at the 1984 Awards:

I had never met Cary Grant before, and I went up to him and introduced myself. I mentioned my Dad, Jim Hutton. We started talking about how much he liked my Dad, and made me feel great. He didn't just say, "Oh, that's nice," and walk away. He sat down next to me and we talked. Despite all the activity in the room, I remember how incredibly gracious and warm and interested in the memory of *Walk, Don't Run* and of my father Cary Grant was. Here was this very, very electric atmosphere, with pages running up and giving last-minute script changes, and countdowns, and loud noises – and there he was. I thought, "If only my Dad could hear this, hear the person that meant the most to him professionally, in his field, saying the things about him that he admired most and looked up to . . ."

I asked him if he would ever want to make another movie, and he just dismissed it. He said, "Absolutely not. I'm having far too great a time doing what I'm doing these days to get back into that." He didn't need to have done what he did, talking to me. It was something I'll never forget. The last of the great gentlemen: Cary Grant.

At home in October 1984, Cary experienced a dizzy spell. Doctors at Cedars Sinai Medical Center in Los Angeles told him he had had a slight stroke. He was warned to ease up on his constant travels and appearances at gala occasions.

But Barbara loved social life, and he always enjoyed showing his amazingly preserved looks. They unwisely continued a non-stop whirlwind of activity, which still included work for Fabergé.

He was wearing himself out. On November 28, 1986, he arrived for another of his question-and-answer sessions at Davenport, Iowa, and checked in to the Blackhawk Hotel. He was in the best of moods, buoyant, looking forward to the evening event, holding hands with Barbara for the photographers. All passion spent, his tension and neuroses seemingly gone for good, he seemed in great form, and everyone he met stared at him in disbelief, noticing his glowing good health. But he was not feeling well. He had a wobbly, unsteady sense of discomfort, and at a rehearsal to set the microphones and lights in the correct positions, at which he was expert as always, he seemed forgetful and uneasy. Beads of perspiration started on his forehead as he moved around the Adler theatre, discussing with the co-ordinator, Lois Jecklin, how best he might handle the two and a half hours of questioning. Towards the end of the discussion he suddenly went pale under his tan and almost fell into an armchair. Barbara, concerned, asked him if he would like a physician. He refused, perhaps aware of the effect a doctor's attentions might have on his image of eternal health and youthfulness. He was determined not to disappoint the audience, and he sat very still in his dressing-room, trying to gather his energies together. Again, Barbara asked him if he would accept medical attention, and again he refused. Finally, Davenport businessman Douglas Miller called Dr. Duane Manlov, who arrived and, much to Cary's annoyance, took his pulse and temperature. Manlov realised Cary was suffering from another stroke. Cardiologist Dr. James Gillson turned up and insisted that Cary go to the hospital. Cary refused. He wanted to return to Los Angeles.

Stubborn, determined in the face of everyone's advice, he became impatient when Barbara, who was in a state of appalling anxiety, absolutely demanded that he go to the hospital. The ambulance arrived; Cary was suffering from chest pains. He was grumblingly taken to St. Luke's Hospital, holding Barbara's hand with expressions of love. When he at last reached the intensive care unit, it was revealed that he was in fact the victim of a major stroke. In a daze of confusion throughout, he probably didn't know the extent of his illness. If so, his passing was merciful. At eleven twenty-two p.m., he was dead.

There was no funeral as Cary had always hated the thought of being buried, particularly at Forest Lawn, where many stars were finally interred, and his body was therefore cremated.

His $80 million fortune was divided between Jennifer and Barbara, who have kept his memory burning bright.

Cary was, and is, mourned. In a barbaric age, he represents a nostalgic vision of much that is lost to us. It is true that his life was tragic, but, though until the last few years he found little happiness himself, he gave unlimited joy on the screen. His performances will never date; their timeless grace is there for all future generations. As for Archie Leach, he never left Grant and Grant never found himself. Someone asked him, "Who is Cary Grant?" and he replied, "When you find out, tell me . . ."

THE FILMS OF CARY GRANT

The director's name is in italics. A (c) shows the film was in colour. Sp denotes Screenplay and b/o – based/on.

1. THIS IS THE NIGHT. Paramount, 1932. *Frank Tuttle*. Sp: George Marion, Jr., b/o play by Avery Hopwood. Cast: Lili Damita, Charles Ruggles, Roland Young, Thelma Todd, Irving Bacon, Claire Dodd.

2. SINNERS IN THE SUN. Paramount, 1932. *Alexander Hall*. Sp: Vincent Lawrence, Waldemar Young and Samuel Hoffenstein, b/o story by Mildred Cram. Cast: Carole Lombard, Chester Morris, Adrienne Ames, Alison Skipworth, Walter Byron.

3. MERRILY WE GO TO HELL. Paramount, 1932. *Dorothy Arzner*. Sp: Edwin Justus Mayer, b/o novel by Cleo Lucas. Cast: Fredric March, Sylvia Sidney, Adrianne Allen, Richard "Skeets" Gallagher, Kent Taylor.

4. DEVIL AND THE DEEP. Paramount, 1932. *Marion Gering*. Sp: Benn W. Levy, b/o story by Harry Hervey. Cast: Tallulah Bankhead, Gary Cooper, Charles Laughton, Paul Porcasi, Juliette Compton, Henry Kolker, Kent Taylor.

5. BLONDE VENUS. Paramount, 1932. *Josef Von Sternberg*. Sp: Jules Furthman and S. K. Lauren, b/o story by Josef Von Sternberg. Cast: Marlene Dietrich, Herbert Marshall, Dickie Moore, Sidney Toler, Cecil Cunningham, Hattie McDaniel.

6. HOT SATURDAY. Paramount, 1932. *William A. Seiter*. Sp: Seton I. Miller, b/o novel by Harvey Fergusson. Cast: Nancy Carroll, Randolph Scott, Edward Woods, Lillian Bond, William Collier Sr., Jane Darwell, Grady Sutton.

7. MADAME BUTTERFLY. Paramount, 1932. *Marion Gering*. Sp: Josephine Lovett and Joseph Moncure March, b/o story by John

Luther Long and play by David Belasco. Cast: Sylvia Sidney, Charles Ruggles, Irving Pichel, Helen Jerome Eddy, Sheila Terry.

8. SHE DONE HIM WRONG. Paramount, 1933. *Lowell Sherman*. Sp: Harvey Thew and John Bright, b/o play by Mae West. Cast: Mae West, Gilbert Roland, Noah Beery Sr., Rafaela Ottiano, David Landau, Rochelle Hudson, Owen Moore, Fuzzy Knight, Louise Beavers.

9. WOMAN ACCUSED. Paramount, 1933. *Paul Sloane*. Sp: Bayard Veiller, b/o magazine serial by Polan Banks, Rupert Hughes, Vicki Baum, Zane Grey, Viña Delmar, Irvin S. Cobb, Gertrude Atherton, J. P. McEvoy, Ursula Parrott, and Sophie Kerr. Cast: Nancy Carroll, John Halliday, Irving Pichel, Louis Calhern, Jack La Rue, John Lodge.

10. THE EAGLE AND THE HAWK. Paramount, 1933. *Stuart Walker*. Sp: Bogart Rogers and Seton I. Miller, b/o story by John Monk Saunders. Cast: Fredric March, Jack Oakie, Carole Lombard, Sir Guy Standing.

11. GAMBLING SHIP. Paramount, 1933. *Louis Gasnier* and *Max Marcin*. Sp: Max Marcin and Seton I. Miller, b/o story by Peter Ruric and adaptation by Claude Binyon. Cast: Benita Hume, Roscoe Karns, Glenda Farrell, Jack La Rue, Arthur Vinton.

12. I'M NO ANGEL. Paramount, 1933. *Wesley Ruggles*. Sp: Mae West and Lowell Brentano. Cast: Mae West, Edward Arnold, Ralf Harolde, Russell Hopton, Gertrude Michael, Kent Taylor, Dorothy Peterson, Gregory Ratoff.

13. ALICE IN WONDERLAND. Paramount, 1933. *Norman Z. McLeod*. Sp: Joseph L. Mankiewicz and William Cameron Menzies, b/o story by Lewis Carroll. Cast: Charlotte Henry, Richard Arlen, Gary Cooper, Leon Errol, Louise Fazenda, W. C. Fields, Sterling Holloway, Edward Everett Horton, Baby LeRoy, Mae Marsh, Jack Oakie, Edna May Oliver, May Robson, Charles Ruggles, Alison Skipworth, Ned Sparks, Jacqueline Wells.

14. THIRTY DAY PRINCESS. Paramount, 1934. *Marion Gering*. Sp: Preston Sturges and Frank Partos, b/o story by Clarence Budington Kelland. Cast: Sylvia Sidney, Edward Arnold, Vince Barnett, Henry Stephenson, Edgar Norton.

15. BORN TO BE BAD. United Artists, 1934. *Lowell Sherman*. Sp: Ralph Graves. Cast: Loretta Young, Jackie Kelk, Henry Travers,

Russell Hopton, Andrew Tombes, Harry Green, Marion Burns.

16. KISS AND MAKE UP. Paramount, 1934. *Harlan Thompson*. Sp: Harlan Thompson and George Marion, Jr., b/o play by Stephen Bekeffi and adaptation by Jane Hinton. Cast: Genevieve Tobin, Helen Mack, Edward Everett Horton, Mona Maris, Toby Wing, Clara Lou (Ann) Sheridan, Jacqueline Wells.

17. LADIES SHOULD LISTEN. Paramount, 1934. *Frank Tuttle*. Sp: Claude Binyon and Frank Butler, b/o play by Guy Bolton and Alfred Savoir. Cast: Frances Drake, Edward Everett Horton, Charles Arnt, Rosita Moreno, Nydia Westman, George Barbier, Clara Lou (Ann) Sheridan.

18. ENTER MADAME. Paramount, 1934. *Elliott Nugent*. Sp: Charles Brackett and Gladys Lehman, b/o play by Gilda Varesi and Dorothea Donn-Byrne. Cast: Elissa Landi, Lynne Overman, Sharon Lynn, Frank Albertson, Cecilia Parker, Clara Lou (Ann) Sheridan.

19. WINGS IN THE DARK. Paramount, 1935. *James Flood*. Sp: Jack Kirkland and Frank Partos, b/o story by Neil Shipman and Philip D. Hurn, adapted by Dale Van Every. Cast: Myrna Loy, Roscoe Karns, Hobart Cavanaugh, Dean Jagger, Bert Hanlon, Russell Hopton.

20. THE LAST OUTPOST. Paramount, 1935. *Louis Gasnier* and *Charles Barton*. Sp: Philip MacDonald, b/o story by F. Britten Austin and adaptation by Frank Partos and Charles Brackett. Cast: Claude Rains, Gertrude Michael, Kathleen Burke, Colin Tapley.

21. SYLVIA SCARLETT. RKO, 1936. *George Cukor*. Sp: Gladys Unger, John Collier, and Mortimer Offner, b/o novel by Compton MacKenzie. Cast: Katharine Hepburn, Brian Aherne, Edmund Gwenn, Natalie Paley, Dennie Moore.

22. BIG BROWN EYES. Paramount, 1936. *Raoul Walsh*. Sp: Raoul Walsh and Bert Hanlon, b/o short stories by James Edward Grant. Cast: Joan Bennett, Walter Pidgeon, Isabel Jewell, Lloyd Nolan, Douglas Fowley, Marjorie Gateson, Alan Baxter.

23. SUZY. MGM, 1936. *George Fitzmaurice*. Sp: Dorothy Parker, Alan Campbell, Horace Jackson, and Lenore Coffee, b/o novel by Herbert Gorman. Cast: Jean Harlow, Franchot Tone, Lewis Stone, Benita Hume, Inez Courtney, Stanley Morner, Una O'Connor.

24. WEDDING PRESENT. Paramount, 1936. *Richard Wallace*. Sp: Joseph Anthony, b/o story by Paul Gallico. Cast: Joan Bennett, George Bancroft, Conrad Nagel, Gene Lockhart, William Demarest, Inez Courtney, Edward Brophy.

25. THE AMAZING QUEST OF ERNEST BLISS. Grand National, 1936. *Alfred Zeisler*. Sp: John L. Balderston, b/o story by E. Phillips Oppenheim. Cast: Mary Brian, Peter Gawthorne, Henry Kendall, John Turnbull.

26. WHEN YOU'RE IN LOVE. Columbia, 1937. *Robert Riskin*. Sp: Robert Riskin, b/o story by Ethel Hill and Cedric Worth. Cast: Grace Moore, Aline MacMahon, Henry Stephenson, Thomas Mitchell, Catherine Doucet, Luis Alberni, Emma Dunn.

27. THE TOAST OF NEW YORK. RKO, 1937. *Rowland V. Lee*. Sp: Dudley Nichols, John Twist, and Joel Sayre, b/o book by Bouck White and story by Matthew Josephson. Cast: Edward Arnold, Frances Farmer, Jack Oakie, Donald Meek, Thelma Leeds, Clarence Kolb, Billy Gilbert.

28. TOPPER. MGM, 1937. *Norman Z. McLeod*. Sp: Jack Jevne, Eric Hatch, and Eddie Moran, b/o novel by Thorne Smith. Cast: Constance Bennett, Roland Young, Billie Burke, Alan Mowbray, Eugene Pallette, Arthur Lake, Hedda Hopper, Virginia Sale.

29. THE AWFUL TRUTH. Columbia, 1937. *Leo McCarey*. Sp: Viña Delmar, b/o play by Arthur Richman. Cast: Irene Dunne, Ralph Bellamy, Alexander D'Arcy, Cecil Cunningham, Molly Lamont, Esther Dale, Mary Forbes, and Mr. Smith (dog).

30. BRINGING UP BABY. RKO, 1938. *Howard Hawks*. Sp: Dudley Nichols and Hagar Wilde, b/o story by Wilde. Cast: Katharine Hepburn, Charles Ruggles, May Robson, Walter Catlett, Barry Fitzgerald, Fritz Feld, Tala Birell.

31. HOLIDAY. Columbia, 1938. *George Cukor*. Sp: Donald Ogden Stewart and Sidney Buchman, b/o play by Philip Barry. Cast: Katharine Hepburn, Doris Nolan, Lew Ayres, Edward Everett Horton, Henry Kolker, Jean Dixon, Binnie Barnes, Henry Daniell, Bess Flowers.

32. GUNGA DIN. RKO, 1939. *George Stevens*. Sp: Joel Sayre and Fred Guiol, b/o story by Ben Hecht and Charles MacArthur, from a Rudyard Kipling poem. Cast: Victor McLaglen, Douglas

Fairbanks, Jr., Eduardo Ciannelli, Joan Fontaine, Montagu Love, Sam Jaffe.

33. ONLY ANGELS HAVE WINGS. Columbia, 1939. *Howard Hawks*. Sp: Jules Furthman, b/o story by Howard Hawks. Cast: Jean Arthur, Richard Barthelmess, Rita Hayworth, Thomas Mitchell, Sig Ruman, Victor Kilian, John Carroll, Allyn Joslyn, Donald Barry, Noah Beery, Jr.

34. IN NAME ONLY. RKO, 1939. *John Cromwell*. Sp: Richard Sherman, b/o novel by Bessie Breuer. Cast: Carole Lombard, Kay Francis, Charles Coburn, Helen Vinson, Katharine Alexander, Jonathan Hale, Peggy Ann Garner.

35. HIS GIRL FRIDAY. Columbia, 1940. *Howard Hawks*. Sp: Charles Lederer, b/o play by Ben Hecht and Charles MacArthur. Cast: Rosalind Russell, Ralph Bellamy, Gene Lockhart, Porter Hall, Ernest Truex, Cliff Edwards, Clarence Kolb, Roscoe Karns, Frank Jenks, Regis Toomey, John Qualen, Helen Mack, Alma Kruger, Billy Gilbert, Marion Martin.

36. MY FAVORITE WIFE. RKO, 1940. *Garson Kanin*. Sp: Bella and Samuel Spewack, b/o story by the Spewacks and Leo McCarey. Cast: Irene Dunne, Randolph Scott, Gail Patrick, Ann Shoemaker, Scotty Beckett, Donald MacBride, Granville Bates.

37. THE HOWARDS OF VIRGINIA. Columbia, 1940. *Frank Lloyd*. Sp: Sidney Buchman, b/o novel by Elizabeth Page. Cast: Martha Scott, Sir Cedric Hardwicke, Alan Marshal, Richard Carlson, Paul Kelly, Irving Bacon, Elisabeth Risdon, Anne Revere, Richard Alden (Tom Drake).

38. THE PHILADELPHIA STORY. MGM, 1940. *George Cukor*. Sp: Donald Ogden Stewart, b/o play by Philip Barry. Cast: Katharine Hepburn, James Stewart, Ruth Hussey, John Howard, Roland Young, John Halliday, Virginia Weidler, Mary Nash, Henry Daniell.

39. PENNY SERENADE. Columbia, 1941. *George Stevens*. Sp: Morrie Ryskind, b/o story by Martha Cheavens. Cast: Irene Dunne, Beulah Bondi, Edgar Buchanan, Ann Doran, Eva Lee Kuney.

40. SUSPICION. RKO, 1941. *Alfred Hitchcock*. Sp: Samson Raphaelson, Joan Harrison, and Alma Reville, b/o novel by Francis Iles. Cast: Joan Fontaine, Sir Cedric Hardwicke, Nigel Bruce, Dame May Whitty, Isabel Jeans, Heather Angel, Leo G. Carroll.

41. THE TALK OF THE TOWN. Columbia, 1942. *George Stevens.*
Sp: Irwin Shaw and Sidney Buchman. Cast: Jean Arthur, Ronald
Colman, Edgar Buchanan, Glenda Farrell, Charles Dingle, Emma
Dunn, Rex Ingram.

42. ONCE UPON A HONEYMOON. RKO, 1942. *Leo McCarey.* Sp:
Sheridan Gibney, b/o story by Gibney and Leo McCarey. Cast:
Ginger Rogers, Walter Slezak, Albert Dekker, Albert Basserman,
Ferike Boros.

43. MR. LUCKY. RKO, 1943. *H. C. Potter.* Sp: Milton Holmes
and Adrian Scott. Cast: Laraine Day, Charles Bickford, Gladys
Cooper, Alan Carney, Henry Stephenson, Paul Stewart, Kay
Johnson, Walter Kingsford, J. M. Kerrigan, Vladimir Sokoloff,
Florence Bates.

44. DESTINATION TOKYO. Warners, 1944. *Delmer Daves.* Sp:
Delmer Daves and Albert Maltz, b/o story by Steve Fisher. Cast:
John Garfield, Alan Hale, John Ridgely, Dane Clark, Warner
Anderson, William Prince, Robert Hutton, Tom Tully, Faye
Emerson, John Forsythe.

45. ONCE UPON A TIME. Columbia, 1944. *Alexander Hall.* Sp:
Lewis Meltzer and Oscar Paul, b/o adaptation by Irving Fineman
of story by Norman Corwin and Lucille Fletcher Herrmann. Cast:
Janet Blair, James Gleason, Ted Donaldson, Howard Freeman,
William Demarest.

46. ARSENIC AND OLD LACE. Warners, 1944. *Frank Capra.* Sp:
Julius J. and Philip G. Epstein, b/o play by Joseph Kesselring. Cast:
Priscilla Lane, Raymond Massey, Josephine Hull, Jean Adair, Jack
Carson, Edward Everett Horton, Peter Lorre, James Gleason,
John Alexander, Grant Mitchell.

47. NONE BUT THE LONELY HEART. RKO, 1944. *Clifford Odets.*
Sp: Odets, b/o novel by Richard Llewellyn. Cast: Ethel Barrymore,
Barry Fitzgerald, June Duprez, Jane Wyatt, George Coulouris,
Dan Duryea, Roman Bohnen.

48. NIGHT AND DAY. Warners, 1946. (c) *Michael Curtiz,* Sp:
Charles Hoffman, Leo Townsend, and William Bowers, b/o life
of Cole Porter. Cast: Alexis Smith, Monty Woolley, Ginny Simms,
Jane Wyman, Eve Arden, Victor Francen, Alan Hale, Dorothy
Malone, Selena Royle, Mary Martin.

49. NOTORIOUS. RKO, 1946. *Alfred Hitchcock.* Sp: Ben Hecht,

Cast: Ingrid Bergman, Claude Rains, Louis Calhern, Mme. Leopoldine Konstantin, Ivan Triesault, Reinhold Schunzel, Moroni Olsen.

50. THE BACHELOR AND THE BOBBYSOXER. RKO. 1947. *Irving Reis* Sp: Sidney Sheldon. Cast: Myrna Loy, Shirley Temple, Rudy Vallee, Ray Collins, Harry Davenport, Johnny Sands, Don Beddoe, Veda Ann Borg.

51. THE BISHOP'S WIFE. RKO, 1947. *Henry Koster.* Sp: Robert E. Sherwood and Leonardo Bercovici, b/o novel by Robert Nathan. Cast: Loretta Young, David Niven, Monty Woolley, James Gleason, Gladys Cooper, Elsa Lanchester, Sara Haden.

52. MR. BLANDINGS BUILDS HIS DREAM HOUSE. RKO, 1948. *H. C. Potter.* Sp: Norman Panama and Melvin Frank, b/o novel by Eric Hodgins. Cast: Myrna Loy, Melvyn Douglas, Sharyn Moffett, Connie Marshall, Louise Beavers, Lurene Tuttle, Reginald Denny.

53. EVERY GIRL SHOULD BE MARRIED. RKO, 1948. *Don Hartman.* Sp: Hartman and Stephen Morehouse Avery, b/o story by Eleanor Harris. Cast: Betsy Drake, Franchot Tone, Diana Lynn, Eddie Albert, Elisabeth Risdon, Alan Mowbray.

54. I WAS A MALE WAR BRIDE. 20th Century-Fox, 1949. *Howard Hawks.* Sp: Charles Lederer, Leonard Spiegelgass, and Hagar Wilde, b/o story by Henri Rochard. Cast: Ann Sheridan, William Neff, Eugene Gericke, Marion Marshall, Randy Stuart.

55. CRISIS. MGM, 1950. *Richard Brooks.* Sp: Brooks, b/o story by George Tabori. Cast: José Ferrer, Paula Raymond, Signe Hasso, Ramon Novarro, Gilbert Roland, Antonio Moreno, Leon Ames, Teresa Celli.

56. PEOPLE WILL TALK. 20th Century-Fox, 1951. *Joseph L. Mankiewicz.* Sp: Mankiewicz, b/o play by Curt Goetz. Cast: Jeanne Crain, Finlay Currie, Hume Cronyn, Walter Slezak, Sidney Blackmer, Katherine Locke, Will Wright, Margaret Hamilton.

57. ROOM FOR ONE MORE. Warners, 1952. *Norman Taurog.* Sp: Melville Shavelson and Jack Rose, b/o book by Anna Perrott Rose. Cast: Betsy Drake, Iris Mann, George Winslow, Clifford Tatum, Jr., Gay Gordon, Malcolm Cassell, Larry Olsen, Lurene Tuttle.

58. MONKEY BUSINESS. 20th Century-Fox, 1952. *Howard Hawks.* Sp: I. A. L. Diamond, Charles Lederer, and Ben Hecht. Cast:

Ginger Rogers, Charles Coburn, Marilyn Monroe, Hugh Marlowe, Henri Letondal, Larry Keating, Esther Dale, George Winslow.

59. DREAM WIFE. MGM, 1953. *Sidney Sheldon.* Sp: Sidney Sheldon, Herbert Baker, and Alfred Lewis Levitt. Cast: Deborah Kerr, Walter Pidgeon, Betta St. John, Eduard Franz, Buddy Baer, Les Tremayne, Bruce Bennett.

60. TO CATCH A THIEF. Paramount, 1955. (c) *Alfred Hitchcock.* Sp: John Michael Hayes, b/o novel by David Dodge. Cast: Grace Kelly, Jessie Royce Landis, John Williams, Charles Vanel, Brigitte Auber, Jean Martinelli.

61. THE PRIDE AND THE PASSION. United Artists, 1957. (c) *Stanley Kramer.* Sp: Edna and Edward Anhalt, b/o novel by C. S. Forester. Cast: Frank Sinatra, Sophia Loren, Theodore Bikel, John Wengraf, Jay Novello.

62. AN AFFAIR TO REMEMBER. 20th Century-Fox, 1957. (c) *Leo McCarey.* Sp: Delmer Daves and Leo McCarey, b/o original story by McCarey and Mildred Cram. Cast: Deborah Kerr, Richard Denning, Neva Patterson, Cathleen Nesbitt, Robert Q. Lewis.

63. KISS THEM FOR ME. 20th Century-Fox, 1957. (c) *Stanley Donen.* Sp: Julius J. Epstein, b/o play by Luther Davis and novel by Frederic Wakeman. Cast: Jayne Mansfield, Leif Erickson, Suzy Parker, Ray Walston, Larry Blyden, Nathaniel Frey, Werner Klemperer, Jack Mullaney.

64. INDISCREET. Warners, 1958. (c) *Stanley Donen.* Sp: Norman Krasna, b/o his play. Cast: Ingrid Bergman, Cecil Parker, Phyllis Calvert, David Kossoff, Megs Jenkins, Oliver Johnston.

65. HOUSEBOAT. Paramount, 1958. (c) *Melville Shavelson.* Sp: Melville Shavelson and Jack Rose. Cast: Sophia Loren, Martha Hyer, Charles Herbert, Mimi Gibson, Paul Peterson, Eduardo Ciannelli, Harry Guardino, Murray Hamilton.

66. NORTH BY NORTHWEST. MGM, 1959. (c) *Alfred Hitchcock.* Sp: Ernest Lehman. Cast: Eva Marie Saint, James Mason, Jessie Royce Landis, Leo G. Carroll, Philip Ober, Josephine Hutchinson, Martin Landau, Adam Williams, Edward Platt.

67. OPERATION PETTICOAT. Universal, 1959. (c) *Blake Edwards.* Sp: Stanley Shapiro and Maurice Richlin, b/o story by Paul King

and Joseph Stone. Cast: Tony Curtis, Joan O'Brien, Dina Merrill, Arthur O'Connell, Gene Evans, Richard Sargent, Virginia Gregg, Robert F. Simon.

68. THE GRASS IS GREENER. Universal, 1960. (c) *Stanley Donen*. Sp: Hugh and Margaret Williams, b/o their play. Cast: Deborah Kerr, Robert Mitchum, Jean Simmons, Moray Watson.

69. THAT TOUCH OF MINK. Universal, 1962. (c) *Delbert Mann*. Sp: Stanley Shapiro and Nate Monaster. Cast: Doris Day, Gig Young, Audrey Meadows, Alan Hewitt, John Astin, Richard Sargent, Joey Faye.

70. CHARADE. Universal, 1963. (c) *Stanley Donen*. Sp: Peter Stone and Marc Behm. Cast: Audrey Hepburn, Walter Matthau, James Coburn, George Kennedy, Ned Glass, Jacques Marin.

71. FATHER GOOSE. Universal, 1964. (c) *Ralph Nelson*. Sp: Peter Stone and Frank Tarloff, b/o story by S. H. Barnett. Cast: Leslie Caron, Trevor Howard, Jack Good, Stephanie Berrington, Jennifer Berrington.

72. WALK, DON'T RUN. Columbia, 1966. (c) *Charles Walters*. Sp: Sol Saks, b/o story by Robert Russell and Frank Ross. Cast: Samantha Eggar, Jim Hutton, John Standing, Miiko Taka, Ted Hartley.

Cary Grant also made unbilled appearances in the following films:

1. SINGAPORE SUE. Paramount, 1932.

2. HOLLYWOOD ON PARADE. Paramount, 1932–1934.

3. PIRATE PARTY ON CATALINA ISLAND. MGM, 1936.

4. THE ROAD TO VICTORY. Warners, 1944.

5. WITHOUT RESERVATIONS. RKO, 1946.

6. ELVIS – THAT'S THE WAY IT IS. MGM, 1970.

ACKNOWLEDGMENTS AND NOTES ON SOURCES

The authors are deeply grateful to the following individuals who gave unstintingly of their time in order to assist us in our research for this biography: President Ronald Reagan, Katharine Hepburn, Dr. Timothy Leary, Stewart Granger, Rich Little, Ralph Bellamy, Sidney Sheldon, Stanley Kramer, Alexis Smith, Richard Brooks, Timothy Hutton, George Burns, Ambassador John Gavin, Douglas Fairbanks, Jnr., KBE, Marlene Dietrich, Margaret, Duchess of Argyll, Milton Goldman, Virginia Cherrill, Phyllis Brooks, Mary Brian, Binnie Barnes, Mike Frankovich, Martin Landau, Jane Wyatt, Johnny Maschio, Constance Moore Maschio, Melville Shavelson, Stanley Shapiro, Martha Scott, Joan Bennett, Janet Blair, Delbert Mann, Edward R. Muhl, Movita, Mrs. Reginald Gardiner, Phyllis Calvert, Frank Capra, Henry Koster, Dane Clark, Rita Gam, Sammy Cahn, John Howard, Laraine Day, Richard Gully, Priscilla Lane, Pandro S. Berman, David Manners, Fritz Feld, Dean Jagger, Jane Wyman, Gene Raymond, Arthur Lubin, Richard Anderson, Ted Donaldson, Irving Fein, Owen Crump, Mrs. Owen Crump, Frances Drake, Craig Stevens, Fay Wray, Jean Rogers, Peggy Moran Koster, Miles Kreuger, William Currie McIntosh, Ernest Cuneo, Curt Gentry, Ted Carpentier, Peggy Shannon, Curtis Harrington, Vincent Sherman, Marvin Paige, Jack Martin, Mrs. Ernst Lubitsch, Nicola Lubitsch, Samuel Marx, Moray Watson, Jean Howard, Robert Cohn, Alexander D'Arcy, Peter Pit, Billy McComb, Ann Doran, Jean Dalrymple,

Michael Harris, Paula Raymond, Alister Hunter, Matthew Kennedy, Max Tishman, Mr. and Mrs. Geoff King, Sally Bulloch, Johnnie Riscoe, Keith Blackmore, Florian Martini, Robin Macdonald, Kendall Carly Browne, Ned Comstock, Seth Green, Madame Olga Celeste, Bert Granet, Berri Lee, Tim Barry, Demetrios Vilan, Guido Orlando, Henry Gris, Kevin Thomas, and Virginia Rowe, and the following, who, sadly, are no longer living: Mary Lee Fairbanks, Noah Dietrich, Marilyn Hinton, Johnny Meyer, Marion Gering, Elsa Lanchester Laughton, Brian Aherne, Howard Hawks, Geoffrey T. Roberts, J. P. Wearing, Joseph Ruttenberg, Casey Robinson, Mae West, George Stevens, Carmel Myers, Delmer Daves, Hal B. Wallis, and Sammy Curtis.

To the following, close personal friends, we are most deeply grateful. Without their kindness and generous help, this book could never have been written: Gavin Kern, Bruce Cohn Curtis, Richard Lamparski, Harold Schwab, Marc Courtland, Daniel Schott, Stephen Breimer, Stephen Ortloff, Patrick Thomas, Keith Hook, John Marven, Bijou Durden, Robert Uher, Pasquale and Veronica Pavone, Philip Masheter, John Leach, Nicholas Armstrong, Peter Moore, Stephen Rattey, Peter Seyderhelm, B.Sc (Econ.), Martyn Shallcross, and Jane and Glen Kern.

Our agent, Mitch Douglas of ICM, proved magnificently supportive throughout. His assistant Jerry Thomas was also a tower of strength. Ray Austin broke a long silence to tell us of his extraordinary friendship with Cary Grant, combining in great degree both honesty and a sincere and lasting respect and admiration for the great star. James P. Maloney did a splendid job of winkling out secret documents in Washington, DC, which had never been declassified. Stuart Halpenn did fine work in New York. Daniel Re'em in London helped us in the difficult pursuit of the matter of the King's Medal awarded to Cary Grant for valour in World War II. Nigel West and Tessa Perfect were also indispensable in tracing this important matter. Herbert Goldman did sterling work in New York, reading through thousands of pages of *Variety* and other show business publications in order to trace the movements of the young Archie Leach in the vaudeville theatre in the 1920s. We would especially like to single out the very important help of Martin Masheter and Christian Roberts, and Mavis Hawkins, who made everything so clear.

We were greatly assisted by Cary Grant's family and friends in Bristol, who were kind, helpful and proud of what had happened to Archie Leach: Valerie Bagnall, Vivian Selley, Nicola Leach England, Betsy Leach Shapland, "Ted Morley", Ellen Hallett, Francis Chivers, and Lillian Pearce.

Ann Splain and Richard Babcock of the Luxury Line in Beverly Hills made so much of this book possible and thanks are due also to Anthony Slide and Richard Goetz, and the staffs of the FBI, State Department, Military Intelligence, Naval Intelligence, US Passport and Visa Divisions, USC Doheny Library, UCLA Research Library, New York Public Library at Lincoln Center, the Library of Congress, St. Louis Opera Company, the *Daily Mail* London (Baz Bamigboye), the British Library, Bristol Public Library, the Colindale Research Library of London (Periodicals Division), and all other British provincial libraries and theatre collections. The staff of the Academy of Motion Picture Arts and Sciences was especially helpful. And finally we would like to express our thanks to our esteemed editors, Ion Trewin and Vanessa Daubney, who have been so kind and supportive throughout.

CHAPTER ONE:
The birth records of Archibald Leach were obtained by Martin Masheter from St. Catherine's House, London. Details of the birthplace were obtained from Bristol registers by genealogist Geoffrey T. Roberts. These included a floor plan and survey map of the house itself. Mr. Roberts secured the family tree back to 1835.

Stewart Granger and Ray Austin confirmed from first-hand knowledge that Cary Grant was circumcised. Mrs.

Sam Jaffe is the source on Grant's declaration that he was Jewish, and this was confirmed by many others. An almost equal number stated that he failed to mention any Jewish origin. His autobiographical statements were published in the *Ladies' Home Journal* (Jan–April 1963) in the series which he published to replace Joe Hyams' authorised work. Martin Masheter obtained detailed particulars of panto-mimes and other theatrical shows in Bristol during Grant's childhood. Particulars of the Pender troupe emerged from period magazines of the early years of the century and from research done by J. P. Wearing for his *The London Stage* (Metuchen, NJ, Scarecrow Press, 1976). An especially valu-able piece was found in the *Pall Mall* magazine of January 1910, which had pictures of the troupe. A small boy watch-ing in the background at a rehearsal may have been Archie Leach.

The Bristol *Times and Mirror* and *Western Daily News* were valuable sources. *Variety* gave a full account of the Pender troupe's European tours. *Popular Mechanics* sup-plied details of the construction of stilts at the time.

CHAPTER TWO:
Shipping lists were obtained showing passenger manifests that accurately established the movements of the Pender troupe. The *New York Times* gave a detailed account of the performances of the Folies Bergère, and *The Stage* and *Variety* filled out the picture. Jesse L. Lasky's memoir, *I Blow My Own Horn* (Garden City, NY, Doubleday, 1956) was especially valuable. Again, J. P. Wearing, in *The Lon-don Stage*, supplied details of the troupe's performances in British pantomime. Mrs. Lillian Pearce, Ellen Hallett and "Ted Morley" supplied much valuable information on his school days. Various histories of magic included accounts of David Devant. Again, research by Martin Masheter and Herbert Goldman pieced together the jigsaw puzzle of the Pender Troupe's further career, supplemented by Grant's *Ladies' Home Journal* memoir. John Marven obtained

details of Charlie Spangles from the late performer's closest friend, interviewed in Liverpool. Various interviews with the late Jean Adair confirmed her friendship with Archie Leach. Sam Marx and Matthew Kennedy remembered Archie Leach on stilts.

Chapter Three

Jean Dalrymple, doyenne of veteran Broadway producers, was a great source here. So was her former partner Max Tishman, now approaching ninety, who, despite illness, supplied vivid memories. The great George Burns was a major source. Lester Sweyd's and Phil Charig's papers, the former housed at Lincoln Center, New York, were drawn from. So was *Act One*, Moss Hart's brilliant autobiography (NY, Random House, 1959). Miles Kreuger and the staff of the Lincoln Center Library provided programmes of the New York musical shows in which Archie Leach appeared. Reminiscences by Jeanette MacDonald were drawn from, and found, in several libraries; Gene Raymond provided more particulars. The Schubert archive was a great source. Many relatives of the late Orry-Kelly in Kiama, New South Wales, Australia, gave his background, and Joel Greenberg in Sydney obtained birth and baptismal records. The staff of the St. Louis Municipal Opera Company provided memorable photographs, programmes and clippings. The late Casey Robinson recalled details of Archie's screen test. Demetrios Vilan remembered the farewell party for Archie Leach and Phil Charig in New York.

Chapter Four:

Files of the *Los Angeles Times* and *Examiner* were consulted for details of Hollywood in 1932. Files of the *Hollywood Reporter* were read from 1932 until 1986. In the 1930s, the publication, which is very different today, provided an extraordinary time capsule of a forgotten world. Studio files provided a detailed account. Ned Comstock of

USC Doheny Library discovered the long-lost files of the store named Neale's Smart Men's Apparel. Arthur Lubin provided a personal anecdote. Mrs. Ernst Lubitsch added much personal data. Budd Schulberg's memoirs were a good source. Anthony Slide and Robert Gitt showed certain films. Roy Moseley interviewed Sam Jaffe (the former agent) in 1975 for Charles Higham's book on Marlene Dietrich, and Miss Dietrich gave long interviews to Charles Higham. Virginia Cherrill, in one of the most memorable and courageous interviews that Roy Moseley has ever conducted, gave for the first time the complete emotional history of her relationship with Cary Grant from the beginning. The Ben Maddox article was drawn from *Modern Screen*. The Mae West material was drawn from Charles Higham's several interviews with Miss West.

CHAPTER FIVE:
David Manners, now aged eighty-seven, recalled the crossing on the *Paris*. The *Hollywood Reporter* was the source of the splendid parties of the era. Edith Gwynn Wilkerson was a social reporter with a Swiftian eye for the peculiar behaviour of the society in which she found herself.

The sources on Howard Hughes' affair with Cary Grant were the late Noah Dietrich, interviewed at his house above Sunset Strip by Charles Higham many times in the mid-1970s, and the late Johnny Meyer, whom Higham talked to at the Drake Hotel in New York City on three occasions in the summer of 1978, in the course of researching a book on Errol Flynn. Guido Orlando, still living, and Hughes' publicist, confirmed the relationship without hesitation, and so did a leading Hughes aircraft designer who prefers to remain anonymous. That same designer fully confirmed Hughes' bisexual activities then and later.

Empire, The Life, Legend and Madness of Howard Hughes, by Donald L. Bartlett and James B. Steele (NY, W. W.

Norton, 1979) is much the best biography of the late tycoon, and has been our main source on particulars of his life as a great airman and aircraft manufacturer. Seth Green in Orange, Virginia, former editor of the Orange *Record*, reminisced on a rain-swept Sunday afternoon about the extraordinary life of his intimate friend, the late Marion duPont Scott. Several other citizens of Orange confirmed the authenticity of his description, and Mrs. Scott's memoirs were also used. The late George Cukor and the late Brian Aherne told Charles Higham of the particulars of *Sylvia Scarlett*. Mary Brian, in her first interview ever on the subject, told Roy Moseley of her love for the actor. The late Noël Coward often discussed Grant with Roy Moseley. Joan Bennett supplied some warm and affectionate comments.

CHAPTER SIX:
The authors regard Phyllis Brooks' long interviews in Maine and London with Roy Moseley as the high spot of all possible research. Miss Brooks opened her heart for the first time with unstinting warmth, decency and generosity. It was not easy for her to reawaken the long-lost past, but for her it will always be with her.

Kendall Carly Browne, Frank Vincent's secretary for several years, confirmed the statements of others that Grant was his own agent. Hal Roach supplied a unique interview on his association with Grant. Jean Rogers, memorable as the girlfriend of Flash Gordon, supplied clear memories. Alexander D'Arcy was a helpful source. CBS, NBC, and SPERDVAC, the well-known radio archive, gave details of the wireless career. The Randolph Scott/Katharine Strother Scott files were found in Room 6E of the Diplomatic Archives. Higham interviewed Katharine Hepburn, Howard Hawks, and Fritz Feld on *Bringing Up Baby*. Mrs. Reginald Gardiner, Douglas Fairbanks, Jnr., and the late George Stevens filled in particulars of *Gunga Din*.

CHAPTER SEVEN:
Howard Hawks in conversation with Charles Higham was the main source on *Only Angels Have Wings*. SPERDVAC supplied useful cassettes of the Grant radio programmes. Ralph Bellamy was entertaining on the subject of *The Awful Truth* and *His Girl Friday*. Rudolph Stoiber and the massive Errol Flynn files at USC, drawn from every branch of the government, supply the full record of Flynn's and Erben's treason to the United States. Sir William Stephenson, in a special cabled message to Roy Moseley, dated June 12, 1987, responded to his question as to whether Cary Grant was a British Secret Agent in World War II. The reply read:

> Your letter, July 2, question, answer is: as Cary was one of a group in constant [touch] and helpful to BSC [British Security Coordination] member Noël Coward. Others in group included Sam and Frances Goldwyn, Alex Korda, David Niven ... all strongly anti-Nazi, pro-Semite. Greetings good wishes, William Stephenson, inter [office] Bermuda.

The late Carmel Myers told Charles Higham of the group of British agents in Hollywood. FBI files confirmed the roles of other agents, including June Duprez and Reginald Gardiner. For full details and documentation on Merle Oberon's role, read *Merle: A Biography of Merle Oberon* by Higham and Moseley (Hodder & Stoughton, 1983). Bert Granet vividly recalled the shooting of *My Favorite Wife*. Sir Douglas and Lady Fairbanks were excellent on the leasing of their house to Cary Grant. The Hilda Krüger documents obtained by Charles Higham from the Diplomatic Archives are in public access and were later lent to Robert Lenzner for his biography of J. Paul Getty. The Cary Grant Special Agent travel documents were obtained by James P. Maloney through the passport office in Washington. The best sources on Barbara Hutton remain C. David Heymann's controversial *Poor Little Rich Girl* (Secaucus, NJ, Lyle Stuart, 1984) and Mona Eldridge's interesting memoir *In Search Of A Prince*. Johnny Maschio and his wife Constance Moore told us much about Miss Hutton. Joseph Ruttenberg and John Howard filled out memories of *The Philadelphia Story* supplied by Katharine Hepburn to Charles Higham in 1975. The Noël Coward quotation appeared in *A Man Called Intrepid*, by William Stevenson (Charwood, 1976), the authorised biography of Sir William Stephenson. The Clifford Odets documents were a great source and were provided by Virginia Rowe, Mr. Odets' secretary, with the approval of Odets' son Walt.

CHAPTER EIGHT:
The documents on Sir William Stephenson are to be found in Room 6E of the Diplomatic Archives. The activities of Bugsy Siegel were recorded in detail in the *Los Angeles Times* and *Examiner*, and in Dean Jennings' biography of the gangster. Numerous State Department documents covered the activities of Dorothy di Frasso in the United States, Mexico and Italy. Joseph Longstreth, breaking a lengthy silence, maintained during the publication of Charles Higham's Errol Flynn biography, at last agreed to confirm (in view of Cary Grant's death) the secret information that Grant had known of Errol Flynn as a Nazi agent and collaborator. Longstreth had never forgotten his meeting with Grant at the 1941 party. The files on Count Cassina are still maintained at the FBI Headquarters in Washington, and in Room 6E. The Barbara Hutton correspondences with Nazi Germany are in Room 6E. So are the von Cramm documents. Priscilla Lane talked about *Arsenic and Old Lace*, and Charles Higham interviewed Frank Capra several times in the early 1970s. Richard Anderson helped us to understand the relationship of Cary Grant and Lance Reventlow. Curt Gentry and Ernest Cuneo told us of J. Edgar Hoover's intense dislike of William Stephenson and, by extension, Cary Grant.

CHAPTER NINE:
Binnie Barnes was extremely helpful during a memorable luncheon with Roy Moseley. Ray Austin described Grant's activities as an agent. Dane Clark and the late Delmer Daves were indispensable on *Destination Tokyo*. The Warner Brothers' files preserved at USC gave day-to-day particulars. Janet Blair and especially Ted Donaldson were excellent on *Once Upon A Time*. Donaldson's account of Grant's fatherliness to him proved to be very moving. Jane Wyatt, the late Ethel Barrymore's memoirs, the papers of Clifford Odets, and Richard Brooks helped us very much in coming to grips with the extraordinary relationship between Grant and Miss Barrymore on *None But the Lonely Heart*.

Alexis Smith was marvellous on *Night and Day*; the Warner Brothers' studio files were a major resource. Jane Wyman and the late Hal Wallis told us more. Miss Smith's statement, "Cary Grant's acting was never an eighth of an inch off," surely said it all. Contemporary interviews with Monty Woolley were called on. Eric Stacy's production notes were helpful.

CHAPTER TEN:
The Louella Parsons quotation is from her Hearst Newspapers column. Material on *Notorious* is drawn from interviews at various times between the two authors and Alfred Hitchcock. The Betty Hensel affair was widely reported in the press. The flight from Los Angeles to New York was described by Johnny Maschio, Constance Moore, and Janet Blair. André de Toth added a couple of details. Myrna Loy wrote of *The Bachelor and the Bobbysoxer* in her autobiography (*Myrna Loy, Being and Becoming*, NY, Knopf, 1982). So did Dore Schary in his memoirs, *Heyday*. Howard Hughes' plane crash was described by his associate Ted Carpentier and confirmed in *Empire*.

CHAPTER ELEVEN:
Again, the FBI files on Hughes have been drawn from. Henry Koster was the main source on *The Bishop's Wife*.

The matter of the King's Medal was researched by the authors based upon an entry in the British Foreign Office Indexes. Nigel West, Daniel Re'em, and Tessa Perfect assisted. Douglas Fairbanks, Jnr., was also consulted in the matter, and Antony Acland, the British Ambassador to the United States, provided some comments. The award was never made public. Much of the material on Betsy Drake was drawn from the Warner Brothers' files of USC Doheny Library. When she was signed to make *Pretty Baby*, both the David O. Selznick and the Leland Hayward files on her were copied and retained in the Warner collection. Myrna Loy's published comments on *Mr. Blandings Builds His Dream House* were drawn from. The shooting of *I Was a Male War Bride* was commented on to Charles Higham by Howard Hawks; Ann Sheridan gave several interviews on the subject over the years. George Jessel's memoirs were a most valuable source on *Dancing In the Dark*. His hatred of Betsy Drake was sustained many years after the event. Stewart Granger was fascinating on the subject of his friendship with Grant and his odd, superficial relationship with Howard Hughes.

CHAPTER TWELVE:

Richard Brooks made possible the section on *Crisis*, and Paula Raymond supplied much detail, some of it contradicting the director's. We decided to run both of their accounts, side by side. Former President Reagan added his own indispensable touch in recounting Mrs. Reagan's disappointment in being replaced. Melville Shavelson was helpful on the subject of *Room For One More*. Sidney Sheldon was very good on *Dream Wife*. The death of Dorothy di Frasso was reported in the *Los Angeles Times*. Charles Higham had a long discussion with Princess Grace on the subject of *To Catch a Thief* at a Lincoln Center tribute to Hitchcock in the 1970s. Roy Moseley also interviewed the Princess on the matter.

CHAPTER THIRTEEN:

Stanley Kramer was, of course, the main source on *The Pride and the Passion*. Melville Shavelson learned much about the production and the personal circumstances surrounding it, and shared the details with Roy Moseley. Mr. Shavelson's novel *Lualda* gives a curious account of some of the matters with which we are concerned, but he is at pains to say that the heroine is not based on Sophia Loren. Sidney Sheldon's novel *Bloodline* also provides a thinly disguised portrait of Cary Grant. The account of the sinking of the *Andrea Doria* is drawn from contemporary newspaper accounts and from Alvin Moscow's definitive *Collision Course* (NY, Putnam, 1959). Mr. Moscow was contacted at his home in Florida on some details. A few touches were supplied by A. E. Hotchner's ghosted memoirs of Loren. Dr. Timothy Leary supplied us with crucial information on the matter of Grant's involvement with LSD and the effect it had on the star. Ray Austin was a rich and varied source on his several years with Cary Grant. His vivid memory for detail helped us considerably.

CHAPTER FOURTEEN:

Ingrid Bergman's memoirs, *Ingrid Bergman: My Story* (NY, Delacorte Press, 1981) were a good source on *Indiscreet*. They were put together by Allan Burgess, with the assistance of Jeanne Bernkopf. Phyllis Calvert talked to Roy Moseley about making the film. Edward R. Muhl gave a unique interview, perhaps the first he's ever given, on his close association with Grant. Martin Landau was vivid on *North by Northwest*. Joe Hyams told Charles Higham of his experiences with Cary Grant and, as mentioned, the *Ladies' Home Journal* series was researched.

CHAPTER FIFTEEN:

Ray Austin continued to be a great help in the matter of Howard Hughes. Moray Watson was the chief source on

The Grass is Greener. The late Sammy Curtis spoke fascinatingly to Roy Moseley about the past. Delbert Mann and Stanley Shapiro gave somewhat different accounts of the making of *That Touch of Mink*. Doris Day's memoirs, prepared by A. E. Hotchner, were again a good source. The account by Greta Thyssen appeared in *Photoplay* magazine. Mona Eldridge's story came from *In Search of A Prince* (Sidgwick & Jackson, 1988). Herbert Sterne's interview on *Charade* was given to his friend Anthony Slide to convey to Charles Higham. Details of the divorce of Betsy Drake and Cary Grant were found in the *Los Angeles Times*. Henry Gris, veteran journalist, interviewed Cary Grant about his LSD involvement for a national tabloid. The quotation from Corinne Introtter about Dyan Cannon's life with Cary Grant was supplied by Kevin Thomas.

CHAPTER SIXTEEN:
The account of Cary Grant in Tokyo was drawn from the *Los Angeles Times* and the Japan *Times*, published in English. Timothy Hutton added some remarks on his father Jim Hutton's association with Grant. The description of Jennifer Grant's birth was very widely reported. The excellent book *The Private Cary Grant* by William Currie McIntosh and William D. Weaver provided a great deal of information that would otherwise not have been available. Tom Stout, former TWA representative, provided the colourful description in these pages. Constance Moore and William Weaver were the sources on the departure of the Grants for England. Nicola and Betsy Leach, Cary's nieces, daughters of his half-brother Eric Leslie, gave an unprecedented interview on their meeting with the Grants. The Weaver–McIntosh book and the Barlett–Steele book supplied information in this chapter. Berri Lee gave an excellent interview on the many aspects of Cary Grant's life at the time. The late William Belasco, Australian Associated Press reports (later withdrawn) and a statement made by Charles Manson on Bill Stout's CBS interview programme formed

the basis of the material on Grant in the grounds of the Melcher house during the infamous murders of Sharon Tate and her friends. The late Marilyn Hinton, who had only six months to live, met Charles Higham and told him of the long-concealed story of Cynthia Bouron.

CHAPTER SEVENTEEN:

Weaver and McIntosh were the best source in the Fabergé association. Berri Lee and Tim Barry provided much detail on the Grant–Maureen Donaldson relationship. Several witnesses proved nervous on the subject of the producer's widow, and asked not to be quoted. Their accounts have been supplemented by details in the Weaver–McIntosh book. Rich Little was his marvellous self in telling hilarious stories of his "becoming" Cary Grant. He also told us of Frank Sinatra's close friendship with Grant. Again, Tim Barry was indispensable on the subject of Maureen Donaldson. Joyce Milton and Ann Louise Bardach provided the best available account of Cary Grant's affair with Vicki Morgan in their sadly overlooked biography, *Vicki*. Both were friends of the late Miss Morgan. William McIntosh was separately interviewed for a description of the final visits to Howard Hughes. He had not supplied these particulars in his and Weaver's book. The maître d' who saw Randolph Scott with Cary Grant at the Beverly Hillcrest Hotel does not wish to be identified. Virginia Cherrill once again proved intriguing as she recounted her renewed, very brief, contact with Grant in the 1970s. Mary Brian also saw him again and talked about that. Sally Bulloch was our main source on the meeting of Grant and Barbara Harris. The Chevy Chase interview with Tom Snyder was, of course, widely reported at the time, as was the Grant–Harris marriage. The staff of the Royal Viking ships described to Charles Higham the charm and considerateness of the Grants on their world cruise. Timothy Hutton provided the moving description of Grant's thoughtfulness towards him at the Academy Awards. Grant's death was best reported in the *Los Angeles Times*.

INDEX

ROY MOSELEY

A LIFE WITH THE STARS

'Roy,
You have known us all so well –
why not write a book?'

Bette

Roy Moseley has been friends with many stars for most of his life. In this latest book, he describes how he first met them while collecting autographs with "The Gang" in London and then, before becoming a well-known journalist and biographer, by working in most areas of the world of show business.

A LIFE WITH THE STARS is Roy Moseley at his most entertaining. Gossipy and enjoyable, it is a unique record of some most unusual friendships.

A Royal Mail service in association with the Book Marketing Council & The Booksellers Association.
Post-A-Book is a Post Office trademark.

MINTY CLINCH

HARRISON FORD

Harrison Ford – world famous for his roles in the smash box-office hits *Star Wars* and *Indiana Jones* – is also reputedly the film industry's richest star.

But behind the fame and fortune is a man whose most valuable asset is his privacy. In HARRISON FORD, Minty Clinch goes behind the scenes to trace his path to stardom. Covering his bleak, twelve-year initiation period, when he worked as a carpenter for his more successful colleagues, to the widespread acclaim he received for *Witness* and *The Mosquito Coast*, this is a true star biography in every sense of the word.

'Refreshingly un-Hollywood and occasionally critical'

Graham Lord in the Sunday Express

'Written with characteristic candour and wit, the book reveals well-researched detail . . . informed and authoritative, while remaining completely readable'

Photoplay

HODDER AND STOUGHTON PAPERBACKS

MORE BIOGRAPHIES AVAILABLE FROM
HODDER AND STOUGHTON PAPERBACKS

MINTY CLINCH

☐ 41200 8   Harrison Ford   £2.95

ROY MOSELEY

☐ 42138 4   Rex Harrison:
The First Biography   £3.95

☐ 42407 3   A Life With the Stars   £2.50

ROY MOSELEY WITH
PHILIP & MARTIN MASHETER

☐ 39380 1   Roger Moore: A Biography   £2.95

JOHN PEARSON

☐ 50598 2   The Life of Ian Fleming   £4.50

CHARLES HIGHAM

☐ 39250 3   Audrey: A Biography of
Audrey Hepburn   £2.50

☐ 41122 2   Orson Welles   £3.95

*All these books are available at your local bookshop or news-
agent, or can be ordered direct from the publisher. Just tick the
titles you want and fill in the form below.*

Prices and availability subject to change without notice.

HODDER AND STOUGHTON PAPERBACKS, P.O. Box 11, Falmouth,
Cornwall.

Please send cheque or postal order, and allow the following for
postage and packing:

U.K. – 55p for one book, plus 22p for the second book, and 14p for
each additional book ordered up to a £1.75 maximum.

B.F.P.O. and EIRE – 55p for the first book, plus 22p for the second
book, and 14p per copy for the next 7 books, 8p per book thereafter.

OTHER OVERSEAS CUSTOMERS – £1.00 for the first book, plus 25p
per copy for each additional book.

NAME ....

ADDRESS ....

....